MANCHESTER
MEDIEVAL
LITERATURE
AND CULTURE

Objects of affection

Manchester University Press

Series editors: Anke Bernau, David Matthews and James Paz

Series founded by: J. J. Anderson and Gail Ashton

Advisory board: Ruth Evans, Patricia C. Ingham, Andrew James Johnston, Chris Jones, Catherine Karkov, Nicola McDonald, Haruko Momma, Susan Phillips, Sarah Salih, Larry Scanlon, Stephanie Trigg and Matthew Vernon

MANCHESTER MEDIEVAL LITERATURE AND CULTURE

Manchester Medieval Literature and Culture publishes monographs and essay collections comprising new research informed by current critical methodologies on the literary cultures of the Middle Ages. We are interested in all periods, from the early Middle Ages through to the late, and we include post-medieval engagements with and representations of the medieval period (or 'medievalism'). 'Literature' is taken in a broad sense, to include the many different medieval genres: imaginative, historical, political, scientific, religious. While we welcome contributions on the diverse cultures of medieval Britain and are happy to receive submissions on Anglo-Norman, Anglo-Latin and Celtic writings, we are also open to work on the Middle Ages in Europe more widely, and beyond.

Titles available in the series

28. *Household knowledges in late-medieval England and France*
    Glenn D. Burger and Rory G. Critten (eds)
29. *Practising shame: Female honour in later medieval England*
    Mary C. Flannery
30. *Dating Beowulf: Studies in intimacy*
    Daniel C. Remein and Erica Weaver (eds)
31. *Enacting the Bible in medieval and early modern drama*
    Eva von Contzen and Chanita Goodblatt (eds)
32. *Riddles at work in the early medieval tradition: Words, ideas, interactions*
    Megan Cavell and Jennifer Neville (eds)
33. *From Iceland to the Americas: Vinland and historical imagination*
    Tim William Machan and Jón Karl Helgason (eds)
34. *Northern memories and the English Middle Ages*
    Tim William Machan
35. *Harley manuscript geographies: Literary history and the medieval miscellany*
    Daniel Birkholz
36. *Play time: Gender, anti-Semitism and temporality in medieval biblical drama*
    Daisy Black
37. *Transfiguring medievalism: Poetry, attention and the mysteries of the body*
    Cary Howie

Objects of affection

The book and the household in late medieval England

Myra Seaman

MANCHESTER UNIVERSITY PRESS

Copyright © Myra Seaman 2021

The right of Myra Seaman to be identified as the author of this work has been asserted by her in accordance with the Copyright, Designs and Patents Act 1988.

Published by Manchester University Press
Oxford Rd, Manchester M13 9PL

www.manchesteruniversitypress.co.uk

British Library Cataloguing-in-Publication Data
A catalogue record for this book is available from the British Library

ISBN 978 1 5261 4381 5   hardback
ISBN 978 1 5261 6718 7   paperback

First published 2021
Paperback published 2023

The publisher has no responsibility for the persistence or accuracy of URLs for any external or third-party internet websites referred to in this book, and does not guarantee that any content on such websites is, or will remain, accurate or appropriate.

Typeset
by New Best-set Typesetters Ltd

This book is dedicated to Robert and Zoë

Contents

List of figures viii
Acknowledgements ix

Introduction: objects, assemblages, affects, ecologies 1
1 Objects of instruction 55
2 Objects of mercy 92
3 Objects of correction 135
4 Testimonial objects 171
5 Objects of liberation 206
Epilogue: fishing for answers 255

Appendix: contents of Oxford, Bodleian Library
   MS Ashmole 61 260

Bibliography 262
Index 277

Figures

1 Oxford, Bodleian Library MS Ashmole 61, fol. 16v: *Sir Isumbras* and the *Ten Commandments* — 13
2 Oxford, Bodleian Library MS Ashmole 61, fol. 17r: conclusion of the *Ten Commandments* — 14
3 Oxford, Bodleian Library MS Ashmole 61, fol. 106r: seal of the *Short Charter of Christ* and title of the *Lament* of Mary [*Lamentacion Beati Mariae*] — 154
4 Oxford, Bodleian Library MS Ashmole 61, fol. 151r: *The Wounds and the Sins* and *Sir Orfeo* — 222
5 Oxford, Bodleian Library MS Ashmole 61, fols. 36v–37r: *The Erle of Tolous* — 257

The included images are copies of photos provided by the Bodleian Libraries Imaging Services at the time of this book's original publication. A complete digitized copy of the manuscript can now be accessed online for free through the Digital Bodleian website: https://digital.bodleian.ox.ac.uk/objects/69462c25-b481-4643-9942-34f7243ea921/. Please consult the digitized copy for full-color images that offer more detail and can be manipulated by the viewer.

Acknowledgements

This book endured a long gestation period spent tracing the affect ecologies of a vibrant situated community. As a result, it owes its very existence to a host of lively collaborations. I will do my best to document them here, although any attempt to recognise a complex living assemblage's many contributors will inevitably leave some elements unrecorded.

This project's early development was supported by various organised thought communities, at a time when medieval studies was undergoing important reflection and renovation. Much of the project's theoretical development occurred in joyful collaboration with others at gatherings hosted by the BABEL Working Group and by the Medieval and Early Modern Studies Institute (MEMSI) at George Washington University; elements were additionally honed through conference presentations and conversations held at the International Congress on Medieval Studies at Western Michigan University, the New Chaucer Society, and the Modern Languages Association. Further refinement and new lines of investigation were made possible at talks generously hosted by the Medieval Club of New York, the English Department at the University of Victoria, the University of British Columbia Department of English, the Emotions in Middle English Literature V conference at the University of Melbourne, and the Center for the Humanities at Oregon State University, all made possible by Valerie Allen, Allan Mitchell, Vin Nardizzi, Stephanie Trigg, and David Robinson and Tara Williams, respectively.

Unsponsored communities of feeling and thought also nurtured the project, among them my two writing groups, one a roving band of misfits comprised of Lara Farina, Dan Remein, and Arthur Russell, the other an internet-enabled virtual workshop with Elizabeth Allen, Lisa Lampert-Weissig, Emma Lipton, and Emily Steiner. Both groups offered solace and vital insight. Other shifting affective communities that left their mark on this book were generated by Suzanne Conklin Akbari, Candace Barrington, Liza Blake, Brantley Bryant, Rory Critten, Holly Crocker, Rick Godden, David Hadbawnik, Cary Howie, Eileen Joy, Asa Mitman, Alex Mueller, Susie Nakley, Julie Orlemanski, Will Rhodes, Karl Steel, and Cord Whitaker. Gratitude for support conceptualising the project goes to Glenn Burger, Jeffrey Cohen, Bruce Holsinger, Tom Prendergast, and George Shuffelton. Special acknowledgement among these beloved colleagues goes to Allan Mitchell, whose tireless support for this project, as it moved in fits and starts and seemed at times to have attained permanent stasis, helped me perceive energising prospects, and he nudged the book forward by insisting that I complete it if only so that he could read it.

My position at the College of Charleston, a public liberal arts and sciences institution, enabled me to share my love of the manuscript and my enthusiasm for new materialism with undergrads and MA students, with special thanks going to research assistant Teresa Hooper, to Alex Ansari for checking the Middle English and correcting numerous errors, to Kaleb Eisele for sharing my fascination for 'Medieval Object Ecologies' in the course he took with me fresh off my sabbatical, to Meaghan Kelly for writing so beautifully about the fused poem *Sinner's Lament* and *Adulterous Falmouth Squire* that her undergraduate work on it was published, and to Molly Lewis for her friendship and for all she has taught me about thinking passionately with compassion.

The book and I were also nourished by colleagues in the College of Charleston Department of English and the Program in Women's & Gender Studies, and by the College's Research & Development Grants that financed the first date I went on with Ashmole 61 fifteen years ago and that more recently provided a reprieve from teaching duties for a semester that allowed me space to conclude the project. Kris De Welde, Claire Curtis, and Gibbs Knotts enriched this final stretch.

Manchester University Press made this book as you experience it possible, especially the labours of Meredith Carroll, Alun Richards, and the editorial team of Anke Bernau, David Matthews, and James

Paz. The anonymous readers for the press gave the book a generous and generative reception, encouraging me to see greater possibilities for it.

The Bodleian Library (that centuries-old wonder-assemblage of objects human and otherwise) carefully sustains the life of the manuscript we know as Ashmole 61, and for that – and for Duke Humfrey's Reading Room, where I first beheld the magnificent book – I am inexpressibly grateful.

Similarly ineffable is my tremendous affection – my love – for Robert Grant and Zoë Seaman-Grant, who sustain me in unfathomable ways. I dedicate this book to them.

Note on the text

When this book was first published, MS Ashmole 61 could be consulted only in person in the Bodleian Library. The included images are copies of photos provided at that time by Bodleian Imaging Services. Now, a complete digitized copy of the manuscript can be accessed online for free through the Digital Bodleian website: https://digital.bodleian.ox.ac.uk/objects/69462c25-b481-4643-9942-34f7243ea921/

Introduction: objects, assemblages, affects, ecologies

> Texts are bodies that can light up, by rendering human perception more acute, those bodies whose favored vehicle of affectivity is less wordy: plants, animals, blades of grass, household objects, trash.
>
> Jane Bennett, 'Systems and Things'

This book is devoted to the emotional allure of textual objects.

When we choose to inhabit the space of a book, we accept an invitation to fashion imaginative worlds with it, in an ongoing creative act that incorporates not only the words on the page as we translate them into our mental landscape but also the physical ecology of the book: in the particular features of its heft, scale, layout, and structure; in the smells and sounds of its turning pages; in its distinct fonts, illustrations, marks of previous readership, and other sensual cues to its unique world. Literary studies has long explored this imaginative textual space and its affective impacts; only more recently have the material site of the text and its effects claimed literary critical attention. More recently, the easy availability of electronic texts, with their own distinctive features, has prompted us to reconsider the full extent of our attachment to the concrete codex: the capacity, mobility, and low reproduction cost of otherwise generic e-texts with their uniform reading environments across diverse platforms weighs against the rich sensual encounter and varied flexible formats of the cumbersome, storage-demanding, resource-heavy book. While certain practical matters may weigh in favour of the electronic text, the emotional pull of the book object is strong.

Medievalists feel particular allegiances to both platforms: we appreciate that digitised copies of medieval manuscripts distribute visual access to books otherwise available to only very few select experts, while we are keenly aware of the material medieval manuscript's extensive somatic range and durability. In this book, I document the emotional attraction of the medieval book through an extended analysis of one fifteenth-century literary anthology that has entranced me for some time now. I trace how that particular book wields this force in collaboration with the inhabitants of its pages – human and non-human, tangible and intangible – and with its readers in manuscript, print, and digital ages. The diverse strains of influence that books exert as material objects are exhibited in this single book's behaviour in the world: the effects of its peculiar material form, the impressions of the assorted texts it contains, and especially the affective responses that the book, including but not limited to its contents, generates. Indeed, this medieval manuscript's agency is witnessed in the very existence of *Objects of Affection*, a book produced centuries later in direct encounter with the realities of the manuscript's physical forms, extending its emotional influences to new cultural, historical, and material environments. *Objects of Affection* models the varied consequences that books have as they participate in cross-temporal collaboration with shifting systems of reading, changing configurations of distribution and archiving, and diverse communities of feeling.

More specifically, this new materialist case study of the physical book that scholars call Oxford, Bodleian Library Manuscript Ashmole 61 (hereafter Ashmole 61) demonstrates the emotional agency of the book through the affective literacy training that Ashmole 61 provided a late fifteenth-century English household. Scholars have recognised Ashmole 61 for its spiritually and socially hortatory interventions in the lives of its earliest audiences through its conduct texts, saints' lives, devotional guides, prayers, didactic narratives, and romances. Reconsidering the manuscript with the assistance of new materialist critical approaches (among them vibrant materialism, object studies, posthumanism, and actor-network theory) draws attention to the prominent pedagogical role of non-human agents, including the book itself: they model exemplary morality and spirituality, encouraging in the humans who appear in the collection, and in those who read it, responses of penitence and sorrow, fear and horror, humility and forgiveness. A full range of medieval ecologies – literary, social, religious, textual, and material – enabled the book's generation of these effects. Apprehended this way, Ashmole 61 broadens our understanding of medieval communities of feeling and of medieval and post-medieval text technologies.

Two central concepts guiding this investigation are 'household' and 'ecology', and the two are, perhaps surprisingly, closely intertwined. Ecology, despite the long semantic history implied by its Greek roots (*oikos*, 'house, dwelling', and *logos*, 'discourse, doctrine'), has had a very short life in English, first used in the nineteenth century (entering from German, rather than directly from Greek) as a specialised term in biology, then spreading to sociology in the early twentieth century. Its current wider usage developed as humans' interest in their damaging effects on the environment (that is, on what is often called the 'natural world') grew, from the late 1960s onwards. 'Ecology' tends to carry with it, today, associations with the 'natural' environment even as it is often deployed more broadly to describe 'the interrelationship between any system and its environment',[1] of which 'natural' ecology is a special case. Making full use of these denotative and connotative possibilities, this book investigates various ecologies bound in this single codex: the ecology of the late medieval English household, the ecology of the medieval book, the ecology of affective spirituality, the ecology of reading.

I thus deploy 'ecology' figuratively and transtemporally as well as what we might consider more literally. The close etymological relation of 'ecology' to 'economy', with which it shares the root *oikos* (and which, like 'ecology', offers many fruitful figurative applications, particularly in the plural), provides opportunities for further clarification: the suffixes *logos* ('discourse, doctrine') and *nomos* ('law, custom') both pull the *oikos*, or household, in the direction of regulation (be it through normative order or through laws); yet their differences point towards the key concerns of each term, especially as used by literary and other scholars over the past twenty-five years: 'economy' attends to the law or custom – the regulation(s) – of the household, while 'ecology' focuses on its discourses or doctrines. The latter of these opens up possibilities for description, the focus of which is not a system of exchange so much as a system of being and becoming, of intersubjective ontology. Given the roots of 'ecology' in 'house, dwelling', the term 'household ecology' might seem a redundant deployment; yet it serves to draw attention to the systems of the household, systems which include but are not restricted to exchanges based on assessments of fiscal or other value.

The household is one ecology of which the medieval book Ashmole 61 is a part. The diverse inhabitants of that household produce the ecology of the book as they are incorporated into it, in the material world they generate and that guides their living, in the social and spiritual desires that shape their influences in that world, and so on. The household ecology is that set of systems invested in the sustenance of a family. In its medieval manifestation, the family is sustained through the interventions of an extended collection of contributors, human and non-human. For instance, in a later fifteenth-century lower gentry household of the sort whose needs most immediately sponsored the production of Ashmole 61, the household would comprise the family who 'owned' the house and its environs, and the people employed to ensure the day-to-day survival of the family and its belongings (including servants and apprentices as well as, in many cases, family members whose primary commitment was to other households): as P. J. P. Goldberg describes it,

> The bourgeois house was [like that of the peasantry] a place for eating, sleeping and supplementary economic activity, but these were not its sole functions. For artisans with their workshops and merchants with their stock and their counting houses, the home tended also to be the principal locus of *all* economic activity associated with the household.[2]

Traditionally, the definition of the late medieval gentry household would stop there, including only the human collective inhabiting and sustaining the household and its environs. From a new materialist perspective, however, non-human elements, organic and inorganic, come into full view as household members – as participants in the system of the household making their own distinct contributions to its ongoing existence. Viewed this way, the household would include not only the gentry family and its human support staff but also the buildings themselves (and the systems that produce these buildings, from systems of inheritance to those mobilising local resources such as wood, clay, water), local varieties of crops, the regional educational resources and histories of linguistic development, and so forth. Such

Introduction 5

a perspective is further encouraged by an observation from P. J. P. Goldberg and Maryanne Kowaleski:

> in later medieval usage, *household* need not mean just people; it could denote possessions. Thus Roger Salways of York left his wife 'all my household holy' and Elizabeth Poynings likewise referred to 'all myne hole apparell and all my stuff of houshold being within my dwelling place' when she made her will.[3]

My work on the medieval household owes much to Vance Smith's *Arts of Possession* (2003), which focuses on household management – especially the skilful ideological management of surplus – and the means by which the household reproduces itself materially. His project is guided by Xenophon's definition of the household as 'the sum of its possessions, a definition based ... on the utility of goods, on the notion that it is objects that constitute our world'.[4] I share Smith's (and Xenophon's) orientation towards the objects that constitute the household, but my primary interest is not in utility as such but in how the household – that is, its shifting community of humans and non-humans – sustains itself affectively. I build on Smith's clarification of medieval English people's attitudes towards the objects they owned, carefully read in terms of the system of ownership inherited and being revised at the time: he demonstrates that '[i]n the English Middle Ages, it is often difficult to know how, or whether, you actually possess your own household',[5] a situation that he shows generates much anxiety concerning the act of possession and the things possessed. My own orientation is towards how one lived with – among, in relation to, in terms of – things (surplus or otherwise), and how this relationship offered challenges and opportunities extending beyond conundrums of naming and claiming to inform the affective ecology of the household.

Household books

The subject of this study is one representative of a type of medieval book that recently emerged from a century of seclusion. Its extant examples were originally produced for and consumed by late medieval lower gentry and wealthy merchant family households outside London. These collections of recycled texts efficiently provided their owners a 'library "in parvo"'[6] – that is, a mini-library, a library contained in a single book. These books gather saints' lives, romances, exemplary narratives, conduct texts, prayers, devotional lyrics, retellings of biblical stories, psalms, and lyrics.[7] Some include chronicles and historical documents relating to the region and the family. These relatively inexpensive books were locally composed and local-facing, their imaginative possibilities appealing to their audiences' individual and collective needs and desires. Produced mostly in the East Midlands in the last half of the fifteenth century and into the first decade of the sixteenth,[8] these manuscript books were soon to be outmoded, manufactured just as the printing press started to offer readers in England a new – not to mention less expensive and more widely accessible – alternative format. (It is, in fact, a time rather like our own, with new platforms providing options alongside the long-standing default mode of textual production and reception, when multiple formats also coexist: incunabula alongside manuscripts then, e-books and audio recording and digitised print and manuscript books alongside paperback and hardcover books now.) In addition to Ashmole 61, other such extant manuscripts are the Heege MS (Edinburgh, National Library of Scotland MS Advocates 19.3.1), Cambridge University Library (CUL) Ff.2.38,[9] and British Library MS Cotton Caligula a.2. These are largely unadorned paper books produced by one or two scribes for what seems (as we are certain of little about the individuals who originally owned these books)[10] to have been a lower gentry, yeoman, or wealthy merchant family.[11] The proportions of the 'pragmatically informative material' vary significantly, sometimes acting physically as 'filler' but otherwise serving the same needs of the household as do their narrative and poetic counterparts.

Based on the domestic audience of manuscripts such as these, Julia Boffey and A. S. G. Edwards assigned them the label 'family books'.[12] Boffey and Edwards offered this category in 2003 to describe books 'compiled for the tastes and purposes of a household or related households, and drawing on available external resources';[13] their aim was to supplement and contrast the already established category of the 'household book', which had been associated with a kind of wholly pragmatic ad hoc reference collection that was 'a repository of practical information of more or less domestic kinds – recipes and remedies and instructions on matters such as dyeing, fishing, arboriculture, and book production – which various members of a household may have wished to consult, or to have recorded, for different contingencies'.[14] Boffey and Edwards thus coined 'family book' to describe books generally containing texts that we tend to call 'literary' and with a noticeably different purpose from those that had been labelled household books, although books of both kinds ('household' and 'family') were 'produced not just for but within the environs of a particular family or household'.[15] In this move their category addresses the full ecology of the book, expanding a narrow focus on the nature of the book's contents (pragmatic information used as an everyday resource by household members) to include as an important taxonomic feature the locus of its audience and producer, in this case 'the environs of a particular family or household'. Through an analysis of codicological evidence, Michael Johnston demonstrates how manuscripts such as Ashmole 61 were probably products of the gentry manor house: 'The household was the provincial institution that brought together a series of individuals immersed in the documentary practices necessary to run a landed estate and maintain a home full of servants, practices that could easily be applied to copying out literary texts.'[16] This production model parallels the one long familiar to scholars in London, with 'in this case, local clerks turning their attention from documentary production for their master to literary production for him'.[17] Therefore, more directly than does 'family book', the term 'household book' acknowledges the range of ways these collections attended to the shifting needs of a particular, local, non-noble household ecology in its fullness, including but extending beyond the human family. The term 'household book' also positions the manuscript materially – in terms of the buildings and land, the non-human inhabitants and fellow producers of the household – and locally: held in place, kept, possessed, even grasped by hand.

Over time, these household books lost their domestic utility and, as a result, their readers; they moved out of households and, in the case of those that have survived the centuries, took up residence in private and then institutional manuscript collections.[18] By the late 1800s their human visitors were limited to editors seeking variants of individual texts and manuscript scholars concerned with medieval books' material composition: for editors, the books contained copies of rare and enduring texts to be refined and recirculated (select texts, that is, from among the many alongside which a given manuscript houses them); for manuscript scholars, they exemplified a waning textual technology. In the late twentieth and early twenty-first centuries, a developing nexus of scholarly concerns drew attention to these manuscripts: cultural studies and New Historicism found much to value in the anthologies' full contents, texts such as Middle English romances, conduct items, and exemplary tales that had promised little scholarly reward for the preceding period's primarily aesthetic and formalist investigations.[19] The deployment of medieval cultural practices and ideologies in such genres offered new insights, and the prevalence of such texts in household books garnered these manuscripts renewed critical attention. Such reading methods can enable more than listening to the past:[20] they can speak with it, an act that recognises that the past is present, that a book born in the Middle Ages but with us still lives in the present as much as in the various past moments through which it has endured.[21] The book ecology of MS Ashmole 61 includes medieval paper manuscript folios and modern ones (now living in the Bodleian Library, then living in a gentry household in Leicestershire); it includes print pages, too (the edition of the book made by George Shuffelton and published by TEAMS in 2008),[22] and electronic ones (the online version of Shuffelton's edition[23] and the select digitised folios available online[24]). The book's ecology similarly includes readers medieval and modern (and all those in between) – along with its community of Middle English verse texts (themselves retellings and translations of previous texts) and their human and non-human inhabitants.[25]

The book ecology of Ashmole 61

Generally unremarkable among medieval manuscripts (which are most often exemplified today via illuminated *de luxe* manuscripts, however unrepresentative those are of books generally across the Middle Ages), Ashmole 61 identifies itself through some distinctive features that appear to be associated with its singular scribe-compiler.[26] Despite having been called 'peculiar' and 'remarkably haphazard' in its production – an assessment that seems to result from a genre-centric critical approach that recognises patterns in the appearance of clusters of a given genre but not in thematic or other associations[27]

– the book's compilation facilitates patterns that suggest thematic as well as generic associations.[28] Such patterns can be seen, for instance, in the early portion of Ashmole 61 that is frequently referred to as the 'Children's Corner'.[29] It begins with the parallel placement of the saint's life *St Eustace* and the romance *Isumbras*. These texts share so many plot elements that they are considered genre remediations of the same story. *St Eustace* appears at the start of the section (which is also the start of the book, and the start of the first quire and of a booklet), and *Isumbras* appears at the start of the second quire, beginning what is the equivalent of a second booklet.[30] In the first quire, following *St Eustace* is a satiric piece from Lydgate (an estates satire-style critique of failures throughout society, *Ram's Horn*) and then two conduct items (*The Wise Man to his Son* and *The Good Wife Taught her Daughter*); in the second quire following *Isumbras* is a poetic version of the *Ten Commandments* and then two additional conduct texts (Lydgate's *Stans Puer ad Mensam* and *Dame Curtasy*). In each case, then, a narrative leads the quire, followed by three texts that are either recognisable conduct pieces or items acting like conduct texts in the way they offer instruction on how to behave to achieve successful social integration. Ashmole 61 has a reputation among manuscript scholars for being 'idiosyncratic'[31] – a euphemism for 'unreliable as a source for authoritative editions' – given the great variation expressed by its versions of multiply attested texts. Certainly, Ashmole's scribe, 'Rate', appears to have been interventionist in his efforts, actively modifying words, deleting lines, combining two texts into one, adding stanzas of his own creation, and so on. Yet while Rate's scribal attitudes and practices collide with modern editing practices and desires, such features of the manuscript as the 'Children's Corner' indicate that they were not simply haphazard, however peculiar.

Ashmole 61 indeed exhibits many peculiarities. The codex has an unusual shape, with tall, narrow pages wide enough for only one column of verse, not sufficient to the two columns per page seen in other extant household books, which are wider and shorter quarto-format codices. At 16 inches (40.6 cm) tall and 5 inches (12.7 cm) wide, the page dimensions of Ashmole 61 have encouraged debate about the possibility that it was a holster book, traditionally conceptualised as a portable manuscript carried in a bag at the belt and commonly associated with minstrels; however, this debate seems to concern our critical terminology more than it does the book's purposes. Lynne S. Blanchfield, in the first modern extended investigation of Ashmole 61 in the early 1990s, finds the 'account-book or "agenda" format' more appropriate to the manuscript than holster book.[32] The paper appears to be account paper that was first folded into an eight-inch by five-inch 'square', possibly to produce a more commonly sized household manuscript, then unfolded before being used for this verse collection.[33] Blanchfield observes that the manuscript's long, narrow shape makes it easier to hold with one hand while doing something with the other, or while reading aloud without a stand.[34] Erik Kwakkel describes how manuscripts with such dimensions were frequently produced for material that would be sung during Mass or used for instruction in monastic schools. However, such items tended be thin as well as narrow, the equivalent of a quire or two and often unbound, to reduce their weight while being held in one hand. Kwakkel notes as well that a late medieval copy of *The Romance of Richard Coeur de Lion* is very slim, which he avers seems to indicate it was made to be used by minstrels.[35] In the case of Ashmole 61, Blanchfield notes that 'the bulk and weight of the volume would have made it cumbersome to carry about, unless in individual quires, in which case more wear and tear would surely be present; only the first quire is likely to have been so used'.[36] Its pristine condition even today suggests that if it had been produced to be carried around as a holster book was, whoever carried it did so with great care rather than treating it perfunctorily as a minstrel's aid.[37]

As it happens, though, there is no need to rely only on the book's size to discern its purposes, since a performance use for Ashmole 61 is also suggested by the fact that all the texts in this manuscript are in verse, at a time when prose was increasingly popular and regularly appeared in other household books (particularly in the chronicle material that Ashmole 61 notably lacks). The modern editor of Ashmole 61, George Shuffelton, finds that the collection's texts 'were chosen on the basis of their suitability for reading aloud' and reaches the significant conclusion that '[w]hat ties the manuscript together is ... a deep investment in oral entertainment as the centerpiece of domestic life'.[38] This is not to say that other household books containing prose were not concerned with domestic life; but in offering texts especially well-suited to public reading in the household, to be shared in an act that gathers the household physically and ideologically, Ashmole 61 announces that '[r]eading was thus a communal duty with a communal purpose'.[39] So even if its account-page format explains its form and the creases on its pages, making unlikely any holster book identity, this doesn't negate the oral presentation or performance orientation of the collection – further supported by the ease it offers for reading aloud without a stand.[40] In this and other ways, Ashmole 61 seems oriented towards inviting communal household engagement through public performance of its contents.

The performative outlook of the collection, with its verse-only texts and its abundant references to minstrels and minstrelsy, is one distinct feature of its materiality; another seemingly contradictory one is the unusual visual presence, even prominence, of its scribe throughout the anthology. When a book like this is being read aloud to a physically present audience, the reader whose speech enlivens the words on the page becomes the local vehicle for the voice of the narrator or, where appropriate, the author; the scribe, in contrast, is directly present only to the single individual encountering the book visually in order to enact the text. Despite the evident focus in the collection on the larger community audience who would engage with the manuscript in its aural form, the Ashmole 61 scribe (whose identity has not been discovered, though some critical consensus swirls around a Leicester ironmonger)[41] took the unusual step of signing his name, Rate – or, once, a variant thereof, 'Rathe' – to half of the items in the manuscript.[42] This gesture points towards an anticipated reader of the book engaging directly with the scribe's visual contributions to the collection. It also repeatedly draws attention to one select member of the household and manuscript ecologies: the scribe.[43]

Ashmole 61's physical features thus raise new questions even as they seem to answer others, maintaining a number of codicological mysteries. These include its most baffling: the illustrations of fish and flowers that fill its pages – 33 of them across 41 items. This is simply exceptional. Household books only very rarely contain even basic marginalia or images (at most, a reader will encounter what Johnston describes as 'sporadic touches of color (typically rubrication) on the first initials of individual lines'),[44] and certainly not repeated images participating in what is a sustained pattern of illustration.

Indeed, of the medieval English manuscripts containing romances (household books among them), the Auchinleck manuscript – a costly collection produced two centuries earlier – is the only one besides Ashmole 61 to contain illustrations. Julia Boffey and John J. Thompson call Ashmole 61's illustration a 'rudimentary, but nonetheless effective, programme of rubrications and decoration'.[45] This distinguishing feature seems all the more insistent because fish and flowers, the recurring images here, are insignificant players in the poems in the manuscript: just one fish is referenced in its texts, and flowers appear only very rarely. Furthermore, the fish all look the same, as do nearly all of the flowers. The images thus cannot be identified as visual adjuncts to individual written texts.[46]

Rate is generally thought to be the producer of the images (in large part because the text and images use the same ink, and also because of the graffiti-like nature of the images). They are thus integrated even more intimately into his act of copying and compilation. Very few textual items in the manuscript appear with titles or incipits. The colophon alone,[47] which appears at the end of each item, consistently indicates the transition from one text to the next, granting this feature special influence in organising the layout of the collection and in guiding the reading experience. Tracing the quick development of this pattern in the first items in the collection helps clarify the significance of the scribal signature in the colophon and its association with the fish and flower images: For each of the first eight items of the manuscript (the so-called 'Children's Corner'), a colophon appears. After the first two texts' colophons – a simple 'Amen' in each case – the scribe shifts consistently to the extended 'Amen quod Rate' ('Amen says Rate'). In this act, he positions himself in relation to the text, marking it with his utterance, inscribing his name alongside the text; he also positions himself in the audience's (later) moment of reading or hearing the text by encouraging a shared response through the 'Amen'. As soon as he inserts himself this way into the colophon in the third item of the text, Rate begins accompanying this verbal signature with a drawing of a fish and, much of the time, a flower (see Figure 1). That is, these accessories rapidly increase in complexity: while items 1 and 2 lack 'quod Rate' or images, all the rest have the full 'Amen quod Rate' tag accompanied by a fish (items 3, 4, and 5) and a stem of flowers (item 4), to the point that item 6 ends with a very large floral braided ring, filling

Introduction

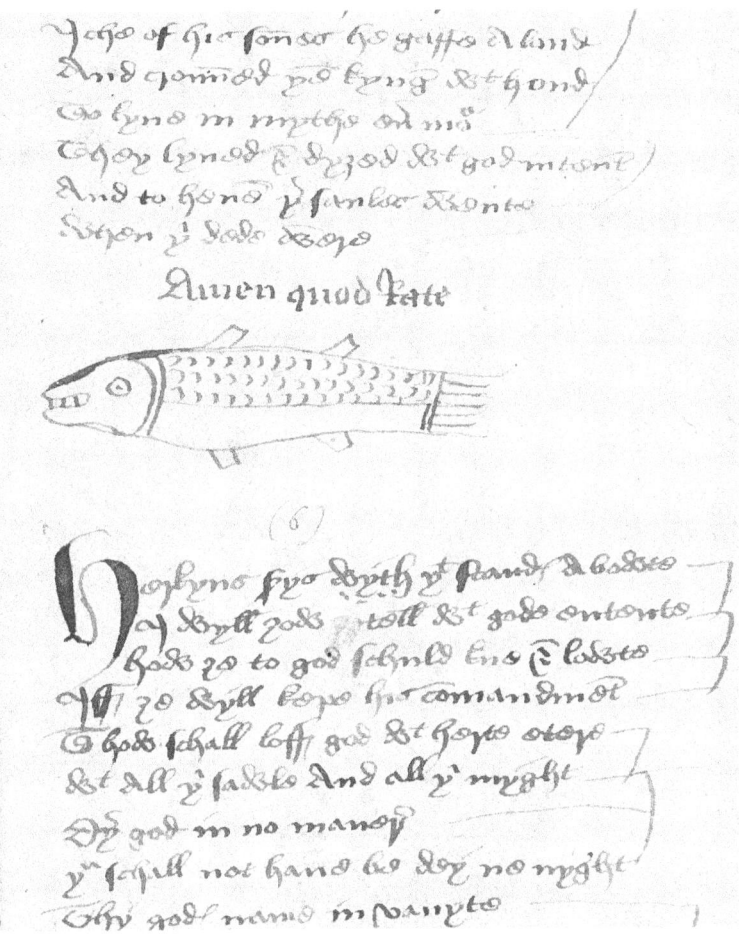

1 Oxford, Bodleian Library MS Ashmole 61, fol. 16v: *Sir Isumbras* and the *Ten Commandments*

most of the blank space between this item and the following – and below the ring-with-flowers appears a fish (see Figure 2). The remaining two items in this section have either a flower (item 7) or fish (item 8).

The Ashmole 61 fish is sometimes relatively symmetrically placed in an open space left between two items in the manuscript, but more often than not it seems to have been drawn before the text it follows

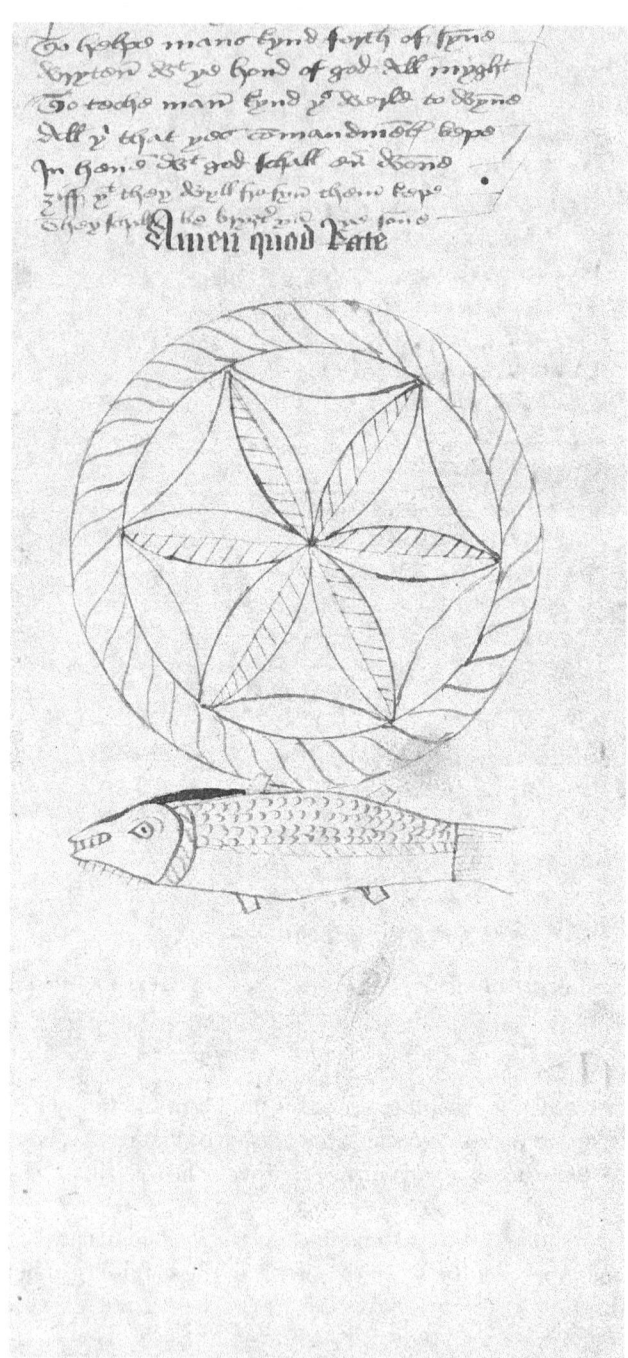

2 Oxford, Bodleian Library MS Ashmole 61, fol. 17r: conclusion of the *Ten Commandments*

was completed, so that the last lines of the preceding poem must be squeezed in, to the point sometimes of nearly preventing independent perception or comprehension of either.[48] The fish, which at these and many other moments appears to be grinning, refuses to defer to the text. Text and drawing intersect, sharing the same space, neither dominating the other – with the effect of flattening traditional hierarchies of text and image. Text becomes extra-textual, image becomes extra-iconic, each moving into spaces and behaving in ways generally disallowed them. The enmeshed elements demand more than separate places and roles, insisting on the interrelatedness of these elements in the book's ecology.

Collectively, these patterns suggest an act of branding on the part of the scribe – a metonymic association between himself and the non-human and non-verbal, offering Rate additional avenues for entangling himself within the world of the book. This enmeshment I am perceiving is not a purely symbolic association – wherein, for instance, the image would be a rebus of the scribe's family name,[49] or a symbol of the Leicester guild of Corpus Christi[50] – that is, where the fish and flower exist only because they can visually represent a person or a human corporation, are present only because they just so happen to convey in graphic shorthand something human that they otherwise do not relate to in any meaningful way. The physical features of the manuscript may be inconsistent, even contradictory, providing texts for oral presentation but building a relationship between the scribe and the book's visual readers; they highlight the range of household inhabitants within the manuscript while emphasising the identity of the individual household member responsible for producing the collection. Indeed, a single coherent meaning for such elements might be exactly what they refuse to offer, however sustained, giving evidence instead of this book's (and all books') rich multiplicity.

Household object ecologies

Ashmole 61 is itself a household object. Produced in a household, apparently by one member of that household for its other members, and engaging the worldly and spiritual concerns of the household collective,[51] the textual collection teems with objects of the household, both real and imaginary: tables, mirrors, beds, door jambs, meat and food, alcohol, household members' bodies and others' bodies – fingers, hands, foreheads – and their products, a stag, a crucifix, demons, a ram's horn, a bird, fiends, chains, tears, a hunting dog, a hawk, two giants, a bridge, an enchanted hall, boiling oil, pieces of the holy cross, two evil dragons, prayer, torture, a human–tree hybrid, a lyre, a death tableau, a fairy castle, deer carcasses, a drinking game. The plenty of this merely partial list accentuates the lively household ecology that extends throughout the anthology – an ecology in which these objects do much more than simply coexist or provide a backdrop for human activity.[52] We might add to the ecology those objects, witnessed by their effects, that are not necessarily materially perceived. In the case of Ashmole 61, such objects would include Catholic Christianity, monarchism, the power of one's word, the power of the Word, hospitality, largesse, patriarchy, monogamy, family. Within texts and across the collection, these objects constitute and reconstitute different household assemblages that serve a range of purposes, from the pragmatic to the philosophical. The scribe-fish-flower synthesis recurring in the book's pages, very tangibly *on* its pages, encourages readers (who in the process of reading become part of the book ecology) to consider the integrations of the non-human and human objects of the household and the various provisional object ecologies generated throughout. In doing so, Ashmole 61 manifests a view of the world in which human institutions and their ethical and moral concerns are produced through interaction with, and often through the intervention of, non-human agents, animate and inanimate.

Such attention to the influence of the non-human challenges contemporary expectations that medieval Christian morality and ethics would be exclusively human concerns. The human soul and its eternal post-mortem experience seem the primary site of Christian moral attention. As Karl Steel notes, 'From the standpoint of *professional, scholarly* texts running through the entirety of the Middle Ages [key examples being Augustine and Aquinas], the difference between having human intelligence and a beast having intelligence is that between a pleonasm and an impossibility.' Steel further observes that such is the case in 'the *systematic* thought of the Middle Ages: outside systematic thought, a vast array of other material teemed'.[53] Evidence from medieval culture suggests that moral agency was often understood much more expansively. As Caroline Walker Bynum demonstrates extensively in her 2011 book *Christian Materiality: An Essay on Religion in Late Medieval Europe*, even medieval theologians – the authorities regularly engaging such matters in the context of institutional religious ideology – spoke of matter as 'organic, fertile, and in some sense alive'.[54] The non-human world was not, first and foremost, starkly divided into the animate and the inanimate; as extensive taxonomies of that world were developed, their central identifier was not, as it would become in later generations, 'the living' and 'the dead'. Matter was not perceived as fixed and non-generative but as 'by definition that which changes': what was inanimate was, in some key features, animate, since it experienced change and did so in ways recognisable from the animate world.[55] Given such understandings of animate and inanimate objects as similarly subject to – and capable of – change and development, certain objects (in this case, human objects) were less likely to be perceived as automatically and naturally the single agential subject, surrounded by multitudes of objects present only to be acted upon and through. J. Allan Mitchell has demonstrated that medieval thinkers understood the human body to be ontologically variant over time, as exhibited during the process of the body's development, during which 'the embryo is in transit between successive species'.[56] Mitchell describes as 'conventional' the statement that 'the [human] embryo lives the life of a plant, then the life of an animal, and afterwards the life of a human being'.[57] As another example, Nicole Oresme observed that 'there are many (or at least several) intermediate *species* between sperm and a complete man'.[58]

These views, however unfamiliar to long-standing modern habits of understanding the material world, share much with the new materialism, a term used to describe a range of affiliated approaches within the humanities and social sciences that promote a renewed materialism in the face of a decades-long emphasis on discourse, language, culture, and constructivism. In its emphasis on materiality, new materialism does not seek a 'return' to a positivist empiricism; instead, it pursues a materialism in ongoing conversation with anti-realist philosophies and informed by dramatic developments in science and technology. Among the new materialisms are some approaches attending primarily to matters of ontology, others primarily focused on biopolitical and bioethical concerns. All include ecocritical practitioners though not all are predominately ecocritically oriented or motivated. They all 'recognise that phenomena are caught in a multitude of interlocking systems and forces'; they 'consider anew the location and nature of capacities for agency'.[59] The multiplicity and diversity of these systems and forces, and the emphasis on previously neglected sites of agency, are central insights of the new materialism.

Generally associated with the new materialism are a cluster of approaches often described as object-oriented (including or in conversation with vibrant materialism, speculative realism, object-oriented ontology, and actor-network theory) that offer methodological and theoretical assistance in reformulating our approaches to reading the physical world in medieval texts. Object-oriented studies have encouraged us to look beyond inherited understandings of objects as inert recipients of human action, agentless entities that exist as drifting victims of the human will. Instead, objects are understood as having effect on others and, in that, having agency.[60] Further, object-oriented studies extends the usual notion of 'the object' to include human and non-human, animate and inanimate, tangible and incorporeal.[61] Clustering these different approaches under the 'object-oriented studies' umbrella highlights the value of their shared features while downplaying the particular qualities that distinguish them.[62] All object-oriented approaches reject the long-dominant concept of the exceptional human and, simultaneously, flatten ontological hierarchies[63] to produce a model of the world that, while making distinctions among its components, removes evaluative association from those distinctions and avoids correlationism, 'the belief that things can only exist in relation to (human) minds or language'.[64] It is a deeply descriptive mode, one that depends on representations of abundant diversity (as in the 'Latour litany' demonstrated via the extended list of household objects that began this section).[65] It fights against traditional and lingering (philosophical and vernacular) 'association[s] of matter with passivity', a view that sees matter as mechanistic, which has long had the effect of 'weakening our discernment of the force of things'.[66] All object-oriented theorists agree upon the force of things; how exactly that force operates in terms of the force of *other* things is where key distinctions are made. Jane Bennett expresses the relationships among things' forces as follows: 'Earthly bodies, of various but always finite durations, affect and are affected by one another. And they form noisy systems or temporary working assemblages which are, as much as any individuated thing, loci of affection and allure.'[67] The emphasis on objects' being in flux, impermanent, and composite – that is, 'built from swarms of subcomponents' – extends throughout vibrant materialism, actor-network theory, and the new materialisms at large.

Bringing both the non-hierarchical ontology of the object and the concept of the object-assemblage to bear on medieval texts helps us to recuperate hermeneutic possibilities that have been lost to our modern encounters with them. Such orientations can enable new possibilities in our relation to the past and in our engagement with the present. I focus especially on generally neglected non-human objects in order to understand how they operate in collaboration (intentional or not) with one another in the particular textual ecology of Ashmole 61, in order to underscore premodern conceptualisations of the physical world.[68] Particularly useful for discerning the effects of collective agency are medieval considerations of stones and minerals, given modern Western conceptions of them as fixed, inert, incapable of development or self-generated change. J. Allan Mitchell shows how medieval models of mineral development reflect those understood for human development: as the human embryo moved across species during its growth – existing as plant then animal then human – the mineral was '[m]etabolizing, coagulating, transforming' and 'emerging in time and spatial environments where they contribute something palpable'.[69] Mitchell and Valerie Allen demonstrate that minerals were understood to develop in ways we would describe as mammalian: for example, Allen shows how Albertus Magnus 'takes stones to be a matrix or "womb", a material cause of metal, "as if the substance of stones were, so to speak, a place peculiarly suitable for the production of metals"'.[70] The stone behaves as surrogate mother to the mineral.

Minerals and humans exhibit shared experiences of gestation, and they are similarly positioned within the moral ecology inherent to earthly existence. Recent work on medieval lapidaries has revealed premodern readings of morality unanticipated by modern natural or ethical philosophy. Kellie Robertson demonstrates, for instance, that the physical intimacy of two differently gendered fire stones is described as generating spontaneous combustion. This characteristic of fire stones is often read allegorically, ultimately transforming into an *exemplum* against (human) lust. But such representations of non-human affective behaviour, Robertson clarifies, were not 'mere analogies' for the human, for 'in a physical world where the rock and the human differ more by degree than by kind, where the divide between the material and the immaterial was not yet so indelible, the reciprocity of moral lessons was underwritten by an ontological connection manifest in the *scala naturae*'.[71] The human fornicator and the mineral fornicator were connected by the relationships among all beings and things – rather than being essentially and fundamentally distinguished by the conscience (and thus moral capacity) of one and the total lack thereof in the other.

This feature appears in medieval writing as *virtus* or *vertu* (the first in Latin, the second in English and French): 'inherent powers and the primary source of ... agency' that '[c]osmic and ecological imprinting' offer all earthly elements, including, in Jeffrey Jerome Cohen's sample, seemingly static stone.[72] Cohen goes on to say that 'lapidaries ... developed a sophisticated vocabulary for the explication of nonhuman agency', including *virtus*, 'a trigger to worldly activity', a term offering 'creatureliness without anthropomorphism'.[73] Medieval associations between generative power and morality demonstrate that the latter was not conceived of as exclusively a human trait.[74] Allen shows that Albertus Magnus understood 'mineral virtue' to be 'the power the stone or metal receives, in the immediate from earthy exhalations, ultimately from the heavens, because (as Albertus explains), "all the powers of things below come from above"'.[75] As part of that power, the stone or metal behaves in certain ways – such as falling when dropped – 'not because of gravitational pull but because the prepondering element of earth in them "desires" to return to base, and thus makes objects move in downward direction'. Further, Allen observes, 'A stone has a sense of place, yet its earthward love is not simple, for the sensible qualities belonging to the other elements compromise its purity, rendering it a microcosm of concord-in-discord.'[76] The innate tendencies and moral lessons offered by stones may be understood by us today as allegorical and thus as simply analogous, because our cultural default is to read rocks as incapable of acting morally (or immorally – or, for that matter, acting at all). Only humans, for us, have that potential for virtue or vice. Not so in medieval lapidaries, or elsewhere: as Holly A. Crocker observes, 'these inherent bodily powers were central to everyday practices that focused on the natural potencies of physical bodies' generally.[77] In Ashmole 61, non-human objects tend to exhibit a capacity for moral clarity that is sometimes greater than that of the humans with whom they are in contact, as we will see in the behaviour of lions (e.g., *St Eustace*), awls (*The Debate of the Carpenter's Tools*), tables (*Stans Puer*), cherries (*Sir Cleges*), kisses (*The Knight who Forgave his Father's Slayer*, *Lybeaus Desconus*), and books themselves in the very performance of this unique textual community.

The texts co-inhabiting the book, and the book itself (as an object including other objects but not subsuming or subsumed by them), have effects in the world, and this is their agency. Contemporary materialist approaches recognise this quality of texts: Timothy Morton, for instance, declares that '[a] poem is not simply a representation, but rather a nonhuman agent'.[78] A text does not just represent the world 'outside' itself; it acts on the world with which it engages, imaginatively and materially.[79] To some extent, this is axiomatic to those who study literature. A text's action, though, tends to be understood as a manifestation and expression of its human author's agency. The ability of a text to have effect in the world is, however, as Jane Bennett observes, 'a function of a distributive network of bodies: words on the page, words in the reader's imagination, sounds of words, sounds and smells in the reading room, etc.'[80] These varied objects in the book ecology can be sensed multiply, by the human eye, ear, imagination – generating a new ecology, wherein the words and pages take on a new instantiation, material and immaterial. Such effects of the material text circulating in the world, building and rebuilding human–non-human ecologies, go well beyond the act of representation, of expressing an isolated human insight or desire. A text's effects can even be such that it 'can help us feel more of the liveliness hidden in such things and reveal more of the threads of connection binding our fate to theirs'.[81] Here Bennett extends the text's liveliness and its effects in the world to the point of a particular ethical influence on readers (one that, again, may or may not be intended or acknowledged by the text's human or non-human producers): causing us to recognise the interconnections of ourselves and others.

Object-oriented interpretation reads all objects with equal attention to their effects, regardless of the recipient of those effects, of the intention behind those effects, of the consistency of the effects. In terms of analysing texts, this means ensuring that non-human objects (including texts, including books) are not acknowledged only in order to examine more extensively their influence on human objects (who thereby retain the position of exceptional subject).[82] This potentiality is of particular concern when investigating the object ecologies of a medieval literary collection such as Ashmole 61, given the strong devotional bent of many of its texts. Our traditions for interpreting the genres in the collection (romance, saint's life, conduct text, *exemplum*, for instance) assume a central human subject whose transformation is the text's purpose – the human subject in the text, and ultimately the human subject addressed by the text. With the combined assistance of contemporary new materialism and medieval ontological reciprocity, however, alternative interpretive orientations are available.

While the religious texts in Ashmole 61 and elsewhere might appear to pose the biggest barrier to a new materialist approach, medieval religious expression shares its larger culture's human/non-human intimacy. Caroline Walker Bynum has demonstrated extensively how 'late medieval devotional objects speak or act their physicality in particularly intense ways that call attention to their *per se* "stuffness" and "thingness"'.[83] She observes that devotional objects' material features are not elided by their sacred meaningfulness but instead are necessary to that very significance. Bynum classifies 'various types of holy matter [that] … were powerful because they were physical presences. It was *as objects* that they conveyed divine power.'[84] She demonstrates through the increasingly common appearance of animated statues and bleeding hosts in the later Middle Ages an enthusiasm for what she calls 'animated materiality'.[85] Thanks to the Eucharist, Bynum explains, theologians (even, importantly, orthodox theologians) maintained that matter was not excluded from holiness. As with Robertson's discussion of the fire rocks' moral responsibility, the consecrated bread and wine are not simply signs of Christ's sacrifice; they *are* Christ's sacrifice.[86] Bynum's argument makes explicit the foundation for the ontological reciprocity that Robertson describes: the ladder of nature includes the divine as well as the earthly, on a continuum of being.[87] In such a cultural environment, detailing the various participants in an object ecology is less likely to reveal only how the non-human elements react to or manifest human will.

Taken to an extreme, an object studies approach to literary texts can risk erasing or overlooking elements that meaningfully demarcate human community. Jane Bennett explains how certain varieties of object studies (in this case, her target is object-oriented ontology, or OOO) insist on 'aloof objects ... positioned as the sole locus of activity'.[88] They depict a cosmos of object-planets cautiously protected by the seemingly vast, empty space in between.[89] In this, feminist literary critic Rebekah Sheldon describes OOO as 'an emphatically anti-relational ontology in which objects recline at a distance from each other and from the networks in which they are embedded'.[90] In its intense focus on the object and as a result of its investment in preserving the integrity of the object's individual agency, OOO seems to require an unchanging object invulnerable to the influences of time, or of other objects, most especially the objects we know as 'society' and 'discourse'.

The incompatibility of OOO with feminism is hard to miss here in a number of ways. For one thing, feminism depends upon change – on the fact that what was and what is will not always be and has not always been such, a situation that makes critique and intervention possible. As feminist rhetoric scholar Jen Talbot observes, 'flattened ontologies ... render illegible the historical and political forces that shape our everyday experiences'; these forces include what she calls the 'agential asymmetries that exist among human bodies'.[91] In other words, flattening ontologies can maintain a specious perspective that is powerfully displaced by Kimberlé Crenshaw's concept of intersectionality, which has recently, belatedly, become fundamental to much feminist thought.[92] Such an approach reveals that not only does OOO tend to focus problematically on the individual entity *as* entity, and downplay, ignore, or even deny the relations between and among entities; in so doing it overlooks and declares insignificant the many ways in which relations among and between entities is structurally lop-sided.

Fundamental insights of Karen Barad's agential realism further support a feminist alternative: for instance, among many other fruitful orientations, she clarifies that 'the relationship of the cultural and the natural ... is not a static relationality but a doing ... that always entails constitutive exclusions and therefore requisite questions of accountability'.[93] In a process ontology such as this, agency is not defined by what the object is, nor does it pre-exist relations – key premises for OOO.⁹⁴ For Barad, '[a]gency ... is an enactment, not something that someone or something has'.⁹⁵ Feminist materialist theories 'foreground the inseparability of the social and [the] material through the lived experience of micro-interactions', Talbot observes.⁹⁶ Such an approach – for instance, the object-oriented feminism promoted by Katherine Behar⁹⁷ or the transcorporeality of Stacy Alaimo,⁹⁸ or the agential realism of Karen Barad, among other material feminisms⁹⁹ – can thus help readers perceive more fully some of the uneven relations that feminism specialises in discerning and that texts regularly document – whether an author so intends or not.

A household is not a random assortment of things occupying a particular shared domestic space,¹⁰⁰ but rather an ecology of inhabitants, human and non-human, whose shared occupancy includes entanglement in collective habits and expectations. This section began with an extended list of some of the occupants of the texts in Ashmole 61, and the rest of this book will aim to demonstrate the myriad forms of enmeshment that these household objects experience within the manuscript. The anthology's household object ecologies meld the fantastic and the everyday in this and other ways, responding to and producing pertinent household affect ecologies.

Book agency

The idiosyncratic physical features of Ashmole 61 multiply and incoherently draw attention to the materiality of its texts, to the space of the paper page, to the ink, words, and objects that share it, and to the range of human–non-human ecologies that generate and sustain it. Arthur Bahr and Alexandra Gillespie observe that contemporary object-oriented criticism – like medieval visual art and like medieval material textuality[101] – tends 'to direct our attention to the text as *a thing among other things*, including the things – pictures, pages, scripts, rubrics, bindings, catchwords – that we must deal with when we notice that our object is a book as well as a text'.[102] A new materialist orientation led me, for instance, to pay a different kind of attention to the 'decorations' in Ashmole 61, so that I did not try to resolve my dissatisfaction with the purely symbolic readings of the remarkable Rate fish that were the only scholarly explanations on offer for this mysterious creature feature.

Scholarly explanation strives to understand these unusual illustrations in terms of human corporations – to read them as a mystery to be solved by discerning how the non-human can convey specifically human significance. Melissa Furrow, for instance, has posited that it might be 'a rebus alluding to where Rate was living or where he was born', offering as example 'a name like Rosgill in Westmoreland County, which has nothing to do etymologically with either roses or fish gills'. Furrow concludes, 'I have no evidence to support that solution to the riddle, and it remains an interesting puzzle to solve.'[103] The seeming lack of a representational foundation for the fish has led one scholar to conclude that '[t]here is no discernible pattern to these drawings, meaning they were likely added according to Rate's whimsy'.[104]

New materialism encouraged me to ask different questions, to follow the fish's lead rather than searching for ways to hook and master it by attaching it to (and explaining it through) human-centred cultural phenomena (the scribe's surname, the symbol of Christ). The unusual relationships among scribe, text, and image suggest that, instead of being a case of doodles-gone-wild or a simple symbolic expression of faith, the distinctive pesco-floral unit operates as a signature-equivalent. This association develops into an interchangeability of verbal signature ('Amen quod Rate') and iconic one (fish-and-flower portrait). Following the fish this way led me to see the preponderance of non-human actors throughout the texts of the manuscript, as well as in the book's composition. It led me to see how, in concert with the verses at whose conclusion they present themselves, the fish and flower operate as a poetic refrain.[105] The flowers (sometimes appearing with the fish, sometimes present independently) may be read through the medieval concept of the *florilegium* (Latin *flos*, 'flower', and *legere*, 'to gather'), a compilation of fine writings gathered together.[106] The flowers present throughout the collection as illustration might thus act as a visual manifestation of the verse, playing up an association between flowers and verse with which readers at the time would have been familiar and once more refusing distinctions between text and image. In other words, the fish and flowers do not appear only as cues to the spatial divisions between individual texts; nor do they appear only as indicators of the less bifurcated system of the text (human and non-human objects in and outside of the text incorporated in/as the book), nor to draw attention to the lines' copyist; they also participate in the literary ecology of the anthology by presenting a variable but easily recognisable actant in the ongoing verse project of Ashmole 61. Simply put, they become part of the poem, whose identity is changed by the inclusion of the image. In this way, the pesco-floral-scribal assemblage enacts the integration of human and non-human, visual and oral, textual and iconic, poetic and imagistic.

A new materialist outlook led me to see that Rate's experience as a scribe may have introduced him to an association between scribal flourishes (such as colophons) and fish images, as can be seen in the fish-shaped cartouche[107] on f. 55v of Harley MS 3744, which is a close sibling, nearly a twin, of the Rate fish.[108] It changed my relationship to the paper on which the words and images appear – a feature I had previously seen as reducing this manuscript's critical currency, lacking as it did the parchment pages that Bruce Holsinger and Sarah Kay have shown hold much potential for readings inflected by work in critical animal studies.[109] Attending carefully to the paper led me to see it as one more household contributor to the manuscript's existence: the appearance of late medieval household books such as Ashmole 61 depended not only on the spread of literacy, but also on the recent rise of paper in England – a relatively cheap and abundant alternative to the parchment required for book production prior to the fifteenth century. It encouraged me to note, further, that paper was a by-product of the household, made from cast-off rags, recirculated just as the very texts such books contain were recirculated in them, and revealing the household's waste to be an important contributor to its cultural prosperity. In these and endless other ways, seeing the text in a manuscript as 'a thing among other things' required me to read differently, to account for the many agents producing the book.

Books did not wait for object-oriented ontologies or Deleuze and Guattari[110] to grant them agency, and scholars working in the late twentieth century prior to the development of the new materialisms exhibited an awareness of the agency of the book even without this particular theoretical scaffolding: 'The master trope of book history', Leah Price observes, 'has always been personification. Elizabeth Eisenstein's *Printing Press as an Agent of Change*, Jerome McGann's "socialization of texts", and Paul Duguid's *Social Life of Information* anthropomorphise books.'[111] Seeing the agency of books in human

Introduction 27

terms, as these phrases indicate book historians and textual scholars did, is an important step towards seeing books' agency in their own terms, as 'book-agency'. Michael Johnston and Michael Van Dussen deploy the same lively model in their 2015 introduction to *The Medieval Manuscript Book: Cultural Approaches*, where their three central theses are presented by applying the analogy of the life cycle of the human to that of the manuscript.[112] Arthur Bahr's 2013 book *Fragments and Assemblages* helps guide us towards a more deliberate recognition of that agency, one that incorporates the contributions of the modern reader to the book's construction. Bahr defines a compilation as 'the assemblage of multiple discrete works into a larger structure'. This assemblage generates further 'assemblages of disparate historical moments: of their individual texts' composition and subsequent, often gradual evolution into the particular material form they now occupy, which itself often differs from its original medieval form'.[113] Human intervention is one factor in this ongoing constitution and reconstitution, with the texts' changing material form influenced by the texts themselves and by factors outside them. But it is just *one* factor, so that compilation is not something a scribe does to texts as he produces a book – and which manuscript scholars simply perceive and describe disinterestedly – but, as Bahr further defines it, compilation is 'a way of apprehending and interpreting objects, rather than … an inherent quality of the objects themselves'.[114] That is, a manuscript's compilation is produced by the relationships among the objects in a given collection, witnessed to by the interpretation that their compilation suggests and that directs (and is the product of) the particular act of compilation. It is not a fixed feature of the manuscript, but one that is produced and reproduced in variant relationships with and within the book.

Bahr's redefinition of *compilatio* provides a solid foundation for an investigation of a household book's diverse actants, one interested in interpreting cross-temporally the relationships among those actants as attested by the material book. Particularly in the case of a collection such as Ashmole 61, typically categorised as a miscellany,[115] attempts to trace connections among its contents have tended to be rejected by manuscript scholars for being the product only of the modern critic's wishful thinking. Margaret Connolly and Raluca Radulescu allude to the ongoing contention over the definition of a miscellany (and particularly the resistance to any reference to a manuscript's texts' bearing witness to scribal or other intentionality) when they note that 'one of the few generic (and "safe") definitions of the miscellany which emerged from the Insular Books conference in 2012 was that of "multi-text manuscript"'.[116] Derek Pearsall insisted, for instance, that despite recent critical attempts to see things otherwise, a miscellany is simply that: a random collection, a feature that he determines is so because it 'looks pretty miscellaneous'.[117] Motivating this critique is a view that interest in finding a guiding principle results from modern scholars' discomfort with the often absent author figure in medieval literature, reflecting the continuing investment in the author in literary studies at large.[118] My interest in the diverse actants that contribute to the existence of Ashmole 61 does not pursue any sort of '"guiding intelligence" ... that turn[s] an apparent miscellany into a continuing thematic meta-narrative'.[119] Instead, I take up Bahr's invitation to see that '[m]iscellaneity is ... most useful as a provocation to further investigation and new modes of reading, rather than as an objective designation'.[120]

Attending to the agency of the book object – which includes any and all scribal and compiler contributions, along with a whole host of other agents – broadens the traditional focus on the human production of manuscripts. As one result, manuscripts that scholars have labelled miscellanies, while 'being vastly outnumbered, perhaps six to one, by manuscripts of single long poems ... *have stimulated exceptional interest*'.[121] They have effects – that is, they have agency – and in the case of household books, those effects are the effects of household agents. Indeed, as Pearsall observes, 'collections that are brought together by choice and chance unpredictably mixed ... provides a rich set of opportunities for "imagining the medieval book"'.[122]

Household affect ecologies

Just as book history's personification of the book recognised aspects of book agency before new materialism developed a discourse to suit, the history of emotions has provided a methodological structure for the activity that some historians and literary scholars were already performing.[123] Sarah McNamer observes that '[l]iterature, after all, is the chief archive of the emotions', while Stephanie Trigg notes of literary critics that 'their business has always been about feeling'.[124] For those studying premodern cultures, that business tends to be oriented towards what Barbara Rosenwein has helpfully labelled 'emotional communities'. Investigating this collective orientation of medieval emotion serves to counteract generalisations based on modern Western norms with their focus on the autonomous individual. A prime site of 'emotional display and engagement' for such investigation is the medieval household,[125] for emotion is hardly the exclusive purview of the royal family or of public political life, both of which as a result of the larger extant archives tend to receive most attention from historians of emotion. Everyday emotional expression in the intimate yet public space of the household offers a rich albeit infrequently visited venue for understanding the 'communal production' of medieval emotion,[126] which is on display in the literature of the household. Rosenwein notes that 'emotions are among the tools with which we manage social life as a whole',[127] and the utility (and risk) of emotions in a setting such as the household is high. Emotions are 'tools [to] manage social life' in Ashmole 61, a place where even literal tools are also devices for fashioning community, themselves direct participants in the emotional life of the household. This society includes, throughout the household that is Ashmole 61, not only people but also animals and inanimate inhabitants, including objects such as the chisel, adze, awl, and hammer of its unique text *The Debate of the Carpenter's Tools*.[128] Social life is here managed through the development of a household-oriented emotional literacy.

The work of Sara Ahmed offers a rich resource for conceptualising emotional literacy as an object-oriented process. Emotions, for Ahmed, have two key distinguishing features: they are affective assemblages, and they are generated through circulation. An emotion is not restricted to a subject's interiority (despite our vernacular tendency to describe emotions this way), nor does it exist in isolation.[129] That is, sadness does not exist as an entity within nor does it infuse and define a given individual.[130] Instead, in Ahmed's object-oriented matrix of emotion, feelings are produced through contact, and the shaping of the subject is not a direct, simple effect of a single cause.[131] An event or experience – a distinct object – does not cause a human to experience pleasure, for instance; the contact of the objects, itself, forms a happy individual. As an extension, objects 'circulate as social goods' and 'accumulate ... affective value as they are passed around'.[132] Among these objects circulating as social goods are not only what we might think of as physical things but also 'objects in the sense of values, practices, and styles, as well as aspirations'.[133] This circulation conveys the social nature of emotion: it depends upon exchange; further, emotion requires contact with objects. Objects are typically excluded from 'the social', which is assumed to be the exclusive domain of (human) subjects. Ahmed's emphasis on emotion as being produced through contact with objects, and through the circulation of such contact and its effects (which are themselves objects), posits a network of interaction that suits new materialist conceptualisations of emotional ecologies as generated by human and non-human objects in ongoing yet provisional contact with one another.

The establishment and maintenance of communities, in Ahmed's conceptualisation, occurs through emotions – which is to say, it results from 'how we respond to objects and others'.[134] This response, which produces the community's boundaries, takes the form of judgements of value, evaluation that results from being affected by something.[135] This evaluation, though, is not autonomously generated and controlled by the subject; it is culturally and socially instructed, for in that contact lie as well prior histories of contact.[136] Emotion produces social subjects, by producing particular kinds of social bodies in response to and in relationship with particular kinds of objects.[137] Rosenwein's emotional communities are thus established and maintained. Discrete social communities are studied by the historian with the goal, as Rosenwein explains it, of

> uncover[ing] systems of feeling: what these communities (and the individuals within them) define and assess as valuable or harmful to them; the evaluations that they make about others' emotions; the nature of the affective bonds between people that they recognize; and the modes of emotional expression that they expect, encourage, tolerate, and deplore.[138]

It is within distinct emotional communities with 'a common stake, interests, values, and goals' that the circulation of social goods occurs,[139] with value judgements adhering and amassing. In emotional communities of the English Middle Ages, for instance, thriving Christian community depended upon the experience of emotions that hold much less cultural prominence (or social utility) in Western societies today, such as contrition and compassion.[140] Circulation within particular emotional communities generates and regenerates the local norms of emotional literacy – which tends to involve what Ahmed describes as a 'slide between affective and moral economies'[141] – such that certain affective states and acts (contrition, compassion) are moral, in the Middle Ages, and not simply individually perceived feelings. Such social norms are not reinforced by active suppression of 'actual' or 'authentic' emotions, with only the rare 'real' emotion breaking through. Norms do not contain and control sincere emotion, which remains unaffected but hidden. Rather, the experience of emotion can occur only in terms of the relevant affective economy.[142] By investigating medieval emotional communities we can expand our concepts of emotion through what Tracy Adams describes as 'the variety of ways ... emotion was understood as a communal rather than private phenomenon'.[143]

The emotional histories of the Middle Ages produced by Rosenwein, Trigg, Adams, and McNamer, among many others, draw attention to features of medieval culture – and resources for encountering it in literary texts – that allow for new ways of thinking. To that, Ahmed's approach adds the vital contribution to emotion-production of the circulating object and the human body's engagement with it. Monique Scheer's notion of 'emotional practices' similarly attends to this involvement of 'the self (as body and mind), language, material artifacts, the environment, and other people ... emerging from bodily dispositions conditioned by a social context, which always has cultural and historical specificity'.[144] Emotional practices are, then, coalitions of human and non-human objects, embodied practices taking effect in the world in terms of the particular cultural norms that become part of the affective object itself, in order for it to have those effects. Bynum observes that 'it is of the nature of objects to carry practices with them'.[145] That is, practices do not exist independently of the objects associated with them, and these objects' identities depend upon the affiliated practices (evergreen trees; hearts pierced by arrows; pieces of cloth with stripes, perhaps some stars or a crescent moon, of particular colours). As a result, such objects – those participating in and thus generating socially meaningful practices, such as sacramentals and contact relics, in Bynum's rendering – are agents causing effects in the world. Such affective agency is contingent upon the emotional practices circulating with the object.

This kind of agency is exhibited not only by devotional objects but also by ordinary household objects. Such objects' agency derives from their existing in community with a range of practices supporting the thriving of the household (such as the aforementioned chisel, adze, awl, and hammer). Objects need not be sacred in order to carry practices and to exhibit affective agency, nor do these practices need to be part of a sacred ecology. Kathleen Stewart describes the ordinary as 'a shifting assemblage of practices and practical knowledges' – that is, the ordinary is itself produced by acts and associated insights understood as serving practical purposes, as determined by and within particular settings. Stewart thus reveals the affective agency of such objects, which she calls 'ordinary affects' and describes as 'the varied, surging capacities to affect and to be affected that give everyday life the quality of a continual motion of relations, scenes, contingencies, and emergences'.[146] Ordinary affects are the effects of objects in circulation, participating in everyday, ordinary practices – what she describes as 'a surging, a rubbing, a connection of some kind that has an impact'.[147] All of this is the product of repetition and practical engagement, 'a kind of involuntary and powerful learning and participation'.[148] As with Ahmed's affective economies, ordinary objects 'work not through "meanings" per se, but rather in the way that they pick up density and texture as they move through bodies, dreams, dramas, and social worldings of all kinds'.[149] Ultimately, ordinary affect (like all affect) is 'not about one person's feelings becoming another's but about bodies literally affecting one another and generating intensities: human bodies, discursive bodies, bodies of thought, bodies of water'.[150] Here, Stewart's affinities with new materialism are most apparent: all bodies – be they material, linguistic, conceptual, hydro – bear agency when in contact, and in their contact lies the circulation of affect. The ordinary household ecologies of Ashmole 61 are generated in just this way through everyday objects' affective contact. The readings of Ashmole 61 that constitute this book will observe a stag initiating a calamitous course of penance, a drinking horn revealing royal infidelity, and out-of-season cherries enabling distributive justice, among other moments of emotional literacy gained through contact that reveals everyday household object agency.

Remediated book ecologies

Over the years since Rate affectionately found the fish and flowers a new home on the pages of this manuscript, contact and affect have generated a new medieval book – not in the case of Ashmole 61 alone, but for medieval books at large. The ecology of the medieval book is very different today than it was just twenty-five years ago, much less 400 years ago. The arrival of the print book transformed the manuscript, and digitisation is transforming both still further. The manuscript itself, as an object, has in most cases not been physically changed by digitisation (except for the rare case where that process threatens damage to extremely fragile manuscripts such as the *Beowulf* manuscript, Cotton Vitellius A.xv), just as it was not itself physically changed by print; yet the manuscript is certainly changed as a result of digitisation, becoming henceforth known by contemporary scholars primarily through that remediation. Only the rarest of medieval scholars has encountered the *Beowulf* manuscript firsthand; most, however, have interacted with the digitised version, which they regularly share with students as well. The manuscript ecology thus now includes thousands more living human participants than it did even in the 1990s. And yet that knowledge is limited to the book's visual appearance, and even that is engaged just one weightless page at a time – with the pages so durable that the investigator can change the size of the page, zoom in on just one brushstroke, and otherwise mangle the manuscript in ways physically and ethically impossible with the single material original. The ecology of the medieval book has, in the case of manuscripts such as Cotton Vitellius A.xv, expanded to include virtual copies that significantly alter the relationship of the reader and the book object.

However, medieval books have long experienced similar kinds of changes to their ecology through the intervention of modern technologies, for their post-medieval life has for the last 150 years been sustained primarily through modern editions in print. The life of Ashmole 61, for instance, changed dramatically in 2008 with the publication of a modern edition (twin editions, really: one in print and one online). Ashmole 61 suddenly welcomed many new readers and found itself participating in conversations from which it had previously been excluded. In that act of remediation, the book became modern and approachable rather than baffling and in need of a guide, left behind with its similarly aged and unfashionable contemporaries, as it had been prior to 2008.[151] Modern editions bring new readers and, in the process, new readings, new compilations – thereby producing, in this case, a new Ashmole 61.

Digitisation contributes to the ongoing life of a manuscript, even as it challenges our traditional estimation of the manuscript's value in terms of its singularity. Literary scholars, like manuscript scholars, often emphasise the uniqueness of a manuscript, of *the* manuscript, as essential to its identity and its worth. Derek Pearsall, for instance, sees this feature as so fundamental that it cannot possibly be emphasised enough, sometimes repeating it three lines in a row, commenting on 'the uniqueness of the artefact' and 'the importance that must be attached to the unique and individual act of making'.[152] The new digital medium's seeming intangibility threatens to replace a personal physical encounter with the unique material manuscript with a purely mental encounter with an unreal object. This concern is apparent in Maura Nolan's analysis in her 2013 *Chaucer Review* article 'Medieval Habit, Modern Sensation: Reading Manuscripts in the Digital Age', where she writes, 'the material book [and here she includes print and manuscript] is a technology that orchestrates habit. Its conventions act as triggers for habitual behaviors, which in turn function as a means of ordering both the physical sensations of reading and the immaterial content of the work':[153] a reader of a medieval manuscript develops those particular human habits that the medieval codex engineers. Thus modern readers' actions and perceptions match those of medieval readers, as they smelled, felt, heard, and saw the weight of the codex, the scent of the animal skins, the creak of the turning folios, which informed their reception of the book's contents. The manuscript ecology, its form and ideas, incorporates the reader, whatever his or her temporal positioning.

But digitisation threatens to deprive the manuscript book of this power. Nolan describes the process of digitisation – that is, as she represents it, non-human reading of the manuscript by the camera and the computer – in very different terms: violent rather than collaborative, and something akin to rape: 'the digital camera acts as a kind of proboscis, wriggling into the hidden crevices of the medieval past'.[154] The camera pries into and invades the body of the book, and then distributes to others the knowledge revealed through that act of aggression: 'From thousands of miles away, readers can now explore the nooks and crannies of manuscripts they have never touched.'[155] Others experience the benefits – the access to previously concealed knowledge – without personal, embodied, human–manuscript contact. For Nolan, touching the text encourages 'a different kind of intimacy, based not on penetration but on sympathy: the effort of the modern reader to understand the experience of the medieval reader'.[156] According to this narrative, ethical knowledge comes through gentle touch, while a reader participating in the ecology of the digitised manuscript inevitably disregards the agency of the manuscript's original readers and even of the 'medieval past' into whose crevices Nolan says the digital camera 'wriggles'.

What is it, one might ask, about reading-while-touching that, for twenty-first-century medievalists, best mimics a medieval reading experience? For many in the Middle Ages, after all, books were encountered only through the materiality of another's voice, distributed by the single reader who was able to see and touch the book – so that the full range of sensory engagement we experience in the manuscript library goes far beyond the limited somatic experience of many, perhaps most, medieval readers. Indeed, one might argue that digitising manuscripts produces a reading situation *more* like a medieval one, with one reader (in this case a technological one) distributing the text visually (rather than aurally) to distant other (human) 'readers'. At issue alongside matters of phenomenology seem to be questions of ontology, concerning this 'new and improved version of the original object'. It seems as if this new version cannot actually 'be' the original, which is displaced, perhaps even destroyed, in the process.

This perceived ontological destruction underlies Nolan's interpretation of the act of digitisation, which follows Walter Benjamin's interpretation of the act of photography: for Benjamin, the painter keeps a 'natural distance from reality' and thereby offers a 'total' picture of it, but the photographer 'penetrates deeply into its web' and offers not a total picture of reality but a reassembling of fragments 'under a new law'. Through Benjamin, Nolan paints a reader of material manuscripts as obedient to the natural laws, and thus sympathetic to the medieval reader, while the reader of digitised manuscripts defies natural laws, and refuses the restrictions of pre-digital reading. Nolan says that

> habits of reading [material books] are manifestations of human limitations as well as expressions of the conventional behavior of the human mind; they reveal the boundedness of life within a body while also demonstrating that cognition occurs in patterns, organising data by means of habitual processes of thought. Books function as visible records of such habits, objects from which cognitive patterns can be deduced.[157]

Electronic reading in this scenario – in which it is positioned as non-human because dependent on advanced technology – presents a threat to the human, asserting a posthuman supremacy.

Such a view assumes a transparency of the *medieval* medium.[158] Even as she previously defined the book as 'a technology that orchestrates habit', Nolan observes that 'digital reading lacks the near-global commonality of holding a book in the hands'[159] – as if books weren't a new and foreign technology when they first appeared,[160] as if electronic reading doesn't involve touch and habituation, as if the human body's senses are fixed and not shaped by culture, as if in the Middle Ages manuscripts were accessible to more than the very, very few.[161] Indeed, the act of digital reading often looks significantly like non-digital reading, with pages that users swipe as they would turn a material book's pages, reflecting the tendency for new technologies to bear skeuomorphs, forms that are traces of prior technologies' functionalities, despite their serving no such purpose in the new context. Further, Jerome McGann observes that while 'the computer [has] greater capacity for simulating phenomena – in this case, bibliographical and socio-textual phenomena', '[b]ooks are simulation machines as well … with hard coded machine languages (we call those typography and graphic design) and various softwares (modes of expression – expository, hortatory, imaginative – and genres)'.[162] Working from Raymond Williams's definition of a medium as a 'material *social* practice' (and not simply material alone, like canvas or screen, and not simply a technique or a technology),[163] W. J. T. Mitchell adds that while both materials and technologies comprise a medium, 'so do skills, habits, social spaces, institutions and markets'.[164] They all constitute a given medium. We have long habits and traditions of including various actants in our understanding of the medieval manuscript assemblage, and of the print text; we simply have yet to develop that understanding of the digital one. As a result, the e-book seems a minimalist – and perhaps anti-human – entity, lacking contributors that we consider central to the book (paper, ink, binding, vulnerability to damage, heft) just as print books lacked features indicative of the manuscript assemblage (a human rather than mechanical producer, uniqueness, idiosyncrasy of size and shape). Indeed, Nolan concludes that '[d]onning the habits of medieval readers allows us to touch them with an intimacy that cannot be reproduced, but without which we cannot understand the past'.[165] Yet the e-book, like the print book before it, incorporates previously absent actants (in this case, computer code, screens, energy and resource efficiency, the ability to preserve fragile originals) as well as those that are very familiar, even as we tend to downplay the nature of their participation in the collective.

Nolan observes that

> Digitization places intense pressure on our presumptions about experience – that is, on the idea that enacting the habits and re-creating the sensations of the past can give us special insight into what it meant to be a medieval reader – because it offers a new and improved version of the original medieval object, the book.[166]

This situation is cautiously celebrated by Susanna Fein and David Raybin in their editorial introduction to the 2013 special issue of *Chaucer Review* devoted to medieval English manuscripts[167] when they acknowledge that a manuscript's 'library setting is itself merely a museum in which to preserve a book already divorced from its original making in a localised setting some six to seven hundred years ago' – implying that perhaps a digital locus may be only similarly divorced from the book's origins – and they offer the possibility that, '[a]s digitized facsimiles become more widespread, they may, with their scientifically enhanced photography, actually lend to the medieval manuscript a freshness to the data it can yield, providing information unknown even to original users and to generations of scholars sitting in manuscripts reading rooms'.[168] This perspective imagines, as Jay David Bolter and Richard Grusin observe, that '[n]ew digital media are not external agents that come to disrupt an unsuspecting culture. They emerge from within cultural contexts.'[169] Our challenge, and opportunity, in this period of the e-incunabulum is to observe, describe, and theoretically conceptualise this new assemblage just as we have done its parchment- and paper-based precursors. We may note, for instance, that as the medieval text took on a different form in each manuscript appearance, depending on the scribe's materials and opportunities, the virtual text takes on a different shape in each encounter, depending on the reader's materials and preferences. The digitisation of our manuscripts and of our print books does not place them beyond sensation, out of the reach of our embodied humanity, but instead keeps the texts they display well within our grasp.

A central aim of this book is to discern this single manuscript's multiplicity, to document and appreciate the whole ecology of the book-in-time. A new materialist transtemporal rendering of Ashmole 61 reads the book's object agency in the array of communities collaboratively generated across its lifespan, circulating among its manuscript, print, and digital iterations. Direct contact with the slender codex's soft paper pages covered in brown ink in the early 2000s transformed what had been a multi-manuscript study of late Middle English romance into a project dedicated to this single manuscript, known at that time primarily for its textual aberrations and misbehaving scribe.[170] Already a devotee when its modern edition appeared in print and online in 2008, I was positioned to observe the adhesion encouraged by the conjunction of Shuffelton's editorial assistance with the reach of TEAMS' series of editions and the field's growing interest in non-canonical literacies.[171] The readings performed here seek to document the emotional literacy instruction generated for audiences in the fifteenth century, doing so with respectful awareness that such readings inevitably indicate still more about how Ashmole 61 affects its unanticipated yet eager reader today.

Notes

1 *Oxford English Dictionary*, s.v. 1.c.
2 Goldberg, 'The fashioning of bourgeois domesticity', p. 135.
3 Goldberg and Kowaleski, 'Introduction', p. 2. They note, too, that 'The object-centered approach to the household as the repository of possessions is also evident in recent archaeological works' (p. 2, n. 8).
4 Smith, *Arts of Possession*, p. 7 and n. 16.

Introduction 39

5   Smith, *Arts of Possession*, p. 19.
6   This phrase comes from Philippa Hardman's 1978 essay on MS Advocates 19.3.1. The term 'household book' has a mixed heritage, about which I will have more to say later in this chapter. For now, I hope that the quick description of this type of book that I provide here will suffice; it will also guide my investigation throughout *Objects of Affection*.
7   Julia Boffey describes such books as including 'a certain amount of pragmatically informative material [that] is amalgamated, in variable proportions, with texts which serve devotional or recreational purposes' ('Bodleian Library', p. 127).
8   Based on its watermarks and script, George Shuffelton dates Ashmole 61 to between 1490 and 1510 ('Is there a minstrel in the house?', p. 55), putting it at the end of this era of household book production.
9   CUL Ff.2.38 and Ashmole 61 share some paper stock (the fourth of four different paper stocks in CUL and the third of three in Ashmole 61) and were copied by a scribe (not the same one) in Leicestershire, and share certain linguistic features (Johnston, 'Two Leicestershire romance codices', p. 87). They also share six texts, but they don't share an exemplar for any of them (Johnston, 'Two Leicestershire romance codices', p. 89). Unlike Ashmole 61, CUL seems to have been produced on commission (Johnston, 'Two Leicestershire romance codices', p. 89, working from Felicity Riddy). Leicester was an active site for book production at this time, with a scriptorium at the Augustinian Abbey of St Mary de Pratis, just outside the city walls (Johnston, 'Two Leicestershire romance codices', p. 88).
10 The Heege manuscript has been convincingly associated with the yeoman Sherbrooke family in Derbyshire, with signatures of three family members appearing in the manuscript in late fifteenth-/early sixteenth-century hands. The Sherbrooke family sold the manuscript to Sir Walter Scott (in service to the Advocates Library in Edinburgh) around 300 years later, in 1806 (see Johnston, *Romance and the Gentry in Late Medieval England*, pp. 142–53, esp. p. 144). Even less is known about the producer(s) or owner(s) of Cotton Caligula a.2 than about Ashmole 61.
11 Johnston argues that romances (and the manuscripts in which they appear) became associated with the landowning gentry as they developed as a class (with early fourteenth-century roots, according to Coss, referenced by Johnston – what he describes as a couple of generations earlier). 'Knights, long the heroes of romance and long the mounted cavalry so important to the English army, had now also become the highest tier of the gentry' ('Romance, distraint, and the gentry', p. 438).

12 The primary book under discussion in their essay is MS Arch. Selden B.24, a Scottish anthology from the late 1400s that includes Chaucer and Hoccleve, Scottish texts and more, all in verse.
13 Boffey and Edwards, 'Bodleian MS Arch. Selden B.24', p. 34.
14 Boffey, 'Bodleian Library', p. 125. The example Boffey and Edwards provide is the Tollemache 'Book of Secrets' ('Bodleian MS Arch. Selden B.24', p. 34).
15 Boffey and Edwards, 'Bodleian MS Arch. Selden B.24', p. 34. Boffey and Edwards twelve years later continued this orientation towards the family milieu, resisting readings of the Findern Manuscript 'as an "anthology" or "miscellany". It needs to be set in its temporal and familial contexts as a "family" book created in a particular place over time to reflect the literary tastes and literary activities in a shared environment' ('Towards a taxonomy', p. 267). 'Family' as it is used today excludes many members of the medieval household, among them servants and apprentices; as a result, its modern use references something different from these manuscripts' arenas of initial production and reception. Further, the term 'family' held ambiguities at the time of these anthologies' production: it could refer narrowly to the 'servants of a household', from the Latin *familia* ('family servants, domestics collectively, the servants in a household', from *famulus*, 'servant') and thus include precisely those elements that 'family' excludes for a modern audience (*Online Etymology Dictionary*, s.v. 'family', www.etymonline.com/index.php?term=family). 'Family' could also, though, refer by the fourteenth century (via Middle French) to a 'group of people living under the same roof, household', and by 1440 more narrowly to a 'group of people related by blood, lineage' (*Oxford English Dictionary*, s.v. 'family'). In the 1540s, a family was a 'collective body of persons who form one household under one head and one domestic government, including parents, children, and servants, and as sometimes used even lodgers or boarders' (*Online Etymology Dictionary*; thanks to Karl Steel for encouraging this line of inquiry). Associations for 'family' varied extensively then, while the term's meaning is exclusive now, making it less useful than it could be to describe these manuscripts. The term 'household', in contrast, consistently refers, from the fourteenth century to the present day, to '[t]he inhabitants of a house considered collectively; a group of people (esp. a family) living together as a unit; a domestic establishment (including any servants, attendants, etc.)' (*Oxford English Dictionary*). Thus referring to these collections as 'household' books includes everyone – and everything – living and working in the household in this period when a home was not, as we would say, nuclear.

16 Johnston finds that the dialect of a manuscript's scribe tends to be similar to that of its early owners, indicating that the manuscript was produced by an employee of the gentry family (*Romance and the Gentry*, p. 98).

17 Johnston, *Romance and the Gentry*, pp. 122–3, 125; see also p. 116. Johnston believes such a production setting 'would best account for the confluence of dialectal and provenance evidence found in these miscellanies' (Johnston, *Romance and the Gentry*, p. 125). I would like to note here that while Johnston regularly uses the term 'provincial miscellany' to describe such manuscripts, which has the benefit of being clear and precise when used among manuscript scholars, I worry about the connotations of such a phrase, for it retains London as the focus of much Middle English literary history, with 'provincial' suggesting they are not only geographically but also culturally marginal (Johnston himself directly refutes this assumption). In addition, 'miscellany' implies a haphazardness and lack of any internal cohesion. While Johnston refers to some of these collections as demonstrating particular production patterns (especially in the case of those produced as a series of booklets), he does not make such a case for all. One aim of the current study is to investigate further the implications of this miscellaneity, which I address in further detail later in this introduction.

18 Ashmole 61, CUL Ff.2.38, Cotton Caligula a.2, the Heege MS; Thornton's Lincoln and London MSS would be categorised this way by some, as well.

19 Providing just one example of this motivation, Nicola McDonald in her introduction to *Pulp Fictions* defends the study of Middle English romance specifically for its 'power to shock us, to unsettle our assumptions about, among other things, gender and sexuality, race, religion, political formations, social class, ethics, morality and aesthetic distinctions', and its utility in the 'interrogation of the norms that order and regulate our lives' (McDonald, 'A polemical introduction', pp. 16–17). See Symes, 'Manuscript matrix, modern canon'; Connolly, 'The whole book'; and Radulescu, 'Vying for attention'.

20 I use 'the past' in terms of Timothy Morton's observation that 'What is called the past is really other objects that coexist with the object in question' ('An object-oriented defense of poetry', p. 220).

21 Carolyn Dinshaw refers to this as a recognition of the 'multitemporality of the *now*' (*How Soon is Now?*, p. 10; italics original). The effects of including post-medieval readers in the ecology of the (medieval) manuscript book can be seen in views such as Jessica Brantley's that '[i]t no longer necessarily matters only how a manuscript was designed to work, if you can see, from the readers' perspective how it did'

('The pre-history of the book', p. 635). Brantley elsewhere observes that '[a] miscellany is most meaningful, not because it was designed to work in a particular way, but simply because it does' ('The pre-history of the book', p. 11). Such statements indicate a move away from validating as authoritative only origins and the intentions of the past (its scribes and collators), and towards an acceptance of the influence of the present (in this case, the readers who later encounter the book) on the past. While Brantley's 'how it did' does imply a prioritising of medieval readers' engagement with the manuscript (as if how it worked then either explains or trumps how it works now), also understood is the contribution of the modern scholar who actively inhabits 'the readers' perspective' – so that the book's readers include not only medieval ones but also those living today who perform the deep interpretation for which Price's definition of book history calls.

22 Shuffelton, *Codex Ashmole 61*.
23 Shuffelton, *Codex Ashmole 61*, d.lib.rochester.edu/teams/text/shuffelton-codex-ashmole-61-introduction.
24 At the time of original publication of this book, just eleven folios were available online (fol. 016v–017r, 105v–106r, 106v–107v, 127v–128r, 150v–151r and fol. iir). A complete digitized copy of the manuscript can now be accessed online for free through the Digital Bodleian website: https://digital.bodleian.ox.ac.uk/objects/69462c25-b481-4643-9942-34f7243ea921/
25 John Dagenais has observed that '[o]ur traditional view of the medieval page sees it as a prepared laboratory cross-section, sprayed with fixative and placed on a glass slide for scrutiny under the microscope'. Perceiving the manuscript as a material object fixed in time and stored in the modern archive to await expert examination places all agency with the scholars and with the present and denies the continuing life of the page, of the text, of the manuscript, throughout the centuries. Dagenais promotes an alternative model: 'The medieval manuscript page and its culture are more like an open Petri dish, a living, growing thing, placed within a fertile, organic medium.' As a result, '[t]here are, in fact, no medieval pages. Whatever medieval pages there may have been were all destroyed in the Middle Ages' ('Decolonizing the medieval page', pp. 39, 67). See, too, Warren, 'Post-philology'.
26 It also contains none of the political, chronicle, or prose items popular in other household manuscripts.
27 '[U]nlike CUL, there is no generic organizational pattern to the manuscript' (Johnston, 'Two Leicestershire romance codices', p. 90).

28 Boffey and Edwards include this manuscript among the '"themed" anthologies' (including Robert Thornton's two collections, Lincoln, Cathedral Library MS 91 and British Library MS Additional 31042), describing it as 'the evidently bowdlerised collection of family reading' ('Towards a taxonomy', p. 271).

29 The first eight items exist independently of the remainder of the manuscript even as they are fully integrated with it; this section has come to be called the 'Children's Corner'. It is the focus of Chapter 1.

30 This mirrors the structure Ralph Hanna has discerned in most of the booklets of the revered Auchinleck MS: as 'top-heavy', that is, with 'the most substantial text coming first' (*London Literature*, p. 76). Arthur Bahr builds on this in his demonstration that *The Legend of Pope Gregory*, the first text in Auchinleck as it now exists, is imitated in structure by the first romance in the collection (which is in booklet 3), *Sir Degare* – both include women who have sons in shameful circumstances; he is raised by a holy man, then he gets the tokens his mother left him; he becomes a knight and goes to claim his birthright, and in the process wins a tournament and thus his (unrecognised) mother as wife (Bahr, *Fragments and Assemblages*, ch. 3).

31 Used by Lynne S. Blanchfield in her title ('An idiosyncratic scribe') and showing its pull in Johnston's use of it in describing, too, the vertical fold used on the paper to create the tall pages (*Romance and the Gentry*, p. 115).

32 Blanchfield has shown that Rate modelled the size of the manuscript on account books ('An idiosyncratic scribe', pp. 13–20).

33 Bruce Barker-Benfield further explains that 'a horizontal crease occurs on every leaf [that is, right in the middle of the long page, extending side-to-side]. The direction of the folds, and the occasional spurt of ink where the scribe's pen has hiccupped over the crease (e.g. fol. 34), suggest that these folds were present *before* writing; a decision must have been taken to change the format of the blank paper from a modest-sized quarto to a "holster" book. This seems more likely than the alternative theory, which posits an unorthodox and awkward mode of carrying' (quoted in Blanchfield, 'An idiosyncratic scribe', p. 14).

34 Blanchfield, 'An idiosyncratic scribe', p. 18.

35 Kwakkel, *Books Before Print*, pp. 165–7.

36 Blanchfield, 'An idiosyncratic scribe', p. 18. The first quire is the only possibly independent quire (i.e., booklet) in the manuscript; all others, beginning with quire 2, end in the middle of a text, which is then continued in the next quire.

37 This entire debate revolves around negative associations with 'minstrel' poetry that linger from the mid-twentieth century but are inappropriate

to current approaches. Shuffelton writes, in a study of the many references to minstrels in Ashmole 61: 'dismissing these references to minstrels as merely tropes or formulaic gestures [as those who want to 'redeem' the texts do] loses sight of their larger significance. Many texts make explicit connections between minstrelsy and the household's generosity' ('Is there a minstrel in the house?', p. 66).

38 Shuffelton, 'Is there a minstrel in the house?', pp. 58, 69.
39 Shuffelton, 'Is there a minstrel in the house?', p. 58. Here, Shuffelton builds on Joyce Coleman's earlier argument (in *Public Reading*) that 'the accounts of reading aloud in English settings tend to emphasise community, bonding "the listeners as a social unit – a family or a household – within an atmosphere of reassuring spiritual and social authority," even as it "functioned as a means of basic social control," and a way to tamp down domestic strife' ('Is there a minstrel in the house?', p. 58).
40 Particularly given Blanchfield's observation that the shape makes it well suited to holding while reading aloud.
41 The LALME places the scribe's dialect just to the north-east of the city of Leicester (Johnston, *Romance and the Gentry*, p. 88). Shuffelton offers that the scribe 'was most likely William Ratte, ironmonger, whose name appears among the free citizens of Leicester in 1509' ('Is there a minstrel in the house?', p. 55); Johnston reaches a similar conclusion, noting there are 'various Rates attested in the city archives' in Leicester, but '[n]one, unfortunately, can be definitively identified as the scribe of Ashmole 61, though I believe William Rott, ironmonger, to be the most likely match' (*Romance and the Gentry*, p. 117). Rory G. Critten notes that 'all but one of the potential candidates for Rate's identity put forward by both Shuffelton and Blanchfield belong to the merchant class' ('Bourgeois ethics again', p. 117).
42 Advocates 19.3.1, a household book produced nearby at the same time and including some of the same watermarked paper, contains some scribal signatures (of its scribes Heege and Hawghton), but only at the ends of booklets, except in very rare instances (Evans, *Rereading Middle English Romance*, p. 76).
43 It is also one of the features that manuscript scholars read as pointing towards an amateur scribe: 'A professional scribe producing a book would hardly have signed his own name repeatedly or drawn a series of what are presumably esoteric illustrations in a volume meant for someone else, suggesting that Rate probably made this for his own household's consumption' (Johnston, 'Two Leicestershire romance codices', p. 90).
44 Johnston, *Romance and the Gentry*, p. 109.

Introduction 45

45 Further, Boffey and Thompson conclude that '[t]hese details, involving little technical expertise and no great expense, are obviously attempts to enhance the appeal of Rate's book for its intended readers. They reflect a conception of "the whole book" and a concern for its visual attractiveness which are not always apparent in other non-systematic book productions of the period' ('Anthologies and miscellanies', p. 298).
46 One image in the manuscript, which is neither a fish nor a flower and thus not part of this ongoing 'program of rubrications and decorations', *is* such a visual adjunct: the shield accompanying *The Short Charter of Christ* (fol. 106r); the fact that in one case an image does provide a visual supplement to the text makes all the more suggestive the fact that the repeated images – 33 of them – do not.
47 That is, the brief annotation at the end of a text (or of a manuscript) in which the scribe, speaking in the first person, asks for or offers a prayer, names himself, or otherwise engages with the audience
48 There appears, among those who have paid attention to MS Ashmole 61 in recent years, to be the sense that Rate's fish appear only between poems. Perhaps this can be traced back to Michael Johnston's description – one of the few published sources on the manuscript – of the fish as appearing 'at seemingly random intervals … at the conclusion of texts' (*Romance and the Gentry*, p. 117). The fish do appear at the ends of texts, but not only there, for they also appear in the middle of texts at the bottom of the page, as for instance throughout item 19 (*The Erle of Tolous*, fol. 27v–38v) at the bottom margin on folios 31r (single fish), 32v (two flowers), 33v (one flower), 36v (two fish) and facing that, 37r (one fish), as well as at the poem's end, on 38v (a flower).
49 See Shuffelton, *Codex Ashmole 61*, p. 3.
50 Blanchfield ('An idiosyncratic scribe'), referenced in Shuffelton, *Codex Ashmole 61*, p. 5.
51 Ashmole 61 has been described as 'an anthology of *domestitia*, texts dealing with family life and family relationships … the scribe has chosen items which deal with all aspects, normal and abnormal, pleasant and unpleasant, of relationships within the family … the emphasis is on middle-class domesticity, manners and morals, on the joys and perils of marriage and ownership of property, on the instruction and education of children and, above all, on the godly life, with a warning against "vanyte", and with a leavening of Romance, slanted also to the domestic bias' (Ginn, ed., *Sir Cleges*, pp. 82, 84–5).
52 In addition, it includes only those items generally perceived as objects. Object-oriented new materialist approaches include, as will be discussed

below, objects not immediately perceived by most people as objects, such as religious faith, hip-hop, or an ice age.
53 Steel, *How Not to Make a Human*, p. 3, italics added; p. 4, italics original.
54 Bynum, *Christian Materiality*, p. 30.
55 Bynum, *Christian Materiality*, p. 254.
56 Mitchell, *Becoming Human*, p. 16.
57 Lemay, *Women's Secrets*, quoted in Mitchell, *Becoming Human*, p. 16. There are many additional examples in Mitchell's chapter 'Being born'.
58 *Nicole Oresme and the Marvels of Nature*, p. 233 (with Oresme's notion of 'intermediate species' following Aristotle's *History of Animals*, pp. 921–3 [8.1], in *Complete Works*, vol. 1), cited in Mitchell, *Becoming Human*, p. 16; italics added.
59 Coole and Frost, 'Introducing the New Materialisms', p. 9.
60 Latour's concept of the 'actant' allows clarification that this agency need not be intentional. See *Reassembling the Social*.
61 It also insists that these things are objects, 'not just amorphous matter', and that 'real things exist' (Morton, 'Here comes everything', p. 165).
62 Internal distinctions have, at times, been a dominant focus among its leading theorists, including Graham Harman, Timothy Morton, Levi Bryant, Ian Bogost, and Jane Bennett. Some object-oriented approaches insist upon the irreducibility of the object (object-oriented ontology, in particular, in which I include Levi Bryant's onticology and Ian Bogost's alien phenomenology) even while recognising the shifting relationships among objects; others perceive the object particularly in terms of the networks or assemblages it participates in (vibrant materialism and actor-network theory, for example).
63 This phrasing is attributed to Manuel DeLanda.
64 Morton, 'Here comes everything', p. 164. Many of these views are shared by new materialists, well beyond those doing object-oriented studies.
65 I should note, even as my project does not depend on such distinctions, that Bogost argues that '[l]ists remind us that no matter how fluidly a system may operate, its members nevertheless remain utterly isolated, mutual aliens' (*Alien Phenomenology*, p. 40).
66 Bennett, *Vibrant Matter*, p. 65.
67 Bennett, 'Systems and things', p. 231.
68 I am assisted by the alternative perspective offered by Jane Bennett: 'there is not so much a doer (an agent) behind the deed ... as a doing and an effecting by a human-nonhuman assemblage' ('Systems and things', p. 28).

69 Mitchell, *Becoming Human*, p. 76.
70 Allen, 'Mineral virtue', p. 133, with quotation from Albertus Magnus, *De Mineralibus*, Book 3, Tractatus 1, chapter 1, the English translation here from Wyckoff, p. 153.
71 Robertson, 'Exemplary rocks', pp. 93, 99–100. Robertson has further pursued her consideration of the *scala naturae*, in 'Scaling nature', where she offers an extended consideration of new materialism, and of Bennett in particular (see pp. 625–8), in relation to ideas about 'microcosmic thinking' expressed by later medieval thinkers such as Alain de Lille, Jean de Meun, Guillaume de Deguileville, and the anonymous author of *Eschéz d'Amours*.
72 Cohen, *Stone*, p. 15. See also pp. 55–6. Cohen notes, among other things, that lapidaries taught that '[t]he topaz prefers chaste companions' (p. 234).
73 Cohen, *Stone*, pp. 232–3. For particular consideration of how the term lost its gendered associations with *vir* (Latin, 'man'), see pp. 233–4, and for discussion of *virtus* generally, see pp. 232–7.
74 See, as well, Jeffrey Jerome Cohen's evocative entry on 'C is causality that *vertu* confuses', where '[s]tones and leaves radiate *vertu* as easily as knights, horses and clerics. Humans may ally themselves with the *vertu* of gems or herbs to accomplish through mineral and vegetal friendship feats otherwise impossible. *Vertu* is a life force: reproduction and vitality, affect and intellect and health, that which moves the flesh' ('An abecedarium', p. 292).
75 Allen, 'Mineral virtue', p. 130; the Albertus Magnus quote Allen cites from *De Mineralibus*, Book 2, Tractatus 1, chapter 3, in the English translation by Wyckoff, p. 63. Cohen similarly discusses this feature of Albertus Magnus's writing in *Stone*, p. 234.
76 Allen, 'Mineral virtue', p. 129.
77 Crocker, *The Matter of Virtue*, p. 3. She continues, 'Virtues are not intangible, theoretical principles; rather, bodies have the potentialities their virtues enable' (p. 4). Crocker's section on 'material virtue' in the introduction to *The Matter of Virtue* offers an excellent overview of this feature of premodern Western European culture (pp. 2–6); her book's chapters trace 'how literary authors, in seeking to represent women's ethical action, end up inventing new virtues through their female characters' (p. 9). Further, see Steel, *How to Make a Human*, esp. pp. 10–15 where he engages with the work of Joyce Salisbury, Dorothy Yamamoto, and Erika Fudge, for consideration of this issue in terms of medieval animals.
78 Morton, 'An object-oriented defense of poetry', p. 215. As Levi Bryant says, 'Texts aren't simply *about* something, but *are* something ... [a

text] is a real thing that circulates throughout the world and does all sorts of things', by 'producing all sorts of real effects' (Coffield, 'Interview: Levi Bryant', n.p.). Such effects aren't necessary for a thing to be 'real', but they are helpful indicators that let us discern the reality of the object. The non-human agent that is the text 'directly intervenes in reality in a causal way' (Morton, 'An object-oriented defense of poetry', pp. 215, 206).

79 The necessity of early print copies of vernacular translations of the Bible to the developments of the Reformation in the sixteenth century is a vivid indicator of this combination of imaginative and material agency.

80 Bennett, 'Systems and things', p. 232. Bogost notes, 'When people or toothbrushes or siroccos make sense of encountered objects, they do so through metaphor. As Whitehead and Latour suggest, this process requires creative effort' (*Alien Phenomenology*, p. 111).

81 Bennett, 'Systems and things', p. 232.

82 The affirmation of human exceptionalism, however unintended, is the fundamental flaw that Harman observes in Bill Brown's thing theory: 'the assumption that "the real" has no other function than to accompany the human agent and mold or disrupt it from time to time' ('The well-wrought broken hammer', p. 193).

83 Bynum, *Christian Materiality*, p. 29.

84 Bynum, *Christian Materiality*, p. 153; emphasis hers.

85 Bynum, *Christian Materiality*, p. 21.

86 Bynum, *Christian Materiality*, p. 158.

87 The 'Prayer at the Levation' (item 17) provides extensive demonstration of these connections through an ongoing metaphoric equation of Christ with earthly elements human and non-human, animate and inanimate: a series of depictions of Jesus as flower, fruit, king, knight, prince, duke, emperor, rose, and pearl is framed in the first and last lines of the poem through the Eucharistic prayer 'Welcom, Lord, in forme of brede' (ll. 1 and 35). The poem indicates that as Christ is present in the form of bread, he is present throughout creation in such other forms, as well.

88 Bennett, 'Systems and things', p. 229.

89 This follows particularly from Graham Harman's key concept of objects' 'withdrawal'. See Harman, 'The well-wrought broken hammer', as well as Bennett's response in which this critique appeared ('Systems and things').

90 Sheldon, 'Form/matter/chora', p. 194.

91 Talbot, 'Flat ontologies and everyday feminisms', p. 87.

92 See Crenshaw, 'Demarginalizing the intersection of race and sex'.

93 Barad, 'Posthumanist performativity', p. 135. Indeed, Barad formulated her theory in the early 2000s, publishing *Meeting the Universe Halfway* in 2007 prior to the appearance of OOO and in conversation and communion with an established community of feminist and feminist-friendly materialist approaches.
94 See Harman, *Object Oriented Ontology*, for an explanation and defence of the OOO perspective.
95 Barad, 'Posthumanist performativity', p. 144.
96 Talbot, 'Flat ontologies and everyday feminisms', p. 89.
97 Behar, 'An introduction to OOF'.
98 See Alaimo, *Bodily Natures*.
99 See Alaimo and Hekman, *Material Feminisms*.
100 And needless to say, not an animated collection of household furnishings as in the Disney version of *Beauty and the Beast* (1991).
101 Bynum's description of medieval visual arts demonstrates how such an enmeshment would be less unusual in the Middle Ages than we might anticipate: 'Medieval art was neither naturalistic nor illusionist. Unlike the painting of a Renaissance Madonna, for example, in which the artist concentrates on making the viewer see paint on canvas as fabric or skin and hence (among other things) admire his or her skill at creating illusion, a medieval image induces the viewer to notice that it is made from paint and wood or vellum and ink. But the stuff of which medieval images were made was not incidental nor indeed was it only an iconography to be decoded' (*Christian Materiality*, p. 28).
102 Bahr and Gillespie, 'Medieval English manuscripts', p. 356; emphasis added.
103 Furrow, ed., *Ten Bourdes*, introduction to *Sir Corneus*, n.p. Consistently, such explanations fail to satisfy even their own proponents, as Shuffelton observes, *Codex Ashmole 61*, p. 5.
104 Johnston, *Romance and the Gentry*, p. 117.
105 More specifically, Dan Remein, a collaborative participant with Ashmole 61, led me to see this.
106 My thanks go to the members of the audience at a talk I gave at the University of Victoria for encouraging me to pursue such lines of inquiry (and to Allan Mitchell for providing the opportunity). Furthermore, the abundant fish (which appear much more frequently than do the flowers) may also re-enact the feeding of the five thousand, with Rate thereby distributing the loaves and fishes to feed the hungry, participating in an assemblage of earthly objects, both human and non-human, with the divine.
107 A cartouche is an illustrated frame for a catchword.

108 Thanks to Bruce Holsinger for drawing my attention to the Harley 3744 catchword fish.
109 Holsinger, 'Of pigs and parchment' (see also Holsinger, 'Parchment ethics'); Kay, 'Legible skins' and *Animal Skins*. Paper manuscripts do seem, by the relative permanence of the ink on their pages compared to the easy erasability of marks on parchment, to be incomplete participants in Stephen G. Nichols's 'manuscript matrix' ('What is manuscript culture?', p. 39). Orietta Da Rold's *Paper in Medieval England: From Pulp to Fictions* (Cambridge University Press) has much to say about paper's agency in literary and non-literary communities in England.
110 'A book is an assemblage … and as such is unattributable. It is a multiplicity' (Deleuze and Guattari, *A Thousand Plateaus*, p. 4).
111 Price, 'From the history of a book', p. 136.
112 Johnston and Van Dussen, 'Introduction'.
113 Bahr works here from Deleuze and Guattari's discussion of book-as-assemblage in *A Thousand Plateaus*, p. 4.
114 Bahr, *Fragments and Assemblages*, p. 11.
115 Seth Lerer clarifies that '[t]he critical consensus seems to be, now, that a miscellany is any collection of texts not necessarily guided by an editorial, authorial, scribal, or patronal aegis' ('Medieval English literature', p. 1265, n. 8; p. 1255). See Margaret Connolly and Raluca Radulescu, 'Introduction', pp. 4–5 for additional and more recent discussion of these distinctions.
116 Connolly and Radulescu, 'Introduction', p. 1. Arthur Bahr, 'Miscellaneity and variance in the medieval book', acknowledges the 'safe' definition provided by Connolly and Radulescu while encouraging alternative types of engagement.
117 Pearsall, 'The whole book', p. 23. He includes in this category, along with nine other manuscripts, as well as 'the various collections of Chauceriana' and all of the output of the scribes John Shirley, Robert Thornton, and John Colyns, 'the romance-miscellanies such as' Cotton Caligula a.2 and Ashmole 61 ('The whole book', p. 17). See the reflections of Bahr on this issue ('Miscellaneity and variance in the medieval book', pp. 187–8).
118 For an example of the ongoing dominance of the author in many medievalist literary scholars' inquiries, even those guided by a deep engagement with manuscripts, see Pearsall's complaint in his 2000 essay of the manuscript work being done (for example with glosses and illustrations of Chaucer texts) that '[i]t was clear I wasn't learning anything new about what Chaucer's text meant' but 'only about the

constraints that the illustrator was under, from ignorance, or from the dominance of conventional models, or from the absence of relevant models' ('The value/s of manuscript study', p. 172).
119 Pearsall, 'The whole book', p. 18.
120 Bahr, 'Miscellaneity and variance in the medieval book', p. 182.
121 Pearsall, 'The whole book', p. 17; emphasis added.
122 Pearsall, 'The whole book', p. 29.
123 Adams, 'Introduction', p. 173.
124 McNamer, 'Feeling', p. 242; Trigg, 'Emotional histories'.
125 Broomhall, 'Emotions in the household', p. 2.
126 Tracy Adams observes that in the Western Middle Ages, 'emotion was understood as a communal rather than private phenomenon', as a 'communal production' ('Introduction', pp. 174, 179). See Downes and McNamara, 'The history of emotions'.
127 Rosenwein, 'Worrying about emotions in history', p. 842.
128 *Carpenter's Tools* has become rather a celebrity since the publication of the 2008 edition of the manuscript, collecting investigations such as Lisa Cooper's in 2011 (*Artisans and Narrative Craft*) and Wendy Matlock's in 2014 ('Reworking the household'). It receives extended discussion in Chapter 3.
129 For Ahmed, 'the nonresidence of emotions is what makes them "binding"' (Ahmed, *The Cultural Politics of Emotion*, p. 119).
130 Ahmed, *The Cultural Politics of Emotion*, p. 119. This depiction of affective economies maintains the subject–object distinction, which I tend to read as an artificial boundary that gives opportunities for granting to those objects that humans determine to be deserving the status of subjects with an exclusive claim to agency. However, this is no limitation to Ahmed's argument, for her treatment of objects (and subjects) weakens that boundary and makes her affective economies useful models for an object-oriented approach.
131 Ahmed, *The Cultural Politics of Emotion*, p. 6.
132 Ahmed, *The Cultural Politics of Emotion*, p. 8; 'Happy objects', p. 31. Ahmed investigates 'how happiness functions as a promise that directs us toward certain objects, which then circulate as social goods. Such objects accumulate positive affective value as they are passed around', and she describes this affective quality as 'sticky' ('Happy objects', p. 31).
133 Ahmed, 'Happy objects', p. 41.
134 Ahmed quickly connects affect and object(s) – in the sense of not subject – when she says that 'happiness also turns us toward objects. We turn toward objects at the very point of "making." To be made happy

by this or that is to recognise that happiness starts from somewhere other than the subject who may use the word to describe a situation' ('Happy objects', p. 31).
135 Ahmed, 'Happy objects', p. 31.
136 Ahmed, 'Affective economies', pp. 6, 10. The evaluation does not occur in the independent now, but within a social – a historical – community. Helpful in visualising this is F. R. Ankersmit's description of sensation, including 'feeling' more broadly, through the experience of holding a vase in our hands: 'We then feel the vase's form because our own hands take on the very same form as the vase's. We are formed by what we perceive, what we perceive leaves its indelible traces on us' (Robinson, 'Touching the void', pp. 130–1; quoted from Ankersmit, *Sublime Historical Experience*, p. 512.)
137 See Trigg, 'Emotional histories', describing Ahmed. Objects include things such as hunger. In her overview of different current and former approaches towards emotion in history, Broomhall notes of the current bodily emphasis that it raises various questions about how things such as hunger in lower-income households influenced emotion, asking the important question 'Were the emotional reactions to such bodily states historically specific, or simply recognised and reported differently?' ('Emotions in the household', p. 8).
138 Rosenwein, 'Worrying about emotions in history', p. 842.
139 Rosenwein, *Emotional Communities*, p. 25. Importantly, 'people move (and moved) continually from one such community to another – from taverns to law courts, say – adjusting their emotional displays and their judgments of weal and woe ... to these different environments' (Worrying about emotions in history', p. 842).
140 King, 'Emotions in medieval thought', p. 2. See McNamer, *Affective Meditation*.
141 Ahmed, 'Happy objects', p. 30.
142 Nagy, 'Historians and emotions'.
143 Adams, 'Introduction', p. 174.
144 Scheer, 'Are emotions a kind of practice?', p. 193.
145 Bynum, *Christian Materiality*, p. 226.
146 Stewart, *Ordinary Affects*, p. 2.
147 Stewart, *Ordinary Affects*, p. 129.
148 Stewart, *Ordinary Affects*, p. 40.
149 Stewart, *Ordinary Affects*, p. 3.
150 Stewart, *Ordinary Affects*, p. 9.
151 The extreme rarity of such an opportunity is apparent in Raluca Radulescu's observation that '[t]he only recent example of a new way of editing such a manuscript is available in the full edition of

the Rate manuscript … There a choice was made to present all the texts continuously, in the order they appear in the manuscript, and only include notes and a commentary separately, thus not impeding fresh independent interpretations of the whole or parts' ('Vying for attention,' p. 121, n. 6).
152 Pearsall, 'The value/s of manuscript study', p. 168.
153 Nolan, 'Medieval habit, modern sensation', p. 467.
154 Nolan, 'Medieval habit, modern sensation', p. 472.
155 Nolan, 'Medieval habit, modern sensation', pp. 472–3.
156 Nolan, 'Medieval habit, modern sensation', p. 473. Note as well that the manuscript is merely a vehicle for human-to-human contact (ultimately a mere instrument).
157 Nolan, 'Medieval habit, modern sensation', p. 470.
158 For instance, Guðrún Nordal began her 2014 plenary address on Icelandic manuscripts at the New Chaucer Society meeting in Reykjavik by saying, 'Manuscripts are our windows to the past. Open a manuscript, and you open the window.' Derek Pearsall similarly describes the encounter with a manuscript: 'There is the manuscript and there am I, and for a moment I have the vivid sense that the past is speaking directly to me. It is difficult to convey the uniqueness of this experience, or fully to express this sense of historical intimacy, of privileged and immediate access to the past' ('The value/s of manuscript study', p. 167).
159 Nolan, 'Medieval habit, modern sensation', p. 465.
160 This situation is humorously represented in the skit 'Medieval Helpdesk' from the Norwegian comedy show *Øystein og jeg*, in which monks are baffled by book technology the way twenty-first-century people were first perplexed by iPads. www.youtube.com/watch?v=pQHX-SjgQvQ (accessed 26 August 2020).
161 My thanks to Lara Farina for pushing my thinking here yet further.
162 McGann, 'From text to work', p. 60.
163 Williams, *Keywords*, p. 158.
164 Mitchell, 'There are no visual media', p. 260.
165 Nolan, 'Medieval habit, modern sensation', p. 476.
166 Nolan, 'Medieval habit, modern sensation', p. 471.
167 The issue, guest-edited by Bahr and Gillespie, included Nolan's essay.
168 Fein and Raybin, 'About this issue', pp. 344–5.
169 Bolter and Gruisn, *Remediation*, p. 19. Lisa Gitelman in a similar vein calls these contexts 'socially embedded sites' (*Always Already New*, p. 6).
170 Perhaps this is not the place to confess that Ashmole 61's peers – including Advocates 19.3.1, CUL Ff.2.38, and Cotton Caligula a.2 – simply

paled in comparison. Admittedly this first contact occurred in Duke Humfrey's reading room, an ideal setting for the start of a love affair.

171 The abundant smiling fish seem to have been powerful participants in this assemblage, showing that Boffey and Thompson's observation of the manuscript's illustrations – that though they 'involved little technical expertise and no great expense ... are obviously attempts to enhance the appeal of Rate's book for its intended readers' – extends to unintended readers, as well ('Anthologies and miscellanies', p. 298).

1

Objects of instruction

Late medieval merchant-gentry households actively established and affirmed human social identity through the exercise of transferable goods. Literal displays of objects – those one inherited (land, houses, goods, arms) and those one acquired (moveable household goods, clothing, court and governmental positions) – substantiated status and the social value bound up in elite identity.[1] Abstract genealogical claims grounded status through perceived biological inheritance, while social worth was professed by tangible – and mobile, and mutable – objects. In such an environment, objects carrying culturally invested significance collectively generated a person's worth and took on heightened social agency. A book such as Ashmole 61 was just this sort of object. Wills regularly attest to the care with which manuscripts and early print books were passed on from one generation to the next, bearing with them into the future perceived material and cultural capital. No evidence of the historical figures who were the earliest owners of MS Ashmole 61 remains, although the like-new condition of the paper anthology suggests that, along the way to its inclusion in Elias Ashmole's collection in the seventeenth century and eventually in the Bodleian Library, appropriate care was taken. The absence of a documented history of the individual book object does not prevent it from speaking of its earliest surroundings; the material and textual components of this manuscript reveal, among other things, how it assisted in the construction of the late fifteenth-century Leicestershire household of which it was a contributing member.

From the start, Ashmole 61 asserts the status-producing powers of its household object ecology. Its first eight texts act as a model household community, establishing methods of status affirmation for the entire collection to follow. *St Eustace*, Lydgate's *Right as a Ram's Horn*, *How the Wise Man Taught His Son*, *How the Good Wife Taught Her Daughter*, *Sir Isumbras*, the *Ten Commandments* (adapted from the *Speculum Christiani*), Lydgate's *Stans Puer ad Mensam*, and *Dame Curtasy*: these texts' largely modern titles emphasise their human elements (a saint, a knight, a wise man, a young man, a good wife, a dame, and so on). Yet in the world of these poems, individually and collectively, the non-human actors are social and spiritual agents in a moral ecology that generates the household and – as one prominent constituent of that – human identity.

An exemplary textual assemblage

The book object of Ashmole 61, and the objects that fill the book, enact a kind of agency some manuscript scholars have been working over the past quarter century to ascribe specifically to scribes. This recent move has challenged long-standing norms of textual scholarship, according to which scribes are a problem to be worked through, with those scribes who are most absent – those whose copying is mechanical and lacks intervention – most esteemed, and those whose presence cannot be ignored, denigrated. In that older model, evidence of agency is understood only as evidence of error. Conceptualising book agency as a collective object agency, however, does not continue to neglect scribal agency, as might be expected: human agency (scribal and otherwise) is itself a kind of object agency, a scribe one of the many actants contributing the unique characteristics of a given book.

In the case of Ashmole 61, the distinctive features of the conduct items, especially, suggest a particularly active scribe: the six non-narrative texts in these first two quires are in nearly every case sufficiently variant to be listed in the *Digital Index of Middle English Verse* (*DIMEV*) as a separate version of the item. For instance, Ashmole 61's version of the *Ten Commandments* (item 6) frames the common text (of ten stanzas) with four additional and unique stanzas, one as a prologue and three in conclusion. Rate appears also to have reworked the more traditional conduct pieces he includes: *Wise Man*, *Good Wife*, *Stans Puer*, and *Dame Curtasy*.[2] Of the twenty-five extant copies of *Stans Puer*, for instance, only two (that is, less than 10 per cent) are sufficiently different to be classified by the *DIMEV* as unique versions, and one of these is the version in Ashmole 61.[3] In fact, Ashmole 61's *Stans Puer* includes an additional prologue of six stanzas, the central effect of which is to make clear its didactic purpose,[4] with the speaker declaring that he wishes to 'teche / That som man therfor the better maye be' and 'ever more all vyces ... may fere and fle', an end he believes will be accomplished by 'tech[ing] chylder curtasy' (5–9).[5] Structurally, this is the only version of *Stans Puer* that is not written in rime royal: Rate presents his modified version of the text in quatrains. The process generates so many stanzas that it doubles the length of the most common version of the poem. Similarly, *Dame Curtasy* is the only unique version of *The Lytylle Childrenes Lytil Boke*. In fact, calling it a version of that more common text (as is generally done) is misleading, for *Dame Curtasy* includes only six of that poem's 152 lines, just 4 per cent.[6] The consistently radical revisions of the conduct pieces suggest that these changes are not the scribal errors critics have regularly labelled them. Further, such differences from the more common version of the text are not present to that degree in neighbouring narratives (*St Eustace* and *Isumbras*); they are in most cases multiple-line additions or deletions, rather than scattered individual aberrations; and they can even involve a change to the poetic form of the entire text. As a result, such distinctions warrant attention as textual adaptations that suit the unique ecology of which these poems are a part. Through such dynamic variations, the texts and their scribe actively and collaboratively generate the unique textual ecology that is Ashmole 61.[7]

Conduct texts orient primarily towards humans' social behaviour; in their particular setting in Ashmole 61, these texts reveal human social identity as consistently entangled with the non-human objects that populate and shape the household. In this, they demonstrate J. Allan Mitchell's observation that 'human agency is distributed among an array of things in [conduct] literature, in which case anthropocentric views of even the most refined behavior cannot be sustained'.[8]

Indeed, Mitchell argues for more than an enmeshment – a metaphor that can seem to indicate a shared community in which agency could continue in its usually perceived single direction, from human to non-human. He reorients conceptions of conduct (and the literature that concerns and constructs it): 'Conduct is the way humans deploy things *as* things, and in that respect, things deploy the human.'[9]

In the opening conduct-heavy poems of Ashmole 61, and given habits of reading exclusively through the human subject, it is easy to overlook the ways in which things might deploy the human: a father instructs his son in how to select a wife who will give him little grief and even perhaps much satisfaction (item 3); a mother warns her daughter against risky public places and dangerous private behaviour, proclaiming the joys of thrift (item 4); young male household members are taught (by a disembodied authoritative voice in two cases, and by Dame Curtasy in another) how to travel efficiently and honourably with one's social betters, how to eat among them without embarrassment, and how to be useful without being noticed (items 7 and 8). Christians are taught, by God in his revealed commandments, how to avoid earthly trouble and heavenly exclusion (item 6) and, by a recurring disembodied authoritative (human) voice, about the disappointments of human society (item 2). In this community of direct addresses to the reader,[10] the first and fourth items distinguish themselves by taking the form of narratives (*St Eustace* and *Isumbras*, respectively), yet they too encourage particular sets of behaviours and beliefs, through the deliberate suffering and deserved success of a future saint and his nuclear family and, in parallel, of a knight-become-king and his nuclear family. Taken as a whole, this section of the manuscript devotes itself to the refining of human behaviour; in so doing, it maps the society of things necessary to the ongoing prosperity of the household collective and promotes methods and orientations useful for achieving prosperous membership in that society.

The first Ashmole 61 texts frequently focus on practical actions that can be taken in specific settings in pursuit of the generally unspoken goals of social comfort and spiritual tidiness. The densely packed environment of social improvement in this initial section of the book can generate an impression of anxious medieval readers filling their weeks with one self-help group meeting after another. Encountering the 'how-to' poems in the company of the socially and spiritually exemplary narratives of Eustace and Isumbras brings into focus the texts' shared investments in modelling identities available to human household inhabitants. Writing about the collective transformative experience that didactic texts can make available to audiences, Eva von Contzen builds on Mary Carruthers' mapping of medieval reading as personal experience – not separate from personal experience, as it is most commonly understood today ('what happens to me' and 'what happened in a book' being two distinct events), but rather reading as an experience that in its very act becomes the audience member's personal experience. As Carruthers puts it, '"what I read in a book" *is* "my experience," and I make it mine by incorporating it (and we should understand the word "incorporate" quite literally) in my memory'.[11] From such an understanding of textual experience, in the case of exemplary texts such as a saint's life or a romance, von Contzen extrapolates that an audience simultaneously acknowledges the singularity of the hero 'as representative – of a group, a community, of appropriate or inappropriate behavior, and so forth' *and* as an experience all audience members share as it becomes their memory, as well.[12] What von Contzen describes here is, in effect, a particular kind of textual community: an exemplary textual assemblage that incorporates the audience as a direct participant in the experience of the text, so that the *exemplum* does not remain what we might call 'only textual' – 'what I read in a book' – but fully animated in the extra-textual world of the readers and listeners. This feature of a text's agency was directly acknowledged in classical and medieval rhetoric, as demonstrated by Carruthers in a discussion of medieval reading practices modelled by Peter of Celle's depiction of reading scripture as 'a series of journeys, a sight-seeing pilgrimage', wherein he 'does not only observe these mental scenes, he lives in them, with a fully sensory as well as rational experience'.[13] A. C. Spearing has described the first-person 'I' of seemingly very personal expressions of a single speaker, 'like most written prayers', as actually 'intended not to express the distinctive feelings of the individual writer but to be available for occupation by many different users'.[14] Similarly, an exemplary text can only fully exist when transformed by the audience, for as von Contzen concludes, it is not within the world of the narrative that the exemplarity is apparent, for there the saint or the romance hero is part of that everyday world; it is in the readers' and listeners' assessment of it *as* exemplary, holding it up as a model, that it becomes exemplary.[15] That assessment is an affordance of the text, known in medieval rhetoric as its *ductus*, 'the way(s) that a composition, realizing the plans set within its arrangements, guides a person to its various goals'.[16]

Considered this way, an exemplary textual assemblage is a site of transformative possibility. This transformation is enabled through an affective network modelled in the world of the text and brought to fulfilment through audience communication with the text, the audience guided by the agency of the text towards that end. Lara Farina describes affective writings as 'textual machines that could be said to bring affect to awareness as emotion and sensation in the service of a particular spiritual programme'.[17] That potential is made evident by the ways the text fails to do so when encountered by an unsuitable audience – for instance, a classroom of twenty-first-century undergraduates in the Global North whose reading of an exemplary medieval text can see it as only dull or obvious. Writing about the affective power of mystic texts, Christine Libby explains how, in the right community (say, a convent), affect can circulate through such texts to 'cultivate dynamic forms of relationality' – that is to say, a text can be a 'transformative object', an encounter with a text creating new community.[18] Libby suggests that 'affect provides a compelling interpretive lens for understanding the pre-modern because of its attention to change and its commitment to multivalent forms of relationality'.[19] Farina further notes that 'the point of affective devotional writings like prayers, meditations, passion narratives, and directive guides is precisely to merge instinctive disposition, emotion, sensation, and thought'.[20] Despite such inherent potential, a devotional text remains inert until an affectively prepared audience activates it. From this perspective, it is possible that non-medieval readers underestimate the intensity of the affective networks generated by exemplary texts such as those inhabiting the first two quires of Ashmole 61. Reading these eight texts together as members of the material collective of this late medieval manuscript – rather than in isolation, in a modern 'best-text' edition, as one example of a distinctly medieval literary mode – might enable greater affective reception in the present.

A children's corner?

The discernible cohesion of the collection's first eight items provides opportunity for investigating the book's agency *in parvo*.[21] One such documented effect on modern scholars is that this section of the manuscript has received its own name, a response no other section of the manuscript has inspired. In her two articles on the manuscript published in 1990 and 1996,[22] Lynne S. Blanchfield called this section the 'Children's Corner', a name that has stuck with scholars working on the collection ever since.[23] In these texts Ashmole 61 combines imaginative and didactic pieces, mixing spiritual with social concerns. This perceived emphasis on social instruction and integration seems to set these texts somewhat apart from the rest, and it seems to modern critics to imply a primary audience of children.

This association of direct instruction with young audiences occurs throughout modern scholarly reception of Middle English literature. In response to a similarly focused portion of Cambridge University Library (CUL) Ff.2.38, a household book sharing many features with Ashmole 61, Philippa Hardman says (echoing Francis McSparran) that it is arranged

> with a programme of religious instruction for children and devotional and meditative material for more sophisticated readers, followed by a set of exemplary tales of practical wisdom and piety, and a collection of ten romances ... This ... aims squarely at the private life of a pious, prosperous family of conventional tastes and orthodox beliefs.[24]

A set of expectations guide this interpretation of the aims and audiences of CUL Ff.2.38 – and similar ones appear to have generated the reconstruction of an audience of children for the beginning of Ashmole 61. Hardman's description seems to assume that children are the primary, perhaps even exclusive, audience for direct religious instruction; that guidance in meditation and devotion is aimed at adults; that exemplary tales and romances, and texts offering 'practical wisdom' and expressing piety, are directed at audiences of all ages. Hardman describes another household book, MS Advocates 19.3.1 (also known as the Heege manuscript), as including three booklets that are 'apparently intended for the use of young boys' – each of them with romances (one *Gowther*, one *Amadas*, one *Isumbras*) accompanied by conduct texts.[25] At least three household books cluster romances and conduct texts – all popular textual forms in late medieval England – and modern assessments of these genres have regularly produced unnecessarily narrow reconstructions of their audiences.[26] The reconstructions are further troubled by the flexibility of the concept of 'child' in the Middle Ages, which could range up to twenty-one and even twenty-eight years;[27] given this, the term 'children's literature' could, if we are considering the medieval notion of 'child', include literature aimed at today's primary school student as well as that oriented towards an adult parent with children of their own.[28]

Critical assignment of particular medieval genres to particular limited audiences is also revealed by Gillian Adams's 1998 survey of scholarship on medieval children's literature: she found that scholars considered conduct texts and instruction manuals to be the only examples of 'children's literature' in the Middle Ages.[29] These results confirm the expectations guiding Hardman's description of CUL Ff.2.38. Elsewhere, Bennett Brockman makes a claim that indirectly challenges those restrictions: 'It appears that we can say accurately, although a bit startlingly, that all the literature of fourteenth- and fifteenth-century England is children's literature.'[30] Not only a few medieval texts but *all* medieval texts are children's lit, Brockman suggests; yet this is a further if seemingly conflicting assertion of extra-medieval assumptions, for Brockman appears to claim that all of late Middle English literature could be described as offering instruction of one sort or another, and thus (given modern expectations), with that purpose, it can all be associated with audiences of children. More helpfully, Barbara Hanawalt observes that in the time of Ashmole 61, '[t]he construction of middle-class behaviour began to coalesce specifically around the adolescent years, and literature of all sorts, high and low, was directed toward an age group that was perceived to be most in need of instruction'.[31]

While the utility of such categorisation varies, the effects are evident. Even medievalists at times need reminding that, as Gillian Adams puts it, 'in certain countries and periods, among them medieval Europe, didacticism has been highly valued'.[32] Further, given its cultural capital, we would hardly expect didacticism to be aimed only at children. A useful critical model exists in responses to another highly valued medieval mode, allegory, which tends today to be deployed primarily in children's texts.[33] Yet interpretive strategies circulating in the Middle Ages lead us to deem *medieval* allegory to be capable of conveying complex, sophisticated ideas, however reduced its modern uses. Medieval didactic texts, with their similar cultural prominence in the Middle Ages, warrant similar interpretive treatment. For quite some time now literary scholars have been using interpretive models adapted from anthropology that, as Claire Sponsler explains, view texts 'not as isolated moments of aesthetic practice nor as inert documents pointing to historical events' – that is, not as either escapist art or historical document – 'but rather as events, incidents, and activities within a complex dynamic of the production and consumption of culture'.[34] In an investigation of the popularity of didactic texts in fifteenth-century England, Juanita Feros Ruys discovers recurring self-contradiction, when such texts are considered as a whole (rather than, for instance, as a content-driven collection of independent proverbial expressions, each proverb understood separately from the next). Where we have often presumed a consistent, hegemonic perspective for the implied speaker of such texts, Ruys finds unanticipated diversity and inconsistency. As a result, Ruys argues, 'the creation of didactic meaning is thereby relocated, existing not now with the author, but rather with the reader/listener who is required to absorb, make sense of, and perhaps resolve, contradictory advice'.[35] These texts were particularly popular in the period Jennifer Bryan encourages us to consider 'readerly England' (1410–1550), its literary identity best understood in terms of its readers (as compared to 'writerly England' [1350–1410], a preceding age better known for its authorial production).[36] When Hardman and McSparran agree that didactic texts, including exemplary narratives, offer a 'pious, prosperous family' affirmation of their 'conventional tastes' and 'orthodox beliefs', such texts' agency is limited to reiterating known truths and the shared values of the status quo. Assuming narrow audiences for such texts prevents us from perceiving the readerly creation of meaning from didactic texts that may differ significantly from the consistent, socially conservative purpose modern readers often anticipate, based on an engagement with distinct individual texts, coupled with a tendency to read through the author rather than through the (medieval) reader.

The special popularity of conduct literature in the fifteenth century suggests that these texts were read from a range of perspectives. Mark Addison Amos argues that they were

> Eagerly consumed by those on both sides of the shifting status border, [so that] many ... reveal an ideological lability as they reflect and affect the new social relationships being negotiated, and so allow us to map out the shared and conflicting interests and reading practices of those at the border of gentility, the nobility and the urban elite.[37]

As a result, he says, conservative readings of conduct literature can be seen among noble readers at the very same time that readings of these same texts by non-noble readers were '"tactical," seeking to colonise meaning in such a way as to enable the commoners to negotiate between their own experiences and an aristocratic text that seeks to exclude them'.[38] Amos explains that this advice does not only support the needs of the lord or master (in the production of an agile and knowledgeable servant), for serving one's lord skilfully also serves oneself; read this way, conduct literature can help one pursue 'one's own personal gain and advancement'.[39] Because audience members positioned differently within the household community addressed by such texts would interpret differently based on their own position within that network, conduct texts and other didactic materials remain open, like allegory, to much more diverse significance than modern readers tend to expect – and thus to produce in their own readings.

Ashmole 61, particularly in this first section with its abundance of conduct items, offers a site for experimenting with different ways of reading didactic texts.[40] While the pursuit of new historicist readings of late Middle English romances, saints' lives, and conduct texts encouraged renewed interest in previously neglected household books such as Ashmole 61 in the last quarter of the twentieth century, such pursuits also entrenched a particular way of approaching these texts that, among other things, left unexamined their emotional investments. We might heed Daniel Kline's warning about the 'hazards of separating didacticism from pleasure in medieval texts'.[41] Kline discourages us from seeing didactic texts as the equivalent of a traditional middle school science textbook, invested in conveying factual information as efficiently as possible. The didacticism of Middle English literary texts takes a very different form, and its possible effects vary as well. Pleasure may not be among those feelings a modern reader personally experiences while reading didactic texts, medieval or modern; and pleasure is not the only emotional experience stimulated for medieval audiences by medieval didactic texts – though it is among the affective responses such texts could provoke.

Some of these responses may be recuperated by observing the methods by which Ashmole 61 encourages particular emotional orientations. On this, I bring to bear Jessica Brantley's observation that '[a]lthough reading practices are shaped by generic expectations, generic categories are equally shaped by readers' habits, and both are indebted to the physical forms of texts in manuscript books'.[42] In the first section of this particular manuscript, these methods involve the ways animals and objects (both rare and everyday) comment on and act in the world, and how the manuscript presents such commentary to the audience, provoking particular kinds of emotional responses and encouraging certain affective habits.[43] These provocations come through the book's non-human inhabitants' interaction with humans within the book and, later, beyond. From the start, Ashmole 61 signals its membership in a network of agential objects: in the traces of a developing ecosystem of inky fish and flower inhabitants; in the new garb worn by its texts to suit this milieu; and in the moral animals and inanimate objects that enliven its pages.

Affective pedagogy via exemplary narrative

The book's orientation towards moral instruction is established by the flagship texts in the first two quires: the legend of St Eustace and the romance of Sir Isumbras.[44] Saints' lives and romances are well known for their shared structures and themes despite their different generic affiliations – such that these seemingly foreign genres (one presumably secular in its themes and concerns, the other spiritual) are at the very least friendly neighbours.[45] In the case of Ashmole 61's *Isumbras* (item 5, fols. 9r–16v) and *St Eustace* (item 1, fols. 1r–5r), not only the romance (as is often the case) but also the saint's life is presented in tail-rhyme verse. This unusual format for a saint's life[46] makes it even more like Middle English romance, and their appearance in Ashmole 61 very near to one another at the start of the collection makes these two narratives' connections all the more apparent; they seem like relatives once-removed.[47] Both edifying narratives present the story of an esteemed man who experiences a dramatic loss of status followed by a time of lonely suffering that offers penitential preparation for the family's reunion and the restoration of its previous position, ending with a final elevation of status in ideal terms legible in each genre.[48] Both do so through the careful intervention of non-human members of the hero's community.

Sir Isumbras's participation in a company of conduct texts appears immediately in the poem's announcement of its central concern with social identity. This focus is expressed not by its human hero, who has forgotten 'what [he] was' (44), but rather by a nearby bird high in a tree. This bird draws Isumbras's attention upwards through its song, and once the knight is properly attentive, the bird explains that Isumbras's pride has displaced his true identity (more specifically, his Christian character).[49] Isumbras's error, the bird elaborates, lies in 'pride of gold and gode' (45). The narrator has previously introduced Isumbras as 'nobull' and 'stronge' (12, 13), 'feyre' (13) and 'hyghe' (15), those physical features and attendant demeanour that a romance hero should exhibit, with the added bonus that he is generous to minstrels (19–21);[50] however, the narrator observes, 'Of Godys werkys he goffe [cared] ryght noght', and 'Hys [God's] mersye he sette nott byghe' (31–2). Isumbras's sin results from an improper relation to things, esteeming earthly goods (and, it is implied, the status they convey and the influence they enable – the powerful elite object assemblage) more than he esteems God and his morally superior works. Notably, this pride is not autonomously generated, for 'inne hys herte a pride was browght' (31). The passive verb implies an absent actor: something or someone brought that pride into Isumbras's heart, and he made the error of accepting it. His sin is thus a group production, and his reform must be as well: to compensate for this error, the bird (notably, an earthly object itself) carefully explains through his 'syng[ing]' (41) (a voice simultaneously described as 'sey[ing]' [43]), that Isumbras must make a choice between experiencing loss now or experiencing loss later. Before departing in flight, the bird succeeds in making Isumbras recognise and acknowledge his error and his involvement in a spiritual (mis)production.

Isumbras understands that he must go without the very objects he has accumulated and improperly valued by prioritising and overemphasising their contributions to his identity. This inappropriate estimation the protagonist identifies to his family as 'oure wyked synne' (107). In a different context, this first-person plural pronoun might indicate an attempt to displace the blame on to others; here, Isumbras's announcement emphasises the poem's focus on the health of the collective. The individual's identity is never purely his own; it is built from the goods he over-values and shares with the family; its dislocation damages and results from the error of the family.[51]

The bird draws Isumbras's attention to the family's failing and encourages him to see the opportunity for penance. In effect, the non-human agent shows the family its neglect of the divine's critical membership in the household. Hereafter, God speaks to Isumbras through a more direct representative: an angel. Isumbras seems to need an earthly translator of sacred agency – whose birdsong is simultaneously human/divine voice – only until he can discern and accept his sin, properly orienting towards the divine agent that he had neglected.

The intervention of the bird is followed by the sudden loss of Isumbras's wealth in the form of his horse (which goes in a moment from 'strong and wyght' to 'Dede' [65–6]) and his hawks and hounds (which go mad and wander off through the forest): the animals that in conjunction with Isumbras's genealogy have generated and maintained his noble status now die on site or lose their domesticated status and return to the wild, leaving him socially unmarked. Isumbras, and the text's audience, watch his visible noble identity disappear.[52] He then learns that his buildings have all burned down and his 'bestys' are slain – all the non-human members of his household ecology have left the human members of the family on their own. At this point, despite the abrupt and extreme catastrophe, Isumbras 'Nothyng yit sory yit was he' (97) – he feels no emotional response, presumably because he has been forewarned by the bird. The double use of 'yit' builds tension, though, reminding readers of the inevitable, and Isumbras's emotional state changes dramatically when he encounters his human family. His first experience of embodied suffering is sparked by seeing his sons and wife flee their burning house, 'when he saw them nakyd be / That he lefte sembly clade' (98–9). The fire has put them at great risk and destroyed their home, but he recognises their loss most directly through their lack of exquisite clothing, that most portable indicator of status. In response, he removes his 'ryche cyrcute of paule' (115) from over his armour, placing it on his naked wife, and then – with 'full drery mode' (117) – cuts his 'ryche mantell' (118) to make clothing for his three sons. Their loss of material indicators of status requires him to physically enact the distribution of those status markers that remain among the collective, and in this case his will (rather than external force) is the agent of change. He must demolish his own remaining signs of status in order to sustain his family – in the process recognising their existence as more than mere signs of status, as meaningful objects presenting qualities previously indiscernible to Isumbras, reorienting his relation to things.

At that first pitiful meeting, Isumbras's wife models for her children appropriate emotional evaluation: in response to the fire, the boys 'had wepyd all ther fylle' (103), but she observes 'yonder I se your fader onne lyve; / For nothinge be ye drade' (101–2). Though she has yet to receive the explanation for this sudden change of events – explanation that Isumbras alone was granted in advance – she values his life over the loss of all they know, and she does so regardless of their extreme reduction in status, their loss of identity. At the same time, the centrality of objects to one's comfort, physical and social, and to one's being are recognised, and that loss is publicly lamented in community. The family's friends 'made a sorowfulle mone / Sore wepyd both olde and yenge' (135–6), seeing the family making their way by begging and depending on others' charity. The narrator observes that 'It was grete dole to se that syght, / That *lady* and that *gentyll knyght*, / How thei dyde sofer wo', the impact of the loss intensified by emphasising the status of the victims, as lady and gentle knight, rather than, for instance, as father and mother (145–7, emphasis added). The audience is encouraged to respond to the family's losses emotionally and to do so through the lens of their reduced status, just as the family and their supporters do, affecting even the strangers who encounter them in their strange new panhandling life. The family wander the forest for three days, without food, and weep. They have lost the household ecology of which they were central members, and 'Ne thing thei saw that come of corne, / Bot fowlys wyld that satte on thorn; / Ne mete ther gete myght he' (157–9). Here, in the forest, the animals and plants surrounding them are wild, inedible. These agents of the natural world do not translate; the family cannot generate a new household identity with them.[53]

The audience is continually reminded of the inappropriateness – despite the unambiguous spiritual justice – of this situation, with descriptions of Isumbras as 'The knyght that was hend and gode' (169) appearing throughout, regardless of his current outward loss of status reflective of past error and necessary penance. The unnatural contrast is affectively presented: 'Herd world is us beforne / That are [before] was wyld [carefree] and cranke [cheerful]!' (188–9).

Isumbras's noble persona remains constant, in the narrator's depiction and strangers' estimation of him, even as his behaviour previously failed to recognise his noble spirit, which required him to temporarily lose the objects that outwardly affirmed that identity. Indeed, towards the very end of the poem as the lonely and suffering Isumbras is finally provided with ample food and water, after much ascetic living, he

> sate and ete nought,
> Bot lokyd onne the haule [hall].
> So myche he saw of game and gle,
> And thought what he was wonte to be;
> Teres he lete doune falle. (589–94)

While he experiences acute need for the physical sustenance that is at long last available to him, Isumbras exhibits a deeper affective need for an object ecology of nobility as it is manifest in the hall, one whose affective benefits – 'game and gle' – trump the 'basic necessities' of food and water and further confirm his true identity, and whose association with him marked him as 'what he was wonte to be'.

A series of actions by animals and non-human others produces the emotional suffering necessary for the ultimate spiritual recuperation of Isumbras's household. The family's experience of profitable suffering is originally triggered by a bird and later supported by a lion and a leopard, who take two of the family's children, and by a sultan, who takes Isumbras's wife, in exchange for which he forces gold upon Isumbras;[54] later, the gold is taken by an angel and the final remaining son is taken by a unicorn. After Isumbras's first son is abducted by a lion, 'With carfull herte and sygheng sore, / … Wepand he wente awaye. / With sory chere and drery mode / … To pyne turned all hys pleye' (175–80). Then, when a leopard takes their second son, 'The lady wepyd all her fylle; / For sorow herselve sche wold spylle, / Sych sorow to hyr was lente' (184–6). The trauma is so intense that the narrator elaborates – in uncharacteristic fashion, given his usual spare description – that 'Lytell wonder thofe thei had care, / For both ther childer leste thei ther / Of the eldyste two' (193–5). This experience of losing beloveds – who also embody the future of the family – instructs Isumbras and his wife in the appropriate estimation of value, estimation that is here affectively expressed and measured.

Later, the affective response of a stranger further instructs audiences in proper evaluation of worth: when Isumbras and his wife, accompanied by their lone remaining son, have wandered for seven foodless days in the forest, they happen upon the Persian sultan's ship just as he and his army are approaching to conquer all of Christendom. Based on the great opulence of the ship, Isumbras determines to seek mercy, believing that such wealth could coexist only with noble human character. His request, however, is rejected by the sultan because of Isumbras's Christian identity. Upon hearing this resistance, one of the sultan's knights says to their ruler,

> Sertys, it is a wonder thyng
> Yone pore man to see,
> For he is both large and hyghe,
> The feyrest man that ever Y se;
> A gentyll man is he.
> With armes long and schuldres grete,
> Wythe browys brante and eyen stepe,
> A knyght semys to be.
> Hys wyffe whyte as whalys bone,
> Hyr lyre [face] as the see fome,
> And bryght as lylé. (247–58)

This estimation of the couple's value reflects a proper reading, in the system esteemed by the narrative: despite the absent markers of clothing, animals, and other objects of nobility, the foreign knight is able to read Isumbras's family's 'true' status in the features of their bodies (the man's based on size and proportion, the woman's associating her with the natural beauty of the ocean and flowers). His observation encourages great pity in the sultan, who upon seeing the couple 'rewyd sore' as well – and, perhaps needless to say, the Christian audience reading this romance would be expected to feel even more. Physical encounter generates genuine affective response. Because of the cultural distance between the two, however – the different systems whose values determine a given object's legibility – the sultan's pity is short-lived, and he reveals himself as lacking his own knight's subtle Christian literacy: the sultan first demands that Isumbras serve him as his knight, and when that is refused, the sultan offers (or, rather, demands) to purchase Isumbras's wife. This untranslatable offer is flatly rejected.

The violent scene that follows, in which all agency is with the powerful sultan, is perhaps the most heavily invested with emotional cues in the narrative. As his wife is abducted, Isumbras is beaten until his ribs are broken, and the lone remaining son must watch the torment in full vivid detail, wailing throughout. His mother, forcibly taken permanently from her family (that is, her increasingly diminishing household community) to be married into a non-Christian society, cries to the point of death and calls out to Mary: 'Schall we now parte in twoo? / Alas, blythe schall I never be / And I my lord no more schall se; / My *joy* is gon me froo. / Out, alas, that I was borne; / My *welth* this dey fro me is lorne. / Thus wakyd all her woo' (318–24, emphasis added). She laments not the loss of the head of her household nor the lack of social position or nobility-affiliated objects, but instead the loss of her joy, in being separated from Isumbras – this is the 'welth' that is taken from her. She seeks permission to see her mauled husband one last time before being sent away, at which point she swoons (351). Such extended attention in this scene to the experience of emotional trauma, as epitomised in the wife's spoken lament, has the primary effect of generating similar reactions in the textual audience. So much sorrow is shared that 'Unethe [Isumbras] myght with eyne se, / So had he wepyd sore' (365–6): his emotional trauma is legible on his body, his eyes made useless by it – actively refusing to allow in more sources of suffering through his visual senses. Isumbras is then even further reduced, with the abduction of his remaining heir by a unicorn – the one son who had to witness his parents' separation and abuse; finally, even the gold that Isumbras refused, which had been forced upon him by the sultan in false exchange for his wife and which Isumbras then hid away rather than using despite his extreme poverty, is taken by an angel. In this scene, the Ashmole 61 *Isumbras* is distinguished from the other eight versions – even from the two in the Lincoln and Advocates manuscripts that are closest to it – in that 'Rate adds or alters a further dozen lines that amplify Isumbras's and his wife's grief at their forced parting'.[55]

Isumbras's previously improper relationship to objects is corrected not only through their loss but also through his years of labour as a blacksmith. During this time, he is able to produce his own armour: he creates the new objects necessary to rebuild his noble identity, even as his visible social identity during the process of creating them is that of a manual labourer. Indeed, his dedication to this lowly labour only confirms his true nobility. He is apprentice and then journeyman, developing the skills necessary to make what in the past others' labour had provided him. But there is no risk that this new identity will become so naturalised for him as to replace his prior noble identity, a situation confirmed by the way this temporary artisan-assemblage allows Isumbras to fight alongside the Christians to thwart the sultan's attack, and it allows him to kill the sultan, getting revenge for the attempted theft of his wife – what he presents as a direct repayment ('yelde' [443]) for the woe the sultan gave him – while simultaneously defending Christendom at large.

In a romance, this valorous achievement – simultaneous personal revenge and political defence of one's lord (and, in this case, Lord) – might well conclude the narrative. However, this knightly achievement, like his years of service as apprentice and then blacksmith before it, is simply one phase of the extended pilgrimage that Isumbras began long ago with his now widely distributed household. He is returned to health by the Christian king he served, and then announces himself 'A smythes man' (485), refusing to see his penance – and restoration of true identity – as complete. The king remains unconvinced that a lowly manual labourer could fight so effectively, but Isumbras refuses his former identity as knight, whatever his self-made armour or praiseworthy performance on the field might suggest. Instead, once Isumbras is restored to sufficient health to depart on pilgrimage, he takes his leave and heads out to face more suffering: he again sleeps outside, 'in heathen land', lacks food and water, and experiences great physical pain, for another seven years. 'Of penans was he never yrke [weary] / For his grete mysded' (539–40). He suffers in his suffering, and yet he continues to insist that the suffering is a necessary good.

Only at this point, as Isumbras lies weeping near Bethlehem, does the angel reappear, offering him bread and wine to announce that his penance is complete and that he is now suitable to commune with God once again. And yet, even as his communion with Christ is affirmed through this sacrament and he is given divine guidance, his original status and accompanying public identity elude him: Isumbras continues to live in poverty. In this state, eventually, he is taken in and given alms by a queen who only the audience knows is his long-lost wife. In her goodness, she commits to provide for him in return for his service to the hall. The queen's knights recognise Isumbras's nobility from his skill with the shot put (625) and in fighting, despite his 'crowkyd stede [decrepit horse]' (633). Even so, Isumbras retains his identity as poor pilgrim until his wife is able to recognise him through a token: the object of exchange for which she was inappropriately taken by the sultan, the gold, is supernaturally returned to Isumbras. He spots the red cloth that contained the gold in a bird's nest, and retrieves it. Deeply attached to the gold – as it is the only extant physical connection he has to his wife – Isumbras is emotionally traumatised by the object, which he hides in his chamber, weeping for his lost family every time he comes near it (659). The cloth's affective agency ultimately enables the couple's reunion: a perceptive knight of the queen discovers the gold and reveals it to her, and she recognises it for what it is and as a result identifies Isumbras for what he is. Isumbras becomes the king of his non-Christian enemy's land: 'A ryche kyng was Syr Isombras, / In more welthe than ever he was, / Of hethyn londys was hee' (723–5). Through the cloth, now transformed from agent of trauma to that of truth, Isumbras's status identity is returned and enhanced, for he is no longer knight but king, a transformation made possible through valorous achievement.

Isumbras's first royal act is to convert the non-Christian inhabitants of his new land, which he does by force. In this, the poem affirms that the violent methods that the sultan had used to conquer Christendom are appropriate, but only when wielded by a Christian – such as Isumbras, who has now been fully reincorporated into the Christian family through God's acceptance of his penance. Such force is necessary, the narrative suggests, not only to convert others but also to maintain them in Christianity, for as soon as a heathen king attacks Isumbras, his (forcibly converted) people abandon him: 'When he was horsyd on a stede, / All thei flede hym fro' (750). Isumbras's wife, unwilling to leave him fighting the 30,000 and more Saracen troops alone, follows her husband's previous path and makes a knight of herself by donning armour (766–7) and joining him on the field. The numbers are significantly against the couple, but the family is suddenly fully reconstituted, powerfully so, with the reunion occurring literally and most dramatically on the battlefield: each son appears on the animal that had abducted him, an act that reinterprets the animals' influence as protective rather than destructive, revealing them to have been actively preserving the sons during their father's testing and now serving the needs of the full household.[56] The whole family – including Isumbras's fully armed wife – are led by angels (notably, the sons are attired as angels at this point) towards their achievement of overcoming other misbehaving (because spiritually misdirected) humans: they slay the two heathen kings and many Saracens, and 'It was comforth for to sene / The gret joys was them betwen / With clyppyng and with kyssing suete' (796–8). The human-animal-angel assemblage that has generated necessary penance through the process of the narrative is here instantiated, empowered to overcome the full force of resistant non-Christianity, a handful against 30,000. Through their fighting the family acquire three lands and crowns to distribute to the sons, and they all 'lyved and dyghed with god intent / and to heven ther saules wente / When thei dede were' (the poem's last three lines, 820–2).

This narrative might well be described as a series of vignettes of loss and affective torment, followed by reunion, presented specifically to trigger emotional responses in the main characters and, by extension, in the audience.[57] When husband and wife are reunited, after an extended encounter at the end of which their identities are made clear, 'For joy thei were wepand. / Joy it was to se them mete. / With clypyng and with kyssing suete / In armes when thei gon folde. / Ather were of other so feyn, / Ther joy myght no man seyn, / The sothe if it were tolde' (702–7). The significance of the losses, and of the reunion, are made clear not directly through the spiritual lessons learned – which are, one might say, not so much learned as experienced anew through the embodied events of suffering and joy. As Isumbras's personal spiritual state benefits from this cleansing, the community at large (his Saracen subjects and those of surrounding Saracen kings) is similarly encouraged to pursue proper communion with God – in their case through an enforced choice, in contrast to the non-violent divine invitation through birdsong that already-Christian Isumbras received.[58] This very state was demanded of Isumbras at the start of the poem by a bird and supported by the actions of lion, leopard, angel, and unicorn, a state he then demands of others by human royal-military force – a state upheld throughout Ashmole 61 as the ultimate good.

Affective pedagogy in *St Eustace*

The parallel narrative *St Eustace* (fols. 1r–5r) follows a similar structure and deploys similar methods of education through emotional trauma, for those inhabiting and those encountering (and in the process themselves experiencing) the narrative. The news at the beginning is delivered in this case by a stag. Elevated by a stone and illuminated by a heavenly light, standing under a linden tree (known for its symmetrical growth patterns offering deep shade with its broad, heart-shaped leaves and deeply aromatic flowers),[59] the antlered deer speaks 'as a man it were' (49) and 'wyth ryght' (51). In this, the stag seems of a kind with the *Isumbras*-bird, albeit with even more confident righteousness, along with a multi-sensory impact that enlarges the bird's singing. The animal spokesperson's positioning is further amplified: the stag says that 'It is Jhesu Cryst of heven / That spekys to thee with myld steven' (55–6) – generating not so much a contradiction between narrator and narrated (the stag refusing the identity claimed for it by the narrator) as presenting a human-animal-divine collective (assisted as well by stone, tree, and light). For full effect, the stag displays a crucifix between its horns.[60] The previously heathen Eustace (born 'Placydas') follows the will of the stag – which by this point, speaking as it claims in God's voice and referring to itself as Christ, urges Eustace to convert 'for love of me and myne' (64). Eustace converts himself and his wife and sons (behaving, like Isumbras, as spiritual delegate for the family corporation); he too suffers sooner rather than later, with an angel announcing to him and his wife and sons, at the moment of their shared baptism, that pains will follow, resulting from temptations by 'the fend' (104). The events to come look like the process in *Isumbras*, with the 'natural' world and human lust depriving the family of their goods (thunder kills the horse [116] and a shipman desires to have Eustace's beautiful wife for himself [135]) and separating children from parents and husband from wife, just as in the romance.[61]

Throughout the saint's life, the fiend to whom the stag refers is never literally present but instead exists as a coalition of agents, human and non-human. Eustace suffers fifteen years alone, labouring as Isumbras does and thereby showing his willingness to lose his personal identity in service to Christ, 'Suynkyng and suetyng' (222) as a hayward, until he is retrieved by the (non-Christian) emperor he once served. Like Isumbras, although for different reasons, Eustace refuses the emperor's men's identification of him as his former self, Placydas, when they recognise a scar on his face; he asserts that 'I may not your feloy [companion] ben; / I ame a pore man' (267–8), but they insist that he deserves the position of privilege he knew before, 'thy honour / That thou were wonte to hane' (270–1). Once the family is reunited, they join together to proclaim their shared faith; while in romance Isumbras's family did this by fighting off non-believers on the battlefield, in this saint's life the family express their faith while tormented by a non-believer, in a brass pot, martyred together and transmitted to heaven.

Despite the greater potential offered by this full-family martyrdom, the affective expression in *Eustace* is muted in comparison to *Isumbras*. Here, the suffering is economically conveyed (for instance, 'Well mekyll was hys care' [159]), with some slight direct expression of emotional pain, as in Eustace's telling his sons upon the abduction of their mother, 'Me thinke my herte wyll all to-bled. / How schalle I you moderles fede? / Now was me never so wo' (151–3). As his heart figuratively bleeds out, he feels his greatest woe for his inability to mother, by feeding, his sons. Upon the family's final reunion, in contrast, much gleeful weeping occurs:

> And sone onne kneys doune thei flewe,
> And thankyd God Allmyght.
> For joye that they togeder were mette,
> All fowre full faste thei dyd wepe,
> And so dyde many a wyght ...
> Than ther was none at that bord
> That fore wepyng myght speke a word,
> Nor none in that inne. (422–34)

After such jubilation at their earthly reunion, suddenly in the last three stanzas the emperor's plan to slay them is revealed, and with the help of the tool of torture, almost immediately – no extended saintly suffering here – 'Ther saulys onto heven went. / Of payn thei were withouten' (456–7).

St Eustace begins the manuscript, the very first of 41 items. *Isumbras* appears at the start of the second quire and has the effect of building on the reader's experience of the saint's life by presenting more vividly and more extensively the emotional trauma and resulting delight of the hero and his family upon their reunion. The first narrative of household penitential loss and reintegration as model of readerly affective instruction, *St Eustace*, is with *Isumbras* expanded in scale: narrative, emotional, and dramatic.[62] Indeed, the Isumbras household's eventual defeat of the sultan and conquering of non-Christendom in item 4 of the collection effectively defeats and displaces the heathen emperor who had martyred the Eustace household in the first text. The narratives thus depend upon a coalition of actors seen and unseen – hero, hero's family, unjust ruler, authorised animal mediator, animal preservers, gold, angels, God – textual and extra-textual, from surrounding sites in Ashmole 61. All are necessary to the process of forgiveness and resulting reconciliation, the modelling of which is a key outcome of the narrative. This modelling gives the audience the opportunity for affective understanding in the present, through the experiences of the household, and to act appropriately in response to that affective engagement. This experience of pain and loss – and of its necessity to the process of penance and forgiveness – emotionally (and this includes physically) affects the audience. Sustained and intimate contact with the narrative object, and its many constituent instructional objects, thus forms the audience, becoming its own exemplary experience and shaping its value judgements.

Affective pedagogy in the conduct texts

All of the conduct items in the manuscript appear in this section and they all blend, to some degree, what Murray Evans effectively labels 'etiquette and religion'.[63] More specifically, they suit Kathleen Ashley and Robert L. A. Clark's description of conduct texts as 'systematizing a society's codes of behavior'[64] – behaviour that, in the Middle Ages, included religious as well as what we might call secular concerns. Conduct texts' methods vary, as Mark Addison Amos describes: 'some resemble more a list of directives than an organized didactic lesson ... others make concerted efforts to support their admonitions with a moral teleology in hopes that their readers will internalize the proscriptions'.[65] The modelling of affective evaluation elsewhere in this first section of Ashmole 61 appears in the form of four texts currently classified as conduct literature – *Wise Man to his Son*, *Good Wife to her Daughter*, *Stans Puer ad Mensam*, and *Dame Curtasy* – and two texts that are typically unaffiliated with conduct literature but in this environment behave as conduct texts too: the *Ten Commandments* and *Right as a Ram's Horn*. Both of these underwent extensive modification by Rate as he included them, and they are especially noteworthy for the way they incorporate non-human actants into the moral ecology typically conceived of as available only to humans.

The *Ten Commandments* (item 6, fols. 16v–17r) starts off with a stanza, unique to its Ashmole 61 appearance, that makes it sound quite like its neighbours – a call to attention in terms of the oral/aural occasion of the hall familiar from the romance in the vicinity – and encourages us to respond to it as a conduct text:

> Herkyns, syrys, that standys abowte
> I wyll yow tell with gode entente,
> How ye to God schuld knele and lowte [obey],
> If ye wyll kepe his commandment. (1–4)

The final three stanzas, also unique to the version of the poem that appears in this manuscript, emphasise the origins of the commandments, particularly their means of transmission to humans: God gave them to Moses 'In two tabullys of ston ryght' (47–9). The stone is not only material suitably durable to convey divine truths, but its noteworthy feature is that it is 'ryght', which is to say, 'correct by moral law', 'in accordance with justice', 'righteous', and more broadly, 'genuine, real, veritable'.[66] The stone's nature, not only its physical appearance, matches the rightness of the moral truths expressed on and through it. The stone tablets, in communion with God, Moses, and believers then and now, circulating among emotional ecologies, 'helpe mans kynd forth of synne' (that is, keep people out of sin) and 'teche mankynd this werld to wynne' (50–1). The stone instructs people in this most important of all lessons. The reading that the book thus encourages includes those moral contributions made to the household by inanimate objects such as stone – which can be as 'right' as the truths divinely engraved on them. Earlier in the short poem, the audience of the manuscript – the household – is also addressed as a whole that includes more than only its human inhabitants: when rest is commanded on the sabbath, the poem clarifies that this means, more specifically, 'Fro werldly werkys thou take thi reste. / All thy howsold the same schall do, / Bothe wyffe and chyld, servant and beste' (15–16). Audience member, wife, child, servant, and beast – all the animate elements that generate the household – must rest (pausing that animation) in honour of the sabbath. Certainly the beasts that work do so generally under the guidance of a human household member. But that assumption doesn't appear to be powerful enough to leave unstated the need for the beasts to rest. Instead, the entire household corporation is delineated. The appropriate response to divine command is to be made by all, not only by human believers, and divine truths may be not only conveyed by means of, but taught through the qualities of, inert material – indicating a conceptualisation of moral community (and moral authority) that expands beyond the human and divine.[67]

If a reader were unaware that the *Ten Commandments* is biblically based – a situation in which modern readers of the manuscript are much more likely to find themselves than were medieval audiences – they would be forgiven for thinking that this text is a close sibling of the four traditional conduct items in this first section of the manuscript (*How the Wise Man Taught His Son*, *How the Good Wife Taught Her Daughter*, *Stans Puer ad Mensam*, and *Dame Curtasy*). Each of these texts exists as a series of proverbial statements presented to an eager listener, a representative sample being 'Gete thi gowd with trewth and wynne [earn your living with truth and honor] / And kepe thee out of dette and synne' (*Dame Curtasy* 79–80). The fundamental truths conveyed in the *Ten Commandments* sound very similar: 'Be thou no theffe ne theffys fere, / Ne nothing wyne thorow trechery' (29–30). The proverbs in the *Ten Commandments* – permanently and divinely carved on the righteous stone – build to the promise of the final glorious lines, apparently added by Rate: 'Yiff that they wyll fro syn them kepe [those that keep these commandments] / They schall be bryghter than the sonne' (55–6).

In great contrast to the directness and simplicity of this poem that follows the lead narrative of quire 2 (that is, the *Ten Commandments* following on from *Sir Isumbras*) is the text that follows the lead narrative of quire 1 (*St Eustace*). *Right as a Ram's Horn* (item 2, fols. 5v–6r) is an estates satire extant in eleven copies and generally attributed to Lydgate, though no individual authorship is indicated in this manuscript. The forthrightly didactic narrative of

Eustace, in audience-friendly tail-rhyme stanza, is followed by a poetically dense allegorical poem in a complex ballade stanza, eight interlocking lines of just three rhymes: ababbcbc. As with the *Ten Commandments*, Rate seems here to have supplemented the text he inherited, in this case adding three stanzas between the original first four stanzas and the last stanza. That is to say, three of eight stanzas – nearly 40 per cent – are there because Rate added them. Henry Hargreaves has described the version of the poem in this manuscript as receiving 'the full Ashmole remodelling'.[68] The poem depicts a world in which vice has departed from all social arenas (high, middle, and low) – for instance, it begins 'Ryghtwysnes do now procede, / And sytyht [sits] lyke a gay emprece' (1–2), with law following suit, 'Kepyng the ordour of perfyte stabulnes' (7) – only to make the satirical cut in the last line of each stanza by noting that each instance of human goodness is 'Conveyned by [directed by, written by] a lyne ryght as a rammys horne'.[69] Given the well-known twists and turns of rams' horns – indeed, this quality is their trademark – this recurring line humorously reveals that the ideal situation described is the opposite of the actual state of affairs, which is as straight only as the most naturally curvy of items. The first definition for 'ryght' in the *Middle English Dictionary* is 'straight' – and this is certainly the primary association in the visual image drawn by the refrain. Yet once more, notions of moral correctness and righteousness are associated with a non-human object, with the association in this case an inverse one, repeated as the last line of each stanza in order to declare various human institutions failed. As with the stone in the *Ten Commandments*, non-human actants are participants in the moral ecology of the world perceived by the Ashmole 61 household – offering material forms for standards (in these cases, rightness and straightness) to be pursued.

In the four traditional conduct texts, one learns to demonstrate one's good conduct – and thus good character – not *from* non-human objects but in relation *to* objects (just as one learns skills for relating to people in these texts). In reading the traditional conduct texts in Ashmole 61, I expand the keen focus on the human in most investigations of the genre, as exemplified in Anna Dronzek's observation that such texts' 'primary focus is behavior in society – interactions between human beings'.[70] I would modify this focus to the social effects of 'interactions among humans and non-humans', for these texts depict the household as populated with abundant non-human objects in a potentially treacherous landscape that the audience must learn how to navigate just as carefully as they do other people: tables, beds, meat and food, alcohol, more alcohol, their own and others' bodies.[71] J. Allan Mitchell observes that conduct texts 'equip humans to do things they otherwise would not be able to do', revealing the human underdevelopment to be not so much an '*autonomous* subject as a *heteronomous* object-oriented one',[72] and the conduct texts in Ashmole 61 exhibit such a methodology. They include many modes of proto-agency that acknowledge the endless possible recombinations of humans, animals, and others – and the dependence of each on the others for a collectively produced affective society.

In the conduct texts of the collection, the assemblages on which one's social identity depends are made very literally present. For instance, in item 8 (fols. 20r–21v), Dame Curtasy's instructions demonstrate that the way to virtuous living – and thus to *being* virtuous, in the text's behaviour-based model – is through treating one's body and one's surroundings suitably: by getting out of bed at the appropriate time (and thus not mistreating one's bed, body, or master), by reactivating one's piety by 'blyss[ing] thi breste and thi forhede' (11–12) and blessing one's mouth before eating (23), by cleansing the face and combing the hair. Foreheads, breasts, mouths, beds, all demand attention, physical *expressing* spiritual. 'When thou comys unto a dore', Dame Curtasy urges, 'Sey "God be here" or thou go ferre' (85–6). Just as one treats non-humans respectfully, so one should other people, saying 'good morning' to them courteously (19–21). Consistently, the way to show appropriate humility to social superiors is the way one treats one's body: 'When thou spekys to any man, / Hand, fote, and fynger kepe thou styll than, / And luke thou uppe into his face … With thi fynger schew thou nothyng' (65–9). One's attitude towards other humans is conveyed not so much discursively as physically, through the appropriate movement (or stillness) of objects. In describing how to eat cleanly, she demonstrates that 'thou may thi wyrschype wyne' (108) by ensuring that your fingers, lips, and chin are clean, and by keeping your food in your mouth. Social success is a matter of effectively reining in (rather like a dog agility trainer)[73] potentially unruly objects in your environment: food, spit, cutlery, limbs, and clothing. 'When thi better spekys to thee, / Do of thi cape and bow thi kne' (137–8).[74] The following rhyming proverb from this text makes the association between actions and qualities clear, as expressed through object relations: 'Ne pley with spone, trencher, ne knyffe. / In honesty and clenys lede thou thi lyffe' (145–6). Not playing with eating utensils – that is, not making the practical impractical – is not only analogous to, but actually *is*, living life honestly and cleanly. The two are, in their parallel positioning through rhyme, equivalent.

Similarly, in *How the Good Wife Taught her Daughter* (item 4, fols. 7r–8v), one's treatment of things will determine the fate of one's soul: 'Borrowyd thing muste nedys go home, / If that thou wyll to heven gone' (191–2). Here it is not simply the parallel rhyme but also the conditional 'If' connecting the two statements that conveys a cause-and-effect relationship between them. Such aphorisms may threaten to oversimplify complex truths: 'Return what you borrow, and you'll make it to heaven' seems to negate the need for any further religious instruction or understanding (much less an extensive multi-century sacred tradition over which countless wars have been fought). However, read in terms of the collection's inclusion of the non-human and the inanimate within the moral universe of the household, the 'borrowed thing' can also be understood as the daughter herself, borrowed from God and ultimately due to be returned back to him, with the mother's duty ensuring that this borrowed thing, her daughter, makes it home to God.

Dame Curtasy is unique to this manuscript, sharing only six lines of its opening with the poem *Lytylle Children*, and it may well have been written by Rate. Portions of it in effect paraphrase *Stans Puer ad Mensam* (item 7, fols. 17v–19v), its predecessor in the manuscript. The two poems share an orientation towards interactions with objects as the means of pursuing virtue and avoiding vice. In *Stans Puer*, for instance, the student is instructed 'Ageyn the post luke not thi bake abyde; / Make not the myrror also of the walle' (58–9). Misuse of material companions (making a bed of a post by sleeping against it, making a mirror of a wall by staring at it as if it might offer a reflection) demonstrates a lack of virtue. Rather than directly pondering Christian virtues (charity, faith, justice, fortitude), one should 'Thy elbow and armys have in thi thought' (186). The extent of the objects with which one must interact in very controlled ways widens hyperbolically in *Stans Puer*, with, for instance, multiple lines on the potential unruliness of salt (133, 146–52). In *Good Wife Taught her Daughter*, the enormous possible influence of inert objects within the household's moral ecology is witnessed in an extended passage on the power of gifts. Matter – once gifted – can overcome even the most extreme human virtue:

> For gode women with gyftys
> Men ther honour fro them lyftys,
> Thofe that thei were all trew
> As any stele that bereth hew;
> For with ther giftys men them overgone,
> Thof thei were trew as any ston. (93–8)

Although it be as true as stone and steel, women's honour can be overcome by gifts – so that objects once gifted (even, presumably, objects as fragile as flowers) can transform a human-steel hybrid or a human-stone hybrid (each of them an epitome of truth, as witnessed in *Ten Commandments*) into, say, a ram's horn-human hybrid. These texts encourage audiences to understand their own agentive potential as one element in a conglomeration of non-human and human agentive potentialities[75] – with one's social virtue directly depending on the outcome.

Throughout these texts, the valuable truths are presented in terms of, or perhaps rather through, affective behaviour. In *Ram's Horn*, women are esteemed when they 'banished away all strangeness [novelty]'; young and old are living rightly when they 'takyn sadnes them to' (27), when they 'lost pride' and 'take them to mekenes, / Whose pacyens is gode both at even and morn' (28–9). The minstrels – the focus of a stanza added by Rate – 'make men myrth for no mede, / Bot for soule helth to sette men in sadnes' (48–9): they make people mirthful without compensation for their labour, for their goal is only to improve the health of the soul by encouraging listeners to seriousness. Sadness, patience, meekness: these are all affective moral orientations that are to be learned and internalised through encountering this text (and the related delivery-system of the minstrel). *Wise Man* (item 3, fols. 6r–6v) instructs in similar affective behaviours: it proclaims that its goal is to make young men 'trew and stedfaste' (6). The praised son in the text is 'meke and myld' (11), and he is encouraged to treat his future wife in terms of emotion-grounded behaviour: 'With love and awe thi wyfe thou chastys' (41), taming her in the way (an implicit comparison) one tames 'Hert and hynd and the wyld ro' (52), with gentleness. Above all, the young man must manage his own emotions: 'be thou not gelos by no weye' (53). Notably, the young woman in *Good Wife* is prescribed the same general affective demeanour as the son in its preceding text: 'meke and myld' (20, and again in 168). Although only this text states it so directly, *Wise Man* seems to share this concern: 'Laughe thou to scorn nother olde ne yonge; / Be of gode beryng and of gode tonge' for 'In thy god beryng begynnes thi worschype' (*Good Wife* 23–5).

Human characters and human experiences in the items in Ashmole 61 – be they narrative or lyric in mode, didactic, devotional, or diverting in purpose – are presented as one element in a household community whose non-human participants collaborate actively as agents of moral transformation. The effects they have, like the effects of humans of various types who appear throughout the texts, can be intense and deliberate, or they can be subtle and incidental. Yet these effects are witnessed repeatedly and are regularly emphasised as crucial contributors to the movement and affective import of the verse. Investigating the human–non-human assemblages that comprise this household book demonstrates the complex effects of a number of mediators that might, read through traditional anthropocentric means, seem only to be vehicles of exclusively human yet so-called universal truths that do not include them.[76] These objects retain their non-humanity – the bird that reveals to Isumbras his moral failing and its remedy sings in a tree and immediately flies away, remaining ever the bird; the leopard and lion that take his children remain wild animals even as they nurture the boys as they would their own offspring and even as their actions produce opportunities for moral improvement; the stone in the *Ten Commandments* speaks through its own lithic solidity and fixity and rightness as much as it does through the words divinely engraved on it. Read differently, the vernacular texts of Ashmole 61 exemplify an affective orientation towards animals and other components of the not-only-human world of the household, one that included them as contributors to the ethical evaluation that generates a distinct emotional ecology.[77] The ongoing production, the continual interchange, pervades Ashmole 61. In what is often read as a fixed, stable, universalising sphere

– that of didactic texts such as conduct literature, saints' lives, exemplary narratives – the fact of change and the opportunity for desired transformation through rather than despite the interventions of others, with moral meaning generated by this very 'interchange', are instead on constant display.

Notes

1. Claire Sponsler offers as examples of this influence 'civic offices, land holdings, houses, household furnishings, coats of arms, seals, and apparel' ('Narrating the social order', p. 266).
2. Blanchfield, 'Romances', p. 73.
3. The other unique version is found in the fifteenth-century Pepys MS.
4. Evans, *Rereading*, p. 73.
5. All quotations from texts in Ashmole 61 are from *Codex Ashmole 61*, edited by George Shuffelton, and indicated by line number.
6. These are lines 5–10, which present the story of Gabriel's creation of courtesy during the Annunciation. Six manuscript copies and a number of early print copies of *The Lytylle Childrenes Lytil Boke* remain (Shuffelton, *Codex Ashmole 61*, p. 446).
7. Arthur Bahr's conceptualisation of compilation and assemblage pertains here; see Bahr, *Fragments and Assemblages*.
8. Mitchell, 'Dining tables', p. 347.
9. Mitchell, *Becoming Human*, p. 157 (italics original).
10. A. C. Spearing observes of the first-person speaker of medieval texts that 'Behind the "I" … there may be no narrator or speaker, no represented fictional person, and in the commonest kinds of Middle English poem, especially up to the middle of the fourteenth century, there is usually none'. Its 'function [may be] to convey proximality and experientiality without specific reference to a pragmatic center or *origo*' (*Textual Subjectivity*, p. 16).
11. Carruthers, *Book of Memory*, p. 211, quoted by von Contzen, 'Why medieval literature', p. 149.
12. von Contzen, 'Why medieval literature', p. 149.
13. Carruthers, 'The concept of *ductus*', pp. 193–4.
14. Spearing, *Textual Subjectivity*, pp. 17–18.
15. von Contzen, 'Why medieval literature', p. 149.
16. Carruthers, 'The concept of *ductus*', p. 200.
17. Farina, 'Get a grip', p. 100.
18. Libby, 'The object', pp. 362, 369.

19 Libby, 'The object', p. 364.
20 Farina, 'Get a grip', p. 101. The appearance in Ashmole 61 of a number of prayers following on the book's cluster of conduct items demonstrates this relationship: an 'Evening Prayer', 'Morning Prayer', and 'Prayer to Mary' (items 12, 13, and 15) request assistance with measured conduct: 'Chryst, gyffe me grace of mete and drynke / This dey to take mesurably' ('Morning Prayer' 17–18) and 'Mary, for thi joys five, / Helpe me to lyve in clene lyve' ('Prayer to Mary' 9–10). Divine intercession is sought in support of generating appropriate human earthly conduct.
21 See the Introduction for a demonstration of this cohesion.
22 Blanchfield used this term in her unpublished 1991 dissertation as well.
23 Murray Evans notes that 'Rate's gathering and reworking of these items [1–8] results in a manuscript context evidently oriented to young readers/listeners, with a "children's corner" at the opening of the manuscript' (*Rereading*, p. 73). He takes this wholesale from Blanchfield, although his use of 'evidently' ('on the basis of available evidence', Merriam–Webster) suggests that he is not fully convinced.
24 Hardman, 'Compiling the nation', p. 67.
25 Hardman, 'Compiling the nation', p. 64.
26 Emily Wingfield observes that in fifteenth- and sixteenth-century England, 'conduct literature commonly circulated alongside romance, and within such collections readers appear to have differentiated less clearly between the literary and the didactic, blurring generic boundaries across folios and quires' ('The literary miscellany', p. 226).
27 See Salisbury, *Chaucer and the Child*, pp. 19–31. Barbara Hanawalt, *Growing Up in Medieval London*, and Nicholas Orme, *Medieval Children*, offer detailed consideration of the 'medieval child'.
28 In *Medieval Children*, Orme uses the term 'young people' in a way that better reconciles medieval and current conceptions (p. 277). He also refers to 'parents and daughters' as readers of texts such as *Good Wife Taught her Daughter* (p. 333), modifying the category productively. Additionally, most of the evidence we have for children reading stories, as for reading non-fiction, comes from the early fifteenth century (p. 281).
29 Adams's goal is to argue for a more capacious model of medieval children's literature.
30 Brockman, 'Children and literature', p. 58, quoted in Kline, 'Introduction: medieval children's literature', p. 2; Kline sees in Brockman's claim a tendency to 'infantilize medieval literature generally as embryonic or incomplete'.
31 Hanawalt, 'The Childe of Bristow', p. 156.
32 Adams, 'Medieval children's literature', p. 6.

33 One need not turn to medievalist C. S. Lewis for examples; the recent Pixar movie *Inside Out* (2015), for instance, is wholly allegorical. Earlier in the twentieth century, allegory was somewhat more common in literature on serious topics for adults, as with George Orwell's 1945 novella *Animal Farm* and Arthur Miller's 1953 play *The Crucible*.
34 Sponsler, 'Medieval ethnography', pp. 1–2, quoted in Ashley, '*The Miroir des Bonnes Femmes*', p. 86.
35 Feros Ruys, *What Nature Does Not Teach*, p. 7.
36 Bryan, *Looking Inward*, p. 26.
37 Amos, 'For manners make man', p. 25.
38 Amos, 'For manners make man', pp. 31–2. I am unsure whether to challenge or to celebrate Amos's use of 'colonise' in this context.
39 Amos, 'For manners make man', p. 39.
40 I discuss some of these texts in Seaman, 'Late medieval conduct literature'.
41 Kline, 'Introduction: medieval children's literature', p. 3.
42 Brantley, 'Reading the forms of *Sir Thopas*', p. 417.
43 From a slightly different (scribe-centric) orientation, Blanchfield notes of Rate that '[h]e tried to stimulate their conscience by visual and imaginative means; he played on their emotions and was himself an emotional and feeling man ... his texts appeal simultaneously to the senses, the imagination and the conscience' ('An idiosyncratic scribe', pp. 166–7).
44 This is the only one of nine total manuscript appearances of *Isumbras* in which it exists in the same manuscript as *Eustace*. I am grateful to Leila K. Norako for pointing this out ('*Sir Isumbras* and the fantasy of crusade', p. 174, n. 20), in an analysis oriented towards the romance's intervention in the late medieval English Crusade imaginary.
45 The connection of the two texts was initially made by Laurel Braswell ('*Sir Isumbras*') and Deiter Mehl (*Middle English Romances*), with later aesthetic amplification by Anne B. Thompson ('Jaussian expectation').
46 As Rhiannon Purdie notes, 'in Middle English literature, tail-rhyme becomes inextricably linked with the romance genre itself in a way that no other verse form does' (*Anglicizing Romance*, p. 1), with roughly a third of all extant Middle English romances (the earliest extant ones in the Auchinleck MS) appearing in tail-rhyme, the only vernacular romance tradition to adopt this verse form (p. 3). Well before the time of Ashmole 61 (from the 1100s through the early 1300s), and in Anglo-Norman as well as Middle English, tail-rhyme stanzas were used primarily for didactic or religious texts (*Anglicizing Romance*, p. 6). Indeed, one such tail-rhyme religious text in Middle English dating from the late thirteenth century was a life of St Eustace (Oxford, Bodleian Library MS Digby 86). Yet while noting the similarities between the

narratives of *Eustace* and *Isumbras*, Purdie concludes that *Isumbras* 'shows no direct textual relationship with either of these tail-rhyme lives of St Eustace' (*Anglicizing Romance*, p. 42). Elsewhere, Purdie posits that tail-rhyme romance was in its 'death-throes' in the fifteenth century (*Anglicizing Romance*, p. 11). Ashmole 61 would beg to differ.

47 Shuffelton, *Codex Ashmole 61*, p. 416. The only other extant copy of this stanzaic version of *St Eustace* (all others being in couplet form) is from the late thirteenth-century household miscellany, Oxford, Bodleian Library MS Digby 86.

48 An influential early contributor to current readings of *Sir Isumbras* as a penitential romance is Andrea Hopkins, *Sinful Knights*.

49 The *Isumbras* bird joins other Middle English birds, such as those making persuasive appearances in Lydgate's *The Churl and the Bird*, Chaucer's *Parliament of Fowls*, and *The Owl and the Nightingale*.

50 George Shuffelton ('Is there a minstrel in the house?') has traced the distinctive attention to minstrels that appears throughout the manuscript.

51 Norako clarifies that, in the Advocates version of the text, upon determining that the family should head to Jerusalem to seek God, Isumbras carves a cross into his own shoulder as well as the shoulders of his sons. Norako concludes that this 'suggest[s] … that the entire family must participate collectively in his redemptive quest' ('*Sir Isumbras* and the fantasy of crusade', p. 179). Here in Ashmole 61, Isumbras cuts a cross into only his own breast (127).

52 Elizabeth Fowler observes that this leaves 'the human body without its social inflections' ('The romance hypothetical', p. 101).

53 In contrast is a romance towards the end of Ashmole 61, *Sir Orfeo*, in which a mourning Orfeo lives in the woods and becomes incorporated into a new ecology.

54 Matlock notes of the sultan that '[h]is miscomprehension places the institution of marriage at the core of the difference between East and West', understanding marriage only 'in material terms' ('Reading family', p. 367).

55 At this point in the narrative, this removal of the one remaining commodity that Isumbras had seems to be the final straw in the gradual destruction of his identity – even in the midst of a narrative whose method is to deprive the hero of all sources of comfort so that he might recalibrate his values and recognise true (divine) worth.

56 This revelation that the assumed threat of the animals that abducted the two sons served instead to preserve them in the face of the family's dangers shares similarities with Marie de France's deployment of the *garwulf* in her lai *Bisclavret* – where her introduction arouses the reader's fear only to demonstrate its inappropriateness to the real

identity of the bisclavret (see Seaman, 'Renovating the household', pp. 74–5). Such a reading is uncommon – Norako, for instance, refers to them as the sons' 'bestial captors' which in the end are successfully controlled and mastered ('*Sir Isumbras* and the fantasy of the crusade', p. 177).

57 Raluca Radulescu takes a different approach in reading *Sir Isumbras* via its fifteenth-century audiences and 'the political idiom encountered in a wide range of texts (chronicles, mirrors for princes, and political documents)' ('Pious Middle English romances', p. 333), which she positions in relation to the War of the Roses, specifically; the absence of chronicles and other prose works from Ashmole 61 (a feature that distinguishes it from other household books of its time and place) reduces some of the call to interpret the romance in terms of immediate political pressures, though she does read a Latin epigram that appears near *Isumbras* in Ashmole 61 as revealing 'anxieties over local governance and relationships', and another item, *Rules for Purchasing Land*, which she reads (working with George Shuffelton) as 'fac[ing] hard-nosed realities' of possession (Shuffelton, *Codex Ashmole 61*, p. 449, in Radulescu, 'Pious Middle English romances', p. 343). Certainly the parallels that Radulescu draws between Isumbras's prioritising his personal spiritual penance over the needs of the larger community he leads and King Henry VI, 'a king widely recognized as unfit to rule, and who gave precedence to his pursuit of religious matters over the matters of state' ('Pious Middle English romances', p. 338), offers compelling insights and helps explain some inconsistencies in this 'penitential romance' – if not wholly pertinent to my concerns here.

58 Upon becoming king of Saracen land – the land of his wife's abductor – he sends out commandments to all that 'Bot thei turnyd to his assentte, / He seyd iche one thei schuld be brente / With sorow and myche care' (730–2) – with the burning, sorrow, and care reminiscent of Isumbras's own suffering that ultimately made him right with God, as it would, presumably, these non-believers as well. As Norako puts it, his 'continual refusal to reinstate himself socially prior to arriving in Jerusalem points toward his appropriate coordination of spiritual and secular aspirations' ('*Sir Isumbras* and the fantasy of crusade', p. 184).

59 Further, all parts of the plant are used for medicinal purposes.

60 We see in Rate's version of *St Eustace*, compared to MS Digby 86's, 'intensified pietistic elements, coupled with a greater concentration on family relationships' (Blanchfield, 'Rate revisited', p. 212)

61 This occurs in the same way Isumbras's were taken, though in reverse sequence: wife by a powerful man and then sons by animals.

62 Wendy Matlock reads in the focus on the father in the two narratives their deep investment in emphasising the significance of the patriarchal figure to the family unit, subsuming the children and wife (who are, as she notes, individually converted in, for example, the version of *St Eustace* in MS Lambeth Palace 306), even as she recognises the poem's emphasis on '[t]he importance of family as a religious unit'. Ultimately, in Matlock's reading, not providing baptismal names for all the family members who convert has the effect of 'emphasizing a hierarchically structured family with a single authoritative man as its head' ('Reading family', p. 355). Matlock does read in Rate's omission of the details of the offer God makes in *St Eustace* – the choice between suffering in youth or in age – 'Rate's lack of interest in the individual', with attention staying on 'the whole family' ('Reading family', p. 358). Indeed, Matlock notes that while other versions of *Isumbras* present the parental grief at the loss of the children through the father's reaction alone, in Ashmole 61, 'only the mother cries' and 'her weeping encompasses the sadness of both parents in one conjugal whole', wherein mourning 'transcends an individual's emotions' ('Reading family', p. 365).
63 Evans, *Rereading*, p. 73.
64 Ashley and Clark, 'Medieval conduct: texts, theories, practices', p. ix. Works more narrowly described as conduct books were also 'abundant in the later Middle Ages, especially the fourteenth and fifteenth centuries' (p. x).
65 Amos, 'For manners make man', p. 34.
66 *Middle English Dictionary*, s.v. 'right', 3a, b, c and 5a.
67 Holly A. Crocker observes, 'Even narratives that prioritize Christian salvation are firmly grounded in a material world that is riven with contingency and violence, but has the potential for improvement and reform. This quotidian materialism is due ... to the sense that human excellence must be set in relation to physical powers that worked, for good or ill, as part of a broader ethical ecology in the premodern world' (*The Matter of Virtue*, p. 5).
68 Hargreaves, 'Lydgate's "A Ram's Horn"', p. 259.
69 Shuffelton lays out the contrasting possible readings of this refrain: 'The Middle English sense of "conveyed" has a range of meanings, including "directed", "guided", "carried on", as well as "written" ... The refrain thus suggests at least two possible senses: that communal life follows a crooked or curved line (and thus has gone awry) or that the text preceding the refrain is as true as a ram's horn is straight. The phrase "right as a ram's horn" is itself proverbial' (Shuffelton, *Codex Ashmole 61*, p. 423).
70 Dronzek, 'Gendered theories', p. 138.

71 In such a material world, Sara Ahmed's emotional society of objects, including but not limited to humans, especially pertains.
72 Mitchell, *Becoming Human*, p. xxix.
73 Gratitude for this understanding of the relationship between human and agility-trained dog goes to Donna Haraway, *When Species Meet*.
74 When modern Western readers take note of such physical expressions of social relationships in these texts, we tend to do so because our own social relationships no longer depend upon them or even recognise them as acts, depriving them of any significance beyond evoking an archaic past. The interdependence of human social status and the objects with which medieval people shared their time and space simply, as a result, does not register.
75 My thinking on this subject has been greatly assisted by J. Allan Mitchell's project on conduct texts, where he powerfully describes his view that 'practical literature for the table *conducts* humans and *composes* new bodies out of a material matrix, betraying the hegemony of individuals and institutions insofar as external agents must be relied upon to *propagate* hierarchy and sovereignty' ('Dining tables', p. 348). Whereas Mitchell emphasises the expression of anxiety about maintaining thresholds in instructional texts ('A dining subject is to move limbs and utensils so as to avoid spilling and polluting bodies' ['Dining tables', p. 350]), in Ashmole 61 I see in these collected texts something closer to an amusement park than an obstacle course.
76 For other considerations of this perspective, see Travis, 'Aesop's symposium of animal tongues'; Tyler, *Ciferae*; and Van Dyke, 'Touched by an owl?'
77 Elizabeth Allen shows the pervasiveness of morally pedagogical textuality throughout medieval Europe and its languages. Even 'Latin commentaries assume that literature – specifically, narrative – should have ethical utility, in the sense of helping to form, or reform, individual understanding' (*False Fables*, p. 2).

2

Objects of mercy

The book that is Ashmole 61 puts a structurally and generically cohesive foot forward from the start, an orderly household manuscript reflecting an adept seneschal-scribe. The eight poems occupying its first two quires reiterate patterns of form and purpose; and they collectively generate an aspirational spiritual-material household identity across a range of situations: aristocratic and common, religious and lay, idealistic and satiric. The conduct texts and exemplary narratives that nimbly fill the first twenty-one folios fail to prepare the reader for the diversity that the collection exhibits immediately thereafter, the cupboard's copious contents spilling out. Particularly on fols. 21v–22v, this variety can appear haphazard, two pages housing very brief Latin texts (four on one page) followed by three short prayers and a false start of the *Ten Commandments* (two stanzas of the fourteen that had already appeared just six folios earlier as item 6). It may be tempting to label these six items 'filler' and thereby remove them from a consideration of the book's agency. Yet this agency is generated by such unexpected elements as well as through the more evidently related ones as in the first eight items. In addition, the physical features of even the seemingly uncharacteristic short Latin poems suggest that these folios, too, were written through, in accord with the rest of the manuscript. Indeed, following on these short Latin poems and four prayers are texts that embody the beliefs that provoke such prayers: these texts take the form of a series of narratives that share a specific affective purpose, to affirm the mercy offered by and through Christ and enacted through human forgiveness.[1] This emotional aim, one that is often but not always primarily and overtly religious, depends upon human actors willingly requesting or granting forgiveness, as one might expect; yet this forgiveness is routinely enabled and even fulfilled in these texts through the intervention of non-human subjects.

The narratives in this second part of the manuscript begin with a trio of *exempla* that vividly depict the necessity of humbly seeking mercy and then manifest the redemptive power of graciously granting it. In this they mark a shift from the role of narrative in the first section of Ashmole 61, which proffered a saint's life and a romance as positive embodied performances of the model behaviours in the surrounding non-narrative conduct texts. In this second section of the manuscript, in contrast, *The Knight who Forgave his Father's Slayer* (item 18) centres on a knight who pursues extreme vengeance for his father's killing. In this, no reader would mistake him for a model Christian – and yet he is, despite this failing, provoked to mercy by his victim's bold expression of religious devotion. That *exemplum* is joined here by *Jealous Wife* (item 22) and *Incestuous Daughter* (item 23), two narratives centred on women whose actions – vengeful suicide and multiple filicide, in one case; and incest, matricide, patricide, serial infanticide, and prostitution (among other things) in the other – present heinous test cases that prove the expansiveness of forgiveness.[2] Items 19 and 20, falling together in between these *exempla*, are longer romances: *The Erle of Tolous* and *Lybeaus Desconus*. The intense focus on moral behaviour and spiritual cleansing in the *exempla* that bookend the romances encourages readers to attend in particular ways to these stories of knightly achievement.

Such an alternative orientation in reading the romances is guided by the focus on knightly conflict in the first *exemplum* that immediately precedes them. The abbreviated narrative of aristocratic discord in *The Knight who Forgave his Father's Slayer* is amplified by the romance that follows it: *The Erle of Tolous* is generally read as a tale of a romantic devotion that survives challenges posed by irreconcilable loyalties;[3] in its Ashmole 61 setting, however, the romance traces in fuller detail the reconciliation between one betrayed and his betrayer. Next, *Lybeaus Desconus*, a rollicking romance comprising a sequence of impressive knightly conquests, emphasises, in this particular household book environment, family and community discord; this includes Lybeaus's being the product of an illegitimate union between his unwed mother and Sir Gawain – a relationship that lasted only as long as his conception required[4] – and Lybeaus's chivalric adventure's being the product of a rash promise by King Arthur that assigns a very young and untried Lybeaus as champion to a maid and her dwarf companion, thus enraging them. The ultimate reconciliation of these various wounded parties and the resulting restoration of community takes on an affective import and intensity that surpasses the more familiar genre-based chivalric romance concern with a knight's achievement of identity, including his ultimate marriage to his lady.[5] Taken together, these five texts offer a range of opportunities for forgiveness and community healing, continually emphasising, acknowledging, and even appreciating human failings. Indeed, these failings seem necessary for the production of compassion – and for the production of art, both in the beauty of reconciliation and in the form of the poem itself.

Exemplary art

Admittedly, 'art' is not one of the achievements usually ascribed to exemplary literature. Instead, it tends to be considered identifiable precisely through its lack of nuanced renderings of human experience – offering simple, controlled, and unquestioning affirmation of conventional but presumably universal moral wisdom to which the potential artistry of a text is held hostage, never to be released. Interpretation of such texts is not only unnecessary, it is impossible: readers themselves are in a position to receive and then to implement, with the text's value inhering in its being an uncompromising catalyst to the reader's moral improvement. Exemplary texts' didacticism is understood as precluding any other purpose, and with didacticism lacking in cultural currency today, such texts are deemed not value-neutral but actively harmful – sustaining hegemonic ideology while failing aesthetically. Despite the energetic work to combat such oversimplification that has been performed by Elizabeth Allen, J. Allan Mitchell, Catherine Sanok and others in the first decade of the twenty-first century, building on that done by Mary Carruthers, Rita Copeland, and John Dagenais at the end of the twentieth, this view of exemplary literature survives even among medieval literary scholars.[6] Significant cultural damage is done by such a limited perception of the contributions of exemplary literature, popular and valued as it was in the Middle Ages. Viewed from this perspective, medieval people and their *exempla* become reductively concerned with moral control and containment, finding relief in the removal of all other possibilities – and, as a result, they are in no position or condition to speak to the present, be it the present of the sixteenth century or of the twenty-first.[7]

Discerning and understanding the relationship between cause and effect are vital to successful moral analysis. As part of her investigation of medieval etiology and the ways literature speaks back to and through medieval *physik*, Julie Orlemanski considers a foundational essay on medieval *exempla* by Frederic Tubac from 1962. Tubac presents a narrative about the dramatic change in the workings of the genre from the early to the late Middle Ages: in his reading, the texts shift from revealing causation in divine power to showing causation in natural sources. Orlemanski examines the data that formed the basis of Tubac's analysis, which is available in the form of his *Index Exemplorum*, gathering 5,400 medieval narratives from the period. A review of the materials revealed to Orlemanski that Tubac's essay claimed for the many thousand *exempla* a rigidity of purpose and expression that the data itself does not support: in the data she witnesses 'a lushly chaotic picture'. Her investigation leads Orlemanski to see in medieval *exempla* not a confirmation of what is assumed to be already known but rather 'a way of thinking about, and playing with, the claims of normative order'.[8]

A productive alternative conceptualisation of the role and effects of exemplary literature in medieval England allows for a broader engagement with often-neglected texts from medieval vernacular traditions. Elizabeth Allen lays a solid foundation for such an approach by observing that 'the effort to enact a general truth in narrative, and the closely related call to readerly imitation, can be found in a range of medieval forms across different genres'[9] – well beyond the texts modern scholars classify as *exempla*. As Ingrid Nelson puts it, this method of enacting a general truth in narrative 'enjoyed a vigorous textual presence'.[10] Allen later builds on this expansion of the exemplary mode by highlighting how late Middle English narrative, in general, 'is particularly obsessed with its capacity to mediate between an imagined world and an actual society – to make vernacular storytelling morally applicable'.[11] This moral applicability, J. Allan Mitchell observes, stretches outside the boundaries of the literal or the textual 'to engage substantive parts of an individual's moral life'.[12] Perceived this way, exemplarity does not remove or displace human moral agency or will – by granting all such authority to the text – but rather provokes moral subjects to deliberate and to act.

Ultimately, exemplary literature's aesthetic behaviour is not neglected or absent but rather is precisely what produces its effects: the moral influence of an exemplary text does not pre-empt but rather is generated by its aesthetic features. Allen reminds us that an exemplary literary text is the product of artistic as well as rhetorical techniques: 'it is not a given that the phenomenological elements of example – as expressed in the narrative details of time, place, point of view – are categorically subordinate to general moral truth'.[13] Concern with art and its effects on human will and desire – its capacity to enact change in people – is attested to in medieval didactic theory.[14] As a result, exemplary art does not lack aesthetic value and interpretive complexity but instead (as Allen observes) is 'a principal site for sophisticated inquiry into the educational methods of poetic narrative, highlighting the limits of authorial control, the importance of narrative as inspiration or seduction, and the possibilities of imaginative freedom'.[15] Medieval hermeneutic theories thus preclude passive readership for exemplary texts. As a result, investigating the operations of exemplarity focuses our attention on medieval attitudes towards reading and the active moral outcomes that this process can generate.[16] Such conclusions about the potential powers of the exemplary mode for medieval readers are encapsulated in the following passage from the *Rhetorica ad Herennium*:

> Exemplification ... renders a thought more brilliant when used for no other purpose than beauty; clearer, when throwing more light upon what was somewhat obscure; more plausible, when giving the thought greater verisimilitude; more vivid, when expressing everything so lucidly that the matter can, I may almost say, be touched by the hand.[17]

The mode offers multiple aesthetically grounded possibilities, one of which is the tangibility of the truths it conveys.

Attending to the 'phenomenological elements of example'[18] in this section of Ashmole 61, with its rich supply of exemplary texts, generates (for readers then and now) the moral influence of each text, and of the collection, showing how it can 'come to order human action'.[19] Reading this way reveals how the unexpected resolution of the various broken relationships (familial and otherwise) in the narratives is made possible and made meaningful through the involvement of fiends, chains, tears, a witch, a devotional icon, monstrous giants, a divine-human hybrid, habitual prayer, magicians, the Blessed Virgin Mary, bare feet, and, most especially, kisses. Emphasis on such an orientation towards forgiveness, redemption, and restoration results in these texts in part from their living in textual community in this manuscript. Further, the successful achievement of acknowledging failings and of conversion to forgiveness consistently depends upon the engagement of non-human subjects who are thereby authorised as custodians of affective edification. Because '[a] mineral', Valerie Allen recalls, 'is the result of a celestial impulse to realize itself in subterranean rock', '[t]he elemental interconnection of things undermines any definitive schism in the kingdom of being between organic and inorganic'.[20] This section of Ashmole 61 encourages readers to observe through a series of particular cases the universality of forgiveness, as it extends through all of creation, an embodied affective experience involving the mediation of community members beyond the human.

Establishing knightly exemplarity

At the head of this sequence of narratives, *The Knight who Forgave his Father's Slayer* (item 18, fols. 26v–27v) establishes these dynamics with the greatest clarity, one outcome of its streamlined narrative. Even for an *exemplum*, *Knight who Forgave* focuses intently in its 116 tetrameter couplet lines on the central conflict and the process leading to its resolution: a disagreement between two knights has led one to kill the other. The dead knight's son seeks revenge, besieging the killer knight for a year, effectively excommunicating him by preventing him from leaving his home to attend church. Everything changes when the imprisoned killer sees parishioners walking to Good Friday Mass. Spiritually moved, the isolated knight risks everything by revealing himself to his awaiting attacker, an act that inspires the vengeful knight to respond favourably to his father's killer's request for mercy, and the two men attend Mass together, their hatred replaced by friendship and their communion with one another and the larger community restored.

Excerpted from the 'Anger' section in Robert Manning of Brunne's *Handlyng Synne* and unique to Ashmole 61, this *exemplum* is a Good Friday story of forgiveness invested in representing the motivations for the feuding knights' actions, in demonstrating the reasons for their change of heart, and in showing the effects of that change. All three knights (including the father killed in the first four lines of the poem) are driven by 'wreth and wo' (3).[21] This wrath leads one of them to kill through ambush (unknightly as well as unchristian behaviour) and the other to seek extreme vengeance. This wrath is not a spontaneously produced, short-lived emotional state but rather is sustained through careful plotting and long-term intimidation, respectively. It is a product of personal inclination as well: the son is 'wyld' (6), which is to say 'headstrong', which leads him to decide ('toke hym to rede' [7]) to seek vengeance. His course is deliberately chosen, and from the start the narrative frowns on it, revealing it to be an expression of personal rage rather than a pursuit of justice. The son methodically assembles the knightly support necessary to sustain a year-long siege of his father's killer (16), and his crew simply waits for the besieged knight to leave his castle, as he eventually must, to allow them the opportunity to achieve the son's revenge. The killer's motivation, when he does finally expose himself to danger, challenges the son's determination, however: it is not resistance to or frustration about being housebound, but the sight of others outside his castle going 'Barefote to the chyrch ... To aske mersy for there mysdede' (25–6), and his recognition that he should be among them, that inspires his father's killer to risk presenting himself in public.

The narrative has informed its audience that this 'was in the Lentyn tyde [time], / When men schuld leve wreth and pride' (18–19), exactly the deep emotional failings of deadly sin committed by the central knights in the story. At this point the narrative moves to the killer knight's interiority, as he recalls how long he has been unable to attend Mass and determines, 'Whatsoever God for me wyll wyrche [do], / I wyll ryse and go to the chyrche' (29–30). The otherwise thrifty narrative attends to the detail of the knight removing his shoes to join the other penitents passing by. The son now speaks, upon seeing his intended victim so vulnerable, declaring to him and to all present, 'Tratoure, now schall thou dyghe / And my faders deth full dere abyghe' (37–8). Because the audience has already learned of the besieged knight's humble obedience, the son's verbal threat at this point sounds all the more vicious, and the audience's empathies shift. The besieged knight kneels and requests mercy in the name of Christ, whose sacrifice on Good Friday he calls on, emphasising that Christ 'forgaffe hym that his blod spylte' (47). He requests that the son do the same in his case: 'Right so thou forgyff me that gylte' (48). With the 'spylte' / 'gylte' rhyme, he puts himself in the position of Christ's killers, sharing their culpability in having spilled Christ's blood, simultaneously highlighting the fact that despite their extreme evil they received forgiveness from Christ. This request he 'praye[d] so reufolly' (54) that it inspires pity in the son, presented as it is in the name of Christ and Mary: in response to the affective submission, the son says, 'For them I grante thee my powere' (58). The knight who, upon first seeing the escaped prisoner, proclaimed that he would kill him, has in mere moments changed utterly, to the point of giving up his newly achieved power at the very moment he has long been anticipating to exert it.

The text doesn't precisely define this power, but it is clear that the son holds a moral advantage over the murderous knight, even if his own pursuit of vengeance is immoderate. This advantage he holds not because of his own or his father's personal moral supremacy, for before he was killed, his father was as culpable as his enemy. The narrative carefully distributes the responsibility for the original conflict: 'Bytwyx two knyghtys ... / Fell a gret conteke [argument] to be' (1–2); 'Bytwyx them fell syche wreth and wo' (3). Both older knights share the blame between them, until 'the one weyted [plotted] the other to slo [slay]' (4). Only at this point does the moral valence of this first encounter between two rival knights shift, for the attack comes not in the context of an authorised space of knightly combat to determine whose claim in their dispute (the details of which remain unstated) is valid, but rather is an act of treachery. No longer are they presented as two equal knights, for one has become a murderer, the other his victim. The son inherits his father's moral claim, which grants him the power to which he refers at the very moment he expressly grants it to his father's killer in honour of Christ and Mary. This exchange of power explicitly redefines their relationship, for the son foregoes his inherited right and, in exchange for nothing but in recognition of spiritual truth, levels their moral status. This act of generosity restores the balance shared by the two older knights at the start of the narrative, free of the unnamed conflict that had kept them both in the wrong. The son then goes further: he 'sone doune lyght, / And in gode love kyssed the knyght' (59–60). This kiss is an additional act of extreme generosity, with the son sacrificing himself – his pride – and translating what was originally an act of emotional superiority (expressing pity) into one of humility (lowering himself to the knight and offering a kiss of peace). The friends head to church together 'In gowd love and perfyte charyté' (63), all for the sake of him who 'ordeynd thus to be' (64). The son proclaims them now in accord with Christ's will – a statement that acknowledges that they previously were not, despite the moral right the son had claimed in pursuing revenge for his father's murder.

The subsequent events in the narrative visibly affirm the knights' new status in communion with Christ. As this is Good Friday, once at church they follow the holy day ritual: 'Befor the cros thei knelyd doune … For to kysse the crosse' (69, 71). In doing this, they re-enact the son's two gestures of humility towards his enemy outside the church moments before, of descending from his horse and kissing his foe. Within the church, the forgiven knight goes first, and then the younger knight follows, described here as the one 'That was become meke and myld' (76). He has been transformed by his actions, just as his former enemy has become his friend. For this deed, the son receives a miracle: 'The crusyfix that there was leyd / His arme fro the crosse uppe brayd [rose up] / And clyped [embraced] the chyld hym betwyx, / and sethe he kyssed the crusyfix' (79–82). And then, as witnessed by the entire parish, 'the crucyfyx hym kyste [the crucifix kissed him]' (85). The humble acts of the wronged knight are acknowledged by the animated crucifix, with Christ reaching up and embracing the knight and returning his Good Friday kiss. It comes as no surprise that the story of 'The merakyll' (96), as the narrator observes, circulates rapidly and widely, with priests preaching about it in their sermons. The miracle, however, is not only the forgiving knight's being hugged and kissed by a normally inert and symbolic crucifix; instead, 'Of thes two knyghtys how it betyde / The merakyll sprong wele wyde' (95–6). The miracle story is about the two knights, rather than about the single knight and the cross; this orientation of the miracle story indicates that such an act of human forgiveness is so rare as to warrant the affirmation of the crucifix. The *human* act is itself truly supernatural, a miracle.

Christ's bodily interaction with the young knight draws attention to and affirms, but doesn't generate, the miracle: it is 'A sygne [sign] … of grete love' (105). The human actions are rewarded with divine love made manifest for all to see. 'God allmyghty of heven above / Preferd [esteemed] hym to kys so lawly [lowly]' (106–7). That is, God the supreme, inhabitant of heaven, so esteems the forgiving knight that he lowers himself to kiss the knight. This observation is followed with 'For he mekyd [humbled] his herte so hye ['high' or 'proud']' (108). Beginning with the ambiguous 'For', this phrase could indicate that the kiss is given *because* the knight humbled his proud heart, or it might mean *that* God humbled his own elevated heart in order to give the kiss. Practically speaking, the first reading seems simplest, but the unclear referentiality of the pronouns in this line – which 'he' is humbling his high heart? Christ humbling his divinity, in kissing the human knight, or the wronged knight humbling his inappropriate pride in kissing his foe? – points to the success of the young knight's *imitatio Christi*. Indeed, priests tell this story specifically to encourage all to 'lyve well the more in charité' (100), to live like the forgiving knight, and through that to live like Christ.

The embodied action of the animated crucifix hugging the knight, in expressing divine approval, demonstrates how embodied human action can perform divine will and, in that act, be an extension of God on earth. In this, a Christian can become a divine-human hybrid reflecting the humanity as well as the divinity of the unified Christ, demonstrating how Christ not only humbles himself in coming to earth in human form but also elevates humanity: as Caroline Walker Bynum puts it, 'God, immanent and immediate in the stuff of the world, might for a moment lift that stuff to exactly the eternity and transcendence it could by definition never fully be'.[22] Here, an act of human forgiveness embodies the mercy of Christ, so that the miracle of transformation of the supernatural has already occurred in that humble act and has been triggered by human, not divine, agency. And in this, it is a miracle: that which is 'not just beyond our current understanding but also outside the ordinary workings of nature'.[23] This is not to say that the forgiving knight – or any human who might follow his example – elevates *himself* to 'the eternity and transcendence' that is beyond his own nature. Rather, in his acceptance of the offer of God's mercy, and in extending it through granting it to others, the human Christian allows himself to become part of and to be elevated by Christ. Both divine and human agency are necessary to produce that networked human-divine hybrid. Notably, the crucifix, which is (using Bynum's words) 'God, immanent and immediate in the stuff of the world', seems here to be literally lifting the stuff of the world, in the form of the knight whose body he enfolds in his own.

Just as God has to offer the opportunity for communion and the forgiving knight has to accept it or else they will remain two distinct entities, the murdering knight had to request mercy and his pursuer had to offer it, in order for forgiveness to be generated. This focus on forgiveness as an affective assemblage the production of which requires non-human agents – in this case the bare feet of the worshippers, the supernatural agent of the sacred, the double kiss – is manifest in a range of ways in the following texts in this section of the manuscript; these suggest as well that other affective virtues in addition to forgiveness may be produced by human and non-human subjects (both earthly and divine) in community. These texts share the embodied experience of complex emotion which is repeatedly generated through the kiss, unforgettably established in this initial narrative by the crucifix's embrace of the forgiving knight.

Romance's kiss of forgiveness: *The Erle of Tolous*

The Erle of Tolous (item 19, fols. 27v–38v), a self-identified Breton lay of 1,210 tail-rhyme lines, follows *Knight who Forgave*, and one might expect that a dramatic shift in style, tone, and narrative concerns would accompany the move from *exemplum* to romance. Certainly, *The Erle of Tolous* lacks the physically present supernatural so central to the effects of *Knight who Forgave*, an absence all the more conspicuous given how typical this feature is of Breton lays. However, this narrative, too, begins with a standoff between two feuding knights. Its manuscript predecessor has powerfully demonstrated the non-violent possibilities for reconciliation between even morally corrupt knights. Although this poem announces at the start that it concerns a lady's misfortune and recovery, audience attention is quickly drawn to her husband, Emperor Dioclesian, and his wicked deeds. He unjustly takes the lands of others, behaving as a conqueror of his own subjects by claiming their lands as his own. His wickedness extends from his actions to his determination to defend them: he tells his wife, Beulybon, when she urges him to return the stolen lands to Sir Barrard, the Erle of Tolous, that 'I schall brek hym, bake and breyn, / as I ame trew knyght' (50–1). Clearly, this is no true knight, and his false claim alongside his violent assertion of his false righteousness draws attention to the competing moral claims of these two knights and the unknightly, unchristian behaviour recalled from the start of *Knight who Forgave*. Here, the narrative presents the violent clash between the two armies that was prevented in *Knight who Forgave* by the catalyst of the captive murderer-knight's sense of religious duty; here, almost 60,000 of the emperor's men are left dead, with just 350 of his great lords surviving, most as prisoners; the earl's side is relatively spared, with 400 casualties. This wrathful action on the part of the emperor, who asserts to his men that they 'leve non one lyve. / Loke that non raunsond be' (75–6), produces significant loss, an excess of blood and killing, concluding this early scene of knightly combat with the sobbing of wives for their dead. The physical and emotional toll when forgiveness is neither sought nor offered is laid out in plain view from the start.

All experience is affectively charged throughout this romance, not just that of war, and it extends from the emperor's extreme wrath – expressed as a reaction to others' resistance to his own wrathful theft – to the treachery among the emperor's men, two of whom conspire to win the love (or rather the body) of their lord's wife, this same Beulybon. The emperor's unjust claim of Sir Barrard's property is imitated by his knights, who treat Beulybon like property that can be similarly claimed through theft.[24] Indeed, their secret plot is an intended double rape of her that involves treachery against the emperor and betrayal of his empress, with one seducing her and the other catching them in the act and threatening to report it unless she shares herself with him as well. When Beulybon refuses seduction, instead declaring them traitors worthy to be burned, the two knights decide – despite her earlier promises to each that she would keep their attempts a secret – to kill her.

While these two triply treacherous knights reveal their so-called love to the empress and require her to respond favourably, the Erle of Tolous provides an alternative model: instead of proclaiming his love to her and demanding reciprocation, the Erle appreciates her beauty anonymously. While he holds the emperor's uncle, Sir Tralabas, captive after defeating the emperor in battle, the Erle asks Tralabas about the reputation for beauty he has heard of Beulybon. When Tralabas confirms this reputation, the Erle asks Tralabas to help him secretly get a glimpse of her. In exchange, the Erle will forgive Tralabas's ransom and release him. He puts himself at risk – travelling to his enemy's territory – and sacrifices wealth (in the form of the ransom) in order simply to see Beulybon; in total contrast, the emperor's own knights put her at risk and plan to betray her, all for their personal physical gratification. The Erle takes more risks than he knows, in fact, for after arranging for the agreed-upon glimpse of his niece, Tralabas reveals to Beulybon the Erle's presence at court, expecting to receive reward from her for outing the enemy; instead, she tells him he must keep the information secret since he gave the Erle his word. Yet again, treachery fails, cut short once more by Beulybon's virtue, and the Erle survives the attempt on his life by Tralabas and justly kills him instead.

The conflict that began the narrative recurs throughout the poem: the emperor betrays the Erle by taking his lands; the knights betray the emperor and his wife by trying to seduce her and by killing (and falsely accusing) one of his subjects; the knights further betray the wife by demanding she pledge to keep their revelations of adulterous love secret and then scheming to make her appear unfaithful to her husband, for which she is doomed to be burned; Tralabas betrays the Erle and tries to kill him. None of these betrayals achieves its desired end, and Beulybon is saved from execution by the interventions of a wise old knight who offers legal insight that gives her a possible way out, and by the Erle of Tolous who offers to be her defender (albeit in disguise, as the emperor still considers him an enemy). Through a series of chance encounters that confirm for him the empress's innocence, and while protected by various disguises, the Erle defeats the two treacherous knights (who then confess and are burned) and successfully defends Beulybon's honour, thus single-handedly cleansing the narrative of its three traitors (Tralabas and the two knights) and creating an opportunity for reconciliation with his own lord, the one redeemable criminal.

The offer of reconciliation is made, in this case, by the one in the wrong: the emperor. As in *Knight who Forgave*, the event is triggered by intense emotion: when Dioclesian learns that it was the Erle who defended his wife, he tells her uncle (this one a good uncle, an abbot who assisted the Erle in his plans to defend Beulybon, allowing him to hear her confession while disguised as a monk)[25] that all will be well between the Erle and him. More specifically, the emperor seems to have been reading *Knight who Forgave*, for he replies to the abbot's revelation of Beulybon's defender's identity with, 'Hath he do me this grete honour? / Anon now I pray thee / After hym that thow wylte wend, / And we wyll kys and be gode frend, / Be hym that dyed on tre' (1170–5). Understanding the depth of the favour the Erle has done for him, and done at great risk to himself, the emperor loses the anger he previously found so intense and righteous that he tried to kill the Erle. That anger makes room for a new emotion: 'Gle ne game lykes hym nought, / So gretly he gan grylle [grieve]' (161–2). His anger does not dissipate and leave him in a neutral state: instead, it is replaced by regret for his own past actions, leading him to seek redemption. He wants the Erle to be returned to him so that they can kiss and be friends in the name of Christ.

In this case, the Erle holds the power that the dead knight's son gave over to his father's killer in the preceding *exemplum*: he justly defeated the thieving emperor early in the narrative. And yet the emperor at that point presented himself as the wronged party and effectively required the Erle to practise his knight's justice, in clearing the emperor's court of three traitors, and to do so incognito and at great personal risk in each case. As the Erle's lord, the emperor should have been doing the opposite: providing him with the resources and support necessary to perform his knightly duties. It takes all of this for the emperor to see his error, which is enabled not by the violent acts of distributive justice early in the narrative but by the generosity the Erle enacted in the face of numerous harms. When the Erle appears, the emperor greets him and says, 'My frend so fre, / My wreth here I thee forgyve, / My helpe, my love, whyll that I lyve, / Be hym that dyghed on tre' (1183–87). Like the forgiving knight, the emperor turns away from the 'wreth' he had against one who he believed (however incorrectly) had wronged him, forgiving the former enemy with the assistance of Christ's love. Further mirroring the forgiveness scene of the two knights in the previous narrative, these two 'Louely togyder gan [did] thei kys' (1188). The speech act of forgiveness here, as there, becomes physically manifest through the kiss, materialising in the world and transforming it.

The central conflicts of *The Erle of Tolous* as described so far share the black-and-white moral scale of the text that precedes it, with the emperor undeniably in the wrong when taking the Erle's lands, an assessment conveyed through Beulybon, who repeatedly presents the voice of emotional-ethical reason. The empress in this way consistently provides *The Erle of Tolous* with what Christ's sacrifice provided in *Knight who Forgave*: a stable alternative to the flawed human will that surrounds her. Yet the moral landscape of *Knight who Forgave* is smoother than is the rocky ethical world of *The Erle of Tolous*, with its varied and challenging topography. Throughout the romance weak versions of love are modelled, as are aspirational ones, asking what loyalty and devotion really are and what they really ought to do. In *Knight who Forgave*, the son understood his loyalty and devotion to his father as demanding vengeance; the poem teaches him otherwise, leading him to express that devotion through showing mercy and forgiveness. *The Erle of Tolous* moves from the flat plains of stark moral truths when it turns away from the battlefield to the private spaces of the castle, where the seeming adultery of Beulybon artificially constructed by the two betraying knights infects the Erle's adoration of her and her response to his desire. Instead of expressing her loyalty to her husband (whose love for his wife the poem is careful to demonstrate)[26] by ignoring the knowledge that the Erle desires to see her, Beulybon actually performs for him during his 'secret' viewing of her, and she later gives him a ring as a token. On the one hand, she gives the ring to the Erle as he seeks alms from the empress while he is disguised as a poor hermit. On the other, she is fully aware of the gift's recipient: making clear that this gift was not made naively, Beulybon later confesses the act repeatedly (to her uncle the abbot, and to the Erle in disguise as a monk when he takes her confession on death row), acknowledging her failing. Indeed, it was because he personally knew of this lapse that the Erle was careful to confirm her innocence in the case with the two treacherous knights before committing to being her champion.

And yet she does keep her word to her husband, and she even keeps her word to the two knights who, at the very moment she gives it, are attempting to seduce and then kill her: she tells each that she will keep secret what they are about to reveal to her, and thus when they later publicly accuse her of having sex with Antor, she does not announce their own actual treachery in defence of herself. The narrative ultimately rewards her for her dedication to truth, for the Erle appears on the scene to be her defender against the two knights and their claim against her honour. Similarly, she and the Erle are rewarded for their devotion to their relationships with the emperor, he as subject and defender and she as subject and wife: after the emperor's death (three short years later), they enjoy a 23-year marriage and produce fifteen children, the poem careful to affirm that the couple earned this victory. Early in the narrative Beulybon had advised her husband, in his attacks on the Erle, 'Be ought that I can se. / It is grete foly, sothly to telle, / To be ageyn the trew quarelle [just cause]' (138–40). The love between her and the Erle endures and is ultimately so productive because of their own just cause – indeed, it *is* their just cause. Just as Beulybon keeps her word despite the danger into which doing so puts her, the Erle seeks just cause before coming to her defence, not solely out of his affection for her but ultimately to pursue justice: 'If he wyst sche had do ryght, / He wold aventour his lyff and hyght / To fyght for that lady so fre' (918–20). Only with that knowledge, the text carefully clarifies, does he act.

The narrative depends on the audience perception of the cause of the Erle and Beulybon as just, and it regularly presents it as such. Indeed, particularly in light of its conduct text neighbours in this setting in Ashmole 61, the poem's extensive and detailed presentation of Beulybon makes her appear the aspirational product of a women's conduct text (35–42);[27] in addition to having the requisite beauty, she continually offers wise advice to badly behaving men (e.g. 136–8 and 151–2). However, both hero and heroine exhibit human failings that they acknowledge. Beulybon does this through repeatedly confessing her sin in giving the ring to the Erle and thereby, even if only ambiguously, promising her love to him, love that she doesn't have the right at that moment to give away. The Erle's error is initially less overt, for his fascination with seeing the empress could be understood as appropriate honouring of the good. And yet he goes to extreme lengths to make it happen, including ransoming – to achieve his own personal aims – a prisoner whose subsequent treachery indicates the benefit that his continued imprisonment would have offered society. Further, the Erle isn't satisfied with the visual confirmation he receives that Beulybon's reputation for beauty is valid, for he immediately prays for an alternative life with her:

> Lord God full of myght,
> Leve that I were so worthy a knyght
> That I myght be her fere [companion],
> And that sche non husbond hade.
> Alle the gode that ever God made
> To me were not so dere. (364–9)

God's real creation falls short of the one the Erle imagines and requests through his prayer. Further, he approaches her for alms while presenting himself as a hermit. His love for her leads him to deception and risky behaviour, behaviour that then creates the opportunity for her own questionable actions in giving him the ring.

And yet the Erle's prayer is answered. Just three years later, Beulybon has no husband and the Erle is her companion. The ongoing narrative support of Beulybon and the Erle for their morally righteous behaviour but also for their moments of ethical slippage intensifies the affective truth while drawing audience attention to the moral impact of the text. Except for the abbot and the merchant, two very minor characters in the narrative, everyone except Beulybon and the Erle exhibits deep human error, rather than mild human weakness – the emperor with his theft, Tralabas and the two knights with their outright betrayal of either their word or their lord, all of it requiring violence to set right. Only the Erle and Beulybon act in ways that support the well-being of the larger community, even if they do so alongside some private demonstration of vulnerability. The societal consequences of individual actions are prioritised in this text: the emperor's forgiveness of the Erle, and the Erle's acceptance of that forgiveness as a statement of responsibility on the part of the emperor – all made material through the kiss between the former foes – doesn't just reunite the emperor and earl. 'All men had joy', the next line tells us, 'withouten mysse [exception]' (1189). The community is whole again, and the people ('All men') are happy about it, as a result of the new relationship produced by the kiss.

Thus far in this section of the manuscript, the kiss–forgiveness combination is a powerful generator of community healing. In the case of *Knight who Forgave*, the two are joined by a physical lowering of the improperly heightened heart, all of which enacts an embodied experience of emotional redemption. In that text, the combination is triggered by an act of ritual religious humiliation evidenced by bare feet in public procession. In *The Erle of Tolous*, the forgiveness, despite its being accompanied by a kiss and resulting in reconciliation, reads as an expression of gratitude rather than the personal abasement in recognition of moral error exhibited in *Knight who Forgave*. The first speech act of forgiveness comes from the Erle, when he forgives Tralabas his ransom:

> Thy ranson here I thee forgyfe,
> My helpe, my love, whyll that I lyve.
> Therto my trouth I plyght,
> If it so be thou wyll bryng me
> In safe werd forth with thee
> Of her to have a syght,
> A hundred pownd with grete honour,
> To byghe thee hors and armour,
> As I ame trew knyght. (205–13)

Here the Erle is not forgiving Tralabas for a wrong done against him, but rather he is excusing Tralabas's payment of a ransom,[28] essentially forgiving a debt. This act of forgiveness – coupled with a request for assistance and the promise of knightly accoutrement – is not accompanied by a kiss, because it is not an affective act but rather a pragmatic exchange of capabilities, of access (to locations, to knowledge, to wealth). The second expression of forgiveness comes from the emperor in a setting parallel to that of *Knight who Forgave*, for the emperor has wronged his subject by taking his lands (and, further, keeping them even when the Erle's success in battle has proven the falseness of the emperor's claim). His act of forgiveness the emperor expresses thus: 'My wreth here I thee forgyve, / My helpe, my love, whyll that I lyve, / Be hym that dyghed on tre' (1184–87). It is the act of giving up one's wrath,[29] a giving over of one's anger, which is an act of granting mercy to someone over whom one has power. It acknowledges no wrongdoing, demonstrates no moral transformation but an affective one, a change of emotional stance towards another. For this, a kiss manifests the shift in their affective relationship – a shift absent from the Erle's earlier exchange with Tralabas. The contrast of these two uses of parallel language within *The Erle of Tolous* – 'My wrath [or Thy ransom, in the case of Tralabas] here I thee forgyfe, / My helpe, my love, whyll that I lyve' – points towards available variants of forgiveness. In the case of the Erle to Tralabas, he follows the forgiveness speech act with a promise of gifts and then concludes, 'As I ame trew knyght' (213); the emperor in his case concludes, 'Be hym that dyghed on tre' (1187). The Erle, making a practical knightly exchange, as witnessed by the knightly accoutrement he offers, calls on his own truth (as knight) as his surety; the emperor, making a moral affective pledge to the Erle – renouncing his own wrath – calls on Christ's truth as the stable foundation for his change. *The Erle of Tolous* thus supplements the forgiveness network of *Knight who Forgave* by demonstrating additional possible applications, towards relationships defined not by affective bonds or moral imbalances as in the case of the emperor and the Erle, and as established in *Knight who Forgave*. All are related in their production of community restoration.

The transformative kiss: *Lybeaus Desconus*

The first romance in this section of the manuscript (and the first not to be attached to a saint's life), *The Erle of Tolous* diversifies the social functions available to forgiveness and enacted by a kiss; the romance that follows it, *Lybeaus Desconus* (item 20, fols. 38v–59v), diversifies the social powers wielded by the kiss, whose agency thus far exists only in conjunction with the speech act of forgiveness. In *Lybeaus Desconus*, as with *Knight who Forgave*, the kiss's agency depends upon non-human participants within its meaning network; indeed, throughout this narrative, non-human agents are crucial to the production of the knightly subject and the virtues, such as nobility and dedication, that sustain it. This poem is perhaps now best known for its stunning human-supernatural hybrid, the dragon-lady that the poem's female protagonist, the Lady of Synadoune, has become as a result of a curse. The kiss of the hero – an example of the *fier baiser* motif, in which a daring kiss and intimate embrace signal transformations – returns her to her true identity. Because of the terms of the curse, it also materially proves to Lybeaus his own (previously unknown) identity, revealing that he is a blood relative of Sir Gawain. Throughout the narrative, in this and other ways, Lybeaus achieves his knightly identity not simply through his own performance but through contact with a range of agents, human and other.

Lybeaus Desconus, in Fair Unknown fashion,[30] traces the development of a youth with an uncertain background as he proves himself through his knightly success in a series of adventures, in the process of which he acquires his reputation and achieves an identity, and ultimately learns his true background (typically this means his paternity, specifically), which serves to confirm the validity of the identity he has produced for himself through his courtly behaviour and valorous deeds. Key moments in the 2,252 tail-rhyme lines of *Lybeaus Desconus*[31] are familiar from the larger tradition, including the *fier baiser* and various of the challenges the hero faces in his adventure (fairy seduction, a battle at a bridge, combat with giants, a sparrowhawk contest, thwarting a rape) as well as the messenger maiden and her attendant dwarf who request aid from the king and thus provide the opportunity for the Fair Unknown to prove himself. In this particular manifestation of the motif, Lybeaus is raised in the wild by his mother, knows himself only through the name Bewfys ('Beautiful Son') that she calls him, and, upon seeing a knight in the woods, determines to become one himself. He heads to Arthur's court, where the king is immediately taken by his beauty as well as his ingenuousness and in response quickly grants the boy's request for knighthood and rashly promises to offer him the first challenge that is presented. This comes from Elene and the dwarf Wyndeleyn, who seek a champion to free the Lady of Synadoune from magicians who have stolen her lands and imprisoned her. Arthur offers them young Lybeaus, which they accept grudgingly, and once underway they repeatedly berate him for his youth and inexperience until he demonstrates his true value as a knight by preserving them from a series of attackers. The adventure involves a number of confrontations with seemingly invincible opponents, until Lybeaus frees the Lady of Synadoune from the curse and from her captors. By the end, Lybeaus has learned that he is related to Gawain, is in fact his son, and the romance ends with Lybeaus's marriage at Arthur's court to the Lady of Synadoune, which gives him the property and position he lacked as an illegitimate son. In the version of the narrative contained in Ashmole 61, the arrival of Lybeaus's mother[32] allows for a reunion of his nuclear biological family and the public revelation of his full identity.

Like the interpretation offered by the romance's two most recently published critics, Eve Salisbury and James Weldon,[33] my reading focuses on the memorable scene of transformation that provides the climax of the adventure narrative. Read in relation to the agency of the kisses of forgiveness in *Knight who Forgave* and *The Erle of Tolous*, however, the kiss in *Lybeaus Desconus* triggers a material transformation that literalises the way a kiss transforms social and spiritual relationships in the previous two texts. Within *Lybeaus Desconus*, the kiss is not distinct from the ongoing production of heroic identity through combat with often non-human opponents, which transforms the Fair Unknown into the knight Sir Gynglain. This combat also transforms each autonomous but abusive figure (human or otherwise) that Lybeaus defeats into one of a sequence of identifiers of Lybeaus's knightly identity: he sends the heads of those he has killed to Arthur as evidence of his success in combat, and he requires, of those to whom he has shown mercy, that they head straight to Arthur's court to tell the king that they have been defeated by Lybeaus Desconus. Transformations producing new identities abound in the narrative.

Lybeaus is a knight-in-the-making who is especially attuned to the non-human from the start. A boy who lives alone with his mother, outside of community, Bewfys heads out to find wild animals being hunted and instead stumbles upon a dead knight. What draws Lybeaus's attention is not the man himself – the knight with whom he will later come to identify – but rather his armour, the material tools that make the knight possible.[34] Like Lybeaus, the text itself here seems to be equating the (dead) knight and the hunted animals that Bewfys sought to observe, as he trades one kind of 'play' for another. His mother has kept her son apart from society because of her fear that he would embarrass them, presumably because he has no father to train him properly:

> For he was so savage
> And lyghtly wold outrage [do harm]

> To his felows in fere [company].
> For doute [fear] of wyked lose [reputation]
> His moder kepyd hym close,
> As worthy chyld and dere. (19–24)

Lybeaus's preference for the armour over the man might be perceived as an indicator of the naivety his mother's protection has deliberately produced,[35] but it might also be read as his proper recognition that a knight without armour is no knight at all (be it himself or a dead man in the woods whose armour can thus no longer serve him). The text affirms the latter significance when Lybeaus removes the armour from the corpse, without any instruction in the complicated task, and then dons it easily. Having thereby transferred the corpse's knightly identity to himself, Lybeaus without a moment's hesitation heads to Arthur's court in Glastonbury, where 'Ymonge lordys and ladys alle, / He grete them with honour, / And seyd, "Arthor, my lord, / Sofer me to speke a word, / I pray yow, par amour"' (44–8). His immediate skill with courtly rhetoric suggests that for some – those with, for instance, the most chivalric blood – training in nobility is unnecessary. He continues, '"I ame a chyld uncouthe / And com nowte of thee soughte; / I wold be made a knyght"' (49–51), demonstrating that he responds to an internal rather than external call – again affirming his congenital nobility – and this despite being just ten years old. Lybeaus (at this point in the text referred to as Gyngeleyn, his true name, which he will not learn until the end of the narrative) has an innate capacity to understand knightly prowess and valour from the moment he has any contact with it, contact that appears in the form of the inert armour rather than in the figure of the human knight's body, whether alive or dead.[36] This contrasts significantly with the event that leads other Fair Unknown figures to seek knighthood in texts such as *Sir Perceval of Galles*, wherein the boy raised in the wild is intrigued by living knights who he spots fighting in the woods (knights he misinterprets as gods) and then on his first appearance in Arthur's court behaves as one might expect of a youth with no prior exposure to this refined world.[37] Lybeaus's alternative perspective is different: from the start, he exhibits a capacity for comprehending the integration of the non-human with the human, the hybrid product that another, better trained knight indoctrinated in the exceptionalism of nobility might misinterpret as a reflection purely of human agency.

Lybeaus interacts with non-human animals in more complicated ways that challenge the status quo but simultaneously demonstrate his nobility, pushing at the expectations of conventional norms. In the first such instance, a familiar scene from the Fair Unknown tradition is itself transformed in the Middle English versions, which inherited from the Old French an episode wherein a sparrowhawk marks the woman who possesses it as being herself the most beautiful of women; it also marks her as the beloved of a knight willing to defend her claim to the hawk. The hawk thus distinguishes the maiden who owns it as both the most beautiful woman and as beloved of a loyal and successful knight. The Middle English version retains the bird (here a falcon) and the competition, but transforms it into an explicit rather than subtly disguised beauty pageant: the knight himself (Geffroun) has a falcon that can be claimed by any knight who believes he has a lady more beautiful than Geffroun's. If the challenging knight's lady fails the beauty contest, the knight must fight Geffroun, and if he loses the fight, he loses his head, which Geffroun then posts on a shaft for all to see.[38]

Given what Lybeaus has done with the heads of the non-human combatants he has met thus far – chopping them off and sending them to Arthur as proof of his success – this version of the episode makes the threat to Lybeaus not simply one of social embarrassment; rather, he risks being transformed from a human knight into an inhuman monster deserving of such treatment. Salisbury and Weldon conclude that 'Lybeaus's lack of chivalric courtesy is notable in this episode', which 'exposes Lybeaus's lack of genuine feeling for Elene and insensitivity to chivalric protocols; his motive for combat derives from a beauty contest to which a mature knight would never have subjected his lady'.[39] Certainly Lybeaus shows little concern for Elene's feelings about being publicly judged physically inferior to another woman, but he also understands that Geffroun's lemman will always be deemed superior. Even at the moment he tells Elene and Wyndelyn about his plan to challenge Geffroun, he knows that he will be required to fight Geffroun, that Elene cannot possibly win. Geffroun's beloved is indeed declared the winner and Geffroun taunts Lybeaus that 'The faukon hast thou lorn' (962), to which Lybeaus replies, 'That was never myn use; / Juste we wyll therforne'

(964–5). Lybeaus understands that the competition is only a ruse, a means to secure opponents for Geffroun. The text's description of Geffroun's lemman presents her beauty as authentic – the 21-line description of her focuses on her face, her hair, her eyebrows, her eyes, and so on, whereas the brief description of Elene mentions only her attire, the various clothes and jewels in which she is bedecked in an effort to make of her something she isn't – and Geffroun's lemman thus legitimately wins the competition. Yet Lybeaus is able to defeat Geffroun in battle despite his own maiden's aesthetic inferiority. He properly reads the falcon, and the lemman, as symbolic distractions from (and cultural euphemisms for) the true focus: knightly violence. The falcon is sent to Arthur, to become part of the largely living monument to Lybeaus's knightly valour.

This episode is followed by another in which an animal plays a key role: Lybeaus's encounter with Sir Otis de Lile, a former supporter of the Lady of Synadoune who, when she was attacked by magicians, fled in fear, leaving her to her own devices. Sir Otis's knightly neglect created the very situation Lybeaus is on his way to rectify. Wyndeleyn recognises the sound of horns as being those of Otis, and at that moment a hunting dog runs through, his coat all the colours of the spring flowers. Elene is so taken with the dog that Lybeaus catches him and gifts him to her. Following this, they ride along in the forest 'all sawght [peacefully] / And told how kempys [warriors] faught / For byrdys bryght and schene' (1083–5), apparently reflecting on their most recent success against Geffroun; this also foreshadows the conflict to come, triggered by a deer being chased by two greyhounds that look just like Elene's new dog. A blue knight following the dogs in chase immediately claims the flower-hued dog as his own, saying it has been missing for a year and demanding its return. Where Sir Otis failed in his responsibilities to the Lady of Synadoune, Otis's blue knight has failed in his responsibilities to a dog appropriately valued and taken in by Elene.

Lybeaus refuses the blue knight's demand, saying 'That schall never betyde, / For with my handys two / I toke hym the meyd to / That stondys here besyde' (1106–9): Lybeaus asserts that in the act of taking the dog in his hands and giving him to Elene, the dog has been transformed and is no longer proper to the blue knight. When the knight won't back down, Lybeaus calls out his inappropriate behaviour as evidence that he is a churl – an identity the knight refuses by announcing that his father was an earl and his mother the Countess of Carlisle (1117–22). Notably, were the tables reversed, Lybeaus would have no such genealogy on which to call. Instead, his reputation depends upon his past deeds – both of which in this episode involve his cleaning up messes left by these less responsible and thus less noble knights. Once again, Lybeaus is revealed to be superior even to those superficially elevated over him. The fight between Lybeaus and Otis (and his 'army' of supporters) is perhaps the bloodiest in the romance; Otis's supporters believe Lybeaus is Satan, given his extreme activity on the field. Meanwhile, Otis and eleven of his men lie in wait all day for Lybeaus and catch him 'As the fysche in the nette' (1184), in a scene evoking the ambush of the Forgiving Knight's father by his enemy. Despite the odds, Lybeaus manages to overcome Otis, who requests mercy, in exchange for which Lybeaus once again requires that he go to Arthur's court as prisoner, marking Lybeaus's knightly identity. Back at Arthur's court, the incoming proofs of Lybeaus's valour have now established him as worthy to be a knight of the Round Table (1294).

In addition to the animals that Lybeaus encounters on his journey to Synadoune which assist him in developing his knightly identity are four giants, the first two of which (a red and a black giant) behave unchivalrously by, first, being caught about to roast a damsel, Violette, for dinner, and then by attacking Lybeaus with the roasting spit when he prevents them from completing their meal preparations. Later, the third giant, Magus, is very knightly in expression and behaviour until well into their combat, when Lybeaus requests a break for a drink, at which point Magus takes advantage of his vulnerability (one that magical Magus does not share) and attacks him. Similarly, this giant seems to appropriately value the lady Denamowre[40] for her beauty, and yet his dedication to her is expressed not through courtly service to her but by trapping her (1325). The near-miss of Magus's knightly performance is subtly conveyed through his behaviour, which is confirmed by his physical affinity to animals: the hair of his 'gryme' beard (which should epitomise his manhood) is like the bristles of a boar (1338); he is further 'grymly ... / As any ox or cow [or] / An asse or any nete [cattle]' (1343–8) and 'Bold as any bore' (1370). His identity is still further contrasted with the ideal identity represented by even the ostensibly genealogically challenged Lybeaus in that 'Hys scheld was blake as pyche— /

Lybeus saw never non syche— / Fowre mawmetys [pictures of idols] therein were' (1371–3) and 'He was blake as any bere' (1376). Here his animal nature is coupled with the non-Christian associations of his blackness and his devotion to idols (conveyed through the Middle English term 'mawmetys') and confirmed shortly thereafter when Lybeaus, having been knocked into the river by Magus, challenges him with 'Wenyst thou, fendys fere, / Uncrystend that I were? / To thee my trought I plyght: / I shall for thi baptyse / Wele quyte thee thy servys, / Throught helpe of God almyght' (1456–61).[41] Idolatrous Magus could only assume that Lybeaus is similarly unbaptised and unchristian, so the logic goes. The Middle English version of this story increases the number of non-human challengers for Lybeaus to pass through, with these challengers reflecting a range of possible subjectivities, defining Lybeaus's humanity as well as his knighthood both in contrast to and in relation with them.

Having thus generated his identity in close contact with giants and taken opportunities produced by questions about the treatment of animals, by him and others, Lybeaus's adventure shifts into the marvellous realm, marked by his being detained through magic by the Lady Denamowre; as Elene eventually succeeds in pointing out to Lybeaus, 'For the love of a woman / That mych of sorsery can [knows], / Thow doyst thee dyshonour' (1538–40). The sorcery, while powerful, can be defeated simply by recognising and rejecting it, rather than requiring an enchanted antidote or similarly supernatural counter-weapon. Indeed, what succeeds in breaking the spell is Elene's reminding Lybeaus of his duty to Arthur and her quick but affecting description of the woe of the Lady of Synadoune, who 'May long lyghe in prison; / That is full grete dolour!' (1541–3). Hearing this, Lybeaus 'thought hys herte wold breke / For that gentyll dame' (1544–5), and he immediately departs for Synadoune. Emotion tends to be a quiet force that is tapped throughout the romance, beginning with the anger expressed by Elene and the dwarf upon Arthur's granting their desperate request to Lybeaus, at which point 'The mey [maid] for ire styll sate. / Sche wold nether drinke ne ete' (235–6). Her righteous anger renders her incapable of any other sensation. Throughout, Lybeaus's encounters can seem to be a series of emotional outbursts, positive and negative. 'Syr Otys', for instance, 'with grete errour [anger] / Rode home in that stowre' (1134–5) and is associated with wrath throughout their battle. Anger is accompanied by plenty of laughter in the poem as well; Elene laughs at Lybeaus's use of litotes to describe Geffroun's threatening castle upon first sight of it (762) – pleasure immediately easing fear – and Lybeaus and the Lady of Synadoune's steward, Sir Gesloke, pass the time on their ride to rescue her by playing: 'They roden forth talkyng, / And so thei dyde syngyng, / And lewgh and made gret game' (1553–5). Magic is no match for true knighthood, be it expressed in the form of valiant battle or emotional correctness.

Having learned the power of enchantment as well as his capacity to defuse it, Lybeaus encounters yet another giant, this one the steward Lambert who challenges Lybeaus to a fight only to prove his worthiness to the task he pursues. Indeed, Lambert presents as a version of the loyal, effective steward, but one able to call up the fierceness of a giant in order to test those who would enter – thus a sort of Supersteward who fulfils his role even more successfully for having extra-human height and power. Nevertheless, Lybeaus handles the challenge with ease, which Lambert suggests might indicate that Lybeaus is related to Gawain, given that he fought like no man Lambert has ever encountered. Lambert explains to Lybeaus that 'Knyght ther is none / That durst hyr [the Lady of Synadoune] awey lede. / Two clerkys ben ther fone, / Fals of blode and bone, / That hath don that dede. / They ben men of mastrye, / Klerkys of nygromansye' (1759–65) – underestimating this kin of Gawain who has already demonstrated his ability to escape enchantment by enlisting the power of his emotion.

Lybeaus then faces the challenge of an enchanted hall (for which he has been well prepared by his previous encounters with magical power), in his pursuit of the magicians Irain and Mabon, the second of whom he kills and the first of whom he wounds. Although Lybeaus is frustrated by not having killed both, his achievement in surviving the enchanted hall (which turns suddenly from minstrel-filled palace of revelry to earthquake-ridden ruin of doom the moment Lybeaus steps on the dais), and in killing Mabon and sending Irain fleeing in fear, is sufficient to trigger the release of the dragon-lady from the magic window of a stone building:

> A worme ther out gan pas
> With a womans face
> Yong and nothing olde.
> Hyr body and hyr wyngys

Schon all thingys
As it were gleterring gold. (2054–9)

This encounter with the dragon-lady is the first challenge that has actually scared Lybeaus – and indeed, despite the monstrously attractive body's shining appearance of glittering gold, he sweats for fear as if he is in a fire and he is afraid his heart will burst as she approaches him (2066–8). Lybeaus's moment of sensory overload is the same moment of the kiss, which she actively takes from him – 'The worme with mough [mouth] hym kyst / And hang aboute hys swyre [clasped his neck]' (2070–1). This vision of the supernatural creature actively kissing and embracing the young knight mirrors, in this section of Ashmole 61, that of the crucifix and the Forgiving Knight;[42] as with that miracle, here the non-human intervenes in order to transform society: the worm-woman loses tail and wings, leaving only a woman 'So feyr in all thing' (2075); Lybeaus is simultaneously transformed, for she tells him the details of her curse – that she would remain a dragon-lady 'Tyll I had kyssed Gaweyn ... Or some of hys kyne' (2093–5) – thereby revealing his true background. Further, she offers herself to him in marriage and, with this, fifty-five castles, providing the privileges of noble birth that his being an illegitimate son prevented him from claiming. Thus (re)juvenated as his true knightly self, Gyngelain immediately tracks down and beheads Irain, and the adventure is effectively concluded.

In these three knightly narratives – *Knight who Forgave*, *Erle of Tolous*, and *Lybeaus Desconus* – a deliberate and boundary-crossing kiss generates social boons, overturning what the world of the text, in its representation of the extra-textual world, deems normative (if undesirable) in human behaviour, be it anger, greed, pride, or another of the deadly sins. A new materialist reading of a text such as *Lybeaus Desconus* reveals that he and his knighthood are part of a community of non-human/not-fully-human subjects who generate with him his knightly identity – and that the worm-lady's active kiss of him transforms him as much as it transforms her.

Forgiving women I

This section of the manuscript ends with two *exempla*, *Jealous Wife* and *Incestuous Daughter*, that also focus on grotesque scenes of transformation, in these cases revealing the monstrous within the human; here, the effects of spiritual filth are materialised, as is the triumphant power of divine mercy, with two sinful female protagonists spared their otherwise deserved eternal exile through distinctive networks of forgiveness rooted in devotion. The ecologies of these two narratives share in the supernatural that infuses *Lybeaus Desconus*, *Knight who Forgave*, and the collection of prayers that precede them, emphasising the transformative power of emotion on a cosmic as well as earthly scale. In the process, they reorient towards the household a series of aristocratic narratives, domesticating their truths.

Jealous Wife (item 22, fols. 62r–65v) in 395 tail-rhyme lines presents the story of a devoted married couple whose prayers to be able to have children are eventually answered, their communion with the divine productive of earthly joys; but these same earthly joys provoke the wrath of the devil, who nearly succeeds in destroying them – failing to do so only because of a powerful sacred assemblage sustained by the husband's devoted private intimacy as part of a human-divine hybrid. This Miracle of the Blessed Virgin Mary appears in Latin, French, German, and Italian, as well as English – with Ashmole 61 containing a unique verse version that lacks a conclusion because of two missing leaves at the end of the text, but that includes a distinctive plot element. Like *Knight who Forgave*, *Jealous Wife* is a 'merakyll' (16) story, and as in that case, the miracle is not solely a product of divine agency but is instead generated by a distributed agency of emotionally entangled subjects both human and supernatural.

The world of this narrative quickly demonstrates the powerful integration of human and divine agency through the happily married couple's seven years of infertility, a situation that makes them 'full sory, / And changyd oft ther chere' (29–30). Their prayers made in good faith prompt Christ to grant their request 'well sone' (36) – seven years of suffering suddenly gone. With two children and a third on the way, the couple's life is full of joy, a situation evoked repeatedly early in the short poem. Their abundant joy, however, provokes the devil's envy, and for him, it's personal: he labours 'Ther trew lufe to abate' (54).[43] But despite his many attempts to intervene in pursuit of his own vengeful ends, he cannot provoke their 'wrothe' (60). The husband's nightly trips to the chapel to pray to Mary are sufficient to withstand the devil's attacks: they create a strong alliance of the earthly and heavenly that the devil cannot dismantle. So he takes a different approach, seeing in the husband's very devotion the potential makings of strife: he wonders 'If that he myght wordys cast / For to wrothe them atwyn' (74–5).

Emotion, as exhibited in the lengths to which the devil's envy of happiness drives him, is a powerful agent, particularly when verbally manifest: immediately, the wife asks her husband, 'Lovyst thou any thing beter than me, / That owhere may be fond?' (89–90), to which he honestly but naively – not to mention ambiguously – responds,

> Sertys, dame … nay
> In no thing me nevyn may [I can name]
> I ne have so grete lykyng,
> Bot of a woman that I wote [know]
> I love wele more, God it wote,
> Than any erthly thyng. (91–6)

Despite everything she knows about her husband, she 'thought a lyther gyn [evil scheme]' (99), assuming that 'hyr lord than / Had lovyd some other woman, / In the maner of synne' (100–2). The narrator steps in to confirm for the audience that 'It was Owre Lady that he ment' (106), but the devil has achieved his ends, casting words that might introduce anger between them and diminish their true love.

Indeed, the devil succeeds mightily, for upon sensing her wrath he fans the flame by generating an association of evil will, collaborating with fiends in hell and a witch in town to provoke the wife to make her suspicion real by providing her with a false interpretation of the reality of her husband's dedication to Mary: the devil tells the witch (in exchange for money) to warn the wife about her husband's infidelity and tell her how to catch him, when he leaves their bed nightly. This carefully crafted manipulation-machine is persuasive, for the wife misreads the situation just as she is encouraged to, and she follows the witch's instructions not to say anything to the husband after she catches him leaving their bed in the night, having been warned that if she did, he would kill her. The devil's plan thus prevents the wife from seeking the truth and pushes her to act on this extreme misreading, with her immediate goal to ensure that 'It schall hym rew full sore' (210). She begins by killing their children – the products of their marriage and of their devotion to Christ – and then turns the knife on herself, certain that her husband will kill her himself for having killed his children.

The devil's initial goal of replacing the couple's joy with wrath, once achieved, generates a desire for her soul: 'The fend of hell was glad of this, / For he wend wele iwys / Of them he schuld not feyle' (235–7). But before he can achieve these ends, the husband, upon seeing the carnage, calls to Mary: 'Lady, helpe—I ame forlorn, / Bot ye that I have ben beforn / Helpe me at this nede!' (256–8). Unlike his wife, he reads the situation properly and knows that her actions were provoked by the devil (259–60). The scene turns cosmic now, as the husband is left behind, asleep, and the fiends depart from hell to retrieve the wife's soul – though 'all ther joy was ternyd to schame / In a lytell throw' (305–6): the situation that they produced in the humans is now replicated for the fiends, as produced by Mary, who comes down from heaven to meet them and present her judgement: 'Wene ye for to have mastry / At your awne wyll?' (332–3). She demands that the devil tell her 'How came this sorow in place, / And in what maner it fyrst began, / Whether that it were thorow fend or woman' (339–41). The devil acknowledges 'Boldly I have it wroght' (346) – which he believes means her soul is then his to claim, since his affective assertion managed to generate the sorrow. In contrast, Mary says that 'ye hyr chermyd to your hond / That lyved in pese and gryght [amity]' (350–1): the wife's sin was created for her by others, rather than self-generated – and Christ has bought her sin, because of this distinction and because of her husband's devotion (355–60): 'Hyr lord and sche be of a blode, / And thorow his werkys trew and gode / To lyfe thei schall be brought' (370–2).

Jealous Wife explains spiritual truths by physically representing the battle over the fate of the individual soul in terms of individual agents of emotion. When the husband, even after the grisly discovery of his dead family, heads straight to the chapel to pray to Mary, the fiends see the possibility that their plans may be ruined: 'the fendys felle, / How that they went oute of hell, / So lothe thei were to tyne [be deprived of (a soul)]' (289–91), and upon seeing this, Mary 'com doune from hevyn hy / Agene the fendys felle' (308–9). At the meeting of the two forces, the poem provides tangible descriptions of the fiends: 'Som were ragyd and long tayled, / Scharpe clawyd and long nayled ... / Som had hornes grete and long, / Oute of ther mouth the fyre sprong— / Withouten lake [disfigurement] were non' (295–300). Their monstrosity demonstrates their lack of divine goodness, something in which humanity – even the jealous, murdering wife, specifically through her sacramental and physical connection to her husband – participates. The fiend tries to argue that because she killed herself and her children, 'Of them thou [Mary] hast no parte' (318) and 'Thou feylest of thi arte [power]' (315). The extent of Mary's power is shown through this 'foule cas' (314), however, with the fiends ignoring her declaration that those who serve her will be rewarded: the 4,000 fiends 'cryed as thei were wode, / "Go we hens with body and blode; / No lenger wyll we duelle!"' (325–7) and begin to take the wife with them to hell. Mary establishes why they have no right to the dead wife's soul (the fiends having pushed her to sin, rather than her having actively taken it); upon hearing her decree, 'Every angell a devyll hente [seized], / And thyrst them that [squeezed them so that] ther rybbys bent, / For tene [anger] of ther plaw [argument]' (382–4). This inspires the fiends to burn the witch's house and break her back, leaving her barely alive – an attack that causes her neighbours to flee (394–6). The poem thus highlights, even here as it ends abruptly due to the missing pages of the manuscript, the powerful effects of others on the individual soul's fate: the agents of hell attempt desperately a misreading in which the human soul is entirely on its own, self-sufficient in its moral identity. The material and extreme representation of the effects of being in community with Mary and a devout family member reveal here the wrongness of that demonic perspective.

Forgiving women II

Though the plot of *Jealous Wife* emphasises Mary's superhero powers, she consistently defers to the agency wielded by the husband's long-term religious devotion, insisting that the rescue of the wife's soul – her forgiveness – is a product of his prayer combined with the sacrifice of Mary's son. The next *exemplum*, *Incestuous Daughter*, continues the focus on the availability of forgiveness even in those situations that appear most hopeless. In this case, ad hoc networks generate the same sacred agency of merciful forgiveness that was produced in *Jealous Wife* through lifelong relationships (there, the husband's devotion to Mary combined with his commitment to his wife). *Incestuous Daughter* (item 23, fols. 66r–67v, in 294 tail-rhyme lines, its beginning missing, starting with l. 118) is, like *Jealous Wife*, a popular medieval narrative, extant in three additional Middle English versions. In this case, an adult daughter has had an ongoing incestuous relationship with her father which has produced three sin-revealing children (this poem's first lines offering a corrupt alternative version of the infertility of the couple in the previous poem). These children the daughter kills, along with her mother upon her presumed discovery of the incest – actions directly echoing the jealous wife's attempts to erase human error (adultery) through removing its evidence (that is, by murdering the union's offspring). At the start of the extant text of *Incestuous Daughter* in Ashmole 61, the daughter murders her father when he reveals his remorse for their shared sin and details his plans to perform penance on pilgrimage, leaving the next day. Having now killed off her entire family, the daughter sets up shop as a prostitute: lacking opportunities to corrupt others in the private space of the home, she turns to the public realm. The narrative attends most to the daughter's experience at church on Good Friday, where she arrives not (like the Forgiving Knight) to seek forgiveness but instead to lure worshipping men away from the Mass to engage them in sin.

Like the fiend in *Jealous Wife*, the daughter seeks others with whom to produce new coalitions of evil will. When she hears her father's plans for penance, the narrator clarifies that 'Thorow the fendys egyng, / Hys doughter thought another thyng / Wers for to do' (139–41). The daughter's sinful acts are the effect of a combination of agencies, not hers alone, and she here seeks more accomplices. Upon her failure, once inside the church, to amass sinners, she becomes available for alternative networks, and the visiting bishop who is presenting his homily seizes the opportunity. Indeed, her presence there – though enabled through her own wicked will – is, also unbeknown to her, part of this alternative: 'To the chyrch thei [she and her prostitute-apprentices] forth wente, / Thorught the grace of God omnipotente / And hys modour Mary' (181–3). This evil-will assemblage becomes literally apparent to the bishop when, upon her entry to the church, 'On hyr he cast hys ey' (186) and 'Fowre devylles that were fals / He se hang [saw hanging] aboute hyr hals [neck], / And by cheynes hyr lede. / Be every cheyn stede hyr one [At every chain one stood by her]' (187–90). In what is the central powerful image in the poem, more than ten lines are spent describing the bishop's vision of the fiends and then explaining their manipulation of her:

> Abowte hyr neke a coler [collar] strong,
> The fendys lede the cheynes long,
> Behynd and before.
> Wele the byschop wyst [knew] than
> That sche was a synfull woman;
> For hyr he syghed sore.
> Sche pukyd [picked] a squyre and on hym lew [smiled],
> And be the sleve sche hym drew,
> And other yonge men mo. (193–201)

These four fiends hang about her neck because she is wearing an iron collar, with the fiends 'leading' her by four chains, one on each side. On seeing this, the bishop recognises that she is sinful – which is to say, visually, he sees that she is being led by sin, by fiends, and he sighs for her in recognition of her situation. The cause-and-effect relationship between the fiends' guiding her and her actions is made very clear, because she immediately smiles at a squire and lures him away by the sleeve – and other men, too. It is worth noting that not all versions of this *exemplum* show the fiends physically leading her by chains – a key narrative feature in this version, and one with no small influence on interpretation. The bishop has 'Grete wonder' (192) at what he sees, suggesting that this is an extreme case, and his response is not limited to pity for the daughter but 'Of the fendys he wold be wreke [avenged]' (208), which he pursues by speaking of God's mercy, 'Both lowd and hyghe' (210).

The bishop's revenge is possible because of the literal power of his words:

> Thorow the grace of God allmyght,
> A word in hyr herte alight [landed]
> That the bysschop spake,
> That a tere fell fro hyr eye
> And be hyr lares [cheeks] it gan don fle,
> And the coler brake [broke].
> The fendys fley [fled] and were adrad [afraid]. (211–17)

In this climactic scene, an assemblage of mercy strong enough to defeat the powerful fiends capable of leading the daughter to commit so many horrific deeds comes into being: a word of the bishop, aided by the grace of God, literally lands on the daughter's heart, the transformation of which leads a tear to fall down her cheek to her neck, where it bursts the collar keeping her in thrall to the fiends, who immediately flee, afraid in their recognition of a greater power. This potent community is composed of the mildest and least aggressive of entities: mercy, a word, remorse, a tear. Not only is God's mercy enough to defeat the most nefarious of fiends, but its success depends upon the collective force of a range of agents, natural and supernatural. This demonstration is extended in *Incestuous Daughter*, for the bishop tells her to wait until the end of his homily before she confesses to him (as she eagerly requests, saying she will soon die for sorrow [246]). As he concludes, her heart breaks (she dies), and the tears of the bishop and prayers of the congregation inspire the voice of God to tell them what is her lot. It confirms that she is in heaven.[44]

Both of these *exempla* can give the surprising impression that a female protagonist who has behaved extremely contrary to nature and divine law gets away with murder. Read only in terms of worldly justice, that would be the case. Read through the way mercy is generated within each text, however, the two poems map out for the audience the interdependency of human and non-human agents in instantiating sin and generating forgiveness. Further, they do so through two different models of sinful femininity that over-esteem the family beyond virtue and, in so doing, appear to the reader to be beyond help. Each poem's overarching concern is with assuring its audience that no matter what one has done, so long as one is repentant – even if this should happen at the final moment on earth, with no priest nearby – one may be shriven and prepared for the opportunity of eternal salvation: 'And if he may do no more / Bot for hys synnes rew sore, / God wyll hym forgyffe' (286–8).[45]

Two missing leaves

The two missing leaves following fol. 65 deprive modern readers of Ashmole 61 – and readers in the past, reaching how far back we do not know – of the end of *Jealous Wife* and the start of *Incestuous Daughter*. In this, the leaves are contributors, in their very absence, to the particular mercy assemblages generated within each poem. When Ashmole 61 readers first encounter him in *Incestuous Daughter*, the father is mid-speech, expressing to them and to his daughter his plans to follow the advice of a priest, to whom he had confessed, that he cease his incestuous activity and perform penance for his many sins. Because of the missing leaf, these sins exist for the audience only conceptually, through imaginative reconstruction, an act that reduces the emotional impact the scenes of the shared commitment to their unnatural acts could have contributed. The daughter's insistence on persisting in their lust-driven evil at the start of the poem in Ashmole 61 appears all the more wilful and thus sinful when contrasted directly with one who sinned and repented; her killing her father for his refusal to sustain with her their life of sexual-social wickedness further heightens the contrast between the two, suggesting that she was the true source of the evil all along. Especially given that medieval tales of incest typically focused on the repentance of the daughter rather than the father,[46] the intensification-through-absence that follows from the missing beginning further prevents Ashmole 61 readers from seeing the incestuous daughter as victim of her father. This makes her aggressive pursuit of, or creation of, partners in sin all the more morally depraved. The missing start of *Incestuous Daughter* directs attention differently by removing from audience consideration the destructive behaviour of the incestuous father. Two other copies of this text remain, along with a number of different versions, all of which allow for the reconstruction of an approximation of what the missing page may have contained.[47] In this case, the missing exposition of the narrative produces a protagonist-in-the-making whose wickedness appears so wilful that it seems impossible to stop. The power of the bishop's words is strengthened, and the forgiveness of God that they represent and enact magnified, as a result.

At the bottom of fol. 65v, readers of *Jealous Wife* are left with her husband still in prayer, anticipating that he will be accused of the murder of his family; meanwhile, the audience knows that his long-term prayerful relationship with Mary has secured his wife's rescue from the fiend and ceaseless damnation. The last images the poem offers are of the relentless fiends racing away from their devastating loss to Mary to wreak what havoc they can on those unprotected by her, first among them the witch who at their urging betrayed the jealous wife and set this tragic pandemonium in motion; they break her back and burn her house, which goes up in flames as her neighbours flee in fear (385–96). The missing conclusion to *Jealous Wife* may be broadly conceived based on other versions of the text that remain, since this version is unique to Ashmole 61.[48] Elsewhere, the narrative follows the cosmic battle between Mary and the fiends with a return to earth, where the husband discovers his wife at home caring for their three children in a scene of everyday domesticity, the family reunited and the wife's horrific violent destruction of their family a fading memory. Rather than reassuring readers of earthly reunion, the poem as it lives in Ashmole 61 emphasises the spiritual conclusion to the story, with Mary rather than the husband the ultimate liberator, the story a religious victory, reader attention focused on the there and then rather than the here and now.

This chapter makes a strong claim – thus far largely implicit – that, when met together in a household community such as the one in Ashmole 61, and more specifically in the second quarter of the collection, romance can give way to *exemplum*. This is not to say, as has been said, that individual medieval romances exhibit features of particular genres that modern readers tend to consider unrelated to romance, as Andrea Hopkins demonstrated thirty years ago in the analysis she presented in *The Sinful Knights: A Study of Middle English Penitential Romance*. This chapter does not aim to argue that romances share literary or other qualities with *exempla*, an argument that has been made very compellingly already. It aims, rather, to recognise a feature of book agency that is often neglected: the pull of textual communities and material idiosyncrasies can be strong enough to make a poem lose its identity. Or rather, the pull can reveal that the identity that modern scholarship has assigned to a text follows from a set of criteria and a reading experience that modern scholars assume held meaning in the past the way they do today. Scholars consistently read *Lybeaus Desconus* and *The Erle of Tolous* as outliers in this manuscript, awkwardly attending a party to which they received a misdirected invitation. Their mere presence in this collection does not, in itself, justify reading them as properly situated among friends in this household manuscript. But the alternative interpretive tools made available by their neighbours reveal features of the narratives generally indiscernible, or deemed minimally meaningful, elsewhere. The absence of the happy family reunion at the end of *Jealous Wife*, for which readers have been carefully prepared by the poem's minimalist narrative structure and initial focus on the couple's years of infertility (a feature lacking in other versions), not only heightens attention to the significance of Mary's actions but also recalls the relative extremes to which the Ashmole 61 *Lybeaus Desconus* goes, two items and three folios earlier, to reunify a family that never quite existed: unusually, in this version Lybeaus's mother returns to the court at the moment of her son's public identification, extending the poem's investment in merciful restitution in ways the *exemplum* itself, in its Ashmole 61 appearance, cannot. Only through the intervention of an editor can the absence be filled and the earthly reunion of the murdering mother with her children and husband serve to erase the stain on her maternity that Mary succeeded in erasing from her soul.

Notes

1 The texts discussed in this chapter are items 18, 19, 20, 22, and 23. They fill folios 26v–67v, which straddle quires 3–7. Quire 3 begins with fol. 19, which contains on its front and back the conclusion of *Stans Puer ad Mensam*. This quire contains a large number of items, since 21v has a series of very short texts. The quire extends from fol. 19 to fol. 30r, and ends with the first four folios of the 15-folio *Erle of Tolous*. *Lybeaus Desconus* fills the rest of quire 4, all of quire 5, and the first folio and a half of quire 6. In other words, there was no attempt to continue anything like the booklet approach established in quire 1 and nearly fulfilled with quire 2 (which bleeds over into the first two folios of the following quire), discussed in Chapter 1. Items 12, 13, and 15 ('Evening Prayer', 'Morning Prayer', and 'Prayer to Mary') are addressed in a footnote in Chapter 1 and item 17 ('Prayer at the Levation') in a footnote in the Introduction; items 16 (*The Debate of the Carpenter's Tools*) and 21 (*Sir Corneus*) are addressed in Chapter 3, along with other poems in this vicinity in the manuscript that are concerned more with correcting behaviour than fostering forgiveness and manifesting mercy, the focus here in Chapter 2. See Appendix for a table listing the manuscript's contents, including information on quiring, foliation, and watermarks.

2 Item 21, *Sir Corneus*, also attends to women's behaviour and the community's moral interpretation thereof, although it does so in a tone that – like *The Debate of the Carpenter's Tools*, also in this section of the manuscript – extends valuable interpretive influence into the next section of the manuscript, which is covered in Chapter 3.

3 One such example comes from James Wade: '*The Erle of Tolous*, in many ways, is an exercise in the proper constraint of erotic desires' ('Ungallant knights', p. 205).

4 At the end of the poem, Gawain observes to the Lady of Synadoune of her fiancé Lybeaus, upon the appearance at court of Lybeaus's mother, 'I gate hym under a forest syde / Of a gentyll lady' (2208–9) – behaviour for which he is immediately rewarded with kisses by the Lady of Synadoune, in appreciation of the noble blood he provided her beloved. Questions of consent are raised elsewhere in the poem, as when the Lady of Synadoune, in the form of the cursed dragon-lady, grabs an obviously terrified Lybeaus and kisses him.

5 These qualities led Lynne S. Blanchfield to conclude that this romance is singularly out of place in the manuscript, 'long-winded and shallow', and lacking in moral orientation ('Idiosyncratic scribe', pp. 66–7). *Lybeaus Desconus* – the English variety of the French *Le Bel Inconnu* – continues to suffer from critical disdain, perhaps even more harmful than the critical neglect which some of its Middle English romance peers experience. Chaucer included Lybeux [*sic*] among the knights in *Sir Thopas* (VII.900), and the bad press persists, including from its own modern editor, Maldwyn Mills (*Lybeaus Desconus*, p. 89). See Wade, 'Ungallant knights', p. 218 no. 27; and see Seaman, 'Thomas Chestre's *Sir Launfal*' and 'Tugging at the roots', for extended demonstration of twentieth-century critical disregard for Middle English verse romance.

6 Elizabeth Allen (*False Fables and Exemplary Truth*), J. Allan Mitchell (*Ethics and Exemplary Narrative*), Catherine Sanok (*Her Life Historical: Exemplarity and Female Saints' Lives in Late Medieval England*), Mary Carruthers (*Book of Memory*), Rita Copeland (*Rhetoric, Hermeneutics, and Translation in the Middle Ages*), and John Dagenais (*The Ethics of Reading*). These critical questions continue to inspire work such as Ryan McDermott's *Tropologies: Ethics and Invention in England, c. 1350–1600*. See Ingrid Nelson, *Lyric Tactics*, ch. 4 (especially pp. 123–4), for a useful summary of the literary historical bases of the *exemplum* as a mode.

7 Catherine Sanok focuses on (and her readings challenge) the temporal fixity assumed of exemplarity: 'Medieval exemplarity is generally assumed to be a form of prescription, one that ignores the historical difference separating the subject of the story from its audience' (*Her Life Historical*,

p. 177). Her work recuperates the exemplary mode of the saint's life by tracing the historically situated renderings of such narratives in the later Middle Ages.
8   Orlemanski, *Symptomatic Subjects*, p. 119.
9   Allen, *False Fables*, p. 2. McDermott challenges Allen's approach (see *Tropologies*, pp. 150–5) by reading it as finding 'the exemplary mode to be disingenuous to authority (because its authority is not *actually* clear and mutable)' (p. 154, n. 22). Allen's rendering of the available operations of Middle English exemplarity, and the flexible interpretations it can invite, nourishes my own readings of anonymous 'everyday' vernacular verse.
10 Nelson, *Lyric Tactics*, p. 123.
11 Allen, 'Episodes', p. 205.
12 Mitchell, *Ethics and Exemplary Narrative*, p. 15. A foundational observation of McDermott's work is that '[a]ccording to tropological theory, interpretation is never complete without action, and that action can take the form of writing' (*Tropologies*, p. 2). For further details, see McDermott's introduction, and then the chapters that follow for various individual demonstrations of that view.
13 Allen, *False Fables and Exemplary Truth*, p. 4. Further, 'particular narratives do not simply support but actively constitute moral generalizations' (Nelson, *Lyric Tactics*, p. 5). Nelson represents the abstract moral of the exemplary narrative as undercutting the details, even as those details inform the moral that displaces them – it 'elides these details and renders them abstract. The contingencies of a story undergird its abstraction but are also erased by it.' This, for Nelson, is the conundrum that 'lyric tactics' address (p. 124).
14 Mitchell, *Ethics and Exemplary Narrative*, p. 15.
15 Allen, *False Fables*, p. 2.
16 Allen, *False Fables*, p. 25.
17 *Rhetorica ad Herennium* (trans. Caplan), pp. 383–5, quoted by Nelson, *Lyric Tactics*, p. 123 – to whom I am grateful for drawing my attention to this rich passage.
18 Allen, *False Fables*, p. 4.
19 Mitchell, *Ethics and Exemplary Narrative*, p. 15.
20 Allen, 'Mineral virtue', p. 151.
21 All quotations from texts in Ashmole 61 are from *Codex Ashmole 61*, edited by George Shuffelton, and indicated by line number.
22 Bynum, *Christian Materiality*, p. 265. See, too, the special issue of the *Journal of Medieval and Early Modern Studies* on 'The Sacred Object', edited by Gayk and Malo.
23 Bynum, *Christian Materiality*, p. 219.

24 In this, the narrative calls back to *Isumbras*, and the Persian sultan's attempt to purchase Isumbras's wife with a bag of gold.
25 This opportunity the Erle requests so that he can discern first-hand Beulybon's innocence of the charges against her. Some read it as morally problematic; Wade, for instance, describes the Erle as 'playing fast and loose with the sacrament of confession' and sees this scene as redundant, since the narrative has demonstrated her innocence, which leads him to interpret the scene as 'interrogat[ing] the Erle's behavior as much as hers' ('Ungallant knights', p. 206), while I see it as the Erle's opportunity to confirm her innocence before supporting her case.
26 See, for example, lines 832–4.
27 Beulybon is 'the fairest lady … Save Mary' and 'therto gode in all thinge / Of almus dede and of god bering / … Of hyr body sche was trew … and therto most bright' (35–42). By the time the Erle first sees her in person, 300 lines into the romance, she is described in detail that makes her an icon worthy of adoration (334–57).
28 *Middle English Dictionary*, s.v. *foryeven* 3a.
29 *Middle English Dictionary*, s.v. *foryeven* 4a.
30 Other Middle English Fair Unknown romances are *Sir Perceval of Galles*, *Sir Degaré*, and Malory's 'Tale of Sir Gareth'.
31 By far the longest poem in the manuscript at this point, with only *Isumbras* (822 lines) and *The Erle of Tolous* (1,210 lines) in the vicinity, though even then *The Erle of Tolous* is just half the length of *Lybeaus Desconus*.
32 Lybeaus's mother never reappears after he leaves home, in the other Middle English strain of the text.
33 Salisbury and Weldon, eds, *Lybeaus Desconus*.
34 Readings such as this one, which see medieval representations as recognising that a knight is not a man with a certain skill set but a man-horse-armour hybrid, the non-human and human together generating the knight, owe much – perhaps everything – to Jeffrey Jerome Cohen, *Medieval Identity Machines*, p. 45.
35 Such a reading is encouraged elsewhere about other Fair Unknowns, such as Percival.
36 In this, this poem has something very different to say than does Italo Calvino's *The Nonexistent Knight* (1959).
37 It contrasts, too, with James Wade's perception of Lybeaus as represented in Ashmole 61 as an 'ill-behaved hero' ('Ungallant knights, p. 203). This assessment comes despite Wade's demonstration of lines extant in other versions of the text that are left out of Rate's version, such as two lines that emphasise the sexual nature of the encounter between Lybeaus and Denamowre (particularly meaningful in other versions is

the narrator's wish 'Alas she hadde be chaste!' [Lambeth Palace 306, line 1475, fol. 95v]) ('Ungallant knights', p. 209). However, Wade's conclusion, particularly its last clause, receives my full support: 'But the fundamental incongruity of an ungallant romance hero might also have been what morally minded readers would have found most interesting about these texts, their moral messiness exposing the tensions between the chivalric ideal and the complexities of lived experience' ('Ungallant knights', p. 218).

38 This modification to the narrative also transforms what had been a recognition of female value (through her possession of a noble animal and of the love of a noble man) into a recognition of specifically and traditionally male knightly prowess in battle.
39 Salisbury and Weldon, Introduction to *Lybeaus Desconus*, n.p.
40 In all other versions of *Lybeaus Desconus*, this figure is named la Dame d'Amore – with Rate's version both extending the anglicising of the French *Le Bel Inconnu* and distancing the direct associations of her as the Lady of Love, the etymology of which is seen in 'Denamowre' only with difficulty.
41 There is much to be said about the racial implications of the representation of Magus here, though to my knowledge it has yet to be said in published analysis.
42 It also is utterly lacking in consent, however much the text seems to assume that all readers would know that of course Lybeaus would welcome the kiss if he knew, as they do, her true identity.
43 The fiend behaves very consistently throughout Ashmole 61. Later in Item 27, *Ypotis*, for instance, he admits to God that he enticed Adam to eat of the apple 'For I had to hym envy, / That thei schuld have that blysse' (268–9).
44 For a reading of this text as a pedagogical tool for 'knowledge building among peers', as in the lines 'All the women that wold be folys, / Fast thei com unto hyr scolys' (157–8) – here what one might describe as dangerous knowledge building – see Harris, *Obscene Pedagogies*, pp. 20–1.
45 Not even every element in the usual forgiveness assemblage – that is, not even a priest to hear one's confession – need be present. Shuffelton offers a brief history of this notion, which 'may seem radical, but scholastic theories of confession upheld this doctrine' (*Codex Ashmole 61*, p. 488).
46 See Archibald, *Incest and the Medieval Imagination*, pp. 188–90.
47 The additional extant copies are in Cambridge University Library MS Ff.5.48 and Oxford, Bodleian Library MS Rawlinson poet. 118. Shuffelton summarises the introduction provided in the missing lines

(reconstructions suggest there were 117 of them) as 'an example of dangerous despair saved by the grave of repentance, and go on to describe how the father was tempted by a fiend into incest with his daughter. The daughter is made pregnant three times, and each time she murders the children to conceal their sin, until the mother discovers the incest. The daughter then murders the mother and the incest continues until the father repents and confesses to a priest, who tells the father he must cease having sex with his daughter and make a pilgrimage to the holy land as penance' (*Codex Ashmole 61*, p. 489).

48 Shuffelton observes that 'even without its ending, *The Jealous Wife* ranks as one of the finest surviving Middle English miracles of the Virgin Mary' (*Codex Ashmole 61*, p. 484). Elsewhere he points to 'its careful structure, skilfully-handled dialogue, and swift-moving plot' that render it 'nothing less than a minor masterpiece of its genre' (pp. 485–6).

3

Objects of correction

Household objects – tools, tables and tableware, vegetation and animals transformed into human sustenance and apparel – can appear to bear agency (for instance, the ability to nourish another physically) only as a result of human recognition or production of that agency. Yet a quilted surcoat, a wooden stool, or a brass spoon is no more a product of the household than is a human member of it, such as a wine merchant, whose very identity depends upon the structures of the household. Similarly, inanimate objects are no more fundamentally 'natural' than are the human bodies inhabiting the household alongside them. In the household ecology, however, cultural and ideological value tends to displace natural value to greater and lesser degrees across ontological boundaries. Analysing such operations and their effects requires pushing towards an assessment of value that weighs extra-artefactual features beyond human intention or expectation. The risk of overestimating cultural and ideological significance is amplified in a book such as Ashmole 61 wherein the concerns of the late medieval gentry or merchant household are foregrounded, guiding the production and retention of the particular texts that take up residence in the codex. Within that setting, however, its texts at times provide readers with the opportunity to recognise that, for instance, a brass spoon is not an object that simply exists. Rather, both hand and utensil, human and metal deliberately formed, must become something beyond themselves in order for the spoon to be enacted and, in the process, for the eating human to achieve dietary decorum.[1] In a literary setting that tends to emphasise certain features of a creature, an item of furniture, a household implement, a part of documentary culture, these items bear with them potentialities that are not always accounted for or contained by that representation. J. Allan Mitchell observes that 'an object that actively holds others in place', such as the spoon in its production of the refined human diner, 'may exhibit a certain kind of *tenacity* in doing so'.² This tenacity may exceed or transform the particular human anticipations within and beyond the instrumental use of the object by the human, and likewise it may exceed or transform a text. Indeed, in this section of Ashmole 61, objects and their relations call attention to the tussle involved in trying to clearly delineate the structures that render household members; at times, the differences – among them, those perceived according to gender – push squarely against such attempts.

At the heart of Ashmole 61, in the centre of the collection, a cluster of texts encourage human audiences to understand their own agency as one element in a conglomeration of human and non-human affective agencies. Across these texts, inanimate objects offer moral instruction vital to human social and spiritual thriving: a community of tools critique and defend their layabout master (*The Debate of the Carpenter's Tools*, item 16), a drinking horn outs misbehaviour (*Sir Corneus*, item 21), out-of-season cherries and gifts distribute justice at court (*Sir Cleges*, item 24), a host of household objects test human commitment to physical and spiritual health (Lydgate's *Dietary*, item 31), and a document embodies religious redemption (the *Short Charter of Christ*, item 29), amid an array of short texts that affirm the tangibility of religious truths (*The Feasts of All Saints and All Souls*, item 25; *The King and his Four Daughters*, item 26; and *The Lament of Mary*, item 30).³ When non-human agents act in literary texts, human readers tend to perceive them as symbolic anthropomorphic figures – as allegorical representations of human qualities (for instance, the tortoise and the hare representing patient dedication and overly confident zeal) or as allegorised representations of human ideals (such as Lady Liberty in New York Harbour).⁴ Through this, potential innate non-human subjectivity is contained, all such capacity restricted to the human. In contrast, for the affective objects residing at the centre of Ashmole 61, their materiality remains indispensable, more than a means to an end or a metaphorical rendering of something else; further, they act in ways legible within their local network, be it the drinking horn in the assemblage of the medieval feast, abundant food and drink in the gentry household, the gift-exchange that sustains royal authority, or the sacrifice that grounds the salvation economy. The diverse affective objects in these texts influence the humans with whom they are in community, just as they are influenced by human and other agents. The texts themselves, like the book that houses them, are affect agents, as well, in this section of the collection, providing moral guidance necessary to sustain the household.[5]

Objects of measure

A tightly structured household community is the focus of a poem called *The Debate of the Carpenter's Tools* (item 16, fols. 23r–26r). Here, everyday objects provide pragmatic moral judgement and much-needed moral instruction to the two humans (one present, one absent) with whom they live and work. Ashmole 61 contains the only remaining copy of this relatively short (288 lines) debate poem, and no other version or analogue of it appears in any other medieval literary tradition. The poem's uniqueness does not end there, for *The Debate of the Carpenter's Tools* is an unconventional example of its type. In medieval vernacular debate poems, animate objects engage with one another in a highly formal debate, typically representing two opposing identity positions and related viewpoints. Often the debaters are birds, with the debate centring on matters of love and courtesy. In the early Middle English poem *The Owl and the Nightingale* (from the twelfth or thirteenth century), for instance, each of two birds argues that his features make him the bird best suited to encouraging socially beneficial forms of human love – and these features are physiological characteristics commonly associated by humans at the time with the given species of bird, qualities to which certain symbolic value adheres. The Owl, for instance, argues that he is superior because he offers practical service (cleansing churches of rats, for example) and doesn't distract with his beauty. The Nightingale, for his part, insists on the value of his own beautiful singing – which reflects heaven and encourages higher thought – while he calls the Owl filthy, a screecher, and a creature of the night who inspires fear and loathing.[6] In contrast, Ashmole 61's debate poem, *The Debate of the Carpenter's Tools*, occurs among everyday tools lacking widely circulating symbolic value and centres not on their own merits (which are not in question) but on those of their human master, the carpenter. Some tools position themselves as his defenders, while others critique him for his constant drunkenness and his resulting insufficiency as a worker and a master. The topic, then, is not love but labour, and the issue not esoteric but practical – one vital to the health of the household. And, in the hands of these tools, the debate pursues the correct evaluation of the carpenter's moral suitability to his occupation and social status, an evaluation of social worth that is here provided, unexpectedly, by things.

The various tools of this carpenter's shop are those he uses every day, in the most mundane, everyday ways[7] – and in this, they are the epitome of 'the thing'.[8] However, they are also his apprentices with their own subjectivity, and in this their relationship takes on a moral valence. Some tools emphasise the servitude and loyalty that each apprentice (that is, each tool) owes its master, while others emphasise the master's responsibility to provide his apprentices with training and social incorporation. Speaking for the second camp and throwing down the gauntlet, the Chip-Ax declares that, as apprentice, he can and will help the carpenter acquire food, clothing, and shoes, but 'for all that ever [the carpenter] kane [do], / [he shall] never be thryfty man' (5–6).[9] Some of the other tools take it upon themselves to prove that such a goal *is* possible, insisting on their commitment to working so hard and well that they will achieve prosperity *for* their master, despite his personal tendencies: as the Groping-Iron (or Gouge) says, 'I suere thee, Compas, by the rode, / Wyrke I schall bothe nyght and dey; / To gete hym gode I schall assey [try]' (36–8). At this point, the debate centres on the distributed responsibility that one group claims is necessary – that is, that prosperity is possible only when tools and master work productively together – and the opposing group's faith that the workers alone can generate the master's identity regardless of the master's actual behaviour. Those insisting on the impossibility of the carpenter's success now redirect the discussion to their true focus: not simply his productivity, but his morality. The Saw insists: 'He wyll not thé [thrive], I sey thee ryght. / He wones to nygh the alewyffe / And he thouht ever for to thryffe' (42–4). No matter what the tools might do, the Chisel adds, the master's 'thryfte fro hym it wyll be take. / For he loves gode ale so wele / That he therfor his hode wyll selle ... / How he schall thryve I cane not thinke' (74–8). Despite that challenge, and without refuting it, the carpenter's faithful supporters commit themselves wholeheartedly to working enthusiastically to produce their master's success.

The debate carries on in this fashion to the point that one supporter claims that they will 'make hym schyreff of the toune' (105–6; the Augur) and another even claims that 'Thof he spend more in a yere / Of gold and sylver than thou may bere [possess], / I schall hym helpe with all my myght; / I trow to make hym yet a knyght' (159–62; the Pulley). Despite their awareness of the master's moral failings in his greater commitment to drinking ale than to pursuing prosperity for himself, his family, and his apprentices, his supporters insist that they will make him a sheriff (overlooking the injustice he would clearly dole out) and a knight (ignoring his thorough lack of nobility of character, much less of blood). The morally invested text gives the upper hand to those who consistently refuse the possibility of this carpenter's achieving prosperity; as the Wynas-Rewle (Windlass) says, 'thou spekys oute of seson; / He may not thé [thrive] therfor by reson. / A carpenter to be a knyght? / That were ever ageyn ryght' (165–8).

Finally, the master's wife appears, in the role traditionally held by the judge in debate poems, coming on the scene well into the progress of the argument to provide an authoritative voice on the matter. In this case, she presents a classic 'wife's lament', complaining that her husband spends on ale not only his own income but also all the money she makes through spinning. P. J. P. Goldberg postulates that, because bourgeois women (in contrast to women of other statuses) 'assisted their husbands' in the economic endeavours of the household, they had 'a more significant voice than their rural sisters in deciding priorities within the household'.[10] The carpenter's wife speaks here from an assumption of such authority. The master's supporters, however, challenge not so much her authority as the morality of her behaviour, claiming she is 'to blame / To gyffe my mayster syche a name. / For thoff he spend more than ye have, / Yit his worschype ye schuld save' (211–14) – that is, she should, like them, support her master's reputation however immoral his actions. In response, she does not answer their claim or their charge against her; instead, she challenges their own moral authority, highlighting its corrupt source in the carpenter: 'For hys servant I trow thou be, / Ther thou schall never thé [thrive]. / For and thou lerne that craft at hym, / Thy thryft I trow schall be full thine' (217–20). Where they present themselves as capable of generating his reputation regardless of his actions, she presents them as mired in and tarnished by his reputation and his behaviour. Once this new rhetorical move is offered, the Draught Nayle (Nail Puller) points to evidence that the carpenter's supporters are morally lacking in precisely the way their master is: they work for just an hour or two before going to the alehouse, and when they do work they work lightly so as not to harm themselves through any exertion. The Draught Nayle concludes that 'thus with fraudys and falsyd / Is many trew man deseyvid ... / They schall never thryve ne thé' (259–62). The carpenter's moral disease infects the entire community.

The objects here tackle matters of immediate concern to the audience of a book such as Ashmole 61: rather than pondering who is the winner and who the loser, in a game of romantic love played by the leisured class, as non-humans like the Owl and Nightingale do, these tools – who know of what they speak, given their total immersion in the labouring world, and without whom the carpenter literally could not practise his craft – address concerns of commitment, responsibility, and authority. In such ways, non-human objects that share the household community with the readers of Ashmole 61 provide their insights and encourage judgement and behaviour adaptation based on their shared investment in and dependence on the health of the household.

The drinking horn in *Sir Corneus* (item 21, fols. 59v–62r) similarly assesses human behaviour and its moral implications, although as a member of the royal hall rather than as part of an artisan's household. In this poem, also unique to Ashmole 61, the drinking horn draws public attention to those at court who fail to maintain the community's shared values. Its means for doing so also differ, for while the carpenter's tools inhabit a debate poem and express the sincerity appropriate to the genre (everyday objects of labour asserting their sober authority), the drinking horn of *Sir Corneus* (a ritualised object of a royal feast) appears in a 'bowrd' (or joke) that is called by its narrator 'full gode and trew' (4, 5). The primarily serious moral register of the debate poem becomes playful and lighthearted, structured around a trick and pushing at the boundaries of social norms. Yet the household object in this poem is intimately tied to the human head of household as well. The drinking horn is notable for standing before Arthur at table wherever the king goes, kept close because 'For mych crafte [skill/tricks] he couth [knew] therby / And ofte tymes the treuth he sey [saw]; / Non other couth he thynke [he knew no other way to get this knowledge]' (28–30). Arthur appropriately esteems the horn for the access it (and only it) provides to truth, and he further values its contribution to his royal assemblage. Given this introduction of the horn's significance to the court, the poem humorously limits the scope of the truth it reveals: 'If any cokwold dryke of it / Spyll he schuld withouten lette [fail]' (31–2).[11]

The horn's agency lies in its ability to reveal hidden truths, but it also exhibits great affective agency: Arthur introduces the horn into the feast specifically 'To make solas and game' (39)[12] – to provide entertainment and joy, pleasure and comfort. Yet those revealed as cuckolds 'Therfor thei were not glade. / Gret dispyte [humiliation] thei had therby' (31–5). Rather than delighting those affected, the horn – as a key participant in Arthur's intended game – causes them to feel shame, a shame that they attempt to distribute away from themselves to one another: 'every cokwold on other leughe [laughed], / And yit thei schamyd sore [were sorely shamed]' (44–5). Each one laughed at the other proven cuckolds but felt deep personal shame at the revelation. Shame, as represented in later medieval English literature, is, Mary Flannery observes, 'social as well as personal, and plays a key role not just in individual emotional experience, but also in shaping and enforcing social expectations and codes of behavior, as well as determining the status of individuals within a society'.[13] The power of shame in this cultural context is seen in how this emotional experience affects the cuckolds; it alters their expression to suit their new status and identity: 'And than changyd the cokwoldys chere [expression]' (40).[14] In such cases the horn wields no instrumental agency, for it fails as a drinking tool, but it holds strong affective agency, transforming men's bodies and selves.

The horn is joined in its public maintenance of private morality by other non-human actants in the royal hall: tables, tree branches, and animal carcasses. The king publicly exiles the revealed cuckolds from the dominant non-cuckold community by seating them at a cuckolds-only table, assisted by the dining tables in a royal hall with their assertion of diners' social status through their hierarchical ordering.[15] On the one hand, this reinforces the men's shaming and offers them (as Arthur explains to the visiting Duke of Gloucester) opportunities for penance. This penance is performed in quite unconventional ways: Arthur places on the head of each penitent 'garlandys of wylos [willows]' (59) and 'Of the best mete ... / That stode on bord befor the kyng ... / To the cokwoldys he sent anon' (61–4). He crowns them with repurposed vegetation and lavishes his own delicacies on them, and then he sends minstrels to 'glad the cokwoldys' (131). Arthur thus seems to recognise the trauma performed by his horn, since he offers the men delights to cheer them and restore their previous facial expression. However, this experience is emotionally complicated for the cuckolds, as Arthur requires that they simultaneously feel and deny their shame and its agency: in addition to treating them so generously, he demands that they 'take no greffe / Bot all with love and with leffe [willingly], / Every man with other' (133–5). He insists that they 'be glad everychon, / For [my] sake make gode chere' (65–6). The king, speaking from his position of royal authority, requires positive public affect and, further, forbids negative private emotion: 'Be never the wrother with your wyves, / For no maner of nede' (68), for 'Of them com owre manhed' (72). From a perspective of noble generosity, a woman's membership in the company of mothers and wives – who enable the production of an individual male's manhood through giving birth and then sustain it as sexual objects and wives – overrides her individual behaviour.

The narrative in *Sir Corneus* focuses on the affective response encouraged by the horn and by the king, the horn's in accord with social norms (embarrassment and displeasure) and the king's in contrast to it (forbidding anger, requiring gratitude). Finally, because this is, after all, a bourd, Arthur himself drinks from the horn and is revealed to be a cuckold, too. In response, the cuckolds at the table 'lokyd yche on other, / And thought the kyng was there awne [own] brother' (181–2). The king accepts this recognition of their shared cuckold identity, willingly joining their dance and seating his brothers at the high dais alongside him. He honours them at the feast through elevating their status to his own. Attention is explicitly drawn to the status differential when Arthur says 'cokwoldys no more I wyll repreve [shame], / For I ame one and aske no leve [exception], / For all my rentys and londys' (193–5). In this, the horn's agency extends beyond the affective and moral. No longer does it merely recognise those who fail to maintain stability within their households, giving them opportunities to perform social and emotional penance in conjunction with the hierarchically marked feast tables and willow wreaths. In finally outing the king, the horn unifies the community by reincorporating the absolved with their leader and even removing prior distinctions of land-based status. In such ways, the drinking horn exemplifies Mitchell's observation that '[o]bjects themselves may assist or resist subjects; some practically enlist subjects, it seems, to carry out their plans'.[16] This poem presents the drinking horn as the ultimate authority in Arthur's hall, doling out moral judgement to which the monarch is then forced to respond. The poem itself similarly carries out the horn's plans: it concludes by stating that a knight who served at the king's dais 'Syr Corneus hyght he [was his name]. / He made this gest [story] in hys gam, / And namyd it after hys awne name' (246–8). The conclusion thus asserts that the poem gets its name from its creator (stating this claim twice in three lines), and yet the poem's events all point towards the horn itself as the one who makes the story possible. As a result, the knight responsible for conveying the story of the horn's revealing truth and flattening of social and moral hierarchies is instead revealed to have himself taken on the name of the powerful horn and only then to have claimed the name, and the story, as his own.

Curiously, this poem shares with *Carpenter's Tools* an orientation towards thrift and prosperity, despite its setting in the royal court, a site not ordinarily associated with thrift, and in this case one actively indulgent in largesse. When Arthur explains early on the logic of the penance he requires of the cuckolds, he clarifies that this is not, as might be anticipated, because they failed to master their wives; rather, it seems, the issue is that their wives were bad businesswomen who mistreated and devalued their goods: as Arthur puts it, 'Ther wyves hath be merchandabull [cheap], / And of ther ware compenabull [generous]' (109–10). In this, the poem combines the affective and moral agency of things with a concern for thrift around which *Carpenter's Tools* revolves. Here, as there, women are held responsible for fairly evaluating the worth of goods (including their own bodies) on the market and avoiding inappropriate generosity.[17] And yet in this moral universe, that of the bourd, focus is consistently drawn to an emotionally satisfying resolution: Arthur declares that 'Me thinke it is non herm' (111).[18] The poem ends with an emphasis on the cuckolds' being 'full blythe' (232), a description of their concluding affective state observed in them by the narrator and then asserted by their own words: 'Every cokwold' then 'seyd to other' that because Arthur is 'owr awne brother; / Therfor we may be blyth' (235–7). This poem presents a world in which the carpenter's supporters are right, however morally misguided: they and their masters share their fate, one in which a carpenter can become a knight and a king can become a jolly cuckold in harmony with his cuckold subjects.

Managing household wealth and health

Attention to the possibilities of fair exchange continues with the short version of Lydgate's *Dietary* (item 31, fols. 107r–108r) that appears here, the concerns of which respond to readers who are well-to-do gentry householders – those who (like the cuckolds in *Sir Corneus*) must manage relations with superiors (King Arthur) and inferiors (their wives). This short version of the *Dietary* appears separated from the other conduct texts in the collection (the last of which was item 8, *Dame Curtasy*) and is just 81 lines long, half the length of most of the remaining copies of the poem in other manuscripts (of which there are fifty-seven). In conduct texts such as this one, readers encounter advice for daily living, advice focused especially on behaviour in public spheres such as at the household table – the non-aristocratic version of the feast table in *Sir Corneus*. There, moral cleanliness depended upon others' appropriate treatment of the (female) body;[19] here, it depends on appropriate treatment of one's own body through the incorporation of things – food and drink especially. Throughout this short version of the *Dietary*, the unidentified authoritative voice encourages beneficial management of the body and the objects with which it interacts: the wealth of the soul as well as of the body depend on it. Claire Sponsler describes the challenge presented in such conduct texts as 'figur[ing] out which and how much of these objects to absorb in order to maintain a state of physical, social, and spiritual well-being'.[20] Speaking outside the particular constraints of conduct literature, Jane Bennett explains in *Vibrant Matter* how digestion is 'a series of mutual transformations in which the border between inside and outside becomes blurry'.²¹ Such absorption holds the potential – and threat – of changing the self, a possible ontological change that the conduct text helps the human to negotiate. While *Sir Corneus* managed the precarious landscape of heterosexual marriage in a patriarchal monarchy, manifest in the material, social, and political obstacle course of the royal hall, the *Dietary* manages the experience of dining with the goal of sustaining human physiological and social survival.

Morality in the *Dietary* is thus expressed through the body's actions and inactions, which affect the health of both body and soul. 'For helth of body cover fro cold thi hede. / Ete non raw mete ... / Drynke holsom drynke, fede thee on lyght brede' (1–3), begins the first stanza. It quickly moves from instructions on physical behaviour that will generate bodily health through what is worn and what ingested to encouraging a certain emotional bearing in order to generate well-being: 'Glad [Go gladly] towerd bede, at morrow also' (7). The same pattern holds in the second stanza, with the directions for eating followed by instructions to have 'Not malas for non adversyté' and to be 'Meke in trubull [discord], glad in poverté, / Riche with lytell, content with suffyciens, / Mery withouten grugyng [grudging] to thy degré [rank]' (13–15).²² The speaker extends the moderation of intake from food and drink to that of verbal and emotional expression, of rest, of psyche (avoid melancholia and excessive joy), and of attire. More expansively, readers are to consider their community, pursuing peace and showing generosity to those less fortunate. As the speaker concludes, 'in two thyngys stondys thi welthe / Of saule and of body ... / Moderate fode gyffes to man hys helthe ... / Charyté to thy saule it is full dewe' (73–7). The body benefits from moderate food, the soul from charitable acts (which also requires the moderate consumption of objects, leaving excess to be shared with others).²³ The body and the soul are not so much separate aspects of the self but rather interdependently comprise – along with those objects it selectively ingests – the individual human subject.

Sir Cleges (item 24, fols. 67v–73r), too, focuses on the day-to-day management of a household family, in this case a family at risk.²⁴ At various points in this narrative, a reader will find numerous examples in the actions of Sir Cleges and most especially his wife, Dame Clarys, of the training and encouragement offered in the

Dietary. She seems to have been an active and effective reader of such conduct literature, taking on the role of the instructional speaker offering guidance to her family in the midst of the challenges it faces. The danger to the family in this narrative comes, however, from the very system of morality that sustains it and that the *Dietary* corroborates. Specifically, Sir Cleges performs with great devotion the cultural value of generosity esteemed there: 'To pore folke do thou no vyalens [violence]. / ... Of sondry metys [be] not gredy at thy tabull' (*Dietary* 19, 21); further, 'Vysete [Visit] the pore with intere [sincere] dylygence, / Upon all nedy have compassyon, / And God schall send thee grace and influence / Thee to increase and thy possessyon' (*Dietary* 45–8). Sir Cleges is *so* generous – in fact, every stanza in the introductory section of the poem emphasises his generosity to all, rich or poor, in hosting a large feast every Christmas – that he eventually loses everything that identifies him and his household.

Sir Cleges is introduced to readers through his treatment of his peers who have fallen on hard times: 'to squyres that traveyled in lond of werre / And were fallyn in poverté bare, / He gaff them gold and fe' (16–18). He shows his social inferiors the same kindness: 'Hys tenantys feyr he wold rehete [support]; / No man he wold buske ne bete [harry nor beat] ... / Hys mete was redy to every man / That wold com and vyset hym than; / He was full of plenté' (19–24). This treatment follows 'Whether thei were ryche or pore' (35). His wife, Dame Clarys, joins him in this service, for 'Grete almysfolke bothe thei were' (31). Minstrels benefit, as well: 'Hors and robys and rych thyngys, / Gold and sylver and other thyngys' (49–50) are their gifts from Cleges in exchange for their service.[25] Notably, the effect of the generosity that the poem highlights is not its lack of moderation; in fact, its merit lies in its determined lavishness. Yet after a decade and more of this degree of generosity, 'Be than his gode began to slake, / Sych festys he gan make' (54–5). Cleges's response to this reduction in income alongside ongoing expense is to continue the feasts by funding them through mortgaging his manors (58–9): 'Hys ryalty [royal estate] he forderyd ay [spent continually] / To [Until] hys maners were sold awey, / That hym was left bot one [So that only one was left to him]. / And that was of lytell valew' (70–3). As he loses the very identity that drew others to him, his supporters depart, leaving him with only his wife and two children (80). Cleges's generosity effectively undoes the household, distributing it elsewhere. His actions demonstrate full faith in the assertions of the *Dietary* that if you do have compassion on the needy and support the poor, 'God schall send thee grace and influence / Thee to increase and thy possession' (*Dietary* 47–8). Cleges, in using his manors as collateral for his loans to support his charity, 'thought hymselve oute to quyte [get himself out of debt]' (60) because he did all of this 'In the name of God allmyght' (63).

Also unusual is the narrative's emphasis on the value of Cleges's generosity as rooted not in the physical sustenance it provides to those in need. Rather, what is repeatedly emphasised is its affective impact: Cleges's goal in his charity is 'To mend with their mode [restore others' spirits]' (51). The narrative focuses, throughout, on the affective agency of things: they improve spirits, as here, but they also, in their loss, diminish spirits. Cleges becomes inconsolable after his family suffers its deprivations, not out of regret that he gave too much and harmed himself and his family, but rather out of regret that he can no longer, in his lack of wealth, donate to others (110–16). It is specifically that he can no longer cheer others, cannot improve their emotional state, that he regrets. On Christmas Eve, when Cleges is at last simply unable to host his annual feast for the poor, he swoons and 'wrong hys hondys and wepyd sore; / Mekyll mon he made ther; / Sygheng full pytewysly [piteously]' (103–5). His sense of loss is enhanced by the sounds of minstrelsy that he hears, a ghostly reminder of past merriment made very present in the material sounds of 'trumpe[te]rs, pypers, and nakerners [drummers] / Of herpers notys and gytherners [guitarists], / Of sytall and sautrey [citole and psaltery]' (97–9) – once again associating positive affect with the objects that make it possible.

As the Cleges family loses its array of holdings and as all of Cleges's men leave him, the narrative constricts and reorients to the domestic sphere. It is here that we see Cleges grappling with the concerns shared by the non-knightly readers of Ashmole 61: indeed, this story provides a very rare glimpse of daily family life in the form of a scene in which Cleges and Clarys, on Christmas Eve, 'When thei had ete … / With myrth thei drofe the dey awey, / The best wey that they myght. / With ther chylder pley thei dyde, / And after evensonge went to bede' (151–5). The family offers emotional sustenance in private, in the face of the sorrow experienced in public.

Clarys responds to her husband's sadness over their losses with hugs and kisses him 'with glad cher' (120–1) – cheer she provides specifically in terms of things: 'now every man schuld be mery and glad / With sych godys as thei had; / Be ye so' (130–2). Material comfort and emotional comfort are conflated in such ways throughout the poem. In private family moments, affective experience gives moral instruction, encouraging an emotional literacy in relation to diverse members of the household, human and non-human.

This orientation continues in the second half of the poem, even as it shifts location from Cleges's household to the public space of King Uther's court. Such a shift is triggered by the appearance of an unexpected and powerful object: out-of-season cherries. These appear when Cleges responds to his feelings of loss by praying (following the advice of the conduct texts elsewhere in Ashmole 61). Rather than asking for divine assistance in his own poverty, Cleges thanks God for what he once had, beginning with the pleasure he experienced while performing charity: 'The myrth that I was won [accustomed] to make / In this tyme for thi sake! / I fede both fre and bond [serfs], / And all that ever com in thi name' (109–12). In expressing gratitude for the very situation that produced his loss, recalling its affiliated pleasurable emotions, Cleges demonstrates the extent of his incorporation of charity's benefit to the self and others – a central lesson of the *Dietary*. Taking to heart his wife Dame Clarys's advice – 'Be Crystys sake, I rede ye lyne [advise you to cease] / Of all the sorrow that ye be ine' (127–8) – he says, 'Now I assent' (139) and goes out to pray alone in his garden, where once again 'He thankyd god with all hys hert / Of all desesyd [wretched] in poverté / That ever to hym he sent' (183–5). Finished, he pulls himself up from his kneeling prayer with the assistance of a tree branch and discovers there berries and green leaves, despite its being December.

Where the significance of the objects that Cleges was formerly able to distribute to the poor was easily legible – his moral responsibility generating satisfaction for himself and his benefactors – these cherries challenge the interpretive skills of almost every human with whom they come in contact. Once he has determined that they are indeed real cherries, by taking a bite and finding 'After a chery it relesyd clene [tasted exactly]' (205), Cleges reads the cherries' import (certain they are sure to have one, since they are ripe out of season) from the perspective of guilt: he fears they are a token, because of 'our grete plenyng' (210), that 'more grevans [injury or burden] is ny' (211). Clarys, who suffers from no such guilt (having herself done no such complaining), is optimistic, seeing it as a token 'Of more godnes that is comyng: / We schall have more plenté' (213–14). Also reading the cherries literally, Clarys sees the potential for profit in them and advises Cleges to share this gift from God with the king, for 'Sych a gyft ye may hafe ther / That we schall the beter fare' (224–5). Her optimism expresses her faith in the goodness of God's material gifts and in the power of the object in the tradition of the gift-exchange – trusting that an act of generosity will provide gifts in return.

In his visit to King Uther's castle on Christmas day, Cleges (accompanied by his son, both of them dressed in 'pore clothyng ... in a symple aray' [249–50]) repeatedly refers to God as 'hym that made all thinge of nought' (264, again in 294), as he had done when praying in the garden (106–7). The connection between divine and earthly objects (including humans) is emphasised and reiterated as one of direct cause and effect, of creator Lord and created earthly subject – whether unseasonal cherries or Cleges himself. This understanding sustains Cleges through his encounters with the king's abusive representatives: each of them (first porter, then usher, and finally steward) refuses to allow Cleges passage to the king unless he will later pay one third of whatever he receives from the king in exchange for his miraculous cherries. The three together thus pre-emptively remove entirely any royal gift Cleges might be able to take away with him. Each of them also threatens violence, upon deeming Cleges to be poor. The porter, for instance, 'seyd full spytously [scornfully] / ... Go stond in begers route [the beggars' crowd]' (251, 256). The porter misreads Cleges's identity through this 'pore clothing' (249), but he appropriately reads the cherries as a gift that will produce a gift in return ('Wele he wyst for his comyng, / For hys presente to the Kyng, / Grete gyftys have he schuld' [269–71]), just as Clarys had anticipated. Unlike Clarys, though, and despite Cleges's direct reference to God the Creator, the porter misses entirely the source and spirit of the gift – its having been a gift from *God*, the maker of the cherries. Instead, he treats the unnatural fruit as a simple commodity.[26] This, coupled with his misreading of Cleges himself, condemns the porter.

King Uther rightly represents good kingship when he sees the great power in the cherries and uses them to secure his own marriage by sending some as a gift to his beloved (374–7); he also properly interprets that Cleges has 'honouryd all my feste / With thi deyntys ... / And worschyped me allso' (401–-3). Effective moral reading is thus modelled for Cleges by both his wife and his king, and Cleges seems through this process to have improved his own interpretive skills: when the king offers to grant him whatever he would like – generously extending to status-changing 'lond or lede / Or other gode' (407–8) – Cleges requests no *thing* in return, so that he will not have to give any reward to the porter, usher, or steward. Instead he requests twelve strokes, and along with this the freedom 'With my staff to pay them all, / Myn adversarys in this hall, / For Seynt Charyté' (419–21). Uther regrets having made such an open promise to the poor subject, observing that Cleges has such need that he should have requested 'gold or fe' (426). Indeed, this exchange takes an emotional toll on Uther, leaving him 'angary and grevyd sore' (431). This emotional response changes utterly, though, when Cleges doles out justice to the misbehaving royal representatives and explains his behaviour publicly at Uther's request. Upon hearing Cleges's report, 'The lordys lewghe [laughed], both old and yenge, / And all that ther were wyth the Kyng, / They made solas inowghe. / They lewghe so thei myght not sytte' (506–9).

Cleges is rewarded by the king for this pleasure-production with knightly accoutrements, the castle of Cardiff, and the position of steward of all the king's lands, 'Of water, lond and frythe ([forest]' (530–8). This he receives in addition to his first reward, the opportunity to distribute justice. In the end, 'Ther fell to hym so grete ryches / He vansyd hys lyne [advanced his lineage], more and les' (557–8). Bearing in mind the debt into which Cleges previously went in order to continue sponsoring the Christmas feast each year, the narrator notes that 'Upon the dettys that they hyght [owed], / They payd als fast as thei myght, / To every man were content' (551–3). Cleges's proper use of goods, presented in terms of contemporary fiscal norms, coupled with his appropriate relationship to his God, his king, and his family, produce this happy ending.[27] Dame Clarys's original appropriate understanding of the object is confirmed not only by this bounty but also by the king's personal gift to her: he sends her, via Cleges, a gold cup, as a 'Tokenyng of joy and myrthe' (541). Like the gift of her heavenly king, this gift of her earthly king is a token not of 'more grievance' (as Cleges would originally have it), but as Clarys foresaw, of 'more godnes' and 'more plenté', of pleasure and happiness.

Documenting sacrificial exchange

Sir Cleges makes 'real' God's material earthly interventions first through the gifts Cleges provides to others in the name of God and then through the cherries God himself provides to Cleges, which Cleges's cleverness and pursuit of justice enables him to exchange for the objects he previously sacrificed through his generosity: wealth, lands, status. A few items later in this section of the manuscript, the *Short Charter of Christ* (item 29, fol. 106r) presents the divine body itself – in the form of the human Christ, speaking from within historical time – as a sacrificial confirmation of the promises and exchanges central to Christianity.[28] In the tradition of the Charters of Christ, the poem itself takes the form and situation of a charter: it follows the steps of the legal process of a charter and ends with a seal, declared in the voice of Christ himself, captured in a binding contract.[29] This poem of 30 lines is titled (in Latin) 'The Lord's Will' (*Testamentum domini*) and declares in conventional medieval legal discourse, 'Wyteh [Know] wele all that ben here, / And after schall be leve and dere [cherished and loved]' (1–2),[30] 'That I, Jhesus of Nazareth, / For lufe of man have soferd deth / Upon a crosse with wondys fyve / Whyle I was man of lyve' (3–6). Through that act, he declares, 'I have gyven and made a grante / To all that askys repentante: / Hevenes blysse withouten endyng' (7–10). To receive the grant, made available through his sacrifice, humans need only be charitable and love their neighbours as themselves – actions he describes as 'the rente' humans owe to Christ. He presents himself in this relationship as their 'cheffe lord of the fe [fief]' (15–16). The 'fe' is not in this case, as Shuffelton clarifies, money – something representing wealth – but the source of wealth itself, a fief, 'an inheritable tenure of land or office held by permission of a lord'. To hold land this way in medieval England – 'in chief' – was 'to hold it directly from the crown rather than from an intermediary'.[31] In this, then, Christ proclaims humans to be in direct relationship to him, the ultimate crown.

The structure of the poem, presented in the voice of the legal actor using the language of an actual charter, makes the object that is the text on the page the legal agreement that Christ signs through his sacrifice on the cross (and through which he produces redemption). This version of the *Short Charter* lacks the final four lines included in other versions of it, wherein Jesus asserts that 'The wounde in my side the seil it is' (British Library MS Harley 237).[32] In Ashmole 61, the final line Christ says four lines earlier is 'Myn awne sele thereto I hynge'. Following this is a large visual image of the heraldic shield of Christ's five wounds, his most meaningful identifier, drawn by Rate.[33] The shield contains a large cross with five suns, with the sun at the centre of the cross enclosed in a heart. These suns as the five wounds of Christ thus visually represent the wound that Christ in the poem says is the seal on the charter.[34] Shuffelton surmises that 'Rate has omitted these last lines [witnessed in the Harley MS] in order to draw attention to the "seal" he has drawn'.[35] This assertion (my wound is the seal) is not verbally necessary, for it is provided iconically in form of the seal that in the Ashmole 61 version Christ says he has hung there. In this, the shield behaves the way the fish and flowers behave elsewhere in the texts' colophons, as a substitute for Rate's name, representing his embodied presence on the page just as this shield represents Christ's embodied presence in and production of the charter.

The stated promises in the *Short Charter* are not only reified by Christ's body but also by the earthly witnesses to this legal declaration, largely non-human witnesses, who are also witnesses to the moment of Christ's death. Jesus concludes the charter with a series of five rhyming couplets each of which begins with the command, 'Wytnes…' In each case, this witnessing – and the great significance of the gift enacted by the grant – is evident in the uncharacteristic nature of each earthly subject's reactions: 'Wytnes the dey that turnyd to nyght / And the sone that withdrew hys lyght. / Wytnes the erth that than dyde quake / And the stones that all to-brake [broke apart]' (21–4). Fundamental elements of divine creation behaved in ways contrary to their nature: day became night, solid stones broke, and stable earth shook. These actions are as contrary to natural law as is the death of God himself. The final witness of the sacrifice and of the charter is Christ, with his word expressed through his wounded body: 'In wytnes of that yche thynge [that same deed – that is, Christ's sacrifice][36] / Myn awne sele [seal] therto I hynge [hang]' (29–30).

Laura Ashe has observed that a charter's purpose, 'as a physical artefact, was that it embodied the event'.[37] The event embodied in this charter is the redemption of humanity embodied through Christ's wounded body as through the body of the document, including the wounds embodied again in the seal. In this, Cristina Maria Cervone adds, 'words and deeds coalesce in action'.[38] The poem thus does not simply represent, allegorically or otherwise, the redemption Christ offers, but enacts it. The reader, holding the written text, holds Christ's promise, the record and the act of his exchange: his suffering, for the redemption of humanity.[39] The *Short Charter of Christ* calls attention to the body of the text as the body of Christ, and the relationship of those non-human bodies to the human reader, through its form, that of a charter complete with seal.

This text and the one that follows it in Ashmole 61 are linked through the visual representation of the seal of Christ: to the right of the image of the seal – that is, enmeshed in the body of the visual text of the *Short Charter* – is written in Rate's hand '*Lamentacion Beati Mariae*', which is the Latin title of a 96-line Marian lament (*The Lament of Mary*, item 30, fol. 106r) that follows (see Figure 3).[40] Shuffelton notes that this poem's direct address by Mary to other mothers is 'quite unusual for both Marian laments and medieval lyrics more generally'.[41] Its placement straight after Christ's direct address in *Short Charter*, particularly with the title of the Marian lament appearing as part of Christ's seal and the visual representation of his five wounds, integrates these two poems into a complementary pair of poetic monologues.[42] Christ spoke directly of his sacrifice in terms of earthly legal discourse in the *Short Charter*, emphasising what his body guarantees for others; in the poem that follows, Mary speaks directly of embodied maternal delight and suffering, ultimately emphasising the devotion that all Christians ought to have to Christ, extending even beyond the commitment they have to their own children. The *Short Charter* conveys Christ's gift through his embodied suffering, and the *Lament of Mary* demonstrates and communicates what Christians owe in return.

3 Oxford, Bodleian Library MS Ashmole 61, fol. 106r: seal of the *Short Charter of Christ* and title of the *Lament* of Mary [*Lamentacion Beati Mariae*]

In her poetic address to readers, Mary presents through the body the contrasting emotional experiences of pleasure and pain – her experiences in contrast to those of the audience of mothers. In repeated visual juxtapositions, Mary sets the way her audience of mothers happily 'Thy chyldys cape [cap] thou doyst [place] upon [your child]' against her own structurally similar activity: 'ever, alas, I make my mone / To se my son as he lyght [lies] here. / Oute of hys hede I pyke many a thorn' (34, 37–9). Most visually and emotionally arresting are the references she makes to her son's wounds: 'Thy chyld lyes sowkyng on thi pappys. / Thereof me thynke it is grete harme / In my sonys brest to se grete gappys [gaps, wounds]' (58–60), rhyming the mother's nourishing breast with her son's deadly wounds (pappys/gappys). Mary requires the listener to live her physical suffering with her, maintaining the present tense in her descriptions, which places her activity in the same temporal plane as that of the audience. She insists that while 'Thou beholdys hys [your child's] fase and hys aray [dress] / Unto thi eye full wele lykyng [pleasing]. / The longyst fynger of my hond beyng [longest finger on my hand] / Throught my sonys fete I may thyrst [thurst] it here, / And take it oute full sore wepyng' (53–5). All of this experience, both the joy and the sorrow, is presented through a series of contrasting yet simultaneous images of physical contact that the emotion produces, with Mary's directly resulting from her somatic sensation of the violence enacted on her son's body. Spoken embodied experience in these paired poems – the suffering of the holy family, in particular – both gives witness to and generates beneficial emotional suffering.

Cosmic ecologies

The Lament of Mary calls attention to the pleasures and sufferings of the bodies of the poems' speakers and listeners. She asserts the inevitability of experiencing the world through embodied social exchange. In this, she builds on Christ's delineation in the *Short Charter* of the nature of the salvific exchange that his human body made possible. Elsewhere in this section of the collection, attention is directed to this central question of salvation as exchange, this attention being directed by means of unconventional embodiments. The dialogue of *Ypotis* (item 27) presents truths of creation, sin, and redemption through the figure of a preternaturally wise child only eventually revealed to be Christ himself; this poem follows on *The King and his Four Daughters* (item 26), an allegorical representation of the salvation assemblage that Christ's embodied sacrifice makes both manifest and possible, presented in the form of a debate among the sisters Mercy, Peace, Righteousness, and Truth, with a vital interjection by their brother, Wisdom. *The Feasts of All Saints and All Souls* (item 25) starts off this trio of texts by establishing the shared human and divine authorisation of the power of intercession that is generated through an earthly human/heavenly saint nexus embodied in a rededicated and sanctified temple. This portion of Ashmole 61 delves much more directly into questions of religious wisdom, presenting truths by deploying literature's varied instructional tools and regularly asserting diverse cosmic ecologies.

As George Shuffelton observes, 'Middle English scholars have either ignored or avoided the odd dialogue *Ypotis*' (item 27, fols. 83r–87v), although Middle English readers did neither. The poem was popular, surviving in fifteen manuscripts and an early print copy, reflecting a wide and long-lasting medieval audience.[43] It popularises Latin texts (translated into Middle English via French) in its 490 lines of octosyllabic couplets (in the Ashmole 61 version, one of two Middle English varieties). This adaptation concerns matters of religious knowledge beyond the Creed and what would have been learned by all Catholics, but still of 'the greatest practical use' for readers lacking formal education and perhaps serving as a catechism for the young, in the form of the story of a young person instructing an adult.[44] The dialogue is framed by an introduction familiar from conduct texts elsewhere in Ashmole 61, and it is historically and religiously situated as having been witnessed by 'Seynt John the apostyll' (4). Ypotis is a child sent to Emperor Hadrian in Rome, who plops the young boy on his knee and asks him his origins. The child mysteriously replies that 'Fro my Fader I com ryght, / Fro my Fader the hyghe justys, / To teche men that be not wyse' (18–20). That response offers sufficient invitation for Hadrian, who begins asking the child questions. One element of this instruction surrounds the Emperor's question to Ypotis 'If that he couth tell hym ought / Of how many thyngys man is wrought [made]' (145–6). The answer:

> Of seven;
> Whych thei be, I schall them nevyn.
> The erth slyme was one of tho,
> Water of the se God toke also,
> Of the sone and of the wynd,
> And of the cloudys, wryten I fynd,
> And of the stones be the se coste,
> And also of the Holy Goste.
> Of the erth he made hys flesch,
> And of the water hys blod so nesch [fluid];
> Of the son hys hert and hys bowellys,
> And of hys other gode dedys;
> Of the cloudys hys wyttis beste [wits],

> And of the wynd breth of breste,
> And of the stone he made hys bone,
> And the Holy Gost hys saule alone. (147–62)

Each human body's flesh is made of earth slime; its blood is made of water; its heart and bowels of the sun; its wits of the clouds; its breath of the wind; its bones of stone; and its soul of the Holy Ghost. People are made of the elements, and thus of the earth, but along with that they are also made of the Holy Ghost. This model of a single human individual reveals the necessity of the earthly and the spiritual to the existence of the human, whose very being depends on both body and soul, on both worldly (in all its material elements) and heavenly. Further, the earthly is also human, just as the human is divine, through these associations – associations that are material as well as conceptual and symbolic.

Despite the appearance that each human is similarly composed of these seven earthly and divine elements, each individual is actually multifarious, for the conclusion to this listing is that 'therfor thei that be here / Be made of dyverse maner' (165–6). In other words, human diversity – the different personalities and other traits exhibited by people – results from the different degrees of mixing of these seven earthly and spiritual elements. One made mostly of earth, for instance, is going to be 'Hevy in thought and dede' (169) – that is, melancholy. The person who 'hath most of the se' (171) will be 'Ever in travel' and 'covet mych of lond and lede [people]' and will be failed by all when he or she is most in need, 'For it farys be an ebe and flod, / As it doth be the werldys gode' (176–7). This continues for those made mostly of wind (light and 'Merry in herte and thought' [179]), clouds (light 'in word and dede' [183]), sun ('Hote and hasty' [186]), stone ('stedfast in thought / And in travell trysty and trew' [190–1]), and Holy Ghost ('He schall have in hert moste / Gode wordys and gode thought and dede, / And the pore cloth and fede, / And love well God and Holy Chyrch' [194–7]). No evaluative preference is given to any one of these seven examples, each with a particular dominant feature, even as one of these features is based in the divine, and although all of them are presented in terms of predominantly moral associations: while he or she of the sea will (naturally) constantly covet, he or she is not condemned for this and in fact is instead, it would seem, provided with a justification:

'For it farys be an ebe and flod'. The training offered for dedicated readers, be they young or old, is not how to behave differently in accord with Christian dogma, but instead how to accept human diversity as natural and divinely authorised, as demonstrating and directly connected to the variety seen among natural elements. Affective generosity to others, rather than strict moral discipline, is modelled, and it is modelled not by other humans but by the basic material elements with which humans share their nature.

The narrative of the dialogue concludes with Hadrian's final question to Ypotis: Are you a good angel, or a bad angel? Ypotis responds with 'I ame he that thee hath wrought / And on the rode [cross] dere have bought' (473–4), after which he departs for heaven from which he came. Ypotis's announcement of his true identity – which hearkens back to the self-identification of Christ in the *Short Charter* – is followed by another, that of the text. It conveys its own origin story, first introduced at the start of the poem and concluded here: the poem was written by 'Seynte John the Wangelyst [Evangelist]' (481) in Latin, 'In holy wryte and in perchemyn [parchment]' (484). Christ and his wisdom are embodied here on earth in the form of the child Ypotis, a form itself unmarked as a divine-human hybrid until the final revelation and despite the mystery that is his knowledge. They are then conveyed to the reader in this textual form, the poem calling attention to its material as well as verbal existence.[45] Set alongside *Short Charter* and *Lament of Mary*, Christ's earthly embodiment legally confirms and emotionally makes tangible the truth of his sacrifice.

Sharing *Ypotis*'s emphasis on the elemental-human-divine assemblage that is the individual Christian, *The Feasts of All Saints and All Souls* (item 25, fols. 73r–78v) – an adaptation of material original to the *Legenda aurea* (*The Golden Legend*) by Jacobus de Voragine, in a version unique to Ashmole 61 – presents two related narratives that share a conception of the eternal cosmos (heaven, hell, purgatory) as thoroughly enmeshed with time-bound earth.[46] In this, it provides an alternative perspective on the deep integration of human, earthly, and divine so directly presented by *Ypotis*. *The Feasts of All Saints and All Souls* presents two realms, that of Christian history and that of divine righteousness, that mutually affect one another – a suggestive alternative to the common conception of this relationship's being unidirectional, from heaven to earth only. In this way, the heavenly is shown to be open to change and thus, implicitly, itself temporally engaged, if not time-bound as earth is. The poem also presents two narratives – one earthly, the other supernatural – whose meanings intersect despite separate development. The first narrative describes and explains the foundations of the feasts of All Saints and All Souls, affiliating the establishment of these twinned holy days with the consecration of the Pantheon temple in Rome as a Christian church.[47] In the second narrative, a living monk's soul is physically taken on a tour of purgatory and paradise as a means of simultaneously receiving full knowledge of the system of saintly intervention and receiving divine approval of the pope's institution of the feasts of All Saints and All Souls.

The poem begins with a justification for the establishment of the new feast day: while there are holy saints who have their feasts 'in the yere / As is wryten in kalender' (11–12), there are 'Many thousands' who do not, except – thanks to the establishment of it – for All Hallows Day. After this quick justification, the scene shifts to pre-Christian Rome and the Pantheon, which originally (we are told) 'Of all godys and devellus eke, / Thus was ordeynd this temple hous / Of all devyllus to have ther cours' (40–2). That is, until Pope Boniface determined to Christianise it. This transformation happens through a new community: the emperor grants Boniface's request, and Boniface 'toke hys clergy and hys power / For to make that temple clere, / And pute oute all that tyrandry,/ And sette therin hys clergy' (67–70).[48] The church was 'made holy' (73) in the worship of Mary, angels, patriarchs, prophets, apostles, martyrs, confessors, holy virgins. 'All Hallow Chyrch was made ther' (78), not by building a new building but by cleansing it of its previous aims and occupants. The new configuration – building plus all the faculty of the Church, plus God's commandment (118) – is an entirely new entity, taking its full effect, as All Hallows Church, when the double feast of All Hallows Day was instituted on the first day of November. The power of this combination of earthly and heavenly authority is clear: once the first Mass was sung there, 'fals errour gan to sese, / And Crystendom for to encres' (89–90). As a result, 'Thys All Hallow Dey be skyll [powerful/effective]; / He may amend hym if he wyll / To com to Holy Chyrch in clenesse / At evensong, matyns, ourys, and messe. / All trespas befor than is forgyffen, / And he be in gode lyffe and clen schryfen' (103–8). This outcome results directly from the prayers of 'All gode seyntys' to Jesus for the souls of the repentant (109).

After this, transitioning to a different mode – introduced by the narrator's call to 'Crystyn man, for Godys ore [mercy], / Herkens now and here more' (115–16) – evidence is offered of God's approval of the pope's institution of such a holy day, in such a place. The subject is 'The solempnyté of this feste, / How hye it is thorow Godys heste [commandment]' (117–18). That 'God was payd [pleased] with that dede' and 'Of his grace he grantyd thereto' (120, 122) is demonstrated through a narrative of a vision, granted on All Hallows Day: a monk's soul is taken up from his body and guided by an angel through purgatory and Eden/heaven. In each of a series of visions, a scene is described in extensive tangible detail, and then the guiding angel explains it to the monk's soul. The monk sees 'a blyssfull thing' (141), a company worshipping a king in his hall – queen, maidens, twelve men, knights, clerks – which the angel then with very little difficulty explains is actually Jesus, Mary, holy virgin martyrs, the apostles, holy martyrs, bishops. The explanation does not offer an allegorical interpretation of the scene but essentially restates it in different terms, simply identifying the figures by name and noting why each is in the position it is, at times offering scriptural foundation for the details of the scene. When the soul is shown purgatory, he sees 'Many men ther were in nakyd' (248), where 'Water and fyre together gan bryn; / It myght be no wey be slakyd' (246–7). Some naked bodies were in water up to their chin, 'Turmentyd so thei had no reste' (253), some to the breast, some to their knees. On another hill he sees a sweet meadow enclosed with jewels, with seats and beds made of shining gold, with a sweet smell; here, the bodies are all young and restful and joyful, eating abundant feasts. Outside the walls are many beggars, to whom the young and restful show no mercy (300): 'For them made no man mone' (302). The angel's explanation for all of this is surprisingly literal: he provides names (the meadow is paradise, where Adam first lived) and explains the reasons for the particular experiences ('Thys men that thou seys in water here / Be saulys to make hem clere. / Water and fyre that thow hast sene, / Of pourgatory it is the peyne' [314–17]). All is just as the soul has seen. 'Thes men that stond and fast callys / Withoute paradys wallys … / Thei be the saules of' people who in life would be kind to none (377–84).

Objects of correction 161

In relation to this vision, the holy day establishes very clearly the ongoing communion of the living and the dead. In order to avoid finding your loved one after the Day of Judgement lingering outside the gates, begging eternally (for 'To bege here it is to late' [402]), the living should pray for the souls of the dead. God deems this holy day 'So that they that no frendys have / Thys is helpe withouten crave / Of ther peynes to have pardon / To com to salvasyon' (417–20). They do not even need to request it: through the mechanism of this holy day, those who are friendless upon their deaths can be aided by those still alive who do not personally know them. The Feast of All Souls generates the necessary congregation of believing bodies past and present. The monk's own believing body is positioned between the two times and places, for when his soul is temporarily taken away by the angel, his fellow monks believe him to be dead and bury him, with the soul returned just in time as they finish the funeral Mass. Following the command of the angel and God, the monk then tells his vision to Pope Boniface, who instituted the day: through this messenger, God confirms the pope's authorisation of the intercessional assemblage. The poem declares, further, that the feast 'How hye it is thorow Godys heste' (118) depends on many participants – including the Pantheon allowing the cleansing to occur – not just one. These two poems exhibit the effects of affective ecologies in which contact generates what Kathleen Stewart calls 'a kind of involuntary and powerful learning and participation'.[49]

Sandwiched between *The Feasts of All Saints and All Souls* and *Ypotis* is *The King and his Four Daughters* (item 26, fols. 78v–83r). A more apt title might be 'The King and his Four Daughters and Son', for the allegorical poem demonstrates that the king's justice can exist only when all necessary elements are harmoniously present, working together in their full affective agency. This poem is a unique 440-line translation into Middle English of a popular section of Robert Grosseteste's Anglo-Norman allegory *Le Château d'Amour*.[50] Shuffelton notes that this translation emphasises the place of the Redemption within history, observing that 'though allegory can tend towards atemporal stasis, the allegorical portion of *The King and His Four Daughters* operates in a carefully constructed historical frame'.[51] In this, it shares the *Feast of All Saints and All Souls*' emphasis on the 'congruity of this world and the next' and on the universal Church's foundations in the historical and earthly.[52] This poem's first half presents an extended summary of the creation of earth and of Adam and Eve, then tells of the original sin and its aftermath; this sets the scene for the allegorical consideration of God's righteousness that fills the second half of the poem. This section begins by introducing the unnamed king and his son 'that was hym lyche. / Of wytte and power lyke hym he was ... in all case' (224–6), such that 'That [what] the fader wyst [knew], the son thought; / All thorow [By means of] the sone the fader wrought' (227–8). Certainly this representation of father and son would leave few readers unaware that God and Christ were being evoked. Yet the poem's central focus is the king's four daughters, each of whom has some part of his wit and power (234–5) and on whom he fundamentally depends: 'For withouten them every dele [all together] / Myght he not reule hys kingdom wele' (239–40). These daughters are Mercy, Truth (Sothnes), Justice (Ryghtfullnes), and Peace – 'Withoute the foure that I named / May nothing right be demed' (249–50).

The allegorical narrative begins when Adam, anonymously presented here as 'a man' of the king's, has broken a commandment and receives his judgement, which 'on hym was leyd / After that the kyng had seyd' (261–2), and which takes the form of four torments ordered by the king: to be robbed, slain, strangled, and put in chains (267–70). With this, the engaged reader may wonder if their previous interpretation of the king and his son as God and Christ was amiss. But this discomfort results from an incomplete understanding of the divine, for in steps Mercy, daughter of the king. As suits her nature, she argues in favour of mercy for the man, since 'Hys enmyse [enemies] for envye / They dyde hym that trecherye' (285–6),[53] and she lays her own existence on the line: 'Mersy I ame: yff thou wyll [have] me, / Thou must have mersy and pyté' (289–90). This brings on Sothnes (Truth), who 'wyll it nought' for 'Yiff all thyng myght savyd be / For whom my syster wyll praye, / Schall non of them stond aye [ever stand, i.e. follow the law]' (304–5). She encourages her father the king, instead, to 'avenge thee of that wyght' (316). Ryght (Justice) asserts her identity and relationship to the king thus: 'Fader, my name is callyd Ryght; / That name I hade of thy myght. / Seth [Since] I ame Ryght and thou hast [begot] me, / As Soth it seys, it muste be' (321–4). Justice and Truth overpower Mercy, and 'Than was that wrech [the man] with peynes schent'

(343). Much torment follows, as 'Soth and Ruyght, withouten les, / Went without Mersy and Pes' (349–50), taking the form of the great flood. It was such 'a reufull syght, / And yit it was bote soth and ryght'. Meanwhile, 'Pes myght nowher be; / Sche was sent out contré, / For sche may for nothyng / Be among wreth and werryng' (361–6). 'And yit', the narrator affirms, 'it was bot soth and right': it was 'reufull', pitiful, but it was truth and justice.

Observing this scene from afar, Peace insists to the king that 'I aught be at thy dese [dais]' (372). And yet, she laments to her father, 'My two systeres Soth and Ryght / At Pes and Mersy thei hold fyght. / All without our asente / Thy don all ther jugement' (375–8). Instead, 'we foure awt be all at one [in agreement]' (381), since 'All we foure, verament, / Schall make one jugement, / Therfor, jugement aught be nought / Tyll we foure at one be brought' (405–8). Only the consolidation of all four of them, she asserts, can make 'Ryght jugement' (410). Further, 'Withouten pes is wroght nothing, / Be it never so grete doyng' (387–8). Peace's interpretation – even this final observation that nothing is made without peace – is affirmed by the daughters' brother, who hears the complaint: 'Of thee, fader, fiyst I com. / Wysdom, fader, my name it is' (424–5). He continues, 'That jugement I wyll onderfonge [take on] / And all that ever to Ryght wyll longe [belongs to Right, i.e. is just]' (435–6). He announces that he will be the sacrifice necessary to justice, taking on the judgement to make mercy and peace possible – as witnessed in the kiss of peace, with which the poem abruptly ends.

Concluding this chapter with *The King and his Four Daughters* provides the opportunity to reflect on the quiet actions with consistently powerful effects that female agents perform throughout this section of Ashmole 61. This final text may seem an unlikely support on which to base such a reading, with its allegorical representation of traits following squarely in the tradition of feminising abstract qualities – Lady Liberty today, Lady Philosophy then, hundreds of others before and after. Encountered in terms of this centuries-long grammatically rooted tradition of personification, Mercy, Peace, Justice, and Truth might be read as gendered without significance.[54] *The King and his Four Daughters*, however, deliberately makes these female figures more than representative entities by identifying them first and foremost as daughters of God – with his son, Wisdom, gendered male and equated with Christ. This family framework emphasises the humanity of the divine; certainly, *The Lament of Mary* accentuated Christ's human embodied suffering as well as her own, in terms specifically of the parent–child relationship. Further, including God's son (in the poem if not in the title) points towards the fact that elsewhere, outside of this allegorical *exemplum*, the daughters of God are, in fact, missing. The poem's central claim, confirmed by God's son in his wisdom at the end of the debate, is that for God to exist, all four sisters must be in accord, made possible by the respectful presence of their brother: the narrator observes that 'Withouten hym on non wyse / Acord may not ryght aryse' (421–2). Their brother hears and acknowledges the claims of each of them – Mercy, Truth, Justice, and Peace – and he prophesies his own divine action: 'I schall cry pes, withouten mys, / And Ryght and Pese I schall do kys [make kiss]. / All contake [debate] leyd [laid aside] schall be; / My wyll it is I schall save thee' (437–40). In this the poem reveals that the sibling rivalry shows the exact mix of virtues necessary for God, the divine hybrid of justice-peace-truth-mercy-wisdom. The father himself is left without a single virtue, containing all. The poem then ends, its final line in Latin confirming the fact of that now-past action: '*Iusticia et pax osculate sunt* [Justice and Peace have kissed]' (441).[55] This kiss brings all in accord, through divine Wisdom, to the benefit of 'thee' who the son's will it is to save.

The necessity to divine wholeness of the four daughters of God points towards the significant roles that women have played elsewhere in this section of the manuscript; this feature is particularly notable given the deep investment in moral living in this vicinity, much of it presented in specifically religious terms. Dame Clarys, the cuckolds' wives, the Carpenter's unnamed wife, the Blessed Virgin Mary and the human mothers to whom she laments: these women all drive and define the moral resolution of the texts in which they appear. Indeed, more often than not they are not only contributors to this resolution but provide instruction or other guidance that leads the reader, along with the other household members within the texts, towards moral readjustment and cleansing. The disorienting step of flattening human/non-human hierarchies can eventually allow unusual entities from all household communities – be they properly interpreted extra-natural cherries, the nexus of elements enabling legal documents to capture divine sacrifice, the missing daughters of God, or wives and mothers saintly and sinful – to emerge as instruments of moral correction.

Notes

1 As J. Allan Mitchell elegantly observes, 'To use a spoon in a controlled manner is to see how the spoon *realizes itself* in the hand's grip, flexed muscle, bent limb, motion and concentration; it is to comport the body to the spoonful' (*Becoming Human*, p. 150).
2 Mitchell, *Becoming Human*, p. 118; italics in original.
3 This chapter addresses items 24–31, which appear across quires 7–10 (fols. 67v–108r). One text from this section of the manuscript is not addressed: item 28 (*Northern Passion*), a lengthy 18-folio retelling of Christ's crucifixion associated with oral performance, lacking the affective elements of the religious material elsewhere in the manuscript and less indicative of relationships across the household community. This chapter includes two items that appear a little earlier in the manuscript, in quires 3 and 6 (items 16, *The Debate of the Carpenter's Tools*, and 21, *Sir Corneus*), which are early expressions of concerns and methods that come to dominate in this later community of texts. See Appendix for a table listing the manuscript's contents, including information on quiring, foliation, and watermarks.
4 Regarding the latter, particularly in relation to emotional expression, see Flannery, 'Personification and embodied emotional practice'.
5 In this I benefit from the methodological model that Mitchell provides when he explains that he is 'interested in tracking some of the ways the literature of the household takes directions from the materiality and minutiae of the dining table, placing physical bodies, including bodies of writing, in relation to them' (*Becoming Human*, p. 122).
6 Chaucer's *Parliament of Fowls* provides more birds, with a greater diversity of perspectives, but with an even narrower focus on courtliness and love. Clanvowe's *The Cuckoo and the Nightingale* continues the debate of love by birds. *Wynnere and Wastoure*, unique to the London Thornton manuscript (a near-contemporary of Ashmole 61), shares with *The Debate of the Carpenter's Tools* a primary concern with prudent thrift and wasteful excess, although it performs that concern in a more learned and deliberately literary mode. Another recurring debate rages between the soul and the post-mortem body, to determine the responsible party for the individual's earned afterlife – a concern on which Rate and his texts concentrate elsewhere in Ashmole 61.

7 For further information on the individual late medieval carpentry tools that speak in this poem, see the episode of *The Woodwright's Shop* (31 October 1998, PBS) called 'The Debate of the Carpenter's Tools', in which the show's host, Roy Underhill (who has a background in theatre and expertise in traditional woodworking, the subject of this instructional series approaching forty years on air), performs the debate by impersonating each tool, with examples of each object shown with his face superimposed on top; this performance is accompanied by Underhill's commentary on the uses and forms of many of the tools. Underhill also produced a line drawing of each speaking tool, which was included in the online newsletter of the *Tools and Trades History Society* in winter 2012. The newsletter includes an article by John Clark that offers extended investigation of a number of the tools.
8 Bearing in mind, as is perhaps unavoidable, Heidegger's famous example of the hammer in *Being and Time*, ch. 15.
9 All quotations from texts in Ashmole 61 are from *Codex Ashmole 61*, edited by George Shuffelton, and indicated by line number.
10 Bourgeois wives 'regularly assisted their husbands in the workshop, and were probably more directly involved in the market economy [than peasant wives], whether selling the products of the shared workshop, engaged in commercial brewing or processing woolen yarn' (Goldberg, 'The fashioning of bourgeois domesticity', p. 137).
11 The poet and, presumably, the audience also appreciate the horn for the ample opportunities for double entendre that it offers, as when it is introduced as follows: 'Kyng Arthour had a bugyll horn / That ever more stod hym beforn, / Were so that ever he yede' (22–4). The ubiquity, intimacy, location, and committed focus of the horn all call attention to its physiological parallel.
12 Indeed the poem here (and, by extension, King Arthur) seems to be trying perhaps too hard, with three appearances of 'solas' in the first 39 lines alone.
13 Flannery, 'The concept of shame', p. 167. Flannery includes in this article a consideration of shame in the conduct texts of Ashmole 61.
14 Guinevere's face is similarly affected when Arthur later fails to use the horn properly: 'Sche changyd hyr colour lesse and more' (188).
15 Mitchell reminds us that banquet tables' 'main courses are conspicuous consumption, camaraderie, disputation, hyperbolic displays of verbal wit and wisdom' (*Becoming Human*, p. 121). He also notes that the wooden table recurs as the central tool for thinking through materiality and human capacity, a 'universal prototype of the designed object' (p. 126), appearing in classical, medieval, and modern intellectual history (pp. 126–30): 'Wood is forever after an archetype of unformed matter,

and furniture – specifically the carpentered table – is an emblem of formed matter and of what humans can achieve' (p. 128).
16 Mitchell, *Becoming Human*, p. 118. Notably, in *Stans Puer ad Mensam*, earlier in the collection, 'When thou schuld drynke ofe coppe or of canne [jar] / Sum [Someone else] wyll drinke, be it thyke or thynne; / Than schall thou be mokyd both of wyff and man' (123–5).
17 As I will discuss later in this chapter, Sir Cleges's generosity to the poor and misplaced provides a meaningful contrast to the undiscerning and morally unproductive generosity exhibited by the wives of *Sir Corneus*.
18 The following lines problematise the situation further, for Arthur observes that 'A man of lufe that wold them [the wives] crave, / Hastely he schuld it have, / For thei couth not hym wern [could not refuse him]' (112–14). In this, Arthur seems to accept the inevitability of rape, even going so far as to call the one pursuing the wife as 'a man of lufe', despite the fact that the woman can't refuse him as he takes 'it' quickly. Later, Arthur publicly thanks the man with whom Guinevere had an adulterous encounter, 'For he me helpyd when I was forth [away] / To cher my wyfe and make her myrth, / For women lovys wele pley' (223–5).
19 Treatment that could be performed only by the woman herself, thus emphasising the powerlessness of the male subject.
20 Sponsler, 'Eating lessons', p. 7.
21 Bennett, *Vibrant Matter*, pp. 39, 49.
22 These lines seem to echo King Arthur's command to his fellow cuckolds that they calmly accept their wives' wandering in *Sir Corneus*.
23 George Shuffelton notes, 'Avoiding flatterers, gamblers, melancholic pensiveness, and arguments with neighbours meant just as much to the well-being of the body as the avoidance of fevers or digestive disorders' (*Codex Ashmole 61*, p. 529).
24 *Sir Cleges* has no apparent source or known tradition in which it participates; it is also a generic hybrid: part romance, part saint's life, part folktale (Shuffelton, *Codex Ashmole 61*, p. 491).
25 The attentive reader will note that minstrels received select attention in *Sir Corneus* as well – being sent to cheer the cuckolds. See Shuffelton, 'Is there a minstrel in the house?' for analysis of the recurring appearance of minstrels across the texts in Ashmole 61.
26 A similar condemnation of a character by the narrative for a misreading of Christian value is seen elsewhere in Ashmole 61 in *Sir Isumbras*, when the Sultan of Persia believes he can buy Isumbras's wife for himself in exchange for gold.
27 At just one point in the poem is this initial loss of status equated to that experienced by Sir Isumbras in the first section of the collection.

After confirming to Uther that he is, in fact, the knight Sir Cleges that the king thought had died, Cleges observes that he used to be Uther's knight 'Tyll God allmyght hath vyset [afflicted] me; / Thus poverté hath me dyght [treated]' (528–9). Here, Cleges adds another layer of interpretation of his experience and God's intervention that has until now not been part of his reading. This layer is also, notably, neither confirmed nor denied by the poem's most astute reader, Dame Clarys.

28 An item appearing a few folios earlier, *The King and his Four Daughters* (item 26), also uses legal terms to represent the sacrifice of Christ.

29 Shuffelton, *Codex Ashmole 61*, provides a helpful summary of the tradition on pp. 521–3. Note that twenty-three other copies of the *Short Charter* are extant. Recent discussions of the *Charter of Christ* tradition, including both the Short and the Long versions, appear in Jill Averil Keen (*The Charters of Christ*), Emily Steiner (*Documentary Culture*, esp. pp. 61–90), Laura Ashe ('The "Short Charter of Christ"'), Cristina Maria Cervone (*Poetics of the Incarnation*), and Eric Weiskott ('A new text'). 'The "Short Charter" carefully and deliberately follows the format of a charter, varying from the form only by giving names rather than seals of witnesses' (Cervone, *Poetics of the Incarnation*, p. 100). Cervone demonstrates (using *Fleta*, from 1290, which simplifies Bracton to explain English common law) how the *Short Charter* moves strictly according to the structure of a legal charter (pp. 244–5, n. 32). Some extant versions of the *Short Charter* (such as BL Sloane 3292) use Latin tags to explicitly identify the different sections (such as *Nouerint presentes & futuri*, *Dedi et Concessi*, etc.). The version in Ashmole 61 does not.

30 'Wyteth wele all that ben here' is a Middle English imitation of 'one of the customary openings of legal charters, "Sciant presents et future"' (Shuffelton, *Codex Ashmole 61*, p. 524).

31 Shuffelton, *Codex Ashmole 61*, p. 524.

32 These four lines date the charter and provide an additional 'seal'. See Shuffelton, *Codex Ashmole 61*, p. 524, for an example, wherein Christ says 'This was gifyn at Calvarye, / Dayt the first day of the gret mercy' (British Library MS Harley 237). The version in Ashmole 61 also lacks other features of other versions: it includes Latin only in the first line, which states that what follows is Christ's will, but does not include the Latin subheadings that are present in other versions at various points later in the poem.

33 This is also the only illustration in the manuscript that is not a fish or a flower.

34 Mary Spalding, the earliest modern scholar of the tradition of the Middle English Charters of Christ, recognised in this image of the shield that the

five suns are 'a common visual representation of the wounds' (*Middle English Charters*, p. xxvi, quoted by Shuffelton, *Codex Ashmole 61*, p. 523).
35 Shuffelton, *Codex Ashmole 61*, p. 525.
36 In this, Cervone notes, the poem 'exploit[s] both senses of the word "deed": an act, [and] a land grant' (*Poetics of the Incarnation*, p. 86).
37 Ashe, 'The "Short Charter of Christ"', p. 35.
38 Cervone, *Poetics of the Incarnation*, p. 86. Cervone further observes that 'agency and action are key to a theological claim grounded in twinned metaphors of lordship'. Admittedly, Cervone here is speaking of the *Long Charter of Christ*, ten times the length of the version in Ashmole 61, including a narrative framework that Cervone reads as vital to that poem's Incarnational poetics: 'It thus situates agent and act at the center of the charter form in the person of Christ, who serves as donor, action, and legal conveyance' (*Poetics of the Incarnation*, p. 95). See Cervone, *Poetics of the Incarnation*, pp. 99–100, for an extended consideration of the implications of this relationship. She reads the *Short Charter*'s 'alignment of the "I"' (that of the poem and that of the charter) as making the poem 'seem more straightforward, even didactic' (p. 98).
39 Ashe, 'The "Short Charter of Christ"', pp. 36, 39.
40 While there is a tradition of Marian laments (also called *planctus Mariae*) extending back to the fifth century, this poem was, Shuffelton estimates, a product of fifteenth-century England that participates in the popularity of visual depictions of the pietà, Christ's post-crucifixion body draped across her lap, emphasising Mary's physical maternal relationship to the adult Christ in direct contrast to the common image of her nursing or otherwise cuddling the Christ-child on her lap, and through that contrast, emphasising her embodied suffering. See Shuffelton, *Codex Ashmole 61*, pp. 525–6.
41 Shuffelton, *Codex Ashmole 61*, p. 526. This unusual Marian lament is extant in two different versions, one in three manuscripts (Cambridge University Library MSS Ff.2.38 and Ff.5.48, and Manchester, John Rylands Library MS Chetham 8009). This version in Ashmole 61 also appears in Bodleian Library MS Rawlinson C.86.
42 This is a move Rate also makes with items 35a and 35b (*The Sinner's Lament* and *The Adulterous Falmouth Squire*), which appear elsewhere as two distinct poems but are here combined into one. This item of paired poems is addressed in Chapter 4.
43 Shuffelton, *Codex Ashmole 61*, p. 505. See Shuffelton's explanatory notes on the text (pp. 505–8), where he describes its diverse generic affiliations, and the roots of the poem in the stoic philosopher Epictetus

(hence Ypotis) who was associated in the third century with a dialogue containing questions, riddles, and biblical trivia that spawned the French dialogue between Hadrian and a wise child, which was a central source for *Ypotis*. At the end of the dialogue, in the Middle English version of the story alone, the young child announces that he is Christ

44 Shuffelton, *Codex Ashmole 61*, p. 507.
45 The reference to parchment is one that Rate might have modified to 'in paper', had he been bearing in mind concerns that his twenty-first-century readers would bring to the poem.
46 Shuffelton surmises that a vernacular version was an intermediate source for this one, and notes that all three Middle English analogues to this text 'radically abridge' the many justifications for All Saints Day offered by Jacobus, and the Ashmole 61 version most aggressively reduces the non-narrative material: 'The implicit suggestion that the Church is subject to historical change appears in a text that in other respects emphasizes the transcendent authority of the Church, particularly the papacy' (*Codex Ashmole 61*, p. 497). Compared to other texts addressing concerns about the afterlife, Shuffelton finds that in this one 'the emphasis given to the congruity of this world and the next is notable' (p. 498).
47 This happened in 609 CE, when Pope Boniface IV was given the building by the Byzantine Emperor Phocas.
48 The building connects Boniface to Emperor Hadrian, who rebuilt the Pantheon c. 125 CE after its original construction in c. 27 BCE. Emperor Hadrian is also present in this section of Ashmole 61 as the one instructed by the Christ-child in *Ypotis*.
49 Stewart, *Ordinary Affects*, p. 40.
50 This section is also incorporated into Langland's *Piers Plowman*, among other literary locales.
51 Shuffelton, *Codex Ashmole 61*, p. 502. He also points out that the 'legal and feudal metaphors' in the original are emphasised in the Ashmole 61 translation, which connects it to the discourse of the *Short Charter of Christ*.
52 Shuffelton, *Codex Ashmole 61*, p. 498.
53 See Chapter 2 for discussion of the consistent relationship between envy and the fiend elsewhere in Ashmole 61.
54 See Paxson, 'Personification's gender', for an extended analysis challenging this understanding – and offering what has in the twenty years since that article's publication displaced the previous axiom.
55 In this, the poem also calls back to the various kiss-agents of the preceding section of the manuscript.

4

Testimonial objects

The third quarter of Ashmole 61 teems with devotional texts that deploy varied strategies in pursuit of the household community's spiritual education and refinement: Maidstone's *Seven Penitential Psalms* (item 32), *The Prick of Conscience Minor* (item 33), a fused poem combining *The Adulterous Falmouth Squire* and *The Sinner's Lament* (item 35), *The Wounds and the Sins* (item 38), and *Vanity* (item 40).[1] A number of these poems were very popular among medieval audiences, yet when engaged by modern readers, they can be rendered effectively illegible. That is, when the poems find themselves in an interpretive environment that lacks vital components (such as familiarity with medieval religious practices, appreciation of repetition, comfort with intense human self-loathing), they can become fixed in place, unable to move or be moved. As a result, they can be and historically have been disregarded, deemed unresponsive to literary analysis. This chapter undertakes to exercise Mark Amsler's view that 'affective literacy challenges the assumption, in the Middle Ages and today, that reading is unilateral consumption and a text is a discrete object'. To read affectively is to commune compassionately with a text and thus become receptive to its varied effects. 'In this respect', Amsler continues, 'affective literacy foregrounds the hinge of reading which opens and closes a gap between reader and text, between the skin of the page and the reading body, between understanding and response, repetition and difference.'[2] That gap between understanding and response, in particular, is one to which these Ashmole 61 poems call attention.

In dialogue with new materialism and affective literacy, shaded contours and alternate prospects can appear in this section of the manuscript. Throughout these poems, a viable community of forgiveness is shown to require the presence of the human, the divine, and the non-human. George Shuffelton has observed of three of these texts (*Psalms*, *Conscience*, and *Wounds*) that 'the suffering body of Christ helps the reader identify sin, develop genuine contrition for sin, and remedy sin'.[3] In conjunction with that strategic process of preparation for penance, variant ecologies are perceptible in all of these texts – in particular, sin assemblages lacking the divine – that demonstrate vividly the necessity of all actants to the production of a forgiveness collective. The texts refuse the view that God's mercy is the only essential element in forgiveness; without elements other than the divine, forgiveness itself – a vital good – would not exist. Further, although penance might seem a purely spiritual issue, the emphasis in this section of the manuscript on the materiality of the agents (including God, in the form of the embodied Christ) reminds readers that penance is an act in the world, a set of earthly affective practices with moral impact. These affective practices also confirm that – as Jane Bennett says of a historic blackout in New York City – 'there is not so much a doer (an agent) behind the deed … as a doing and an effecting by a human-nonhuman assemblage'.[4] The doing, in the case of these poems, is the penance enacted by an ad hoc forgiveness apparatus, whose rarity is underscored by the impossibility of penance when one element (pride, for instance) compels the exclusion of the divine.

Affective literacy: reading (against) sin

A short, widely distributed, fourteenth-century Middle English poem, *The Wounds and the Sins* (item 38, fols. 150v–151r, straddling the break between quires 12 and 13), exemplifies the ways in which Ashmole 61 consistently materialises religious truths.[5] In particular, the metaphysical abstractions that make penance necessary and absolution possible – sin and grace, respectively – become in this section of the manuscript material agents collaboratively generating new spiritual states. Among these agents are the illicit desires of humans and the sacrificial love of God, both elements expressed in full-on affective embodiment in *The Wounds and the Sins*. This poem serves as a tool for practising the Devotion to the Wounds, which claimed its greatest support during the historical period of the original audience for Ashmole 61, as witnessed by the establishment of the Mass of the Five Wounds in the fourteenth century.[6] The poem begins with the incipit *Sequitur septem peccata mortalia* ('Here follow the seven deadly sins') and consists of eight tetrameter quatrains, each of which is preceded by a heading centred above the stanza, surrounded by abnormally abundant white space in which it floats, grabbing attention and declaring the showcased sin (the first, for instance, is 'Agens pride', the second 'Agens envy', and so on).[7] The preposition that recurs in each subheading – 'agens' or 'against' – seems to imply an oppositional relationship; in this poem, it suggests as well the possibility of a turning, a conversion.[8] Each subheading's call to consider the particular deadly sin seems to have included each respective quatrain's goal of turning the reader against the sin and thus converting them through the following lines that counter the sin. The poem is primarily spoken by Christ, each quatrain describing one of his wounds as well as its source. Structurally, Christ asserts a direct cause-and-effect connection between the moral actions of earthly agents and the suffering of the divine body, and with this the poem justifies the call for turning away from each sin.

Immediately in the very first stanza ('Ayens pride'), Christ vividly reminds the reader that 'Wyth scherp thornys that be kene / My hede was crounyd [crowned], as ye may sen [see]. / The blod ran done be [on] my cheke [cheeks]; / Thou, prowde man, therfor be meke' (1–4). That the sharp, cruel thorns enact the pride of the sinful human being addressed is conveyed through the structural positioning of the two objects (thorns and pride) on one side of 'therefore' and the advised contrary human action (to 'be meke') on the other. Three lines delineate the physical torture and its effects; the final one admonishes the sinner and encourages alternative spiritual behaviour to prevent physical agony. Later in the third quatrain ('Ayens glotony'), the speaking Christ observes that 'In all my thirst upon the rode [cross] / Men gaffe me drynke that was not gode, / Azell [Vinegar] and gall for to drynke; / Gloton, theron I rede [advise] thou thinke' (9–12). The glutton being addressed, like the men at the cross, misuses the resources necessary to life by hoarding them for himself. In this act he not only demonstrates his sin through his improper treatment of material objects but also in producing others' suffering.

Sin, the poem demonstrates repeatedly through presenting a series of such cases, is the active and inappropriate participation in moral-material compounds that cause others harm. In this, not only the human but also the non-human bears responsibility, in its particular distinctive destructive qualities. In line 5, for instance, the 'scherp spere was full *yll*' (that is, 'evil'; italics added); in line 1, the 'scherp thornys' are 'kene' ('cruel, savage').[9] These items, like the human sinner, are acknowledged to have emotional agency and even intent. The objects in conjunction with the sinful humans past and present carry certain affective practices that cause real, damaging effects that are simultaneously and inseparably physical and spiritual.

Each quatrain presents a specific sin assemblage in which misdirected human desires (pride, gluttony) and misdirected non-human agents (vinegar pretending to be water, thorn acting as a knife) combine with the vulnerable human-divine body (head, cheek, blood, throat) to produce bodily torment and moral harms. Further, the poem connects the crucifixion – specifically, the wounds on the body of Christ – affectively to the sins that the Church teaches made his sacrifice necessary in the first place. Christ requires that the audience acknowledge the effects of sin, taking seriously the agents that make possible its genesis and experiencing it through their sorrow at having contributed to Christ's suffering: he says, in those vibrant first two lines, 'Wyth scherp thornys that be kene / My hede was crounyd, as ye may *sen*' (1–2; emphasis added). All demand witness: the speaking voice of Christ, the direct reference to the attacks on his body through seeing the wounds themselves (requiring imaginative visualisation on the part of the reader), and the act of *making* the wounds, including the resulting blood, thirst, and pain, through the acts of the vicious objects. The reader, to experience the forgiveness necessary to be incorporated once again in an affective divine-human community, must (as ordered in the final line of each quatrain) think (4, 12), learn (8), be meek (12), cease (16), forgive (20), and – in the last line spoken by Christ – 'Behold' (28).

The poem concludes that the act of reading – like the act of beholding, like the act of praying – is a penitential act. In this, it demonstrates the late medieval experience wherein 'texts were understood to inspire mental images, and ... reading and seeing "were part of the same bodily operation, involving perception and cognition in the search for knowledge"'.¹⁰ Its final quatrain differs from some other versions of the poem, in this case presenting a prayer in the voice of the human who has been listening to Christ's verses, now speaking back to Jesus, who has himself become the listener: 'Jhesu, for thi wondys fyve, / Kepe hem wele in ther lyve / That this lesson wyll rede / And therwith ther saulys fede' (29–32).¹¹ The prayer request is made in the name of Christ's bodily suffering as evidenced in each of the wounds, to feed the soul of the willing human reader, who will be fed 'therwith' – fed with this lesson, it implies, but also, reaching back, fed with the five wounds. The syntactical and temporal multiplicity are enabled by the poetry of the commentary, with 'for' and 'hem' playing diverse semantic roles that turn the human listener's prayer into a request that the wounds – the products of human sin, as each stanza has articulated, and thus presumably a problem, a wrong – themselves be well kept by Christ in order that they might feed the souls of those readers who learn the poem's truths, the readers in turn being kept well through that nourishment.

The material-affective approach made possible through poetic play is supplemented by the hybrid schema of the poem, in which the five wounds are indivisibly connected to the seven deadly sins – five quietly transformed into seven. The left hand's wound is associated with covetousness, the right hand's wound with wrath; the bleeding feet with sloth; the heart (presumably equivalent to the wound in the side) with envy. From there, the wounded head is associated with pride, although Christ's head is not among the conventional five wounds; further, the other two 'wounds' are the soldiers' feeding him vinegar (associated with gluttony) and his being born to a human mother (associated with lechery). Christ says 'Of a clene meyden [pure virgin] I was born / To save mankynd that was forlorn [lost], / And suffyrd deth for manys syn [man's sin]; / Lecher, of luste I rede [advise] thee blyne [cease]' (13–16). The feeding of vinegar and the being born of a virgin are even less like the five wounds than is the unconventional wound of the head pricked by thorns; they are certainly torments, however, the former (drinking vinegar) more familiarly evoking physical suffering than the latter (being born human). Shuffelton notes that the equivalent line to 'Of a clene meyden I was born' (13) is, in Cambridge University Library MS

Ff.5.48, 'Alle my body was beten for sin', which he observes seems 'a clearer allusion to the Scourging' than is the earthly human birth of Ashmole 61's *Wounds and Sins*.[12] Focusing on Christ's taking on human physicality appears here to be itself a wound, standing in for the beating he received as part of the crucifixion, otherwise absent here. Human birth can be acknowledged as a diminishment of Christ's usual full apparent divinity, yet it is an uncommon point of attention within the poem's repeated structures.

The poem makes a number of such puzzling assertions: the five wounds are equal to seven sins, in a poem of seven stanzas (one per sin) with a final concluding stanza; each sin is a direct cause of a wound (that relationship emphasised through 'therefore' and 'thus' adverbs) that in most cases bears no clear physical relationship to the effects of the sin. Rosemary Woolf has said of the poem that it exhibits a 'lack of congruity in subject matter', and indeed the logic is obscure even as it is asserted.[13] Shuffelton observes that the production of this poem 'involved taking some liberties with the representations of the wounds … but the appeal of making these two lists correspond seems to have outweighed the difficulties'.[14] Those difficulties, however, remain significant and unaddressed by the poem: since '[t]he mnemonic potential of these kinds of schemes was widely appreciated by the laity, and such numerical schema offered a useful means of catechism',[15] the individual penitent reader of *The Wounds and the Sins* would be all the more likely to notice the expansion from five to seven. Indeed, the five wounds were ubiquitous in religious textual description and visual iconography. Making such a change to the anticipated schema in such a highly conventional setting drew attention to itself and thereby encouraged thought, reflection, questioning.[16] The final stanza's focus on the act of reading as prayer suggests that the act of reading the poem and meditating on the possible relationships between the given wound, a product of individuals living at the time of Christ, and the sins performed by temporally present readers was itself a practice that made possible penitential cleansing. The poem is a penitential object, circulating with penitential possibilities and practices attached, and available for adaptation in every instance. And it reveals that the sacrificial love of God and the desires of humans are not abstractions expressed *through* the material world; rather, in the appropriate combination, they together *enact* forgiveness *in* the world.

Affective literacy: reading as embodied penitence

Perhaps the most emotionally wrenching poem in this affectively attuned collection, Maidstone's *Seven Penitential Psalms* (item 32, fols. 108r–119v) displays the shared participation of humans and the divine in generating forgiveness. This outcome is naturalised through and grounded in similarities between humans and Christ, and it is further identified through Christ's affiliations with non-human elements of creation. This 909-line poem is a vernacular translation of the psalms traditionally thought to have been written by David to atone for his having committed adultery and murder.[17] By the time of Ashmole 61, these psalms (6, 31, 37, 50, 101, 129, 142, in the Vulgate), which came to be considered the 'penitential psalms', had long been associated specifically with Lent.[18] Maidstone and others (in later medieval England, Richard Rolle and Eleanor Hull)[19] combined these psalms with commentary provided by Ambrose, Augustine, Cassiodorus, pseudo-Gregory the Great, Alcuin, and Peter Lombard. Maidstone's poem consists of a series of stanzas in which the first two lines present a portion of the psalms in Latin, the next 2–4 lines translate this into Middle English, and the following 4–6 lines provide commentary on or expand obliquely the idea presented in that translation, often turning to the Passion, Incarnation, and Redemption, all wholly absent from the original psalms, given their Old Testament provenance.

In Maidstone's rendering of these psalms he extends their poetry through the commentary, where he mingles historic and religious past with the present and the local, in terms of language, culture, and species. Lynn Staley highlights what appears to be a deliberate detachment of Maidstone's *Psalms* from their historic source. While most of these psalms begin with a first line referencing David (for instance, Psalm 6 begins 'Unto the end, in verses, a psalm for David, for the octave'), '[n]o version of this poem [that is, Maidstone's] opens by locating the Psalms within the context of David's life, *as almost all other translations do*'.[20] Further, this is one of the texts in the collection where Rate 'has extensively altered the language of the text' and 'introduces a large number of idiosyncratic readings' by, for instance, leaving out four lines from each (that is, half) of Maidstone's stanzas on Psalm 129.[21] Maidstone and Rate together enable the commentary to manifest emotion by highlighting the spiritual and emotional enmeshment – even similarity of subjectivity – provided by non-human creatures and entities (among them, the divine-human hybrid Christ himself) with whom humans share the earth.

These psalms earned their name for being imposed on penitents, holding the promise of God's mercy; that is, appropriate affective practice in conjunction with this circulating object produces absolution. Staley observes that the *Penitential Psalms* 'offer a path for conversion that begins in measured and empathetic reading',[22] a manner of reading encouraged by poems throughout this section of the manuscript. The verses here express the suffering of the human speaker, often presented in terms of Christ's experience of suffering on the cross – which is, in one extended section of the poem, expressed directly by Christ (again, notably missing from the Old Testament original), in dialogue with the human speaker. Following on the original psalms, this poem emphasises in its translations and commentary the experience of the individual speaking voice, which represents Christians broadly, just as in this section of the manuscript (in *The Wounds and the Sins*, for instance), the speaking Christ or Mary represents religious truth within the community of believers, as it does elsewhere in Ashmole 61 (the *Short Charter of Christ* and *The Lament of Mary*, among others). The experience of the speaker is presented first-hand, in their own voice, describing the pain and making it available to become a cause of the reader's own embodied understanding, their com-passion, their empathy, with the emotion deployed to achieve a particular end.

Maidstone's *Seven Penitential Psalms* performs the work later continued in the collection by *The Wounds and the Sins* to detail how Christ's physical pains are a literal product of an immoral human/non-human violence assemblage. Alongside this, however, this poem repeatedly rests lyrically in shared moments of physical suffering, emphasising Christ's humanity through humanity's Christlikeness. The penance of the (representative) human speaker occurs through emotional and physical torment that echoes Christ's on the cross, as when the human speaker laments, addressing God: 'On me thy hond lyghet hevyly [lies heavily], / And I ame turned in my wo, / With thornes priked grevosly. / Ther prykyth perylous thornes two / Of synne and peyn – this fele wele I' (106–10). The pricking of the thorns recalls Christ's crown of thorns, and the pains are tangibly felt by the speaker; though for the human sufferer, these perilous thorns are specifically sin and pain – which were, *The Wounds and the Sins* demonstrate, the true sources of Christ's suffering as well: human sin, manifest in material violence, producing corporeal pain for God. Shuffelton describes this poem as '[s]trongly Christological', repeatedly using 'the Passion as a way of allegorising the suffering spoken by the speaker of the psalms'.[23] This allegorising enacts a shared moment of physical suffering with moral origins, putting Christ and humanity – as represented by the single human voice, detached in Maidstone's version from the historical David – in the same position.

This physical experience of spiritual pain continues for the repentant but not yet absolved human speaker, echoing throughout Christ's experience of spiritual torment made possible specifically through his human embodiment: 'For thy arwys [arrows] ben in me ipyght [placed]; / Thou hast sette fast on me thy hond' (201–2), recalling Christ's wounding and beating in the crucifixion; and 'For in my flessch is ther non hele [health] / In presens of thi wrethly face. / My bones wanten [lack] pese and wele / For synne that me thus deface' (209–12), the flesh and bones lacking peace and health because of anger and sin. Poetry enables the physical expression of the effects of sin on the human subject, simultaneous agent of sin as well as its victim: in one commentary, the speaker observes,

> And thei that thought to do me skathe
> Spoke wordys that were veyne.
> And all the dey, both late and rathe,
> They thought on gyle and upon treyne [tricks],
> Bot when thei fynd mosse and mathe [maggots]
> And brymblys growyng upon ther breyne
> Than wyll the soth hymselve unswathe [the truth reveal/uncover itself]. (289–95)

The spiritual truth ultimately reveals itself in this prophecy through the grotesque, if entirely natural, actions of non-human antagonists: moss, maggots, and brambles, growing on the human attackers' brains, post-mortem.

Just as human sin defaced Christ by requiring him to take on human form, necessitating that he be distant from God in his incarnation on earth, it defaces and distances the embodied human from God. The loose (mis-)translation that the poet offers with

'My wondys ben all roten and ranke / After the face of my foly' (225–6)[24] increases connections to Christ through the 'wounds' (associated so fully with Christ's bodily torment on the cross) while marking human distinctions in the corruption-by-sin of the speaker's wounds, produced 'After' (226), or 'so as to resemble',[25] the 'face', the embodied appearance of the speaker's folly. Christ's wounds, in direct contrast, though caused by human sins as well, are themselves so pure that they are a site of comfort to humans and are capable of cleansing sin. Here the wounds and sins (for the sinner, not for Christ) are equivalent and depend for healing upon Christ's mercy.

Christ also recounts his own suffering here, as he did in *The Wounds and the Sins*.[26] Notably, this is a significant shift in voice from that of the original psalms, voiced by a human speaking in an Old Testament setting wherein there is no extant Messiah. In the case of Maidstone's *Seven Penitential Psalms*, transferring the words of the human speaker of the original to those of Christ in the translation and commentary structurally equates the position of the human speaker and the divine. More specifically here, while the human speaker busily presents his own suffering through Christ's, Christ conveys his experience of physical woe by turning to the experiences of other animate and inanimate earthly objects, and not to those of humans.[27] For instance, 'I was made lyke the pylicane [pelican] / In wyldernes ther hymselve slethe [slays]. / So redyly to the rode [cross] I rane / For mans saule to sufyr dethe' (585–8). The first line begins to translate the Latin ('I am become like a pelican of the wilderness; I am like a night raven in the house')[28] but adds the reference to the self-slaying that is absent in the Latin and in the psalms and instead comes from popular tradition dating back to before Christianity.[29] The stanza's third and fourth Middle English lines capitalise on the added reference to the pelican's suicide, observing that it is Christ's nature, as it is the pelican's, to sacrifice himself in the wilderness – the pelican for its young, Christ for sinful humanity. A comparison that represents Christ as engaging in suicide is potentially tarnished by associations with despair and is thus a morally risky comparison (as it was not in the original psalm, which lacks both a divine speaker and a suicide reference). Yet the comparison with a non-human subject enables the central shared quality to predominate: the willed yet naturally impulsive production of one's own death to save others (emphasised by his running to the cross), in the wilderness.

The translation of the second half of the Latin line then appears in the fifth line of the stanza: 'And as a nyght crow in hyr hous can / By nyght se to holt and heythe [in woods and heath], / So soveryd [suffered] I to save man' (587–91). The comparison here is not rooted in a clear if unanticipated parallel the way it was with the pelican: instead, it seems that Christ suffered in the way the crow has the ability to see in the darkness. The next line of the psalm (in the Vulgate, Psalm 101:8) reads, 'I have watched', but the situational connection with Christ's suffering in this stanza seems to reside specifically in his being able to see in the dark – perhaps the metaphorical darkness of the human sinner's existence. The associations evoked by this simile seem to offer little to enhance Christ's action of willed sacrifice, beyond emphasising the innate clarity of his perception and thus the wisdom of that sacrifice. Maidstone's *Psalms* delays the 'I have watched' until the following stanza, which begins with the Latin lines, 'I have watched, and am become as a sparrow all alone on the housetop'.[30] Christ says, 'I woke in wo, made lyke the sperow [sparrow] / That in the rofe is solytary. / Upon the tre my nest was narrow: / Theron myght I no brydys carye [chicks carry]' (593–6).[31] His experience hanging, alone, on the cross, with no room for others, is that of the sparrow: solitary woe. Christ says he was 'made like' each given bird, with the experience transforming him into a different animate object, imaginatively expanding the more familiar model of his having become human. The larger effect seems to be the association of Christ's actions and qualities with those of recognisable earthly creatures, however overextended at times the poetic reach.

Christ's body is even like the earth, in this stanza, tilled for the benefit of others: 'As erth is hurlyd under the harow [the ground is turned] / So was my flessch that sprong [was born] of Mary' (597–8). Violence to a body – be it earthly or divine – paradoxically engenders life, in both cases, with an emphasis on Christ's own earthliness through the reference to his body's being born of Mary's. Christ powerfully finds all of creation available for intersubjectivity: at the start of his second spoken stanza, he describes himself as 'Smyten I was lyke gresse [grass] or hey' (569), a close translation of the Latin that precedes this line, though here spoken by Christ rather than by a human speaker as in the original.[32] Christ thus shares in full humanity and, as something more than simply an extension of that identity, full earthliness. His first spoken stanza begins, 'For my lyve deys, lyke the smoke, / Have feyled and aweywerd hyed [fled]. / My bones be dryed and all thrught soke [sucked dry] / Lyke a thing that were forfryghed [fried]' (561–4). This translation develops and intensifies the imagery suggested by the Latin: 'For my days are vanished like smoke, and my bones are grown dry like fuel for the fire'.[33] It provides the smoke with intention, now not only vanishing as in the Latin but actively fleeing away, even as it removes the instrumentality of the dried wood of the Latin simile, with the bones now actively sucked dry (not only 'growing' so) and fried – presumably to a crisp and beyond what would be useful as fuel.

The human speaker responds to Christ's 71-line speech – all prompted by nine verses of Psalm 101[34] – in the following stanza, the Latin at its head conveying verse 13. The human voice here responds,

> *Tu autem, Domine, in eternum permanes et* [But thou, O Lord, endures forever and]
> *Memorial tuum in generacionem et genercionem* [thy memorial to all generations].
> Thy mynd abydeth in every kynde,
> For thi godhed was noyghed [affected] never;
> Ther was no schowre [suffering] that it myght schend [ruin].
> Thy manhed myght men wele dysever [destroy];
> Therof thei made a reufull ende.
> Therfor ilke man is thee lever [dearer to you]
> That this matyr wyll have in mynde [will meditate on this matter].[35]
> Bot sertys, Lord, thou lyfyst ever. (633–40)

The Middle English translation offered for the first Latin line reads 'Your mind abides in every nature'.[36] This is a dramatic departure from the literal modern English translation of 'But thou, O Lord, endures forever'. It seems similarly to have little to do with the next Latin line, 'and thy memorial [endures] to all generations'. The divine quality of endurance is all but left behind – delayed until the last line of eight in the stanza – and the multi-generational perspective is completely ignored. Instead, the translation attends to the distribution of the divine throughout all of creation (temporally horizontal rather than vertical in orientation) – God's mind residing in 'every kynde'. It also insists that such distribution alters the divine itself not at all, affected 'never'. The next lines draw attention to God's human embodiment in the form of Christ, with no suffering able to tarnish that divinity, despite the attempts of humans to destroy Christ's humanity. The stanza concludes with the end result of that situation: whatever person appropriately ponders God's 'mynd' – including its residence in all of creation – will be beloved by God.

Later, following on the section of Christ's speaking, the poem further establishes the relationship between the divine and the earthly in surprisingly mundane ways that are right at home in the household. Here, Psalm 101:27 spreads across two stanzas. The Latin lines are:

Ipsi peribunt, tu autem permanes, et omnes / sicut vestimentum veterascent.
They shall perish, but thou remainest, and all of them shall grow old like a garment. (740a-b)

Et sicut oportorium mutabis eos et mutabuntur; / tu autem idem ipse es et anni tui non deficient.
And as a vesture thou shalt change them and they shall be changed; but thou art always the self-same, and thy years shall not fail. (748a-b)

In the Middle English translations and extensions that Maidstone/Rate present for this verse, the relationship between God and the humans he created appears in terms of everyday materials crafted and used by humans. The speaker translates *sicut vestimentum veterascent* ('all of them shall grow old like a garment') as 'all schall elde [grow old] *lyke a cloth*' (741–2). The more specialised significance of 'garment' is widened to reference, very generally, any fabric. The noun can be modified in Middle English as today to indicate certain qualities, adding 'of gold' or 'of blue', or to indicate certain purposes, as 'of religion' or 'of widwehod', or compounded with an adjective, for instance to produce 'bordcloth' (tablecloth).[37] 'Cloth' on its own points functionally towards any and all such fabrics. While 'cloth' enables an end-rhyme with 'loth' two lines later, the poet and scribe demonstrate no resistance to increasing the generalisation in order to create that rhyme. The speaker a few lines later prophesies, in translation of the second half of the Latin line, 'And thou schalt *as a coverlyte* [bed sheet] / Them change, and thei schall changyd be' (749–50; italics added). In the Latin here being translated 'coverlyte' is *oportorium*, or 'covering', which the Douay-Rheims English translation presents more specifically as 'vesture'.[38] While the Latin might imply an aristocratic or clerical register, and the alternative translation as 'covering' remains very general, Maidstone/Rate take the opportunity to rhyme with 'perfyte' and narrow the image to that of the 'coverlyte' or bed sheet.[39] The Middle English domesticates the fabric in both of these cases, making it everyday, generic cloth in the first case, and then the cloth that protects the bed, as well as the sleeping human, and is regularly changed, in the second.

Serving similarly to diminish the distance between the mundane and the divine, the commentary in another section deploys earthly imagery that is not in the Latin on which it expands: 'Withcalle [Recall] me nought in the halvyndele [halfway point] / In my deys throughoute the yere, / For thei passe oute [away] as the myddey mele [mealtime], / And slyden out as cloudys clere' (725–8) are the first two lines purportedly translating the Latin *Ne revoces me in dimedio dierum meorum; / in generacionem et gereracionem anni tui*, or (in modern English translation) 'Call me not away in the midst of my days; the years are unto generation and generation'.[40] In Ashmole 61, these lines and what follows shift the scale from looking towards future descendants, taking a centuries-long view of the sort only God can truly see, with the 'generation and generation' with which the psalm concludes. The Middle English instead moves towards the intimate, personal perspective of the days of the year and their passage, compared to the universal experience of a meal that leaves one hungry too soon, or the vision of clouds that pass away from the sky – turning instead towards a much more immediate and human temporal scale immersed in the embodied present.

Christ in his appearances in Maidstone's *Psalms* fully experiences earthliness, sharing in the human perspective through his human embodiment. This builds to the strongest and most common association of Christ's body with earthly objects: the Eucharist. Christ announces that on the cross, 'For als it were brede [bread] of askys [ashes] I ette, / Wepyng I mengyd [mixed] with drynke among' (609–10). This translation seems to convey the verses of the psalm quite closely: the original (in modern English) is 'For I did eat ashes like bread, and mingled my drink with weeping'.[41] The more meaningful transformation here is not linguistic, nor does it rely on figures of speech; instead, the significance depends on the fact that these words are now spoken not by David or another repentant human but rather by Christ himself, and they are uttered in the midst of his detailed description of his experience of physical suffering during the Passion. Literally transforming while in process on the cross, Christ's ashes are bread, his tears drink. The rich earthly imagery of the psalms encourages extensive contemplation of the various aspects of God's union with the human and the non-human – with this union being based in shared suffering and generating forgiveness in the world.

In the midst of building such mutual experiences and qualities, however, the poem also presents contrasts between humans and animals. Following the lead of the Latin that heads two stanzas (Psalm 31:9), humans who indulge their desires and concern themselves only with how they live here and now are likened to mules and horses that lack understanding. The first half of the verse becomes, in a close translation, 'Ne fareth not as muyle ne hors / In whych non understondyng is' (163).[42] In the following stanza, the first two lines of the Middle English translate the Latin there closely as well, so that those who are kept away from God because of sin are presented as being led like horses: the speaker says to the Lord, 'In bernacle and brydell [bit and bridle] thou constreyn / The chekys of them that negheh thee nought [who do not draw near to you]' (169–70).[43] The divine agent is forced to treat the rebellious human soul just as humans treat horses, physically limiting their agency to guide them productively, ultimately to lead them (in the case of humans) to God. Maidstone and Rate elsewhere bring in, through the commentary, comparisons that highlight the shared experiences of agents across what are typically thought of as different strata of subjectivity; here, however, the continuation of the Latin verse's equation of sinful man and mindless, labouring beasts indicates that the earthly world beyond the human retained its use as negative, undesirable contrast to ideal human identity. Such a sinner 'doyth no better than beyste or byrde' (86).

Similarly, worms, those without conscience, are constant reminders of the future of the human body after death; while the worms are not condemned for this behaviour, there is a confident assumption that all would prefer to avoid becoming a human-worm hybrid living in the earth. One stanza, for instance, ends its reflection on the psalm with 'When he is closyd in a cloute [wrapped in a shroud]

/ To woune within the wormys walle [the worm's domain]' (343–4). Here the body is living within the walls – in the community of – the worm, but also within the walls of the worm itself, that is, inside the worm's body after being eaten, for the commentary on Psalm 31:9 observes (warning against being like a horse or mule, with no understanding), in a sharp expansion on that verse, 'thi courruptabull corse [body] / Is nought bot wormys mete, iwys [indeed)]' (165–6). Such imagery is certainly in line with the *contemptus mundi* mood of this section of the Psalms (the biblical as well as the Maidstone/ Rate versions), as seen in depictions of the frailness of the human body: 'For freylty hath full fyllyd my reynes [organs], / And in my flessch ther is non helthe' (241–8, a translation of Psalm 37:8), not to mention the disgust it engenders: 'Behold, in synne I was consevyd / Of my modour as men bene all / And of my fader not resevyd [received nothing] / Bot flessch full frele to synne to fall' (416–20).[44]

Throughout Maidstone's *Seven Penitential Psalms*, the emotional distress that the speaker of the biblical Psalms exhibits in response to his and others' torments – physical as much as spiritual – is amplified in the choices for translation of scripture and in the commentary to follow, commentary itself translating and adapting the writings of other commentators. The recurring patterns across the Middle English poem reflect not a discernible intention of its poet and scribe but rather a set of discourses for experiencing and understanding spiritual pain and necessary suffering. Lynn Staley describes the voice throughout Maidstone's *Psalms* as that of one experiencing 'anguish'.[45] It is a voice expressing 'abject terror' followed by 'gratitude'.[46] In this context, these are all morally grounded emotions – that is, feelings produced by a recognition of spiritual danger. The conclusion of the poem includes this stanza that, in its development of the psalm it translates, draws together the poem's affective purposes:

> *Expandi manus meas ad te; anima mea* [I stretched forth my
>   hands to thee; my soul]
> *Sicut terra sine aqua tibi* [is as earth without water unto thee]
> To thee, Lord, my hondys I sprede.
> My saule is lyke lond waterles;
> I may not wepe, I ame so bade,
> So bareyn and so sorowles.
> Synne settys [besets] me full sade;

Therfor, I pray thee, Prince of Pese,
Helpe that I some teres hade,
That gostly frute myght have encrese. (836a-43)

Elsewhere in the poem, the speaker has an excess of tears produced by the intensity of his feelings of shame and guilt. Here, in contrast, the speaker's soul is so dry that he cannot weep and prays to God requesting tears so that he might increase his spiritual 'frute'. Specifically, it is sorrow that is lacking – his soul 'so bareyn and so sorowles' and, in conjunction with that, 'bade'. The poetic expansion of the psalm takes the representation of the soul as an incomplete creation, earth without water, and associates this lack of water with a lack of tears that thus reflects a lack of true sorrow, a land barren and unable to yield life. Sorrow conveyed, according to the *Middle English Dictionary*, 'Emotional or mental distress, grief, sadness; anxiety, care'.[47] The speaker's plea is itself a product of his sorrow, and yet he feels lacking in sorrow without the tears that his dry soul cannot, itself, generate. Lynn Staley observes of this poem that in it, 'Sorrow produces a new way of seeing both the self and God.'[48] The speaker here seems to be right in the thick of that process, working towards a new way of seeing, and yet the speaker finds it impossible to reach fulfilment without the physical affect-agent of tears to complete this spiritual transformation. This experience manifests for the speaker and, ultimately, the reader the necessity of the body – the tear-producing object – to the process of sorrow, penance, and possible redemption.

Affective literacy: rendering mundane monstrosity

In *The Prick of Conscience Minor* (item 33, fols. 120r–128r), material agents emphasise that penance is possible only in the earthly world (and its extension, purgatory) and vividly communicate the tangible horrors of eternal damnation – including what happens to the human subject existing independently of the non-human divine. The 'prick' of the title is quite literal in this regard: in the previous two texts penitent readers must behold the sufferings of Christ, and share the suffering of the sinner, and through the emotional trauma of imagining those images perceive the violence of sin; here, the focus shifts to beholding the repulsiveness of sin directly and sensing it physically (rather than perceiving it through its effects on others) so that the reader might as a result 'begyne thi pride to sese [stop]' (376) – that is, leave the pride that is the foolish belief in the possibility of human independence and self-integrity. To achieve this goal, the poem's depictions of the human reveal that when deprived of the divine – as when steeped in unrepented sin – the subject is *insufficiently human*. The human–divine union that *Wounds and Sins* and Maidstone's *Psalms* actively represent as the aspirational model appears here in its reduced form, as a monstrosity produced by the estrangement that sin generates.

The Prick of Conscience enjoyed enormous popularity in the Middle Ages, extant in over 115 manuscripts, more than any other Middle English verse text. It was even translated into Latin prose and copied many times in that form – all of this despite being more than 9,600 lines long and a relatively late production composed in northern England in the mid-fourteenth century. The poem was quickly abridged, one of those abridgements being the version in Ashmole 61 (produced in 1380 or earlier) and extant in seven other copies: *The Prick of Conscience Minor* (called 'Stimulus Consciencie Minor' in some cases such as Ashmole 61, with that title used for the text by its most recent editor, Shuffelton). Only about half of this poem – its first 424 lines (of 784) – uses *The Prick of Conscience* as its source, the section wherein the complete long poem adapts Innocent III's *De miseria*, which inspired the textual branch of the *contemptus mundi* tradition.[49] The middle section of *The Prick of Conscience Minor* (lines 425–648) has no clear source; the source for the final lines (648–784) is the *Compendium theologice Veritatis* of Hugh Ripelin of Strasbourg, which was in wide circulation. This abbreviated *Prick of Conscience* moves from a focus in its first half on the afterlife to what Shuffelton describes as the 'messy physicality of human existence' in its second half.[50]

The Prick of Conscience Minor presents the human-sin agent through its ongoing limited materiality, from conception to death (referred to throughout in terms of that death-state, the human subject identified with the compound 'wormys mete' and, literally rather than metonymically, as 'rotyn erth and stynkyng cley' [403–4]). The poem requires the reader to recognise the incomplete and corrupt nature of this alternative, ultimately powerless entity. In the first two stanzas, the anonymous human speaker calls on God for assistance in living on earth sufficiently well so as to be with God after death, the immediate focus and ultimate goal of the poem. The speaker – simultaneously the member of the household who was reading the text, speaking these words to God – prays, 'Gyff us grace folys [sins] to fle, / And wele to lyve, and kepe us chaste / So that oure saulys may redy be / To god when we schall yeld the goste' (5–8). With this conventional preparation, the work of learning gets underway: the earth is 'this exile' (10), a place where the human prepares itself in order to go home to heaven, in the end, by making the self 'redy' for God (13). This life in exile is not just a lesser alternative to life with God: it is 'nought bot a ded lyvand [living death]' (18). What humans think of as 'living', which leads them to fear death, is itself dying (24), with 'Deth ... of endles lyve begynning' (33).

In order for death to paradoxically start life, one cannot simply 'be good' and 'live well', for that outcome requires knowledge that can be learned only through God: 'No man to dyghe [die] can be herdy [confident] / Bot [except] he that lyves wele throughe skylle [knowledge]' (15–16). This 'skylle' requires that the reader 'wyll lere [learn] / To lyve wele and ryghtfully, / And of gode and evyll hafe knawynge clere' (41–3). In order to learn clear understanding of good and evil so as to live properly in this living death, the reader must 'Weynd out [Depart (in one's mind)] every dey of thi lyve here / Throught thought, and forgete thi bodye' (45–6). The skill to learn and the knowledge to be gained can be done, the poem says, only through a practice of daily mental detachment from the fallen earthly body which will, it is then demonstrated, only drag down the human mind and its potential improvement.

The method and mode of the preceding text, Maidstone's *Seven Penitential Psalms*, offers a stark contrast, with intense 'emotion' repeatedly represented through visions of Christ's suffering as well as the human speaker's; Shuffelton describes the *Seven Penitential Psalms* as being 'balanced by ... logical scholastic structure'[51] in being followed by *The Prick of Conscience Minor*. Certainly the latter poem emphasises the human actions of 'learning' and 'knowing', 'thinking' and 'seeing' in place of the *Psalms*' singular sustained focus on 'feeling'. The only emotion *Conscience* calls on is being angry at sin: upon seeing heaven, 'At thi synne sore schuld thou tene [be sorely angry]', for the way sin 'pute thee fro that feyre cyté' (267–8). Where the penitent human speaker of the preceding poem pursued cleansing tears, a requisite physical culmination of the process of repentance and reconciliation, this poem presents no embodied human experience as productive of spiritual improvement: the body must be left behind for this achievement to be possible. The reader is encouraged from the start that 'if thou wyll knaw to lyve ryght, / Thou schall thi *thought* send unto helle' to 'se thorow *gostly syght* / More sorow and peyn than tong can telle' (81–2, 85–6, italics added).

And yet this knowing and thinking and spiritual sight are not performed through abstract contemplation. Rather, as Howell Chickering notes of the full-length *Prick of Conscience*,

> Many passages are explicitly designed to stimulate physical fear … in the reader or hearer as a first step toward contrition [and they] achieve this goal by an obsessive emphasis on bodily suffering, the pains of death, and the tortures of hell … by the frequency and intensity of their imagery and the repetitive pressure of their rhetoric … [that] seems intended mainly to scare its audience.[52]

Ellen K. Rentz puts it more bluntly: 'The *Prick of Conscience* aims to terrify.'[53] The central premise of the poem is that it is not enough to flee from sin in fear: one must intellectually learn to loathe it for its loathsome nature. The physical fear makes way for deep learning and knowing. In order to experience this new consciousness, the sinful reader must feel *now* the pains of hell that their sins merit, so that repentance and penance can take place before death and the reader's spiritual literacy may be improved, internalising a safe way of engaging with the world: feeling wholly disgusted by its seeming delights.

As George Shuffelton puts it, 'these comparisons rely on sensory experience in an attempt to make the afterlife palpable'.[54] In this, *Conscience* makes use of earthly elements, as did Maidstone's *Psalms*. There, the birds, grass, and smoke highlighted the deep connections between humans, Christ, and creation, in order to lead the reader to share in a vital emotion, recognising empathetically Christ's suffering and the reader's responsibility for that undeserved pain. Here, sensory experiences are again engaged, in this case with disgusting objects encouraging the necessary 'feeling now' through comparisons of the dire version in hell to the already painful version on earth: just as fire in the world is much hotter 'Than is the fyre that is peyntyd on a wowe [wall]' (98) – or, for that matter, than is described in words in a poem – the well-known and extreme pain of childbirth is but a 'bath of water clere' (168) compared to the 'peyn of fyre [in hell that] is so mekyll [much] to clens synnes sere [diverse]' (161–2). All that is painful abounds 'within helle gate', without restraint: 'of all that peyn is grete plenté, / And that peyn schall never abate' (90, 91–2), its fires everlasting, even if doused with 'all the water in the see' (95). All is richly represented through palpable material intensities. The souls burning in the fire of hell 'schall ther be ever duelland [dwelling] / To thei be fined [refined] clen therby / Als is the gold in fyre meltand' (174–6). The souls being purified in hell are presented here as objects – gold melting in fire that is the opposite of (and completely lacking the relief of) clear water. Gold that, like the soul, should be so valuable is instead laid waste by the fire. In response, there is only 'hungour, thyrst, and throng' – physical suffering – and in response, 'wepyng and dolefull song, / Gnastyng [Gnashing] of tethe and grysly chere [grim countenance]' (107, 109–10). Upon being urged to 'send thi thought furthermore / To purgatory' (153–4), that physical and emotional suffering continues, so strong 'That all the martres sufferd here ... / As to that peyne are nought to telle' (164, 167). At least purgatory's torments offer the possibility that 'In that fire thei schall duell there / Tyll that they of synne clensyd be' (157–8).

In demonstration of its cynical view of humanity as only potentially – and ultimately only post-mortem – in communion with the divine, *Conscience* finds much on earth that can be used to depict the horrors of hell. Earth is, this poem maintains, a reduced, less intense version of hell. Heaven, in contrast, cannot be represented through the fallen earth and is thus presented far less tangibly, in terms of 'myrth that passyth all manys myght' (211) and 'perfyte lufe that never schall sesse' (212). That it endures and is perfection and is beyond human possibility can be communicated; *what* has these qualities, however, cannot. At times the poet attempts material extremes to help convey it, by turning the scale beyond measure: 'ever grete fulnes of lyght' is there (209), 'Largenes of rowme [room] withouten prese [crowding]' (210), 'all maner of welthes endles, / And of all delytes grete plenté' (225–6). Generally speaking, heaven is a place lacking the limitations of the good (light, space, wealth) that earth requires. 'Ther is medys of halowys sere [many hallowed fields] / So mykell [much] that non them mesore [measure] may' (233–4): what is good on earth, abundant fields, is there without restriction. Ultimately, heaven's 'flowyng of more ryches / Than ever myght eye in this werld se' (227–8) is just that: impossible to see based on earthly experience. Hell, however, can easily be represented in its terms.

In deep contrast, earthly existence inhabits a series of circumscribed places, all of them bad and inappropriately esteemed by the misguided embodied human soul: 'Thinke wher thou arte and know in hast: / Thou arte here in a exile sene [seen] / That is the world that thou lovyst most' (377–9); the reader must 'think' and 'know' to perceive the true reality of their beloved home, which is actually 'a dale of sorow to tayst [experience]' (381), 'a wyldernes weyst [desolate]' (383), all of it 'Full of travell [labour], tarye [struggle], and tene [anguish]' (382) and 'full of angres [agonies] and of myschevys [afflictions]' (392). This programming continues, line after line, some softened by taking the form of similes, others direct renderings: the reader is in a forest of robbers and thieves (385–6), a 'se flowand [surging] / Full of wawys and stormys that grevys [injures]' (387–8), a burning oven 'full of fyre of synne that grevys' (389–90), and a foreign land of afflictions (380–92). Instead of demonstrating God's mercy through the suffering of Christ on the cross, *The Prick of Conscience Minor* reminds the reader of the human torment of the alternative, of what happens when mercy is not sought and the human is on its own: 'els had thou bene / Dampned to helle wihoutyn mersy' (455–6).

Not only are the different locations, tangibly presented, extreme in their sensory assaults, but the depiction of the human in its earthly form is utterly infected by the sinful nature of its home: 'And sethyn were thou conseyved and wrought / Of a porsyon of fowle matere [portion of foul matter]' (349–52) – and further, the reader is told, in your weakness at birth you were merely 'a skyne all blody dyght [skin made all bloody]' (360), and now 'Thou arte bot stynkand slyme withine, / And a sake [sack] full of fylthe pryvye [hidden filth] / That over is coveryd with a skyne' (362–64). To make matters worse, foulness begets foulness: 'Than comes of thee, both thyke and thine. / Ther comes non other fruyt of thee / Bot only fylth, stynke, and synne' (366–8). It is not simply contact with the contaminated earth – being composed of it at its basest, and of nothing else – that produces this awful object of filth: the individual human machine continually generates more and more of the same. This is first manifest purely physically, in a stanza forcing the reader to witness that 'on every partye [part] / What comes fro thy mouth and nose, / And fro other partys of thi body / When thou lyst [wish] here thi body es [to ease] / A fouler donge hyll of thi body / Saw thou never' (369–74). The effect of this endless and utter foulness is harm to the soul: 'What schame and vylonye / Thou doyst thi soull, bethink thee swythe [quickly]', the reader is urged. 'How foule thou makyst it [the soul] and uglye / Thorow syn that thou doyst here oft sythe': created in sin and of sin, the human befouls its own soul all the more through repeated sin. Thus the human makes the soul 'How pore, how nakyd and how nedye / Of all gode that schuld make it blythe [happy]', depriving it of good and destroying its potential bliss. Instead, 'How thrall thou makys it to thi bodye, / That to thi sawle schuld serve swythe [readily]' (513–18). The potentially complete human 'makes' the soul foul; lacking the divine, here in exile on earth, the deficient, overly physical human can produce only filth and sin and prevent its soul from reaching bliss.

There is no other possibility, the poem notes, in earthly exile: 'When thou schall anything begyne, / Withouten God thou may not spede [succeed]' (465–6). Repentance – the path to reunion with God – is necessary to reintegrate the matter of the sinful human with the divine object, restoring it to its appropriate state, and this is to be pursued on earth, where both human and divine are available for integration into this desired assemblage. Instead of demonstrating God's mercy as it was manifest in the suffering Christ on the cross here in the world, *The Prick of Conscience Minor* reminds the reader of the human torment of the alternative and its long-term effects, being 'Dampned to helle withoutyn mersy' (455–6). The sinful human will not simply not be *shown* mercy by God, but that unrepentant sinner will be free of – will *lack* – mercy, literally living without God. This temporary exile could become permanent, as this is the automatic progression of the sinful soul that lacks the benefit of a spiritual education made meaningful through sensory consciousness raising and cultural rehabilitation. Ultimately, after properly seeing and understanding these places – hell, purgatory, earth, and heaven – the reader will 'Behold thiselve than, flessche and felle [flesh and skin], / And this wrechyd world unserteyne. / When thou hast done as I thee telle, / Thou turne unto thiselve ageyne' (333–6). The reader will, upon completion of this training, see a different self, who will thus *be* a different self, one pursuing the prospect of reunion with the divine.

The delightful, hyperbolic disgust provoked by reading the abbreviated *Prick of Conscience* today, coupled with the intense popularity of the poem in the late Middle Ages, renders the dearth of modern literary analysis of the poem – in any of its lengths or varieties – surprising. Over the past century, the text has been addressed in published form by few scholars, the majority of whom have attended to dialect features or have announced additional manuscript copies newly discovered or have described a single manuscript or its scribe. In the 1990s the poem's contents gained attention as part of the developing scholarly study of vernacular theology, in which setting it has continued to contribute to understandings of medieval lay piety.[55] More recently, four literary investigations of the text have appeared in the second decade of the twenty-first century, which may signal a new critical popularity for the poem.[56] Among them is Moira Fitzgibbons's demonstration, as part of her in-depth reading of the full-length *Prick of Conscience*, of the poet's participation in a late medieval conversation (engaged in by Langland, Nicholas Love, and others) about human capacities of reason and thought.[57] As Fitzgibbons observes, tracing the kinds of learning assumed by the poem and the sorts of knowledge required to follow its teachings, 'Mental soundness is an unstated prerequisite for inclusion in the Christian community that the *Conscience*-poet envisions.'[58] Her observation affirms Shuffelton's assessment of this poem's turn from the emotional orientation of Maidstone's *Psalms* which precede it in the collection. And yet the learning is itself affective, rooted in the fear that is repeatedly generated for the reader by the relentless images of filth and corruption, nearly all of them features of the human subject, with very little pause for the delights that heaven might ultimately and eternally provide.[59]

Affective literacy: sensing sin

In the *exemplum* of *The Adulterous Falmouth Squire* (item 35b, fols. 136v–138v), Ashmole 61 provides an individual narrative portrait of the mercy-deprived sinful human existence of all humans that *The Prick of Conscience* so amply describes. This 195-line quatrain poem appears in seven manuscripts, which Rate precedes with a poem that elsewhere appears independently, *The Sinner's Lament* (item 35a, fols. 136r-v). Here, the two are presented as one. The lament, which originates in the first half of the fifteenth century, remains in six manuscripts and is presented in 99 lines of eight-line stanzas. The two poems Rate combines into one – an act that hid the separate sources of each poem from modern scholars for some time[60] – and together the text 'belongs to a widespread class of penitential lyrics in which the dead speak from the grave and deliver a warning to the living'. Susanna Fein observes that '[s]uch poems appeal directly to the emotions, to innate trust in what one sees, to sensorial knowledge of pain, and to each individual's primal sense of corporeal wholeness'.[61] In this, its methods have much in common with *Conscience*, but with a different orientation towards a unique representative human subject. Like *Conscience*, it encourages the reader to 'behold' and 'see' so that they might 'wyste' and 'thinke' (2, 37, 35, 85). More directly than does *Conscience*, this text emphasises emotional impact on the reader as an additional goal: repeatedly from the start, the figure is a 'dollfole wyght' (4) producing a 'dulfull syght' (2), describing a 'dolefulle deth' (34). The man, the sight, and the death they represent are sorrowful and evoke sorrow in the reader.[62] The knowing and thinking result from seeing – through the process of feeling – the speaking human subject's loss and its suffering.

This fused poem materialises morality in two different registers (one a lyric lament, the other a narrative *exemplum*), demonstrating faith in the affective agency of materiality. This agency extends even to Rate's naming the adulterous Falmouth squire, who is anonymous in other versions, 'Sir Wyllyam Basterdfeld' (7). By doing so, and doing so with such punning significance, Rate grounds and individualises this universally applicable example. Further, the speaker announces in the first stanza that he was 'Some tyme in Ingland duellyng' (5). In a line uttered between announcing his location and his name while alive, he asserts, 'Thys was trew, withouten lesyng' (6). The truth-claim combines with the individual and the local to encourage the reader to attend very closely to the figure as a representative of the self. Later in the poem, the adulterous squire observes that his horrible fate was decided 'Thirti wynter sene the dede' (55) in Falmouth, and he 'take[s] wytnes of Kyng Rycherd [II]' (18), deposed within the preceding century. The speaker is thus both geographically and temporally local to the reader, requiring very little emotional stretch and thus nearly guaranteeing empathy. Of the textually represented sinner, penance again demands direct acknowledgement of what the sinner would rather refuse, as the speaker commands at the start of his lament: 'All Crysten men that walke by me, / Behold and se this dulfull [doleful] syght' (1–2). The harms of sin must be witnessed, and the emotional impact experienced, and through that the painful truth learned, by the viewer.

By being provoked to sorrow with this doleful sight and story, the reader will not end up in the position of the speaker, who bemoans that for him, 'Than was to late of "Had I wyste!"' (35). Importantly, the speaker does eventually reveal 'I thought to amend me in my age' (65), despite having said earlier that 'I had no hape [occasion] whyll I was here / For to aryse and me repent' (20–1). The reader is aware that he had every occasion, and had full knowledge, since he had planned to repent at a more convenient later date. In this, the listener is shown that recognition must lead to immediate action. As with *The Prick of Conscience*, this poem emphasises the urgency of repenting: 'amend you whyle ye have space [time]. / For I have lost everlastyng lyght, / And thus of mercy can I gete no grace' (9–11). Over and again he asserts that for him, it is 'to[o] late' (23, 40).

Beyond mercy, 'thus' (36) and as a direct result, one becomes ontologically other, as seen in the torment of hell that he experiences: 'Thus ame I lappyd all aboute [surrounded] / With todys [toads] and snakys, as ye may se. / I ame gnawyn [gnawed] my body aboute' (36–8). The accursed speaker, and the poem, thus reveal in tangible terms what happens when, as *The Prick of Conscience* warned, one is 'Damned to hell without mercy'. One must eternally 'abyde as best [beast] in stalle' (73). An existence apart from the divine is not a fully human existence. Later, the soul of Basterdfeld's brother is seen in heaven, 'a creatoure / Als bright as any sonebeme' (180–1), contact with the divine generating a more-than-human existence.

When Basterdfeld's pious son prays to Mary and Jesus to see his father and to learn his eternal residence (85–7), an angel guides him through a hole in the ground to hell, showing him his father hanging by the genitals, burning, as 'Fendys bold with crowkys [crooks] kene / Rente hys fader fro lyth to leme [limb to limb]' (104–5). The lesson of this journey is that a forgiveness assemblage is possible only if it originates on earth: once he has died, the adulterous squire's soul is beyond reach, his pious son's daily prayers for his soul deprived of any positive effect. Hence the speaker's announcement in the very third line that 'It helpys not to calle ne cry, / For I ame dampned' (3–4). The benefit to be gained here is for the reader's soul, whoever will 'bewere be me' (54), and not for the speaker's, which is beyond assistance.

The angel next takes the son to heaven and shows him a beautiful meadow with one hundred thousand singing birds (pelican, popinjay, 'tymour' [songbird], turtledove, and nightingale [152–5]) that recall the speaker's reference to 'when I was in my flowres, / Than was I lyght as byrd on brere [briar]' (44–5), his rendition of life on earth prior to his damnation, now rendered far superior to his life in hell's flames. Angel and son walk on crystal paths to a garden whose walls are bright gold, with the sounds of angelic song coming through the gates. There, the son sees the tree of knowledge, which has a strong and pungent smell and a pale colour, lacking fruit and flower (156–8). The son considers this a 'ruefull syght' (160) – hardly what one expects of heaven – and wonders that 'The blode [blood] of this tre lokys so rede' (163). As the angel explains, this tree's flowing red blood further demonstrates the monstrosity of the disrupted human–divine alliance: it is the tree of the forbidden fruit, that through which Adam was driven from the garden to live on earth (164–7), and 'When any synfull [sinful person] come hereine ... For vengawnce of that cursyd synne / The blode ryneth oute of this tre' (172–5). Even in heaven sin tears at the tree – and not simply the symbolic significance of the tree-as-future-cross – just as it does the embodied Christ, destroying the harmony possible only through repentance on earth.

The lesson in the second half of the poem (adapting *Adulterous Falmouth Squire*) seems to pertain not as much to preventing the reader from sharing the adulterous squire's fate as to educating the reader about the operations of prayer and intercession, particularly in relation to those souls damned to hell. The speaking father observes that his son will be a priest in seven years' time (129), and he warns him 'For ever the more thou prayst for me, / My peynes schall be more and more' (134–5). The poem thus shows the limits of the family, of the household of which this manuscript is a part: the human members of this family are in three separate arenas, with the young son on earth, his adulterous father in hell, and his faithful uncle safely in heaven. That future distribution depends only on the education and, ultimately, the spiritual behaviour of each individual member. In this, *The Adulterous Falmouth Squire* refuses, or at least limits, the mercy-machine carefully established by *The Feasts of All Saints and All Souls* (item 25) earlier in the manuscript. In this scenario in which family members are only on earth, in heaven, or in hell, even purgatory does not provide possibilities. Instead, hundreds of thousands of saints cannot change the eternal fate of those souls who refuse to repent when they have the means and opportunity while alive on earth. After that, no matter how pious the son you leave behind to pray for you, you are doomed to eternal hellfire. The poem thus presents complex moral matters from a distinctly earthly focus, with the son able to see his blissful uncle in heaven only very briefly, with no conversation of the sort that hell supports, with earthly engagement leading the tree of knowledge to show the 'upside-down' nature of life on earth.

Affective literacy: assessing intensities

This upside-down quality of earthly existence is at the root of the poem *Vanity* (item 40, fols. 156v–157r), which begins (after the first line's restatement of Ecclesiastes 1:2, 'O vanyté of vanytés, and all is vanité'), 'Lo how this werld is turnyd up and downe' (2). This poem of eleven rhyme royal stanzas is unique to Ashmole 61, a fifteenth-century northern/north Midlands composition. It is largely a paraphrase of Ecclesiastes, which was at the basis of the *contemptus mundi* tradition, and in this, *Vanity* shares much with *The Prick of Conscience Minor*.[63] Every stanza ends with a variant phrase leading to vanity: 'ende in vanyté' (7, 21, 28), 'turne to vanyté' (14), 'was vanyté' (35, 70), '[not] bot vanyté' (42, 56, 63, 77). Poetically, the lyric is thus a rarity in the collection, where only Lydgate's *Right as a Ram's Horn* (item 2) indulges in similar sharply refined poetic structures. However, its concerns and participation in the *contemptus mundi* tradition and its goal of converting its reader away from an inappropriate and naive desire for worldly pleasures makes it right at home in this section of the household collection.

The moral purpose of the poem is to discourage pride,[64] a pride that in the ecology of this poem is, more specifically, a pride in controlling earthly objects rather than, as in *The Prick of Conscience Minor* or *The Adulterous Falmouth Squire*, a pride in human independence from the divine. For instance, stanza 2 address the reader – having just announced that 'The best thereof schall ende in vanyté' (7) – to call out the fact that that despite that inevitable end, 'Yit beldys [builds] thou castellus, haulys [halls], townys, and towerys' (8). The remainder of the stanza details the cities and towns, walls, lodgings, chambers, bowers, and the tapestry, gold, and jewels that decorate them, creating a gorgeous image of medieval aristocratic material culture, only to conclude that 'Yit schall all waste and turne to vanyté' (14). Following stanzas address the desire for and pride taken in fame; female beauty and youth; noble birth; good marriage and family; and one's own youth, only for it all to be overturned by the wheel of fortune, which appears in line 50 at the start of stanza eight, so that loss and ageing and death are the only possible conclusion: 'all was vanyté' (70).

The pedagogical logic here is that of direct cause and effect (as in *The Wounds and the Sins*), with each stanza depicting the human folly of pride beginning 'Yiff thou' and then ending, in its final line, 'Than [or sometimes 'Yit'] schall…' And yet, unlike the other poems discussed in this chapter – particularly *The Prick of Conscience Minor* and to a lesser extent Maidstone's *Psalms* – there is no disgust for the world being represented. Instead, in its copious descriptions of these various earthly ideals there is a recognition, even an esteem, for the things that are lost through the turns of the wheel of fortune. The vanity seems here to be in thinking that they were the ultimate good rather than a lesser good, not in thinking that they held any beauty at all. In this, the poem varies distinctly from the full-on *contemptus mundi* of *The Prick of Conscience Minor*. Here, it is not that the foolish humans see themselves surrounded by sacks of dung that they believe are their spouses and children, as *Conscience* would maintain, and it is not that they attempt to live outside of God's moral structures. The reader is not to contemplate death as the moment of moral decisiveness – utterly predictable in its arrival and its finality – but instead, the vanity of all things results from the 'changeabull' wheel of fortune (50). The term 'vanity' carried associations of the thus-described item's being 'worthless, transitory, or illusory; also, that which has no purpose'.[65] The young are not encouraged to see their beauty and strength as truly ugly and weak, compared to the power of God. Instead, they are to see them as temporary and to see pride in them as, thus, foolish.

The final stanza switches dramatically away from the 'thou' addressed by the preceding 10 stanzas and here the first five lines begin 'We'. This 'we' is not a collective first person incorporating the 'you' addressed by the previous stanzas, with their orientation to noble possessions and passions. Instead, 'we' labour, in particularly agricultural ways, and have no rest. In one line alone, 'We dyge, we delve [sow], we saw, we scher [shear] also' (73), and other people benefit: 'We geder [gather] the corn [grain] hom for other mens ryches' (74). The final two lines conclude: 'Bot [we] labour in poverté to the tyme that we dyghe [die]. / Yit is our labour not bot vanyté' (76–7). On the one hand, this concluding stanza alters the previously appreciative tone of the descriptions of the aristocratic earthly delights in stanzas 2–7, showing that all of that luxury depends upon the constant, painful and unrewarding labours of many others – with whom the reader is encouraged, or even assumed, to empathise, through the repeated 'we'. But on the other hand, this undercompensated labour 'in poverté' is shown to be, similarly, 'not bot vanyté' (77). In this, the concluding stanza seems to work metaphorically to make all of the previously presented striving for earthly success the equivalent of labouring in vain the way the poor worker does.

Vanity is the penultimate item in the collection, followed only by the incomplete and unique narrative *King Edward and the Hermit* (item 41).[66] *Right as a Ram's Horn*, the only other Ashmole 61 item in the French lyric tradition, is the second item in the collection, following the narrative of *St Eustace*. These two lyric poems depict the folly of placing faith in the values of this world, and they do so through carefully wrought verse. This parallel structuring suggests the possibility that Rate saw in this penultimate poem shared sympathies, poetic and moral, with that early one, the second in the collection.

Ashmole 61 presents in other sections of the manuscript affect assemblages that include non-human objects – birds and stags, cherries and unicorns – which provide moral guidance (which is also to say spiritual guidance) to the human actors within the text and the humans who, in reading, enter the text. Compared to those saints' lives, romances, conduct texts, and satires that focus on the direct emotional insight modelled by non-human agents, this section of the manuscript with its explicitly and singularly religious concerns can read as a fixed, stable, universalising sphere. However, the opportunity for desired transformation through the interventions of non-human objects similarly reminds readers of the mutability of the human/non-human moral ecology and the need to develop emotional literacy. Affect, Sara Ahmed explains, is 'what … sustains or preserves the connection between ideas, values, and objects'.[67] In terms of this medieval book's appeal to its fifteenth-century household readers and the operations of the emotional community it shares with the late medieval English household, this section of the manuscript, with its penitential lyrics, narratives, and didactic texts, reveals how the act of reading these circulating texts is itself an act of penance, a relationship continuously generated and sustained by the 'connection between ideas, values, and objects' – between the forgiveness of Christianity, the corruption of sin, the faith in the good of God, the power of reading. Finally, this relationship is vitally dependent upon the shared materiality of all.

Notes

1 These items (32, 33, 35, 38, and 40) appear in quires 10–13 (the four final quires of the manuscript) on fols. 108r–157r. Items 37 (the life of *St Margaret*) and 39 (*Sir Orfeo*) from quires 12 and 13 are addressed in Chapter 5. Not addressed in this chapter, or elsewhere in this book, are items 34 (*Stations of Jerusalem*, which fills all of quire 11, fols. 128r–136r, except for a portion of its first and last pages) and 36 (*Legend of the Resurrection*, in the middle of quire 12, fols. 138v–144v). Each long poem (eight and six folios, respectively) is a unique version of the text, and neither participates actively in the affective or collaborative multi-ontological community building that this book traces elsewhere in the manuscript. See Appendix for a table listing the manuscript's contents, including information on quiring, foliation, and watermarks.
2 Amsler, 'Affective literacy', p. 84.
3 Shuffelton, *Codex Ashmole 61*, p. 577.
4 Bennett, *Vibrant Matter*, p. 28.

5 *The Wounds and the Sins* is extant in nine manuscripts and was 'among the most popular lyrics of late medieval England' (Shuffelton, *Codex Ashmole 61*, p. 575).
6 Shuffelton, *Codex Ashmole 61*, p. 575. The current Pope Francis has encouraged modern Catholics to revive the devotion, which he noted 'may sound a bit medieval' (Wooden, 'Pope urges revival').
7 All quotations from texts in Ashmole 61 are from *Codex Ashmole 61*, edited by George Shuffelton, and indicated by line number.
8 The Middle English 'ayen(e)s', of which 'agens' is a variant, is particularly multivalent, according to the *Middle English Dictionary*. Only its fourth sense suggests this being 'in opposition to' the noun it modifies, with the first sense 'opposite', as in 'facing'; the Old English predecessor of 'ayen(e)s' could offer the sense of 'in active hostility or opposition to' (*Oxford English Dictionary*, s.v. 'against', s.II.2.a.), suggesting that the sense perceived by modern English readers might well have been regularly understood in the intervening years as well.
9 *Middle English Dictionary*, s.v. 'kene'.
10 Williams, *Middle English Marvels*, p. 549, citing Camille, 'Before the gaze', p. 216. For more on medieval experiences of orally and visually encountering a text, see Coleman, *Public Reading*.
11 Both Cambridge University Library MS Ff.5.48 and Cambridge, Jesus College MS 13 retain Jesus in the speaking role; the other nine extant copies (including Ashmole 61) do not (Shuffelton, *Codex Ashmole 61*, p. 579).
12 Shuffelton, *Codex Ashmole 61*, p. 578.
13 Woolf, *The English Religious Lyric*, p. 224, quoted in Shuffelton, *Codex Ashmole 61*, pp. 578–9.
14 Shuffelton, *Codex Ashmole 61*, p. 576.
15 Shuffelton, *Codex Ashmole 61*, p. 577.
16 In this, my reading runs counter to Shuffelton's assessment that 'The poem provides a very simple way to contemplate the Passion while enumerating (or identifying) one's sins, and this utility must have been the source of its appeal' (Shuffelton, *Codex Ashmole 61*, p. 575).
17 Adultery is a focus throughout Ashmole 61, including in this section (as will be apparent in the discussion of *The Adulterous Falmouth Squire* to follow), and familial murder is committed by both sinful women in the *exempla Jealous Wife* and *Incestuous Daughter*, addressed in Chapter 3. Staley reads these features of the psalms in terms of the affair that John of Gaunt had with Katherine Swynford, since Maidstone was John of Gaunt's confessor by the time he was producing this poem (Staley, 'The Penitential Psalms', p. 251).

18 Staley, 'The Penitential Psalms', p. 221. Staley gives information on the sources, distribution, and readership of the Penitential Psalms, studying adaptations by Maidstone, Thomas Brampton, John Fisher, John Donne, and Jonathan Edwards, along with possible influences on Julian of Norwich. Staley's focus is on lordship and earthly authority (ranging from Richard II and John of Gaunt to Henry VIII). She also traces Langland's focus on these psalms as 'tools' of labour to perform intercessory prayer, itself a recurring object of religious concern in Ashmole 61. See also Edden, ed., *Richard Maidstone's Penitential Psalms*, for further consideration, and Kuczynski, *Prophetic Song*. All biblical quotations are from the Douay Rheims translation of the Latin Vulgate, unless otherwise noted.
19 Maidstone's was most popular in the fifteenth century, being displaced in the sixteenth by Sir Thomas Wyatt and others (Shuffelton, *Codex Ashmole 61*, p. 534).
20 Staley, 'The Penitential Psalms', p. 250, italics added.
21 Shuffelton, *Codex Ashmole 61*, pp. 534, 535.
22 Staley, 'The Penitential Psalms', p. 235.
23 Shuffelton, *Codex Ashmole 61*, p. 533.
24 The Latin is *Putruerunt et corupte sunt sicatrices mee, / a facie insipiencie mee*, or 'My sores are putrified and corrupted, because of my foolishness' (Shuffelton, *Codex Ashmole 61*, p. 286). 'A facie' seems to have generated 'the face'.
25 *Middle English Dictionary*, s.v. 'after' (adv.) 6.
26 This section fills lines 561–632.
27 This Maidstone and Rate do by calling on Psalm 101 for its rich earthly imagery, which is the source for all of the following Christ–non-human comparisons.
28 *Similis factus sum pelicano solitudinis; factus sum / sicut nicticorax in domicilio* (ll. 584a–b; these are Psalm 101:7); modern English translation is Shuffelton's (*Codex Ashmole 61*, p. 298).
29 Saunders, 'The symbolism of the pelican'.
30 Shuffelton, *Codex Ashmole 61*, p. 299.
31 Lines 593–4 translate the second half of *Vigilavi, et factus sum sicut passer solitarius in tecto*.
32 *Percussus sum ut fenum, et armit cor meum* (ll. 568a–b) ('I am smitten as grass, and my heart is withered', Shuffelton, *Codex Ashmole 61*, p. 298).
33 Shuffelton, *Codex Ashmole 61*, p. 298. The Latin reads *Quia desfecerunt sicut fumus dies me et ossa / mea sicut cremeum arverunt*.
34 Verses 4–13.

35 I here silently emend Shuffelton's proffered gloss of 'manner', which must be a typo for 'matter' ('matyr').
36 The ninth sense listed in the *Middle English Dictionary* for 'kinde, n'. seems most apt in this usage: '(a) A class of creatures; human beings, birds, reptiles, etc.; ... (b) a species of plants or animals; a genus; also, the animals that belong to a given family; (c) a kind of thing, element, disease, humor, medicine, gem, etc.; a category, a general type; also, a general term'.
37 All examples taken from *Middle English Dictionary*, s.v. 'cloth, n'.
38 Shuffelton, *Codex Ashmole 61*, p. 304.
39 It should be noted that the *Middle English Dictionary* includes, after an associated quotation in the entry for 'coverlyte' taken from Maidstone's *Psalms* as it appears in London, British Museum MS Add. 39574 (the Wheatley MS), '[rime: parfiʒte]'. Noting the rhyme word in this entry seems to imply that the use of 'coverlyte' is done to rhyme rather than to convey a particular sense. While this is possible, these are not mutually exclusive concerns.
40 Shuffelton, *Codex Ashmole 61*, p. 303.
41 *Quia cinerem tanquam panem manducabam, / et potum meum cum fletu missebam* (ll. 608a–b).
42 The Latin is *nolite fieri sicut equus et mulus quibus non est intellectus*, or 'Do not become like the horse and the mule, who have no understanding' (Shuffelton, *Codex Ashmole 61*, p. 284).
43 Here the Latin reads *in camo et freno maxillas eorum constringe qui non adproximant ad te*, or 'with bit and bridle bind fast their jaws, who come not near unto thee' (Shuffelton, *Codex Ashmole 61*, p. 284).
44 Perhaps a mild reduction of the misogyny of the original – 'For behold I was conceived in iniquities; and in sins did my mother conceive me' (*Ecce enim iniquitatibus conceptus sum, / et in peccatis concepit me mater mea*, Psalm 50:7) – but bleak in its representation of human existence, in any case.
45 Staley, 'Maidstone's *Psalms* and the king's speech', p. 255.
46 Staley, 'Maidstone's *Psalms* and the king's speech', p. 260.
47 *Middle English Dictionary*, s.v. 'sorwe'.
48 Staley, 'The Penitential Psalms', p. 223.
49 Shuffelton, *Codex Ashmole 61*, p. 539. Had Chaucer's translation of this text survived, one wonders how critical conceptions of his authorial concerns might have developed differently than they have in its absence.
50 Shuffelton, *Codex Ashmole 61*, p. 540.
51 Shuffelton, *Codex Ashmole 61*, p. 534.
52 Chickering, 'Rhetorical stimulus', pp. 194–7.

53 Rentz, *Imagining the Parish*, p. 126. Like Chickering, Rentz speaks of the full-length version.
54 Shuffelton, *Codex Ashmole 61*, p. 540.
55 See Watson, 'Censorship and cultural change' and, more recently, Rice, *Lay Piety*. In 2005, ten years after Watson's early work on the text, Howell Chickering said of its 'status in vernacular theology' that it 'remains uncertain' ('Rhetorical stimulus', p. 191).
56 See Fitzgibbons, 'Enabled and disabled "myndes"'; Killian, 'Menacing books'; Minnis, '*The Prick of Conscience* and the imagination of paradise'; and Rentz, *Imagining the Parish*.
57 Fitzgibbons, 'Enabled and disabled "myndes"', p. 72.
58 Fitzgibbons, 'Enabled and disabled "myndes"', p. 73.
59 Chickering points to the 'long and rich tradition of describing the New Jerusalem in material terms (bejeweled turrets, streets of gold)' while noting that in *Conscience*, 'the poet gives such details only cursory allegorical treatment ... [and] promotes a desire for the physical (and also social) joys of Heaven rather than a desire to love God Himself' ('Rhetorical stimulus', p. 214). While this may be a valid reading of the full-length version of the poem, it seems less appropriate to *The Prick of Conscience Minor*.
60 Shuffelton, *Codex Ashmole 61*, p. 558. For an aesthetic reading of Rate's synthesis of the two poems, see Kelly, 'Affective reading'.
61 Fein, *Moral Love Songs and Laments*, p. 363.
62 *Middle English Dictionary*, s.v. 'doleful': 'Full of sorrow, sad, sorrowful, distressed'.
63 Shuffelton, *Codex Ashmole 61*, pp. 587–8. Beyond Shuffelton's edition, the poem appears in only one modern edition, from 1924 (reprint 1957), Carleton Brown's *Religious Lyrics of the XVth Century*.
64 Pride was the first sin addressed in *The Wounds and the Sins* (item 38), and it was also the error of Sir Isumbras (item 5), the first individual human figure whose sin was resolved in Ashmole 61. In this, as the penultimate poem of the collection, *Vanity* returns to a moral concern in which the collection has been consistently invested.
65 *Middle English Dictionary*, s.v. 'vanity'.
66 This poem is discussed in Chapter 5.
67 Ahmed, 'Happy objects', p. 29.

5

Objects of liberation

The later part of Ashmole 61 consistently draws attention to human attempts to sever communion with non-human others, earthly and divine. Such malfunctioning earthly and cosmic relationships are documented in Chapter 4. Having extensively demonstrated the pervasive defects, the collection concludes with three vivid narratives of successful human reincorporation.[1] *St Margaret* (item 37) provides a transitional model, with the saint's body a sacred battleground on which acts of torture are transformed into sacraments through the heroine's alliance with a piece of the holy cross, an angel, two evil dragons, her many converts, and her own prayer. This poem integrates previously ruptured material and spiritual components essential to Christian community. *Sir Orfeo* (item 39) models selective adaptation through the transformation of a classic story of tragic loss into one of hopeful recuperation, wherein a saint's life, in tandem with romance, rewrites an inherited model. In this genre-composite, the human-tree hybrid Orfeo performs penance as he unites with his harp to live harmoniously among wild animals, creating a salubrious inverse community of the human courtly household, one that models a regenerative alternative to the fairy king's dangerous court. The collection ends with the unique text *King Edward and the Hermit* (item 41), in which a scene of potential discord – dormant in deer carcasses that in a different climate would have generated royal ire – is prevented through the intervention of a game that, with the aid of alcohol, successfully reconstructs a relationship and thereby the kingdom. These three final narratives actively transform inherited texts and traditions in ways made possible and meaningful through prominent human–non-human coalitions.

The medieval *Life of St Margaret*

St Margaret (item 37, fols. 145r–150v) presents the story of late medieval England's second-most popular virgin-martyr saint, who starred in 'manuscripts, amulets, wall paintings, icons, reliquaries, and embroideries'.[2] As this range of venues suggests, St Margaret spoke in voices institutional and lay, soteriological and mundane.[3] Material evidence demonstrates that her popularity was growing in the fourteenth and fifteenth centuries, that is, in the years leading up to Ashmole 61's time of production.[4] The outlines of St Margaret's story (for which there is no historical documentation)[5] do not themselves suggest why such attention might have adhered to her: Margaret was a virgin living in the Antioch region when she was pursued by the Roman administrator Olibrius to be his wife or mistress. She resisted his appeals, calling on her commitment to Christ, at which point Olibrius imprisoned and tortured her, none of which had any effect, and she was eventually martyred. In this, her life could be mistaken for that of St Lucy or St Agatha, St Juliana or St Barbara, or St Katherine of Alexandria.[6]

St Margaret's story, however, includes remarkable distinctive features. While imprisoned by Olibrius, Margaret is attacked by a demon-possessed dragon that she successfully defeats. One early Latin version of the story presents Margaret making the sign of the cross in the direction of the dragon, in response to which it disappears. In a different early Latin version – the one with which the Ashmole 61 version generally accords and whose story has come to be known as the 'Mombritius recension'[7] – Margaret is literally swallowed by the dragon, rather than only approached by it, and then quickly emerges out of the dragon's belly, unaffected by the experience and ready to take on a second demon that she also overcomes. These plot details help elucidate why her story was so frequently represented in images across medieval England, with as many as twenty painted scenes devoted to the events of her life.[8] Episodes such as her encounter with the dragon, which becomes St Margaret's most recognisable feature, reward visual representation, vital to the success of a religious narrative in the Middle Ages.

George Shuffelton notes that the Mombritius recension's more dramatic version of St Margaret's life 'remained very popular, no doubt for the spectacular entertainment it offered audiences'.[9]

Certainly readers today respond strongly to the action-adventure elements of her story, and her physical defeat of the dragon provided a useful iconic identifier for the saint. However, as work by Katherine J. Lewis, Wendy R. Larson, and others has shown in recent years, evidence from the full assemblage of cultic participants – laywomen alongside anchoresses and Church authorities[10] – suggests that the popularity of this virgin saint in the later Middle Ages followed especially from her symbolic defeat of the dangers of childbirth in her literal bursting forth from the dragon's belly free of harm. In earlier versions, including those in Old English, St Margaret's victory over demons was associated with her intercessory capacity to drive out demonic possession. By the thirteenth century, Middle English lives of St Margaret extended the saint's association with childbirth that was first extant in Wace's twelfth-century French version.[11] With this, St Margaret became the patron saint of childbirth and protector against birth defects,[12] demonstrating a particular appeal to lay Christian women in addition to the female religious to whom her story was presented by clerics as a model for chaste living in accord with Christ.[13] As evidence of Margaret's appeal to laywomen, Larson presents the story of Anthonius Guainerius of Pavia, a fifteenth-century physician who advised those assisting women in labour to have the legend of St Margaret read aloud, that the labouring woman should wear relics of the saint, and even prescribed that 'the text itself [be] placed on the mother's belly in order to invoke St. Margaret's aid'.[14] Larson notes that Guainerius might have been encouraging the focus on St Margaret as an 'emotional balm' for women rather than as an expression of his own faith in the saint's interventions, but she finds it significant that he 'makes no effort to eliminate her' from his instructions for guiding the birthing process.[15] This Pavian physician, living at the time of Ashmole 61's production, encouraged the story's use based on women's belief in its potential health effects. St Margaret's life thus offered various possibilities to medieval women depending on their position, experiences, and challenges.

At least six different versions of St Margaret's life were produced in Middle English. Extant versions include a stanzaic one (originating in the thirteenth century) from which the Ashmole 61 version descends (having been in the intervening centuries transformed into a couplet version also extant in the fifteenth-century Brome Commonplace

Book); this joins other later medieval English versions of her life: one early fourteenth-century version appearing in the Auchinleck manuscript, another among John Mirk's late fourteenth-century sermons (circulating in at least twelve manuscripts in the fifteenth century), and fifteenth-century products by John Lydgate and Osbern Bokenham.[16] The extensive variety exhibited by these texts affirms the ongoing appeal of the key scene with the dragon, alongside localised discomfort with it. Jacobus de Voragine, author of the *Legenda aurea* (compiled around 1260), for instance, called Margaret's being swallowed by the dragon and bursting free after making the sign of the cross while within its belly 'apocryphal and not to be taken seriously'.[17] And yet Voragine did not, as a result, ignore the key scene, as other versions (such as the *Old English Martyrology*)[18] did: he included it, unable to deny its appeal even while renouncing it. Meanwhile, readers of the so-called Mombritius recension were many, and these included Ashmole 61's scribe Rate, who found in this story material for his own and, it would appear, others' pleasure and improvement.

The making of a saint

St Margaret is just one of two saints' lives in this 41-item anthology, a feature notable given the collection's fondness for narrative combined with the prominence of religious matters across its contents. *St Margaret* is the female saint's life, accompanying the male saint's life of *St Eustace*, which appears as the first item in the manuscript. Ashmole 61 thus begins and very nearly ends with a saint's life (just four items follow *St Margaret*), with none appearing in between. These, however, are hardly the most distinctive or compelling features of the Ashmole 61 life of St Margaret. While Jacobus de Voragine had expressed two centuries earlier, in a text still in wide circulation in the fifteenth century, a preference for a version in which no dragon appears, Rate in Ashmole 61 provides readers with not just one but two dragons: in this, he goes one further than do other versions of the life in the Mombritius recension. Those follow the dragon scene with the arrival of a demon – lacking the disguise that the first demon appeared in – which Margaret forces, using physical restraint, to tell her the story of his and his associate's true identities, purposes, and history. The Ashmole 61 St Margaret, in contrast, meets and subdues a second and still scarier dragon after she defeats the first, and learns all she needs to know about his identity in the process.

This intensification of the very element in the life that others had decried indicates a particular investment on the part of Ashmole 61 in its deployment of the story of St Margaret. In this, Rate might be found guilty of simply increasing the 'spectacular entertainment' to which Shuffelton ascribed the legend's appeal. However, Shuffelton also observes that the narrative is concerned with 'the proper relationship of the physical and spiritual worlds'.[19] In the Ashmole 61 presentation of the life of St Margaret, this relationship is managed through, and thus narratively represented in the form of, different human figures' interactions with material objects. This chapter argues that features unique to the Ashmole 61 *St Margaret* exploit the legend's central investment in that 'proper relationship' through heightened attention to assemblages that have the effect of further strengthening Margaret's qualities present in the Mombritius recension, actively justifying her late medieval status among laywomen as patron saint of childbirth.

The poem's human–non-human relations establish this particular orientation. As is not uncommon in the case of a saint's life, the saint's pagan opponent – here, Olibrius – is condemned by the text for an insistent literalism, misreading objects as themselves holding sacred power. This foe is first introduced in terms of his earthly authority: 'He was a kyng of grete myght', and 'All Azy [Asia] ... Was hys awne to gyff or selle' (75, 77–8).[20] The nature of this representation sets him up for failure, in a saint's life, for though it is not a bad thing to be a powerful king (whatever the medieval genre), this king treats his land and people as his personal commodities to give or sell.[21] Similarly condemnatory of Olibrius is that his attempts to persuade Margaret to accept his faith and be his wife are all presented in purely material terms: in addition to offering her all of Asia, he also promises 'Sylke and gold and purpull paule ... Welle furryd with ryche ermyn' (180–2) and the 'beste metys that is in lond' (184), all of which he feels confident will 'Jhesu Criste pute oute of thi thought' (186). When these inducements fail to weaken her commitment, he attempts to belittle her God, again in material terms: 'We dyd Jhesu Cryst to dede / And dyd hym streyn upon the rode / Tyll he suet water and blode / ... And [If] thou leve on hym, thou arte lorn [lost]' (149–53). When Margaret calls on Jesus' 'mykyll myght' (155), evidenced, she explains, by his metaphysical abilities (his salvation of all believers, including some who had been in hell [155–61]), Olibrius tortures her continually, pausing every now and again to see if the torment has been enough to change her mind. Needless to say, it never is.

Margaret ties Olibrius's obsession with physical power and material luxury to his idols: 'thi godys that thou belevys onne, / Thei are dom [dumb] as any ston' (258–9). His own actions seem to support this recognition, for whenever he demands that she 'Beleve on my god' (256) and she refuses, Olibrius threatens her not through the power of his god, but through his own physical might: after he has one of his men blind her, he boasts that 'For before thou had thi syght; / Now hast thou non thorow my myght' (254–5). Not only has he performed this deprivation of her visual agency by means of his own earthly power – requiring his 'sergeantys everychon / They schuld turment hyre anon' (222–3) – but she publicly challenges him on the limits of this physical power: 'To rente the flessch fro the bone, / Power of my saule getys thou non' (264–5). Offering further evidence of the truth of her observation, all he can do in every case is order still more tortures of her body.

Despite Olibirius's protracted campaign to overpower Margaret physically in order to dominate her mind and thus her soul, he succeeds only in enabling the *imitatio Christi* that is Margaret's implicit goal. The poem emphasises this effect in its depiction of her body as she endures his attacks:

> They bete hyr with scowrgys strong,
> And turment hyr with grete wrong.
> They bete hyr, both man and wyffe,
> And fast with hyr thei gan stryffe,
> Tyll the rede blod felle a doune
> To hyre fete fro hyr croune [head],
> Tyll thei wend sche hade be dede;
> So fast on hyr thei hade leyde. (196–203)

She experiences scourging, like Jesus, and the blood streams down her body from her head – her 'croune' – visually evoking the image of Christ on the cross, blood running down from the crown of thorns. When this fails, they continue their abuse, this time effectively sending her to hell: 'With there nayles thei dude hyr flessch drawe / Lyke as hundys [hounds] had hyr gnawe ... And rent hyr lyer [skin] fro the flessch tho' (226–7, 230). It is as if she is being gnawed on by demons, torn apart, as are the inhabitants of hell depicted elsewhere in Ashmole 61, as in *The Adulterous Falmouth Squire* just two items earlier, where the 'Fendys bold with crowkys [crooks] kene / Rente [the squire in hell] fro lyth to leme [limb to limb]' (104–5). Where Christ, after his crucifixion, liberates crowds from hell, from her position of hellish torment Margaret liberates pagans by converting them – 'Many a thousand or it were eve [before it was evening]' (482).

While Olibrius had pleaded with Margaret to 'Have mersy on thi feyre fleche / And onne thi skyne that is so nessche [tender]' (208–9), she demonstrates consistently that her orientation extends through the physical to the spiritual, in the mercy she grants to Olibrius's people, including even his executioner, Malcus, when he 'axyd mersy' (516) upon seeing her attending angel providing her with support and honour. While the conflict between the pagan administrator and the Christian virgin is presented through her spiritual superiority to his physical power, St Margaret's abilities are not purely metaphysical. Instead, they take effect through her supernatural physical endurance. Like Christ, she can survive extreme bodily torment through which – this a direct effect of Olibrius's expression of his earthly power – she is seen, as Lewis observes, 'suffering to obtain divine favour for her followers and ultimately taking her place in Heaven'.[22] Her opponent's attacks serve only to allow her to demonstrate the power of faith in Christ and, through this, to accumulate converts for Christ and followers of her cult in the making.

The nature of the combat between Olibrius and St Margaret – that is, between pagan error and Christian truth – shifts when he foregoes his belief that his superior physical power can ultimately prevail and she is attacked by demons in the dungeon. Readers were told early on that Olibrius 'servyd dey and nyght / Hys fals godys' and 'the devyll of helle' (79–81), by which he is driven 'Ever to strew the Crysten men' (85). His attempt to destroy Christians is evident in his interminable torture of one representative Christian, Margaret. His being a servant of the devil (the ultimate force behind his false gods, themselves impotent while the devil himself is not) allows the narrative to shift orientation when both combatants – Margaret and Olibrius – are assisted by members of their respective spiritual communities. First, an angel of Christ brings Margaret a piece of the cross (278) and says it comes to her from the Trinity, 'Thy enmys therwith to defend [ward off]' (285). Arming herself for the battle to come, Margaret requests from the angel the return of her sight which Olibrius has previously destroyed. As soon as Margaret's vision returns, the angel disappears – and Margaret learns that she has been granted supernatural vision, so that she can see 'What thei be that thus hath turment me' (291).

This vision brings the first opportunity for Margaret to feel fear: where she had no concern about the violence done to her body by Olibrius and his representatives,[23] at this point 'Sche lokyd a lytell be hyr syde / And saw a dragon be hyr glyde / That was of colour as grasse gren, / Margaret hyr for to nem [seize]' (302–5). This description, with the vividness of the green dragon gliding just beside her, coming to snatch her, enhances the threat to Margaret and intensifies the audience's emotional connection. Margaret sees 'Out of hys mouth fyre bryning bryght' (307) and 'was agryfed of that syght', falling on the ground, at which point he immediately 'sualowyd up hyr body and bone' (312). Her ability to see the truth seems to have the primary effect of making her vulnerable to the dragon, rather than resistant to it. Beating and blinding and gnawing were sufficiently familiar earthly experiences to Margaret; being eaten by a dragon takes her to a new arena, one full of emotional tension and uncertainty, building on the empathy for Margaret previously stimulated in the audience by her spiritual resistance in the face of her physical torture. The piece of the cross provided to her moments before by her supporting angel, however, creates with her an inedible combination, so that immediately the dragon 'byrst upon the ground / The mayden com forth save and sound. / And it was Cristys wylle' (315–17).

That line 'And it was Cristys wylle' might seem to remove all agency from Margaret, making her only an instrument in the service of divine authority. Indeed, in the stanzaic *Life of St Margaret*, the closest version to the one in Ashmole 61, she responds to her defeat of the dragon by singling out just one source of power, that of the cross as material purveyor of Christ's might: 'Iblessed be Thou, Jhesu Cryste; Thi myghte is fulle good. / Now slayne is this dragon *thorugh vertu of the Roode*' (189–90; italics added). In Ashmole 61, however, Margaret presents a different understanding of the source of the powerful agency witnessed in that scene:

> [She] thankyd Jhesu of hys myght
> That sche hade overcom that foule wyght.
> And understode welle that it was
> Thorow the vertu of the croysse.
> That foule dragon was sleyn ther
> Thorow Godys myght and hyr prayer. (321–6)

She thanks Christ that 'sche hade overcome' the dragon, not that the dragon had been overcome and Margaret rescued. Further, Margaret 'understode welle' that the power ('vertu') of the cross, the power of God, and the power of her prayer collectively killed the dragon.[24] The poem is careful to map out this potent assemblage capable of overcoming a fiendish dragon even from within. This rendering of the victory over evil modifies in the extreme the alternative presentation of Margaret elsewhere as defeating the dragon by simply making the sign of the cross in its general direction: not only does it provide an entertaining spectacle – which it certainly does – but it does so consistently through representing supernatural power as a palpable product of human–non-human interaction, wherein the supreme power of the divine is not only metaphorically represented on earth but is tangibly manifest in earthly inhabitants.

In the Mombritius recension of the life of St Margaret, this moment of resolution is only temporary, with a foul fiend next attacking the saint and being physically overcome by her. In Ashmole 61, this fiend is uniquely replaced with a second dragon, this one scarier than the first: 'A fouler best never man se' (330), not even the one from which she burst moments before.[25] The depiction of her feat here can sound surprisingly, to a modern reader, like that of a comic book superhero:

> To hym sche went, I understond,
> With the holy crosse in hyr hond,
> And smote hym so upon the fynnes[26]
> That he myght not abyde her dynnes [endure her blows].
> That staff that was so long [i.e., the cross]
> That thorow Criste myght [through Christ's might] so strong
> Downe to the grond sche hym caste,

And with hyr wymple [headscarf] bond hym faste.
In [On] hys neke sche sette her fote. (331–9)

St Margaret sees this still fouler beast and, instead of falling in fear as she did before, or depending on a sacred object to take the lead, she heads straight for him, holding the piece of the cross – made strong through Christ's might – and hits the dragon with it beyond his endurance, tying him up with her wimple and holding him down by standing on his neck. In this action, the poem reminds readers of the saint's gender precisely as it is a source of power – her wimple a makeshift weapon – and not weakness. Margaret then demands that the captured dragon share his information with her: 'I conjure [command] thee, / What thou arte thou telle me ... What thou arte I wyll have knowyng' (341–4). She physically overcomes him through her faith and demands knowledge as her reward.

The education of a saint

This emphasis on Margaret's deep understanding harkens back to her first characterisation in the text: from the very start she is associated with knowledge as a source of power, for her father ordered her killed when he learned through necromancy prior to her birth that she would become a Christian. Knowledge threatens to lead to her death, but it is also a vital sponsor of her survival; her mother sends Margaret away to preserve her and to ensure her education and thereby her access to heaven: 'The messanger forth wente / To a norys [nurse] that wonyd [dwelled] ther / For to putte hyre to lere [educate her]' (36–8). Young Margaret has inherited her mother's investment in education, for while she is described with the fairness, beauty, and good conduct required of a female hero, the emphasis is on her 'understondying and knawelege' (48), both reflected in her actions: 'She toke hyr to Crystys lore / And belevyd in hym ever more' (49–50). This characterisation of Margaret is further intensified by some provocative ambiguity in the representation of this period of her development:

> The norys that kepte hyr fro dispare
> Had seven chylder that were fare,
> And well sche kepte this chylder seven –

> The eighth was Crystys meyden of hevyn.
> Both of heven and of helle
> Full gode tayles sche cuthe telle,
> ...
> Of many seyntys sche told the lyffe
> Both to man and to wyffe.
> And when sche was fiftene yerys old
> Sche was feyre woman and bold. (51–68)

The life of St Margaret traditionally presents the source of these stories as the nurse, to whom Margaret was sent with the explicit goal 'to putte her to lere', to educate her. And yet in this passage, the 'sche' who is telling good tales in line 56 seems to refer back to the closest antecedent, 'Crystys meyden of hevyn' (that is, Margaret), rather than the more distant one, 'The norys'. In the stanzaic version, the verb in the rendering of this scene is 'herde [heard]' (23) (rather than, as here, 'told'), so that there, young Margaret is clearly hearing these tales. While Shuffelton reads the nurse as the source of these stories in Ashmole 61,[27] in line with other versions of the stanzaic life, the depiction of the saint throughout this particular version of her story, along with the ambiguous syntax in this passage, supports reading young Margaret as herself the teacher of the seven other children. The Ashmole 61 version on various occasions emphasises the saint's pure reception of the truth of Christianity, a responsiveness rooted in her wisdom and learning.

Olibrius effectively perceives the power of Margaret's mind, for the second dragon's forced confession reveals that 'In dragons wyse we com to thee / To spyll thi wytte and make thee wode to be. / The kyng, Syr Olybryus, / In this lyknes sent us thus' (361–4). Olibrius has learned that harming her body does nothing to reduce her power, so her 'wytte' must be disabled. Olibrius attempts to turn her mad through a fear that goes beyond the physical. This attempt, too, fails utterly, and in the process Margaret's *imitatio Christi* is further enabled. She says to the second dragon, 'I conjure thee, by Cristys myght / And in Godys holy name, / That thou do never more schame, / Bot synke doune into helle, / Forever more ther to duelle. / Synke done, thou foulle fend'; and 'He sanke adoune by Godys myght, / Thorow the prayer of that virgyn bryght' (406–14). Having been torn at by hellhounds and then trapped in a dungeon to be attacked by demons, Margaret enacts divine judgement through her prayer, returning the fiend to his proper home and releasing herself from his power, a variation of Christ's harrowing of hell.

In further imitation of Christ, Margaret's saintly purpose ultimately depends on her sacrificing herself in order to facilitate her followers' access to divine succour. In inadvertent support of this, Olibrius orders hot lead and oil to be poured on her, from head to foot. His goal is her conversion to his pagan belief and acceptance of his earthly power over her; instead, these liquids 'had no power hyr to quelle' because 'The holy crosse kepte hyr welle' (467–8) and in effect turned this intended torture into a sacrament: St Margaret is thus anointed prior to her death. Following this, as she continues to refuse the order to convert, her torturers at Olibrius's command submerge her in a vat of water. St Margaret expresses again her transformative power: 'Anon as sche the water gan se / Sche thought therein crystynd to be, / And seyd, "In Crystys holy name, / Here I take baptysm and defy ther blame!"' (474–7). In confirmation of her declaration of this sacrament, thunder cracks and 'The angell toke hyr out of the water than; / They myght it se, every man' (479–80); in response to her miraculous baptism, multitudes convert, 'Many a thousand or [before] it were eve' (482), including her executioner, Malcus.

Twice, Olibrius's earthly tools of torture are transformed into apparatuses of sacred truth. Divine affirmation of St Margaret comes again as she is about to be burned to death outside the city – Olibrius attempting to reduce the effects of her martyrdom by staging the act away from the public, but once again actually enabling further Christian conversions among his people. Indeed, the direct divine intervention in the earthly (as the thunder cracks again and the sun turns black [501–2]) strikes great fear into the people who followed Margaret out to her execution, who 'were ferd [afraid] in that stound [moment] / That for fere thei fell to grond. / They were so afreyd tho / That thei knew nother wele ne wo' (503–6). The narrative emphasises the full extent of their fear by repeating it three lines in a row – effectively combining their reverence with the Trinity that inspires it. Whereas earlier St Margaret's fear of the first dragon immobilised her and made her initially susceptible to the dragon's power (and her success all the more astonishing), the masses' fear here is evidence of an appropriate acknowledgement of divine power, an awe that leads the previously pagan people to the act of proper worship.

Reflecting her prior ability to defeat the dragon through her prayerful collaboration with the piece of the divine cross and God's might, Margaret calls again on that potential power, this time to the benefit of her followers, carefully establishing the process through which this spiritual assemblage can be reactivated.[28] She offers a long public prayer requesting the protection of those present converts as well as all in the future who honour her, hear or read about her torments, or do alms in her name (529–67). She highlights women in childbirth (546–53) and requests specifically 'that the fend do them no skathe [harm]' (562) and that they 'never in syne dyghe [die in a state of sin]' (559). The poem affirms that 'Oure Lord herd hyr prayer son / And grantyd hyr all hyr bone' (566–7), and the trio of Michael, Gabriel, and Raphael bear her soul to heaven. This process turns Margaret into 'other people's object as relic, as text, as patron, as example', Lewis observes, and in this she might be read as ultimately reduced, whatever her mental, physical, emotional, and spiritual achievements, to the traditional feminine purpose of serving others. But, Lewis argues, such 'possession of her does not elide her subjectivity. Rather it is reiterated and strengthened, whenever a devotee who invokes her name and her intercession enacts that possession.'[29] Lewis observes that in the Ashmole 61 version this intercessory power is more strongly materialised, for this poem 'includes a plea [from the saint] on behalf of those who "beryth on them my lyffe" (563), those who "carry" or perhaps even "wear" her life', and who 'through actually wearing her life in the form of amulets' could gain her intercession – their bodies and thus souls marked by her story. In this the 'texts of her life could become contact relics'[30] – a capacity for the object, an alternative identity and agency, enacted through the saint's life and her prayer.

In its extended establishment of the saint's cult, to which it commits 15 per cent of its lines, the Ashmole 61 life resists the trend of contemporary fifteenth-century versions of St Margaret's life that Sherry L. Reames describes as 'water[ing] down the contents of her final prayer' so that the 'bold promises in the stanzaic account' become in Mirk and Lydgate mild 'assurances of comfort and grace'.[31] Mirk's sermon strives to redirect attention to St Margaret's institutional authorisation by the Church, and thus her cult's direct dependence on the sacraments, fighting against her use in 'private observances at home'[32] – which is to say, at the very site where childbirth occurred. Lydgate's life of St Margaret, from the first quarter of the fifteenth century, was produced at the request of Anne Mortimer, Countess of March – requested by a woman during the period in her life when she was vulnerable to the dangers of childbirth.[33] And yet, Karen Winstead observes, Lydgate makes St Margaret into 'a model of humility and piety', placing 'greater emphasis on exemplary virtues' and reducing significantly her victory over the devil, 'transform[ing her] into a demure and retiring figure' who is 'as benign toward demons as she is toward her human adversaries'.[34] Fifteenth-century adaptations of St Margaret's life exhibit a tendency to reduce the female saint's public agency as well as her powerful gendered association with women in childbirth.

It is in this cultural moment that Ashmole 61 amplifies Margaret's power over the dragons – by including two of them, one that scares her but another that, despite being more gruesome and fierce, does not – and also carefully delineates the ways her followers can call on her intercessory powers through an embodied connection to her life, wearing its text on their bodies. Of such moves towards the physical in some saints' lives, as in the vernacular versions of the virgin martyrs' lives generally, Winstead sees that '[t]he concreteness of the Middle English legends makes readers less ready to look for the theological significance of the saints' struggles and to read the legends as stories with lessons for the here and now'.[35] This is precisely the feature of Margaret's legend that Mirk's sermon attempts to control – and that Ashmole 61 further unleashes. The Ashmole 61 version uniquely details the origin of a shrine around the saint's body in Antioch,[36] where 'all that were seke and lame / Thether fast gan thei gon; / Hole and sound hom thei come, / Thorow grace of God allmyght / And be prayer of that meyden bryght' (599–603). In a number of such moves, this late medieval rendering of the life of St Margaret asserts the female saint's agency and her embodied connection, through her gender and despite her own virginity, to childbearing mothers across time.

Lewis argues that Margaret and Olibrius, like most opponents in virgin-martyr lives, 'are given clearly gendered attributes and activities to heighten the dichotomy between them, and ultimately to privilege femininity over masculinity, in a divinely sanctioned reversal of the gender hierarchy of this world'.[37] Pagan belief is represented by Margaret's father and Olibrius (as well as by his men who torture her); Christian belief is conveyed (through instruction) by Margaret and her nurse (and she is sent away for safety by her mother, who dies in childbirth in most other versions and is thus unable to protect her daughter as she does here). In the context of the textual life of St Margaret, Christianity is something to be distributed and nurtured in private, away from the public pagan power of the father – and is in this and other ways feminised.[38] Being embodied in a saint attached to women giving birth in the private space of the home makes explicit those gendered associations common across the lives of virgin-martyr saints.

In this, Ashmole 61 further emphasises St Margaret's powerfully collaborative production of a lay female Christian community. The sacrament of baptism, Rentz explains, was vital to the generation and sustenance of the late medieval parish – of the community of believers: it was 'central to lay spirituality and to the construction and representation of the parish and parochial identity', the baptismal font 'the source not only of parochial identity but of an extended sense of spiritual kinship among parishioners, both living and dead'; she further explains that 'churchyard burial … represented a renewal of that vow, a homecoming or return to the place of one's baptism, and a lateral move into the fellowship of the dead'.[39] From this perspective, the Ashmole 61 life of St Margaret, with its special attentions to the saint's management of her own baptism amid her pagan setting and her careful delineation of how she should be honoured after death, shows her joining that community of believers through this claim to spiritual kinship with the living and the dead, across time and space. In support of this, throughout the process of her encounters with Olibrius, she transforms his attempts to change her body and thereby convert her belief and thus her soul into her own enactment of sacramental rites. This ongoing project of building Christian community through enduring physical torture the saint performs very deliberately: Lewis notes that it is 'something that she allows to happen to herself' so that she 'appropriates it and directs its meaning'.[40] The Ashmole 61 life of St Margaret appears in its distinctive features to draw audience attention to Margaret's active transformation of masculine violence into female survival, both earthly and spiritual, individual and collective.

Transformation and *Sir Orfeo*

Following *St Margaret* in Ashmole 61 is the 32-line lyric *The Wounds and the Sins* (item 38, fols. 150v–151r), six of whose stanzas share fol. 150v with the saint's life, the final two sharing fol. 151r with *Sir Orfeo* (item 39, fols. 151r–156r). It thus serves as a bridge between the two poems, one that offers the opportunity for the reader to perform penance for their sins – each deadly sin listed along with a penitential response confirmed by Christ – action whose need St Margaret's selfless sacrifice would have made evident for each reader (see Figure 4.)

St Margaret concludes with the narrator's blessing appearing just across the gutter from the first 42 lines of *Sir Orfeo*. The two narrative poems share depictions of intense violence against the female body that spark a consideration of the transformative possibilities of human death. Much recent criticism (including my own)[41] has focused on the poem's attentions to the threshold between life and death: in the hiatus from human living that Orfeo imposes upon himself, self-exiled to the wilderness on the loss of his wife to the Fairy King; in the suspended figures in the display in the Fairy King's courtyard wherein individuals hover at the moment of death or abduction; in Heurodis's own suspension in fairyland, living yet unable to return to her human home; in her continued silence upon her actual homecoming, displaced as heir-producer by the loyal-steward-proclaimed-heir. Much of that criticism has concluded that while the poem appears to exchange the classical story's tragic conclusion for a happy medieval romance ending, this new conclusion is ambivalent and may reveal that even genre reassignment cannot enable Orfeo to retain his lost wife.[42] Such readings in their teasing out of the poem's conflicting investments further substantiate its long-standing position of esteem among modern readers. However, in its home at the end of Ashmole 61 – where it is the 39th item, followed by just two unique texts, the short poem *Vanity* and the incomplete narrative of *King Edward and the Hermit* – the narrative's emphases appear somewhat different. Its physically violent and

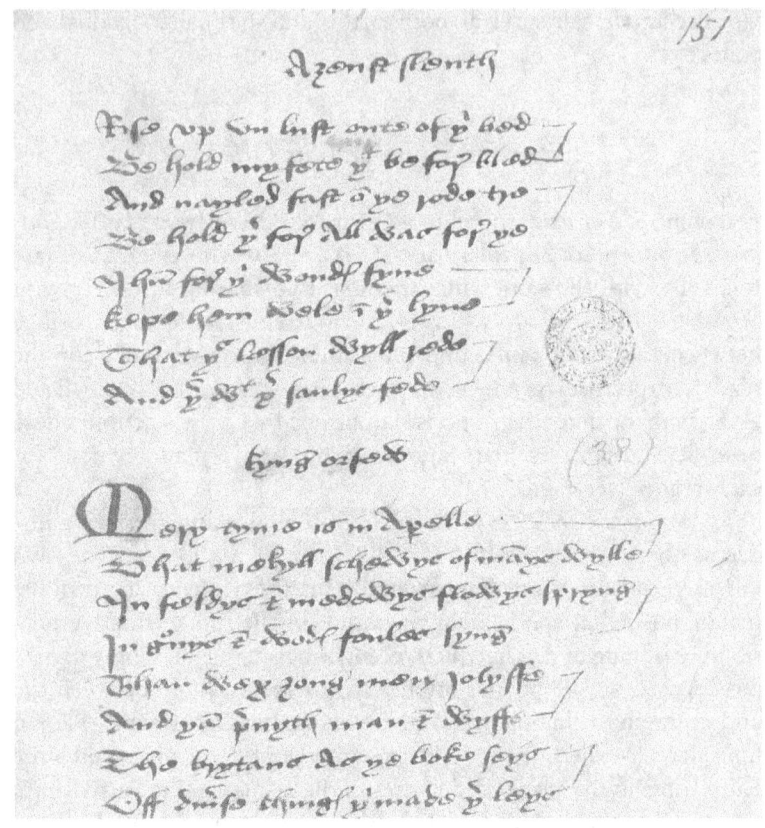

4 Oxford, Bodleian Library MS Ashmole 61, fol. 151r: *The Wounds and the Sins* and *Sir Orfeo*

emotionally intense representation of a woman being tortured for not turning away from the cultural norms of her community takes on a particular valence that associates *Sir Orfeo* not primarily with the tragedy that is its classical heritage but with the opportunities for conversion and rebirth made possible in the saint's life that is its neighbour – the ending of one poem and the beginning of the other resting face to face in the closed collection over the centuries, saint's life become contact relic facilitating Meroudys's safe rebirth.[43]

Critical analyses of *Sir Orfeo* vividly demonstrate a feature common to all acts of reading: interpretation is generated in collaboration with elements of any given text – its words and images, its layout

Objects of liberation 223

and material form – as well as with extra-textual agents that participate in the hermeneutic production, sometimes by invitation, sometimes not. In each new encounter, reader and text are joined by additional collaborators who inform any given experience of a poem such as *Sir Orfeo*. In the past thirty years or so, for instance, readings appearing in academic scholarly publishing communities have been produced in collaboration with medieval theories of visual art and music (Seth Lerer), modern theories of deconstruction (Oren Falk), documented medieval encounters with fairy (Neil Cartlidge), modern theories of wonder (Tara Williams), medieval discourses of late medieval Christianity, astrology, and fairyland (Alan J. Fletcher), and late medieval political culture (Elliot Kendall).[44] Across these readings, modern scholarly hermeneutic communities have tended to include as a prominent contributor the classical story of Orpheus and Eurydice as told by Ovid and Virgil.[45] In such interpretive ecologies, the meanings of the Middle English *Sir Orfeo* are perceived in the ways its author is understood to be 'exploit[ing] this literary inheritance'.[46] In addition to key plot points that *Sir Orfeo* shares with the earlier Latin versions, compelling echoes from the classical stories of Orpheus appear: in the bodily fragmentation experienced by Heurodis (transferring to her the Maenads' tearing Orpheus apart in Virgil's version); in Orfeo's saying upon departure from home after his wife's disappearance that 'I wyll never woman sene [see]' (218) (as Orpheus in Ovid's *Metamorphoses* refuses women after his wife dies). In Virgil, Eurydice is fleeing from another man, Aristaeus, when she is bitten by a snake and dies; for readers familiar with Virgil, these associations infuse the Middle English story of the Fairy King's abduction of Heurodis, whose attempts to escape the fate determined for her by the Fairy King are rendered impossible by his magic, her forced disappearance from her human community a fate equivalent to death – and the Fairy King's unstated reasons for requiring her to join them explained via Virgil as potentially stemming from sexual desire. Reading the Middle English poem in relation to its culturally powerful classical predecessors further enriches an aesthetically and emotionally affecting artwork.[47]

Interpreted in collaboration with its housemates in Ashmole 61, as enabled by the fifteenth-century scribe Rate, *Sir Orfeo* produces some meanings that happily coexist with those absorbed from the classical tradition (which the poem never directly references) and the medieval romance genre (which it does); some meanings that the poem suggests, however, are generally imperceptible in other reading communities such as, for instance, the Auchinleck manuscript, the J. A. Bliss edition from 1966, or the 1995 Laskaya and Salisbury edition as presented in the 2014 *Broadview Anthology of British Literature, Volume 1: The Medieval Period*.[48] In Ashmole 61, the fairy kingdom to which Heurodis – here, Meroudys – is taken carries with it associations with the underworld of the classical tradition, implicitly in its manuscript appearances and overtly in the scholarly modern editions where it is accompanied by footnotes that supply that classical interpretive framework. Additionally, in Ashmole 61 this fairy otherworld calls to mind a number of vivid depictions of the Christian underworld of hell and otherworld of purgatory that appear in texts earlier in the collection, as in *The Prick of Conscience Minor*, *The Sinner's Lament*, and *The Adulterous Falmouth Squire*.[49] Such associations, like the poem's allusions to the ancient Roman underworld, are indirect. Spiritually transformative possibilities generated through violent human bodily suffering appear in these texts and elsewhere, including in the collection's two saint's lives – figures physically performing penance on earth or in purgatory, or readers being inspired to perform their own acts of penance in response to the eternal tortures experienced by unrepentant sinners in hell.

Among these fellow household-book inhabitants, *Sir Orfeo* translates for a medieval reader the deeply familiar Christian moral ecology to an alternative setting, one also imbued with the supernatural, in this case the extra-Christian world of fairy. The surprising transformation performed by the poem is not only a genre shift from classical myth to medieval romance but also a change in emphasis and purpose, from life-affirming tragedy, to affecting Celtic love story, to spiritually vital Christian devotional aid. The collection's recurring concern with penance extends into the simultaneously familiar and alluring but also foreign and dangerous space of fairy, all of it occurring through the moral capacity of materiality – earthly and otherwise – in the poem. In reading environments that do not include the other forty inhabitants of Ashmole 61, it is certainly possible to read *Sir Orfeo* as demonstrating how 'wonder-inducing spectacles might have moral significance and effects', as Tara Williams has done.[50] Neil Cartlidge observes, in support of such an interpretive framework, that 'by the fourteenth century there was a long tradition in medieval literature of reading the fairies' incursions as a symbol of moral or social disorder'.[51] Reading *Sir Orfeo* alongside its textual companions in Ashmole 61 can also draw particular kinds of attention to the moral questions it raises – moral questions not regularly central to modern readers' interpretations of the poem.

For a reader of the Ashmole 61 anthology encountering *Sir Orfeo*, St Margaret has just finished performing a series of 'wonder-inducing spectacles' that struck fear into the hearts of observers and, as a direct result, generated great moral effects: thousands of conversions. Martyred virgin hagiographies such as Margaret's share structural elements with Meroudys's character and experiences in *Sir Orfeo*: Ellen Caldwell has observed parallels in

> the virgin's wealthy, noble upbringing [daughter of prince Theodosyas in *St Margaret*; queen of Thrace, in *Sir Orfeo*], the rebuffing of a tyrannical/pagan suitor [Olibrius there, Fairy King here], the punishment of the heroine to urge her compliance with the suitor's sexual desires [physical torture, there; permanent abduction to fairyland here], and finally the 'rescue' by Christ, the true bridegroom [exactly that in *St Margaret*; here, earthly bridegroom Orfeo's retrieval of Meroudys from the fairy court], and the carrying to heaven/death of the bride [literal death and assumption there; return to Thrace here].

All have analogues in *Sir Orfeo*, as noted in square brackets, 'albeit in secularized and Celtic-influenced form'.[52] Encountering these elements in the supernatural setting of *Sir Orfeo*, in the wake of St Margaret's defeat of demon-possessed dragons and conversion of thousands of unbelievers, translates the genre affiliations of Christian hagiography to a complex hybrid poem collaboratively produced by classical legend, Celtic myth, and courtly romance. In this fecund environment, the poem exhibits a 'capacity … to digest and transform the familiar',[53] taking the opportunity granted by medieval romance's *aventure*, as Jeffrey Jerome Cohen suggests, to enact 'a collaboration with the strange'.[54]

Prefacing morality

From the start, Ashmole 61 orients readers of *Sir Orfeo* to questions of morality even as it immerses them in the elsewhere world of romance. It does this in a way that no other remaining copy of the poem does – and does so at a notoriously confusing spot in the poem that results from the dramatic variation among its three extant copies. The earliest, the fourteenth-century Auchinleck *Orfeo*, is missing its first page and thus the original beginning of the poem there is uncertain; the version of *Sir Orfeo* in MS Harley 3810 (early fifteenth century) – where it is the first item in the manuscript – begins with an 18-line passage extant in the Auchinleck *Lay le Freine*; Ashmole 61's version of this poem includes this passage extant in Harley 3810 and Auchinleck's *Lay le Freine*, but preceding that passage and starting the poem proper, it offers six lines that are not present in the other extant versions of the poem – although they do appear in a different Middle English poem also housed in the Auchinleck, *Arthour and Merlin* (where they are lines 259–64).[55] Shuffelton describes these first six lines as containing 'a formulaic description of springtime' and concludes that they 'have little apparent connection to the lines that follow'.[56] What follows these six lines in Ashmole 61 is the incorporated prologue it shares with Harley 3810, which emphasises the genre affiliation of the poem, describing qualities common to the Breton lay (in terms of subject matter, tone, and the supernatural, associating the poem's origins with the Bretons) and presenting this poem in terms of that tradition.

Before thus positioning the poem in relation to the Breton lay, Ashmole 61 first presents readers with a brief description of the seasonal setting in these six lines apparently unique to this version of *Sir Orfeo*, though borrowed from elsewhere. The first two lines announce the 'Mery tyme is in Aperelle [April] / That mekyll [much] schewys of manys wylle' (1–2). Shuffelton suggests with the gloss in his edition that the merry time of April 'shows much to man's liking', reading 'wylle' as 'liking'. While April indeed often has the effect of pleasing people in both lived experience and poetic tradition, the following couplets suggest an alternative reading for the first two lines: lines 3–4 describe flowers blooming in meadows and fields and birds singing in groves and woods, standard elements of a *reverdie* situationally parallel to the merry April time of line 1; these flowers and birds, though, lead to the lines 'Than wex yong men jolyffe [joyful], / And than proudyth man and wyffe' (5–6). In its concluding focus on human participation in this seasonal assemblage, the couplet draws attention not to the reproduction ultimately encouraged by and vital to springtime but instead to desire itself, especially in the unusual verb 'proudyth' (4). Shuffelton glosses this word as 'grow amorous', which sufficiently conveys the general sense. But it is an uncommon Middle English word, and for the verb form, 'prouden', the *Middle English Dictionary* offers '(a) To be or become arrogant or haughty; (b) to make (sb.) proud; (c) to be vain; (d) to be pleased, be happy'. The first three of these are associated with pride, a deadly sin; only the last refers more generally to a morally neutral emotional experience. The beginning of *Sir Orfeo* in Ashmole 61 seems to be evoking the familiar season of springtime to draw attention to the ways it encourages not just joy but lust and pride, specifically.[57] After all, the manuscript layout places these introductory lines right below a stanza of *The Wounds and the Sins* on the final deadly sin, sloth, and then a closing stanza calling out to Christ to 'Kepe hem wele in ther lyve / That this lesson wyll rede / And therwith ther saulys fede' (30–2). Willingly reading spiritually educational texts feeds the soul and makes possible future well-being. In this setting, the unique beginning of *Sir Orfeo* might well present 'wylle' of line 2 in terms of the *Middle English Dictionary*'s primary definition for 'will': 'The appetitive and volitional faculty of the soul'. This merry time of April shows much of man's will, of the faculty of the soul that desires and manages that desire and, as often as not, leads to sinful emotional activity – such as that which is the focus of the unique poem that follows *Sir Orfeo* in Ashmole 61: *Vanity*.

After raising the stakes this way, the poem consistently requires the reader to manage their emotions in response to the series of affecting scenes on display, some of them highly morally charged. Indeed, the poem's hero, Orfeo, is first presented not in terms of his great nobility, as would be expected in a romance, but in terms of his own emotional experience: he 'most luffyd gle and herpyng' (28). The ability of his harping to make people 'wene [think] that it were a blyssedfull note of paradys' (38–9) means that listeners are transported by his musical art to heaven even as they remain squarely on earth. Orfeo enacts here in this introductory scene what the poem as a whole manifests: 'art's power to reshape experience'.[58] That reshaping, or transformation, or conversion, is made possible through objects generating human emotion. At times, the object is a musical harp in collaboration with a beneficent person, such as

Orfeo; at others, the object is magic manipulated by a nefarious figure, such as the Fairy King, in collaboration, say, with an ympe-tree and 'undrentide'. In all cases, emotion is generated – within figures in the poem, and within readers of the poem – that has the potential to fundamentally 'reshape experience', depending on what the art of the narrative 'show[s] of man's will'.

After a quick introduction of Orfeo's learned and skilful harping and an even quicker introduction of his queen, the poem immediately hurls its audience into emotional turmoil, the song they are hearing – the poem itself – giving no impression that they are in paradise. Meroudys is discovered by her attendants, upon waking from a long nap under an ympe-tree, screaming, wringing her hands, scratching her face until it bleeds, and tearing her gorgeous garments to shreds (66–70). The whole community tries to restore her to herself – for she 'was ravysed out of hyr wytte' (70) – but to no avail. In this, the Fairy King has succeeded where Olibrius, in his attacks on St Margaret, did not. Meroudys's terrible transformation is conveyed in further detail by Orfeo, who tells her, with both his wife and the reader as the shared audience for his trauma, how she appears to him, now 'becom wode and wyld' (92), her slender fingers covered in her own blood (94–104), her 'lyppes that were so bryght rede / Semys as wan as thou were dede' (95–6), her eyes looking on Orfeo, he says, 'as I were thi fo' (100). Orfeo asks mercy from her, his 'God leman' (101), indicating that she holds power over him through this transformation, returning him to the position of the courtly lover – or, like Olibrius's subjects pleading for mercy from St Margaret, the penitent sinner.

When Orfeo asks, 'What thing may thee helpe now?' (104), he raises the possibility of a remedy. Meroudys speaks, spending nearly all of the following 60 lines telling him (and the reader) that it is much worse than he fears, explaining the Fairy King's demand and accompanying threat. The extended description detailing what thus far only Meroudys knows, through frightening first-hand experience, is all the more horrific for being presented by the victim in such a matter-of-fact way. In response to Orfeo's question, the Fairy King (as quoted by Meroudys) pre-emptively warns that 'Nothyng helpe thee ne schall' (172) and asserts that there is no way to hide: 'If that thou make us any lete [hindrance], / Wherever thou be thou schall be fete [fetched] / And to-torn thy lymys [limbs] all' (169–71).

This position of helplessness, in the face of magical omniscience in league with a mysteriously authorised demand and a willingness to cause great pain to achieve those ends, is felt sharply by the reader along with Orfeo, unable to intervene whatever his will: he can only lament, 'Alas ... I ame wo!' (179). All he can do is verbally articulate his emotional experience. Despite the thousand knights Orfeo has gathered to try to protect Meroudys when she waits at the meeting spot, inevitably 'The quen was awey twyght [seized] / And with the feyry awey inome [taken]' (194–5). No one knows where she has gone, and 'Ther was cry, wepyng, and wo' and 'grete sorow' (197, 200). The fear and empathy generated by that encounter, as evidenced in Meroudys's deeds and words and proven by her abduction, are then transferred to Orfeo, who in effect himself abducts the king, right after the queen has been taken: he tells his people to 'Chese you than a new kyng / And do your best with all my thing' (213–14) and departs for the wilderness. In response, 'Ther was wepyng in the halle / And grete sorow among them alle' (221–2). There is only more crying, more weeping, more sorrow.

A wilderness home

Having prepared the audience for a strong emotional experience with moral overtones, and having delivered it in its first 215 lines, the narrative locus changes with Orfeo in the wilderness. Here, emotion – all human experience and expression of it – disappears. Emotion is sensed only by the audience, in response to the vivid and detailed representation of Orfeo's losses. The dire nature of his situation in the wilderness is first introduced through a series of material contrasts to his previous life of appropriate, natural nobility: where he once 'sate in boure and halle' and wore 'purpull palle', he now lies 'in herd heth' wearing 'levys and gresse' (244–6); he once had castles and towers, forests, rivers, fruits, and flowers, but now he has to dig for his food of berries and bark (256–62) and 'may not make hys bed in es' (251–4); where he once was served by knights and knelt to by ladies, his only neighbours now are beasts and birds (247–50). In this, the poem vividly recalls for the reader of Ashmole 61 the experience of Sir Isumbras's family during their years of penance, separated from one another and living in destitution in the wild, lacking all their previous material markers of nobility, itself an extended narrative depiction of a feature also familiar in this collection from *St Eustace*. This interpretive community provides evidence which the poem itself does not, concerning the mystery of the motivation for Orfeo's self-imposed exile. The audience empathy generated by this montage of Orfeo's losses can, in this Ashmole 61 context, point towards a possible expression of sinful culpability for which penance might be served through the loss of his wife. His experience in the wilderness maps on to the periods of penitence in both *Isumbras* and *St Eustace* – with his bare feet at his departure from his kingdom (234) evoking the penitent Good Friday procession of the murderer in *Knight who Forgave*. Modern readers tend to esteem the poem's reluctance to offer a precise explanation for the characters' motivation and experiences, leaving much of the narrative enigmatic, inviting further empathetic investigation, and in the process heightening the feelings of loss shared by the reader. Perhaps for a medieval audience experiencing *Sir Orfeo* in Ashmole 61, some of those uncertainties were satisfied by the presence of other interpretive collaborators participating from elsewhere in the collection, offering a productive penitential purpose for Orfeo's period of self-exile.

Orfeo himself is so transformed by this relocation that he loses grasp of external points of reference. Among the series of material contrasts evoking reader sorrow for Orfeo is the observation that 'He sey not [saw nothing] that hys herte lykyth / Bot wyld bestys that by hym strykyth [stalk]' (249–50). Nothing that he sees pleases him – except for the wild beasts moving nearby. These are the beasts that his collaborations with his harp are able to charm; their shared appreciation of the music makes of them an alternate community.[59] Orfeo expresses himself only through his harping, once he is in the wilderness: '[He] harpyd after hys awne wylle [own desire]' and 'temperyd [tuned] hys herpe with a mery soune', playing very loudly (274–6). His will directs his harping, and the result is a strong, merry sound. One might, given everything, expect a lament. Yet a jolly melody it is, and it appeals to the wild beasts, who 'com aboute hys harpe to here. / The bestys of that forest wyld / Com aboute hym, meke and myld, / To here hys harpyng so fyne – / So mych melody was thereine' (277–82). They are drawn to the music, 'coming about' him – an action stated twice in three lines in an almost ritualised repetition – calmly despite being wild, so that they can experience the richness of his song.[60] While he plays, they are transformed into the household animals he left behind. And then, 'When he hys harpyng stynt wylle [wished to stop] / No lenger ther abyde [linger] thei wylle [wished]' (283–4). These lines make clear that the animals are not simply physically entranced but instead choose to stay with Orfeo so long as he is harping – an activity he chooses, as he wills, to stop. Gillian Rudd reads the harp in such moments as being the single way Orfeo is signalled as continuing in his humanity; it is also, perhaps ironically, the means through which he is able to host this alternative ad hoc community in the wild.[61]

Over the period of years of his absence, Orfeo has fully relocated, temporarily domesticating wild beasts and, 'In a tre that was hollow, / Ther was hys haule [hall], evyn and morow' (269–70).[62] The poem thus pitifully makes of a simple tree Orfeo's outdoor castle – entirely lacking in all noble luxuries, and yet marked by his presence and thereby itself converted into a royal hall. Orfeo is, as well, transformed by his harp, which is the one thing that goes with him from his courtly home and holds extensive symbolic significance throughout the poem. The harp seems to contain certain features of Orfeo himself that he lacks when separated from it – and the harp is a more reliable indicator of his identity, upon his return to his kingdom, than is his own body.[63] He has by that point been changed by the experience in ways the harp has not: as expressed through the perception of his subjects upon his incognito return, Orfeo appears as wilderness itself: 'thei seyd everychon / How the mosse grew hym upon … "Hys body is clong [gnarled] as a tre!"' (495–7). Indeed, the steward recognises Orfeo only by the harp he carries, not even by its sound while he strums it but by its very physical reality: 'The stewerd the harpe knew full suyth [immediately]' (522). Orfeo's body, no longer fully, or rather no longer only, human, has the features of a tree and, most convincing, is a natural host to moss, evidence of his successful immersion in his wilderness identity.

During this period of gradual yet deep transformation, Orfeo spends his time, when not communing with his wild neighbours through their shared appreciation of song, observing the sporadic appearances of fairy folk in the area. He sees the Fairy King and his hunting company, complete with barking hounds and glowing horns, 'Bot no dere ne best thei nom [captured]' (293).⁶⁴ At other times, armies of knights pass by. In each case, 'He wyst [knew] not were thei were becom [gone]' (294) and 'he wyst not whether [where] thei wold wend [would go]' (302). These essential events from his prior noble life have no discernible meaning to him here as he witnesses them in progress. But then dancing knights and ladies draw his attention to sixty ladies riding on palfreys, 'Not a man among them, iwyse' (308). Furthermore, 'every lady a faukon bere' and 'Of game [prey] thei found well god haunte [gathering]' (309, 311). The falcons successfully chase the birds through the sky and the river, 'Every faucon hys pray slowgh' (315). Now and only now is Orfeo able to express emotion, which he does in abundance: 'Than sate the Kyng Orfeo and lewgh [laughed]' (316). His emotion so intense that he cannot stand, Orfeo adds to this unexpected expression by speaking for the first time in ten years: 'This is gode gam [sport]! / Thyder [There] I wyll [go], be Godys name. / Sych game I was wont [accustomed] for to se' (317–19).

Orfeo's period of exile has been sustained by his communion with the wild beasts and birds, untouched by his visions of noble knights on their way to war, of the noble hunt performed by men and dogs who are strangely unable to catch their prey. Yet a vision of ladies successfully hunting with falcons abruptly transfers Orfeo back to his prior existence, to his human courtly identity, acknowledged through the physical immediacy of joyful laughter. This embodied emotional experience returns him to human social exchange and, simultaneously, to his lost wife: 'Up he rose and thether went he. / To a ladé he come tho [then]; / He beheld hyr face and body also. / Hym thought that it was in all wyse / Hys awne quen Dame Meroudys' (320–4). The vision allows him to return to human culture, which Elizabeth Allen describes in this case as 'a ritualized courtly order within which death is predictable, tolerable, even benign'⁶⁵ – as enacted in the hunt, in which certain noble animals are deployed by humans to help kill other, wild animals.

This experience, Allen further observes, 'reframes his time in the forest as a mental and emotional passage from past to present, that is, as a labor of memory in time'.⁶⁶ The emotional passage becomes especially apparent in the wordless exchange of the couple: they behold one another 'And never a word to other thei speke' (326). Seeing his transformation written on his body – 'For the poverté that sche on hym se' (327) – Meroudys's emotional expression transforms her husband's prior joy: 'The terys ran doune by hyr eyghe' (329). Her body speaks to him through its emotional experience and expression; it communicates to the fairy ladies, as well, so they lead her away from the cause of her sorrow. Orfeo's return to humanity is apparent in his own emotional response, uttered in words just as he lamented his loss of his wife as soon as she was returned from her fateful nap: Orfeo laments his inability to die (340) in the wake of this wordless exchange, asking, 'Why wold not myn herte breke a-two?' (334), a rhetorical question posed again just four lines later. Instead of dying, however, this return to emotion generates action, and he races after his wife, following the ladies as they 'In a roche of stone ... ryde' (349); he 'folowyd and not abyde' (350). His decade in the wilderness, that 'labor of memory in time', may also here be a period of penitential poverty. And it is finished. The present is no longer on hold[67] but instead reactivated, with the possibility that it might unite past and future.

This possibility is made real through Orfeo's determined negotiation with the porter, his brave walk along the wall of abducted victims, and his successful deployment of his harping ability – his artistry – to generate a clever transaction in which the Fairy King unwittingly relinquishes his stolen prize of Meroudys.[68] Orfeo's music has the effect here that it had in the wild: 'Wele hym [the Fairy King] lykyd to here hys gle; / The ryche quen, so doyd sche' (428–9), with others coming to 'felle doune to hys fete, / They thought hys herpe was so suete' (432–3). They hear and choose to remain calmly nearby, just as the beasts and birds had done. It is only after Orfeo stops – by his own will – that the Fairy King makes his rash promise, enabling the return of Meroudys to her husband and her kingdom.

Restoring Sir Orfeo

Returning to the kingdom reveals Orfeo's continuing hybrid state: he has been removed from the wilderness, but he is no longer who or what he was. The experience has transformed him. His people see him as part-tree, moss-bearing, and the poem further demonstrates that their king has been altered by his experience as part of this alternative ecology. Eleanor Griggs reads the time in the wilderness as having trained Orfeo in how to tend his kingdom appropriately through what she calls 'transformative gardening'.[69] Further, she sees Orfeo and the Fairy King as both dismembering and grafting within their own kingdoms. In the case of Orfeo, the ympe-tree[70] in his royal garden, combined with his learning in the wild, has potent results once he returns home: the steward becomes his 'heir [by being] "grafted" onto Orfeo's rootstock', Allen says,[71] with Orfeo's kingdom, as Griggs puts it, 'forever altered through the discontinuation of primogeniture'.[72] This transformation is consistently read by recent critics as preventing the poem from achieving the happy ending promised by its new genre: Elliot Kendall interprets this fundamental alteration of the kingdom as evidence of 'deep troubles with the family as a political structure';[73] Oren Falk emphasises the childlessness of their marriage as indicating that the recovery of Heurodis is ultimately a failure, and Williams, like Fletcher, sees the queen's silence once she is returned to human society as thwarting the usual reading of the ending as happy.[74] Allen sees in the dramatic scene of reunion, where Orfeo tests his steward's loyalty by first pretending to be a stranger who found the harp with the king's dead body a decade ago, another sign of the strained conclusion: upon eventually learning that this man is his missing king, the steward 'over the bord anon he threw / And fell anon doune to hys fete' (574–5). The conclusion's being achieved through an artificial grafting of the steward on to Orfeo's lineage, Allen says, is 'a rupture that the poem insistently mystifies, but the crashing furniture reminds us of the more thoroughgoing destruction of Heurodis's body and of her life itself'.[75] Reading the Middle English transformation of the poem into a romance in terms of the expectations generated by that genre and the poem's Celtic setting, analysts find the attempt a failure – or a deliberate demonstration of the failures of the cultural norms traditionally supported by the romance genre.

The conclusion of *Sir Orfeo* in Ashmole 61 does not successfully translate the classical story to a romance environment either. But because of the specific moral framework provided by the proximity of the life of St Margaret and by the unique guiding framework that the version of *Sir Orfeo* in this manuscript offers, the ending provides indications of a 'happy' resolution. In one of just two references to Christianity in the narrative, the king and queen escape the Fairy King's control 'thourow Godys grace' (465). The only other reference to God in the poem appears even more generally, when Orfeo proclaims 'Thyder I wyll, be Godys name' (318) upon seeing the fairy ladies' falcons catch their prey. Elsewhere, these references would rightly be deemed purely formulaic, given their tag-line positioning. However, this version of the poem calls on God directly in its final lines:

> And all that this wyll here or rede,
> God forgyff them ther mysded,
> To the blysse of hevyn that [so that] thei may come
> And ever more therin to woune [dwell]. (598–601)

While concluding lines conventionally call out to the reader requesting prayer for the good of the soul of the author (or scribe), here they request that those who willingly become an audience for the poem be forgiven their sins by God so that they may live in heaven eternally. In this, the poem makes the same request that St Margaret made in support of those who hear the story of her life. And in this gesture, it recalls for a reader of *Sir Orfeo* the earlier life of St Margaret, while also transforming the seemingly religiously empty story of Orfeo and Meroudys that the voice has just presented into a religious agent. Read as a single actant tethered only to what readers today can reconstruct of its earlier hermeneutic environment, *Sir Orfeo* can suggest differently: 'it is precisely by deliberately prompting so many different registers of interpretation at once, without actually authorising any of them, that the text brings us so effectively to the brink of moral and interpretative entropy',[76] Cartlidge suggests, leaving only disorientation for the audience facing what Fletcher deems a 'morally vacant space', their only refuge 'a trick of fiction' presented in the form of the happy ending.[77] Yet Seth Lerer observed that what he calls the 'Ashmole coda' – its final four lines, quoted above – 'may imply a certain celestial sense in the restoration of the kingdom'.[78]

This 'celestial sense in the restoration' is reinforced within the poem through the parallels between St Margaret and Meroudys. Margaret hovers in a space between temporary, earthly, embodied Christian faith and eternal life with God, the death of the earthly body vivid, final, and meaningful; Meroudys's earthly body, meanwhile, temporarily ceases to exist, sequestered in fairyland, and remains in a kind of hovering in-between upon its return to human community in its apparent inability to reproduce and its silence. Allen concludes that '[i]n the very process of playing out its existential fantasy of "crossing over", the poem depicts the mortal limits it seeks to transcend',[79] a conclusion richly appropriate to versions of the poem travelling without the Ashmole preface and coda. Here, however, the 'crossing over' is modelled successfully by St Margaret, and Meroudys performs an *imitatio Margaritae*: she scratches wildly at her face (l. 94, in Orfeo's vision of her) the way Margaret was scratched (as if in hell); the Fairy King shows every luxury to Meroudys just as Olibrius did to Margaret (155–74), though these are not presented as bait to lure her to believe in his god and become his wife (as did Olibrius) but instead as proof of his own power – with the threat that should she ignore that power and refuse his call, her limbs will be torn. This is precisely what happens to Margaret when she arrives but refuses to convert, with Meroudys here performing on herself the torture that the Fairy King threatens. Orfeo tries to resist the command by protecting his queen with all his knights; questioning the true power of such earthly might is what preserves Margaret, who trusts only in her own God, on whom no one calls in the narrative of Orfeo until the end. It could, then, be said of each woman, neither of them resident of a traditional romance, that '[b]y surrendering to *aventure*, to that which arrives unwilled and unforeseen, to a world where things exert uncanny agency and human lives follow erratic, sometimes ecstatic tracks, she is transported out of human time but not out of body'.[80]

Reorienting *King Edward and the Hermit*

The final poem in this section of the manuscript – which thus concludes the collection as a whole – is a text that, like *Sir Orfeo* before it, infuses an inherited literary tradition with attention to spiritual concerns that the tradition generally lacks. In this case, the text models everyday religious charity in the midst of a comic tale that reveals and pardons a crime against the king's court, itself in need of some spiritual cleansing. This 521-line incomplete poem (item 41, fols. 157r–161v), thought to be missing one or possibly two final leaves,[81] appears in no other manuscript and is known variously as *The King and the Hermit* and *King Edward and the Hermit*.[82] Despite its uniqueness, the poem shares certain features with other poems in a tradition that has come to be called 'King and Commoner' tales. Most of these are, like *King Edward and the Hermit*, extant in unique manuscript or print copies from the fifteenth century or later: *King Edward and the Shepherd* (c. 1400–50), *John the Reeve* (c. 1450), *Rauf Coilyear* (c. 1460), *The King and the Barker* (c. 1468), and the last two fytts of *A Gest of Robin Hood* (c. 1495). These narratives share a standard plot in which a king is out in the countryside, typically hunting, and is accidentally separated from his entourage. He meets a subject, most commonly a peasant, who resists the unidentified king's request for food and drink and instead expresses his anger at the king's men who unlawfully abuse peasant land and goods. Eventually, the peasant agrees to the king's request and ends up offering him good wine and, among other unexpected delectations, venison poached from the king's own forest.[83] In rare cases, the king and commoner enjoy a drinking game.[84] In exchange for this hospitality the unidentified king invites the peasant to the royal court, where the peasant is provided with a banquet during which he is mocked by the king's retinue and becomes fearful of execution once the king's identity is revealed. In those poems in the tradition that have extant endings,[85] the peasant is ultimately rewarded with goods and improved status.

As the outlines of the standard plot suggest, these narratives focus primarily on status: they typically begin with an aristocratic hunt whose tenor unexpectedly shifts with the king's separation from the others and the appearance, and the narrative foregrounding, of a commoner who makes complaints directly to the unknown king against the very noble class he represents – and more meaningfully, for the audience, against the social power structures that the king authorises. As Mark Truesdale has carefully traced through representative narratives, King and Commoner tales initially manifest a carnivalesque rule reversal, with a feast hosted by the commoner that 'melds together the political complaint … with a merry inversion of the folk carnival', the commoner become the authority.[86] When the commoner appears at the king's hall at the end of the tale, however, everything shifts back: at this court feast, the king is clearly in control; even as the peasant sits at the head of the table and is indulged with attention and delicacies, this positioning is used to mock him by emphasising, in the observations of the king's attendants at court, its utter inappropriateness. The 'hierarchical inversion' that the tradition celebrates in the early banquet in the wild is in the end overturned: 'The commoner has been placed in the absolute center of official culture and under direct surveillance', Truesdale concludes.[87] The court is once again, as it was implicitly at the start of the narrative, 'a place of death, oppression, and betrayal' in contrast to the 'liminal forest' that had been 'a place of life, feasting, and rebirth'.[88]

King Edward and the Hermit shares this plot, with two significant exceptions: the poem ends abruptly when the king invites his subject to visit him at court the next day and then departs for home, reunited with his knights; and the king's exchange occurs not with a peasant but rather a hermit. Both of these features contribute to a poem that in a number of ways alters some of the common concerns and effects shared by the other samples of the comic genre. The poem's Ashmole 61 neighbour, *Sir Corneus*, is set at the court of King Arthur and focuses on the public outing of cuckolds through a magic drinking horn (with Arthur himself the final outed cuckold); the text self-identifies as a 'bourde', tempering its potential class critique by presenting it as a joke.[89] *King Edward and the Hermit*, notably, does not so self-identify, even as modern editors of the poem continue to classify it as a bourde. In contrast, the poem self-identifies as 'this romans' (14), implicitly calling on *Sir Orfeo* rather than *Sir Corneus*, and along with that, generically resituating otherwise identifiable features of the King and the Commoner tradition. In addition, the poem transforms the particular identity of the subject: rather than an agricultural labourer, a peasant, this partner in the king's wilderness feast is a hermit, which means that he was probably originally of a noble or gentry family rather than a peasant one,[90] with his current status placing him 'outside the bounds of class'.[91] This single feature effectively removes the poem from the standard thematic framework of the King and Commoner tradition, as there is no true commoner here, even while the text maintains a number of the familiar plot points. Further, the narrative places the text generically elsewhere: the encounter of a mounted nobleman with a hermit in the wilderness is such a recognisable romance event that those readers familiar with the King and Commoner tradition must have felt themselves abruptly yanked out of that comic territory.[92]

Those not familiar with that tradition, meanwhile, are through this initial king-and-hermit encounter prepared to anticipate a romance, the very generic affiliation that the poem explicitly claims for itself.

Asserting its textual affiliations appears to be a prominent concern of the poem: its first hundred lines position this narrative in relation to an array of texts, near and far. It recalls for the Ashmole 61 reader the king-in-the-wilderness setting of the middle section of *Sir Orfeo*; at the same time, its first few lines reach back to *St Eustace* – the first text in the collection – with the notable appearance of an impressive stag under a tree.[93] Here, the king is so eager in his hunt that he presses his foresters, who assure him that there is no need to strain since his royal forest is so loaded with deer that one can see 2,000 of them in a single night (34–5). While flattering the king's royal power, this description deprives him of the challenge he seeks. At that moment, though, an 'old foster' steps up to describe a deer he saw under a tree, with a huge rack, twice as large as any other, 'Sych one saw I never are [before] / No feyrer myht be' (40–1). The king chases this mystery prey so long and so fast, 'Fro mydey to the evynsong' (73), and so fruitlessly, that he gets separated from everyone else, even the hounds, and finds himself lost. Fearful that he and his horse will be thrown in the dark, the king calls on St Julian, because he has heard 'pore men' request the saint send them 'god harborow' (84–5) when they are in need. As he himself has never been in such need, the king looks to the peasantry for religious guidance and physical sustenance. He is rewarded, for as soon as the prayer is uttered, assistance appears in the form of a hermitage, which the king first mistakes for a chapel – a process familiar to romance readers of, among other texts, *Sir Gawain and the Green Knight*.

Quickly, then, the poem calls itself a romance and evokes a series of familiar aristocratic genre markers. These it offers in place of the complaints typical of the first section of King and Commoner tales, where the narrative frames the encounter between the two in terms of the everyday abuses by the powerful committed against the peasantry. At the start of *King Edward and the Shepherd*, for instance, immediately upon meeting, the shepherd tells this stranger representing himself as a merchant, 'I am so pylled with [pillaged by] the kyng / That I most fle fro my wonyng, / And therfore woo is me. / I hade catell; now have I non; / Thay take my bestis and don thaim slone [have them slain]' (31–5). The two have an extended exchange in which the unidentified king seeks information from the shepherd about his perceived mistreatment, with the shepherd detailing the harms against him. In *King Edward and the Hermit*, only a strange stanza (ll.153–64) that is also rhythmically aberrant (with an additional half-line at 153) seems to linger from that tradition: after the stranger makes his way to the hermitage gate, he asks the hermit for lodging, and in response the hermit asserts – to this man he has never before met – that 'I have ete up all the hyre [consumed all the wages] / That ever thou gafe me. / Were I oute of myn hermyte wede [hermit's garb], / Of thi favyll [guile] I wold not dred, / Thoff ther were sych thre [three such of you]. / Loth I were with thee to fyght' (154–9). Here, the hermit references insufficient wages, presenting himself in a position of status-based precarity and referencing past deception, none of which is elsewhere supported by the narrative – and which is out of place for a voluntary ascetic such as the hermit in any case. These seven lines seem a vestige of a genre with which the poem in its current form no longer affiliates. Immediately thereafter, though, the hermit offers the king lodging and whatever food he can provide (having confessed to his guest that he eats only 'rotys and ryndys [roots and bark], among wyld bestys' [127]).[94] In this, the hermit leaves behind whatever nascent complaint those seven lines might contain. From there, the unidentified king proves himself a supportive guest, cutting wood and cleaning the stable where his horse has been housed and fed.[95] Gentle class-based humour is generated when he, for instance, feeds his horse with the barley straw that the hermit gave the king to eat for his own dinner. In such characterisations and tone, the narrative calls on the gentle romance *Sir Isumbras* much more than it does on the starkly comic *King Edward and the Shepherd*, the poem to which modern critics most often compare it.[96]

The poem's sometimes ambiguous hybridity is regularly evident and renders the King and Commoner analogues less useful as interpretive guides than they might otherwise be. Over a simple dinner of bread and cheese, the king tells his hermit-host how he, 'And I sych an hermyte were / And wonyd in this forest' (190–1), would wait for the foresters to fall asleep and then would take his bow and arrows and – because 'The kyng of venyson hath non nede' (198) – well, he just might 'hape to have' some meat that he could provide himself and his guest (199–200). That is, the unidentified king, in the hermit's position, would feel justified in taking the king's excess, regardless of the stated legality of the situation, and in sharing it with his guest. Whatever assurance is provided to the audience by the king's offering an interpretation that only he could make legally binding, in pushing the unwitting hermit this way he generates fear that the hermit will be lured into violating the king's laws right in front of him. Narrative concerns thus shape-shift again, the dramatic irony allowing the audience to sense the serious threat about which the hermit himself is ignorant. In manifesting this disparity of legal agency, the narrative may implicitly allude to the class complaint usually expressed by the peasant against the king's foresters in the King and Commoner tradition. The king continues his pressure, reasserting his sense that poaching would be appropriate: 'I wold hold it for no skath [shame], / Thoff thou had bow and arowys bothe, / Allthoff thou be a frere' (243–5). Unable yet to determine the king's motives, the audience is left on edge until the hermit responds, offering relief. Here as earlier in the poem, the king is educated by his social inferior about behaviour suitable to the situation: previously, he recalled that poor people pray to St Julian for aid, and was rewarded; here, his provocations are contained by the hermit's proper response: 'I schall be trew to hym [the king], I trow, / For to weyte [guard] my lordys prow [honour] / For dred of sych a thing' (252–4), further explaining that were he caught, he would end up in prison, and ultimately be hanged for his deed. The king continues his attempt to embolden the hermit, insisting that hunting while others are at rest is perfectly legitimate (and ignoring the hermit's concerns about his own vulnerability to royal justice).

The hermit having effectively asserted the boundaries of his own behaviour, the king then promises, 'be hym that dyghed on tre' (267), that he will not tell anyone if the hermit offers him some venison to eat. With this secrecy assured through an eternal rather than worldly authority, the hermit shifts tack: leaving behind the legal jeopardy in which poaching would place him individually with the king, he observes that as a hermit, he and his order have taken vows to pray and live on charity. He claims to have eaten no flesh since arriving at the hermitage in deference to that commitment. This moral framework thus established, however, the hermit next references his loneliness and observes that his guest 'semys a felow [friendly companion]' (285). With this, the narrative changes shape once more, moving from an *exemplum* in which a Christian refuses the temptations of a fiend dressed as a hunter into the comic mode: after all this, the hermit departs briefly to return with exquisite 'bred full whyte, / And venyson ibake tyte, / … Venyson salt and fressch he brought, / And bade hym chese wherof hym thought / Colopys [Fried or roasted meat] for to dyght [prepare]' (291–6). Having verbally constructed his required identity, the hermit demonstrates his faith in the secure community that he and his companion have built together.

With the revelation that he in fact has deer meat of various kinds, the hermit admits – admits, not confesses – that he performs exactly those criminal deeds that his guest insisted were appropriate.[97] The king, in response, eats, and eating what is actually his own venison, he laughs: indeed, 'grete laughter he lowghe' (299), confirming to the audience that his testing of his subject has been all in play. The two drink and eat and laugh, the shared truth of the hermit's poaching drawing them close, the king gently ribbing his host by saying, 'Now Crystys blyssing have sych a frere / That thus canne ordeyn our soper / And stalke under the wode bowe! [forest's boughs]' (305), with a simultaneous nod to the audience in the king's assertion that 'The kyng hymselve, so mote I thé, / Is not better at es than we' (306–7). The pair enjoy their new freedom – and the audience along with them, the pure playfulness further supported by the host's bringing out the better drink and laying out the rules for a drinking game (testing one's ability to say the nonsense words 'fustybandyas!' and 'stryke pantner!' at the appropriate time).[98] They spend the night and nearly a quarter of the narrative enjoying their freedom from social constraints as generated through the game and drink. This shared pleasure seems to be the narrative's objective, everything that leads up to it serving to make this exchange possible. Eventually, as the night wanes, the hermit describes the guest's future opportunities to share the drinking game with his own fellows – 'jentyll men' (387) – at home, and to return one day for more 'wyld dere' (392) at the hermitage. The hermit begins to return them to their appropriate separate ecologies, the forest and the court. At this point, the king introduces himself. However, his introduction is simply a more specific disguise: he says his name is Jake Fletcher (447), and he invites the hermit to visit him the next day at court where he serves the king, so he can 'quyte' his kind host for the forest feast (397).

The possibility of actual royal approval of extra-legal consumption, suggested to the audience through the laughter and the drinking game, loses some of the comfort it had promised, as the king continues to misrepresent himself to his host. At the same time, though, he claims through his particular chosen name an intimate affiliation with the hunter-hermit, representing himself as a maker of arrows, the very tools that make possible the hermit's poaching. In this, the king insists that they are deeply compatible companions, 'fellows' engaged in the same enterprise. For his part, the hermit continues to insist on his own distinct identity, separate from Jake's, for when the guest says that the two of them will meet at the king's gate and quickly be let in and served the best food available (399–404), the hermit retorts that he doesn't need the king's charity – for charity that 'comys thorow sych menys hend [such men's hands], / He havys full lytell [gets full little] that stond at hend [nearby] / Or [before] that he go away' (414–16). Further, and implicitly as a result of this lack of royal support for his subjects, the hermit continues, he has created his own reliable support network, exchanging poached venison for his neighbours' bread and ale (420–4). The reader, aware of the guest's true identity, is shown in this contrast that the hermit's thriving (thieving) community effectively exists outside the bounds of the king's insufficiently charitable legal realm – presumably as a direct response to the limits of royal largesse.

And yet despite this further admission on the part of the hermit and simultaneous attack on the character of the (presumably absent) king, the king asserts, 'So mote I thé, / Hermyte, me pays wele with thee [you please me well]: / Thou arte a horpyd [splendid/bold] frere' (426–8). He affirms his host's particular identity as 'friar', while affirming his performance of his role, however deviant. The king invites his wilderness host into a future romance, saying that 'Yit myght thou com sum dey / Unto the courte for to pley, / Aventourys for to sene, / Thou wote not what thee betyde may' (431–2), and in fact, the king says, the hermit might finish up the better for it. As a final expression of their intimacy, his host shows Jake Fletcher a special chamber, where 'The king saughe aboute the hermytys bed / Brod arowys hynge' (457–8). Here, in what is in effect the inner chamber, the hermit reveals his tools of the criminal trade and challenges his guest to pull a huge bow, which the king cannot manage, thereby demonstrating the hermit's great skill (one utterly inappropriate to his religious identity) – and inviting his guest to make him some arrows, to which Jake says, 'I schall' (473). In this act, they are functionally in league. After another pledge of fidelity, the king is taken to see two large tubs of venison, and they spend the rest of the night with their drinking game. In the morning, in the final two stanzas of the poem, the hermit promises to visit his guest at court the next day, and the king heads home. His knights and squires, who had hunted all night for him 'With sygheng and sorowyng sore. / They cryghed and blew with hydoys bere [hideous noise]' (512–13), are 'glad' to hear the king's horn. Reunited, they all head back to town, and the poem ends exactly at the bottom of fol. 161v, rather cleanly, if abruptly, concluding Ashmole 61.

The poem as we have inherited it offers an ambiguous conclusion: on the one hand, other King and Commoner narratives provide an extended final scene wherein the commoner makes his way to the king's court and is ceremoniously welcomed and dined, while also being mocked for his (inevitable) lack of courtly etiquette. In this move, Truesdale with the assistance of Bakhtin argues that, in direct contrast to the earlier feast, this concluding 'official feast asserted all that was stable, unchanging, perennial'.[99] This official feast mirrors and thus supplants the unofficial one, reasserting the proper order. In Ashmole 61, whether as a result of deliberate human intervention or of physical deterioration, the poem concludes at the unlikely pair's harmonious parting, leaving them eternally at play in the forest, the king improved by his encounter with the hermit and the hermit continuing in his poaching, having literally if unwittingly been confirmed in his activity by regal justice incarnate. This poem leaves king, hermit, and audience in the 'place of life, feasting, and rebirth'[100] – which is also the locus of the conclusion of the entire collection.

This conclusion enables a reading of this revision of the King and Commoner tradition that prioritises the carnival elements while providing, through the figure of the hermit, some opportunity for religious alongside social transformation. The hermit reveals himself as failing to meet his religious commitments in a number of ways, among them feasting outside of the religious calendar (that is, when he should be fasting) as well as hunting – which, taking the form of poaching as it does, is simultaneously social and spiritual misconduct. And yet, Truesdale suggests, 'While he is flawed, the hermit's charity nonetheless sets a better Christian example than Edward's court.'[101] In this, *King Edward and the Hermit* redirects the King and Commoner bourde: it 'takes this carnival, carnal hermit and transfigures him into a vessel that both holds and corrects the sins of the court'. In the process, Truesdale suggests, the hermit's critique of the charity of the king's court (ll. 405–19) 'serves as a mocking summarization of the usual second half of the King and Commoner plot, displaying a self-awareness and even weariness with the tradition'.[102] Had the hermit later visited 'Jake Fletcher' at the king's court and discovered the true identity of his guest, but only after himself having been mocked for his inappropriateness to the courtly environment, this might have offered the hermit opportunity for penance. The narrative's apparent lack of interest in providing him with this chance seems to affirm his priorities just as the disguised king did. Such summary, containment, and rejection of the usual second half of the narrative within the first would seem to confirm the ending as it currently stands in Ashmole 61. Read this way, the effect of this poem's contribution to the tradition provides the king with an unexpected model for improved religious expression, of hospitality as well as charity, a new orientation with which he leaves the hermitage and the narrative, with no reassertion of the ultimate authority of the royal court.

An analysis that pursues authorial or scribal intention would be thwarted by this ending of the text and of the manuscript. Such a pursuit would aim to fill the perceived gap, to determine if one or two leaves are lost from the manuscript and, based on that, how many lines are missing from the poem and what they might have originally conveyed. The aim would be to perform the duties of the second, official banquet, even in its literal absence, reasserting the tradition's control. An approach tracing book agency, however, finds in this assertion by the book's ending a refusal to participate according to expected norms for the King and Commoner tradition. The end that the book actually has, on fol. 161v, celebrates the irreconcilability of the multiple genres and traditions at play in this individual text and sustains the moment of achieved harmony resulting from the opportunity for carnival in the wild. In this, it extends the transformations occurring within and performed by the narratives that precede it. The unlawful venison and forbidden fine alcohol appear not as sins to be forgiven but instead as agents of permanent if unplanned community building. With it, Meroudys is returned from Hades and from the King of Fairy, relieved through the sovereign security promised by the steward of the maternal responsibilities otherwise expected of her – and this is managed through unexpected affiliations of man and beast enabled by harp and hand. With this end, St Margaret creates Christian community through alliances with a sacred stick, improvised sacraments, and prayer. The refashioning of genre expectations is, with the conclusion of Ashmole 61, ultimately made possible through unanticipated, and even undiscerned, ends.

Notes

1 These three narratives occupy the final quire and a half of the manuscript (quires 12 and 13), fols. 145r–161v. Each narrative except the last is followed by a lyric filling one to two folios (items 38 and 40), both of which are considered in Chapter 4. See Appendix for a table listing the manuscript's contents, including information on quiring, foliation, and watermarks.
2 Larson, 'The cults of St Margaret', p. 31. Larson offers extended description and analysis of a number of texts, images, and statues depicting the story of St Margaret, addressing lay and clerical receptions of the saint, particularly the utility of the fantastic/dragon elements in different settings. See also Lewis, '"Lete me suffre"', p. 72.
3 Over 200 medieval churches were dedicated to her, more than to any other female saint (Lewis, '"Lete me suffre"', p. 79).
4 Lewis, '"Lete me suffre"', p. 79.
5 Furthermore, the earliest extant *vitae* are ninth-century Latin and Greek texts (Larson, 'Who is the master?', p. 96).
6 Shuffelton, *Codex Ashmole 61*, p. 570.
7 This version was printed in the fifteenth century by Mombritius, hence the modern scholarly reference to this version as the 'Mombritius recension'.
8 Reames, ed., *Middle English Legends*, n.p.
9 Shuffelton, *Codex Ashmole 61*, p. 570.
10 See Larson, 'Who is the master?', for an extensive discussion of this unconventional consideration of patronage in a saint's cult – including 'the full range of practices and the artifacts those practices produced

that were associated with promoting or drawing on the subject's sanctity and efficacy as an intercessor' (p. 95).
11 Larson, 'Who is the master?', p. 97. For more on the role of St Margaret and others in medieval English childbirth culture, see Morse, 'Alongside St Margaret'.
12 The latter of these concerns – currently benefiting from readings informed by disability studies – seems to have grown out of her power against demons (Larson, 'Who is the master?', p. 97). They are also generally diminished in later versions of the story, which emphasise the childbirth experiences of mothers more narrowly.
13 See Lewis, 'The *Life of St Margaret*' and '"Lete me suffre"'; Larson, 'The cults of St Margaret' and 'Who is the master?'; Winstead, *Virgin Martyrs*; and Robertson, 'The corporeality of female sanctity'. A number of scholars have noted that the *Book of the Knight of the Tower* offers the story of St Margaret not only as a model of good (female) living but also 'as a reminder that "many grete and evylle temptacions shall befyght and assaylle yow"' (Shuffelton, *Codex Ashmole 61*, p. 571, including quote from Caxton, *Book of the Knight of the Tower*, p. 92).
14 Larson, 'Who is the master?', p. 94. Such activities are part of the 2015 historical novel *The Anchoress* by Robyn Cadwallader.
15 Larson, 'Who is the master?', p. 95.
16 Reames's *Middle English Legends of Women Saints* includes the Stanzaic Life, Mirk's *Sermon on St Margaret*, and Lydgate's *Life*. Further detail about all of these texts can be found in the footnotes of Lewis, 'The *Life of St Margaret*'.
17 Cited by Reames from the English translation by Ryan, 1.369. For more on Jacobus de Voragine and the *Legenda aurea*, see Reames, *The Legenda Aurea*. Prior to that and in the eastern tradition (where St Margaret appears as St Marina), Simeon Metaphrastes called the dragon and demon scenes 'malicious interpolations' (quoted in Larson, 'Who is the master?', p. 98; see Larson for further examples of the reception of the legend throughout the Middle Ages in a range of media). More recently, the cult of St Margaret was suppressed by the Vatican in 1969, along with those of Saints Christopher and George – whose strong legends had little or no historical evidence.
18 Larson, 'Who is the master?', p. 98.
19 Shuffelton, *Codex Ashmole 61*, p. 570.
20 All quotations from texts in Ashmole 61 are from *Codex Ashmole 61*, edited by George Shuffelton, and indicated by line number. Shuffelton glosses this phrase as 'in his control', which is a valid rendering even as it diminishes somewhat the market lens through which the original presents Olibrius as viewing and valuing his land and people.

21 This very error was exhibited by the Persian sultan in *Sir Isumbras*; see Chapter 2.
22 Lewis, 'The *Life of St Margaret*', p. 141.
23 Emphasised by Olibrius's complaint that 'Sche felys nothyng of all this wo!' (l. 219).
24 See the Introduction for discussion of medieval *vertu/virtus*.
25 Shuffelton notes that this manuscript version 'appears to be unique in making this second assailant another beast' – in even the stanzaic version that is the ultimate source of this version, the second figure is a devil (*Codex Ashmole 61*, p. 574).
26 In this depiction of the second dragon, which is represented in no other version of the story, appears the first use attested in the *Middle English Dictionary* of the word 'fin' to refer to part of the body of anything other than a fish (a point observed by Shuffelton, *Codex Ashmole 61*, p. 574). The image is intensified through the word's appearing as a rhyme word (fynnes/dynnes) – the saint's blows hitting the dragon on its fins, specifically. The preponderance of fish images throughout Ashmole 61, including a multitude of fins, makes this first appearance of this extra-piscine usage particularly intriguing.
27 'The nurse who raises Margaret outside of Antioch includes saints' lives in her oral instruction' (Shuffelton, *Codex Ashmole 61*, p. 571).
28 Lewis notes that 'The audience would also be trained to read and understand Margaret's torture, like Christ's, as part of a bargain which she is striking with God for the benefit of those who are moved by it to ask for her intercession' ('"Lete me suffre"', pp. 77–8).
29 Lewis, '"Lete me suffre"', p. 81.
30 Lewis, '"Lete me suffre"', pp. 79, 81. For more on texts and images that acted as relics to assist in childbirth in medieval England, see Morse, '"Thys moche more ys oure lady mary longe"'.
31 Reames, ed., *Middle English Legends*, '*Margaret of Antioch* Introduction', n.p.
32 Reames, ed., *Middle English Legends*, '*Margaret of Antioch* Introduction', n.p.
33 Reames, ed., *Middle English Legends*, '*Margaret of Antioch* Introduction', n.p.
34 Winstead, *Virgin Martyrs*, pp. 122, 124, 131.
35 Winstead, *Virgin Martyrs*, p. 47. In this, Winstead responds to Elizabeth Robertson's observation that most female saints' lives include 'an emphasis on physical experience' including 'intimate acquaintance with both the inanimate and animate physical world' (Robertson, 'The corporeality of female sanctity', p. 268). Robertson reads this move

as essentialist and reductive, while Winstead and Lewis a decade or so later read it very differently.
36 Lewis, '"Lete me suffre"', p. 80.
37 Lewis, 'The *Life of St Margaret*', p. 131.
38 Lewis, 'The *Life of St Margaret*', p. 133.
39 Rentz, *Imagining the Parish*, p. 11.
40 Lewis, '"Lete me suffre"', p. 78.
41 Seaman, 'Disconsolate art'. This essay addresses two poems wherein an attempt at consolation involves a rewriting of a classical story from Ovid: Chaucer's *Book of the Duchess* (the story of Seys and Alcyone) and *Sir Orfeo*.
42 Elizabeth Allen writes, '*Sir Orfeo* also depicts, in symbolically laden terms, the queen's tragic and irremediable death' ('Death and romance', p. 127).
43 In Ashmole 61, Heurodis is, uniquely, referred to as 'Meroudys'. I will refer to her as Heurodis when talking about the poem as a collective of its three different extant manuscript appearances, and as Meroudys when referencing the Ashmole 61 poem specifically.
44 See Lerer, 'Artifice and artistry'; Falk, 'The son of Orfeo'; Cartlidge, 'Sir Orfeo in the Otherworld'; Williams, 'Fairy magic'; Fletcher, '*Sir Orfeo* and the flight'; and Kendall, 'Family, *Familia*'. These readings have also, as this list acknowledges, contributed to the reading generated and conveyed here.
45 Virgil, *Georgics* IV; Ovid, *Metamorphoses* X.
46 Cartlidge, 'Sir Orfeo in the Otherworld', p. 226. Such exploitation was performed by many in the Middle Ages, among them Christine de Pizan, Boccaccio, William of Conches, Nicholas Trivet, the author of the *Ovide Moralisé*, and Robert Henryson. 'Through medieval commentaries, Christian re-readings of the narrative became well-known: 1) Orpheus's backward glance and his consequent loss of Eurydice becomes emblematic for temptation and sin; or 2) Orpheus becomes a Christ figure and the tale foretells redemption' (Laskaya and Salisbury, Introduction to *Sir Orfeo*, n.p.).
47 Shuffelton summarises this status well: 'Of all the texts in Ashmole 61, none has attracted the amount of critical attention that *Sir Orfeo* has. Though much of this attention stems from the poem's beauty and ingenious construction, a large portion of the scholarly interest can also be attributed to the poem's mysteriousness' (*Codex Ashmole 61*, p. 579).
48 That said, Elizabeth Allen – without explicit consideration of the poem's Ashmole 61 neighbourhood and in terms of Middle English romance generally – notes in her reading of *Sir Orfeo* that Sir Isumbras 'is

initially described as a grand lord who likes to hear minstrels singing in his hall' ('Death and romance', p. 143, n. 14). That *Sir Isumbras* is the fifth item in Ashmole 61 makes this association textually as well as generically pertinent.

49 Such a recollection is similar to that performed in the depictions of St Margaret's *imitatio Christi* outlined above.
50 Williams, 'Fairy magic', p. 537. Williams describes wonder as 'an active and productive response'.
51 Cartlidge, 'Sir Orfeo in the Otherworld', p. 200. His essay offers examples from twelfth- and thirteenth-century clerical and vernacular texts.
52 Caldwell, 'The heroism of Heurodis', pp. 296, 297. Caldwell is here associating these features of *Sir Orfeo* with virgin-martyr lives in general, not St Margaret's in particular.
53 Fletcher, '*Sir Orfeo* and the flight', p. 144.
54 Cohen, *Stone*, p. 185.
55 These lines are not included in *Arthour and Merlin* in its appearance in London, Lincoln's Inn, Hale MS 150 (early fifteenth century).
56 Shuffelton, *Codex Ashmole 61*, p. 584.
57 The *Middle English Dictionary* does not list this appearance among its associated quotations. It does list the Auchinleck appearance, in *Arthur and Merlin*, and associates it with the fourth meaning. The passage's role there in the midst of the romance is rather different from its role here, appended to the start of a different poem.
58 Lerer, 'Artifice and artistry', p. 94. This is a key observation of the poem's workings in Lerer's reading, setting the artistry of Orfeo in contrast to the artifice of the Fairy King.
59 In this, the poem offers an alternative assemblage to the one St Margaret experiences with the two dragons, the first of which glides near her in a structural echo of the wild beasts around Orfeo.
60 It is difficult to resist observing a parallel with the triple repetition of the fear felt by the crowds at St Margaret's execution.
61 Rudd, *Greenery*, p. 99.
62 Of the Auchinleck version, which contains a half-line absent in line 269 in Ashmole 61 that specifically indicates that the harp is stored in the hollow tree, Griggs observes that '[b]y placing the symbol of his art and his courtly life within the body of a tree, the wild forest literally swallows up human society' ('The orchard and the "ympe tre"', p. 106). While less vividly represented here, the effect is fundamentally the same.
63 Cohen describes objects in the poem – he references the tree and the stone, though this is appropriate to the harp as well – as 'material

objects that are literally metaphoric and irreducible to symbol' (*Stone*, p. 183). These objects, that is, carry symbolic significance in the text in which they appear, even as they carry significance that is super-symbolic, as well.

64 Neil Cartlidge observes that 'the Otherwold breaks into the everyday world in the form of a hunt-without-prey' elsewhere in medieval texts as well, as in the extended *Peterborough Chronicle* example he provides ('Sir Orfeo in the Otherworld', p. 201).
65 Allen, 'Death and romance', p. 134.
66 Allen, 'Death and romance', p. 134. This calls to mind Cohen's description of the ympe-tree and the rock in this text as 'transport devices', for they both enable in undisclosed ways the movement of humans from their familiar world of the orchard and the forest to the unfamiliar world of fairy (*Stone*, p. 183).
67 Elliot Kendall describes Orfeo's wilderness period as 'death-likeness, stasis, and sterility' ('Family, *Familia*', p. 319).
68 Orfeo's arrival at the Fairy King's castle and encounter with the porter, where he presents himself as a minstrel, is all reflective of the same trick in *Sir Cleges*, where it provides Cleges with access to King Uther. Here, as there, the entry leads to a redistribution in moral terms – enabled by the harp here, by divine cherries there. See Chapter 3 for a discussion of that poem in Ashmole 61.
69 Griggs, 'The orchard and the "ympe tre"', p. 97. In striking contrast, Kendall focuses on Orfeo's relationship with the fauna (rather than the flora) in the wild as a 'parody of Adam's naming of the animals in Eden', because 'instead of confirming his dominance or stewardship, Orfeo pays them no attention' – what Kendall calls a ten-year 'loop of potential mastery unfulfilled' ('Family, *Familia*', p. 321).
70 An ympe-tre is not a particular species of tree but rather one that has been grafted. See Jirsa, 'In the shadow of the ympe-tre', for detailed analysis of the history of modern criticism of this feature of the poem.
71 Allen, 'Death and romance', p. 141. Allen reads Heurodis as literally dead, with the first self-destructive scene and the tableau scene (where Heurodis is under the ympe-tree, presented right after the list of deaths of women by childbirth and madness) indicating that this – death in childbirth and through madness – is Heurodis's fate and is both why she is gone and why Orfeo has no heir (see esp. 'Death and romance', pp. 135–7).
72 Griggs, 'The orchard and the "ympe tre"', p. 110.
73 Kendall, 'Family, *Familia*', p. 289.
74 See Falk, 'The son of Orfeo'; Williams, 'Fairy magic', p. 554; and Fletcher, '*Sir Orfeo* and the flight'.

75 Allen, 'Death and romance', p. 142.
76 Cartlidge, 'Sir Orfeo in the Otherworld', p. 225.
77 Fletcher, '*Sir Orfeo* and the flight', p. 164.
78 Lerer, 'Artifice and artistry', p. 106.
79 Allen, 'Death and romance', p. 128.
80 Cohen, *Stone*, p. 184.
81 Bruce Barker-Benfield attempted, during the manuscript's rebinding in 1986, to reconstruct the quiring of the manuscript in its original form (made less discernible through resewing and pasting in the centuries following Rate's day). He determined that the final quire, the manuscript's thirteenth, which this text concludes, originally had 16 leaves, with the final five folios now missing (Shuffelton, *Codex Ashmole 61*, p. 2). Based on the patterns of other King and Commoner tales, Shuffelton and others posit that there may be 1–2 folios of the original *King Edward and the Hermit* now missing.
82 The poem appears in Ashmole 61 without a title (unlike *Sir Orfeo*, which here has the title 'King Orfew'). The king in the poem is referred to as King Edward in line 13 ('It befell be god Edwerd deys'), but that identification holds no apparent significance in the remainder of the poem. Another poem in the tradition is called *King Edward and the Shepherd*, and in that case the king is distinctively Edward III, given the specific references to Edward's reign made in the poem, which was written for 'one of Edward's many court celebrations and includ[es] prominent members of the court in its storyline. It appears to be indebted to the Latin *Speculum Regis Edwardi III* by William of Pagula, a pair of open letters from 1331 and 1332 that castigate Edward and his court for abuses of purveyancing' (Furrow, 'Kings and Commoners: introduction', n.p. Further, see Truesdale, *The King and Commoner Tradition* and 'Robin Hood'.) Most critics working with the text in the modern era use the title *The King and the Hermit*, including recent editor Melissa Furrow, although Ashmole 61 editor Shuffelton chooses *King Edward and the Hermit* (used previously by a German editor in 1905), as does the critic who has had most to say about the poem in the past century, Mark Truesdale, probably following Shuffelton.
83 *King Edward and the Shepherd* is found in Cambridge University Library MS Ff.5.48 (late fifteenth century); *John the Reeve* remains only in the seventeenth-century Percy Folio; *Rauf Coilyear* (a Scottish text wherein Charlemagne visits a collier) remains in a print copy from 1572; *The King and the Barker* is extant in Cambridge University Library MS Ee.4.35 (c. 1468); *A Gest of Robin Hood* remains only in printed editions from 1495. Estimated dates of production for the texts are

provided by Truesdale, *The King and Commoner Tradition*. Melissa Furrow observes that 'Looked at as a group, the poems evidently enjoyed a very broad audience: royal and noble, clerical, bourgeois; Windsor, Staffordshire, Leicestershire, Scotland' (Furrow, 'Kings and Commoners: introduction', n.p.). Truesdale notes that King and Commoner tales and Robin Hood tales were 'related literary traditions [that] were often recorded in similar forms, preserved in the same manuscripts, and became inseparably merged at the end of the fifteenth century in *A Lytell Geste of Robyn Hode*, whose seventh and eighth fyttes adapt the King and Commoner narrative' ('Robin Hood', p. 69). Sir Walter Scott adapted scenes of the king and the friar from this poem for scenes between Friar Tuck and King Richard in chapters 16 and 17 of *Ivanhoe* (1820) (Truesdale, *King and Commoner Tradition*, p. 198).

84   *King Edward and the Hermit* shares this feature with *King Edward and the Shepherd* – though it should be noted that the games have different rules in each poem. The roots of a drinking game between a king and an unexpected partner go back to Gerald of Wales's *Speculum Ecclesiæ* (thirteenth century), where the king is a disguised Henry II who is hosted by a Cistercian abbot. Walter Map and King Alfred also told 'king and commoner' style stories. For more on the latter, see Truesdale, 'Robin Hood'.

85   A number of them, including *King Edward and the Shepherd*, considered the closest analogue to *King Edward and the Hermit*, do not.

86   Truesdale, 'Robin Hood', p. 76. Truesdale adds that the peasant's lament about injustices regarding food 'transforms the banquet table into a site of class warfare' ('Robin Hood', p. 73).

87   Truesdale 'Robin Hood', p. 77.

88   Truesdale, 'Robin Hood', p. 78.

89   The title of the TEAMS collection in which Melissa Furrow's editions of *The King and the Hermit*, *King Edward and the Shepherd*, and *John the Reeve* appear (alongside seven other comic texts) is *Ten Bourdes*.

90   Furrow, 'Kings and Commoners: introduction', n.p.

91   Shuffelton, *Codex Ashmole 61*, p. 591.

92   In the more common narrative, the aristocratic orientation of the narrative's introduction via the hunt is 'quickly disrupted by the intrusion of the commoner (a figure decidedly not common in romance)' (Truesdale, 'Robin Hood', p. 71). In this way, *King Edward and the Hermit* seems to be removing in a single character reassignment both the genre disruption and the class intrusion generated by the commoner.

93   See Chapter 1 for an extended discussion of *St Eustace*. The poem is set in Sherwood Forest, with whom Robin Hood was associated by

the early 1400s; Jeffrey L. Singman observes that 'the unparalleled and otherwise unnecessary reference to Sherwood [in *King Edward and the Hermit*] could well be a deliberate allusion to the Robin Hood tradition', one that by the time of Ashmole 61 included Friar Tuck (*Robin Hood*, p. 83).

94 Echoes of *Sir Orfeo* fill this poem as abundantly as deer do the king's royal forest.

95 Here, Sir Isumbras's time as a blacksmith and St Eustace's as a hayward come to mind. Not to be overlooked is George Shuffelton's saying that King Edward 'performs his chores ... with the enthusiasm of a visitor to a dude ranch' (*Codex Ashmole 61*, p. 592).

96 Shuffelton observes that 'usually the host combines crude, rustic manners with pompous self-satisfaction'; for instance, Rauf Coilyear 'knocks [his guest] Charlemagne to the floor for a perceived breach of etiquette' (*Codex Ashmole 61*, p. 591).

97 Truesdale calls this hermit a blend of the 'tradition's trickster poacher with a carnal, pleasure-loving religious figure who is partially drawn from the carnival Abbot of Misrule, anti-clerical satire, and comic literature'. Gerald of Wales's *King Henry II and the Cistercians* also used a religious figure in this tradition – but that is unusual (Truesdale, *King and Commoner Tradition*, p. 106).

98 For some hypothetical explanation of this word choice, see Furrow, *Ten Fifteenth-Century Comic Poems*, on which Shuffelton bases his note to line 340 (*Codex Ashmole 61*, p. 595).

99 Bakhtin, *Rabelais*, p. 9; quoted in Truesdale, *King and Commoner Tradition*, p. 4.

100 Truesdale, 'Robin Hood', p. 78.

101 Truesdale, *King and Commoner Tradition*, p. 108.

102 Truesdale, *King and Commoner Tradition*, p. 109.

Epilogue: fishing for answers

> Most manuscript scholars trust that there are answers to be found in books and that careful research will turn these answers up.
>
> Alexandra Gillespie, 'Manuscripts'

This book has argued by example that the simple act of reading an everyday household manuscript collection seriously muddies the waters of our placid hermeneutic pools. Immersion in the full ecology of the manuscript stirs up items previously settled at the bottom, rendering a pond murky, and maybe even menacing, in its renewed opaqueness. This project set out to discern what happens when we read a single medieval manuscript as a living anthology of literary texts functioning collaboratively, rather than treating it as a static historical document fixed in the past, or as an archive of textual variants to be consulted and corrected. The 'careful research' performed through reading the household ecology of Ashmole 61 this way discovered, for instance, that a poem's layout could exert agency on interpretation that challenged normally reliable hermeneutic guides such as genre study or historicism. Again and again, it revealed that answers were not waiting to be unearthed and identified; instead, seeking them yielded entry-points to alternative topographies – as does an ympe-tree, or an angel.

An array of recognisable non-human features of the collection appeal to readers of the physical manuscript Ashmole 61, most notably the fish and flowers distributed throughout the codex. The manuscript is generally typical in terms of its literary contents, offering an assortment of romances, conduct texts, saints' lives, and devotional texts as do other fifteenth-century household books produced in the English Midlands. In terms of its physical features, however, it is exceptional, taking the form of a tall account book (otherwise interpreted as a holster book) and presenting not only illustrations, themselves very rare in household books, but an extended series of images of fish and flowers. Indeed, among medievalists familiar with the manuscript, 'the Rate fish' is easily recognised out of context – say, when it appears in the form of a tattoo on a person's forearm. As a result, readers of the manuscript might be more receptive to a particular line in *Lybeaus Desconus* than would be those reading the poem in another material environment, for instance, in Naples, Bibliotheca Nazionale MS XIII B.29, or in Shuffelton's modern print edition or its online twin, all of which lack the images of fish and flowers.

Lybeaus Desconus, halfway into the poem in its Ashmole 61 setting, has an encounter with Otis de Lile in which Lybeaus is 'besette [trapped] / As the fysche in the nette' (1184). The action of the 'grymly gromys [fierce young officers]' (1187) who capture him seems likely, at the very least, to prevent Lybeaus from reaching the Lady of Synadoune and achieving his quest. Yet in that very moment of overcoming him, Otis's men reveal their intense fear of Lybeaus, having just witnessed his superior knightly valour: they proclaim, 'This is the fend Sathan!' (1180). This stanza can appear overloaded with figurative associations – Lybeaus the fish possibly calling to mind affiliation with Christ, even as he is perceived by his wicked opponents as the devil. In this cosmic ecology stretching from earth to heaven and hell, Lybeaus is rendered a kind of supernatural hybrid potentially mingling the sacred and the profane.

Appearing on folio 49v of the manuscript, the verbal image is further saturated with possibilities, for the fish that the scribe appears to use as his brand throughout the manuscript has begun behaving differently here in the midst of *Lybeaus Desconus* and its neighbour *The Erle of Tolous*. In the previous section of the manuscript, that is, in the first two quires (and as described in detail in Chapter 1 of this book), a fish and sometimes one or more flowers appear alongside, or eventually at times in place of, the abundant scribal signature (a simple 'Amen' developing to a thereafter-repeated 'Amen quod Rate') at the end of most items. After following this pattern for 48 folios, Rate's fish start acting differently. In the long poems in this section of the manuscript, the fish appear mid-text, positioned no longer exclusively as a signature equivalent participating in the colophon at the text's conclusion.

It is tempting to posit that Rate felt the need to assert his presence in the midst of these extended narratives. The shorter texts in this section of the manuscript follow the fashion established in the preceding quires. For instance, *Knight who Forgave* (item 18) concludes, as has by this point become typical, with a fish and 'Amen quod Rate' squeezed together between that item and the next. The following text is the 11-folio *Erle of Tolous*, at that point the longest text in the collection. The text ends with 'Amen quod Rate' and a flower; it does present fish, too, but does so on its internal pages – one on fol. 31r a few folios in, and then three across the seam of 36v and 37r, with two fish appearing as a tiny school on the left, and another on the right (see Figure 5). The conclusion of the poem appears on 38v, just two turns of the page later. The next item, *Lybeaus Desconus*, fills 21 folios (38v–59v) – nearly twice as many as the already uncharacteristically long *Erle of Tolous* – and reaches a reduced colophon of just 'Amen quod Rate' with no image, not even a flower as in *The Erle of Tolous*. Prior to this, though, fish have swum through the narrative not only in the verbal image of battle recalled above but also in the form of a little pug-nosed fish on 46v and a portly fish on 58r, once again right before the conclusion of the poem.

This is another instance of the ways the fish in Ashmole 61 calls attention to itself – or, rather, the fish call attention to themselves

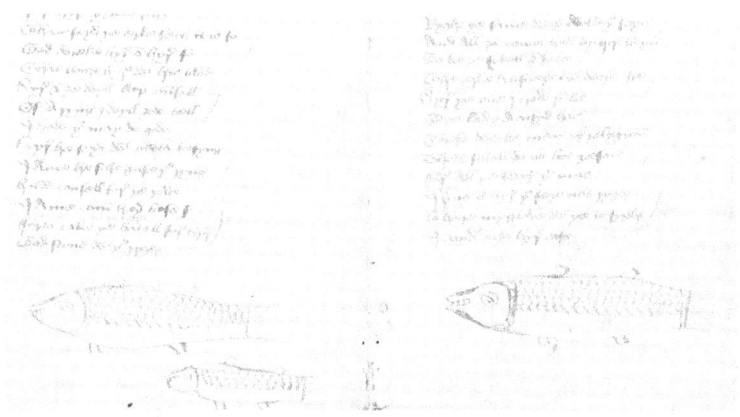

5 Oxford, Bodleian Library MS Ashmole 61, fols. 36v–37r: *The Erle of Tolous*

– and by extension to the non-human contributors to the manuscript throughout. Despite my having pointed towards the possibility of Christian figurative associations in the image of Lybeaus as a fish about to be caught – associations possibly, if paradoxically, further encouraged by the reference to Lybeaus as Satan in the same stanza – readers of this book's introduction will recall that in relation to the repeating Rate manuscript fish iconography, I resist such explanations. Above all, what I am not positing here or elsewhere is a consistent significance, symbolic or otherwise, for the fish that inhabit Ashmole 61. The reading strategy that I discern Ashmole 61 to be suggesting to its readers lacks such a fully consistent or cohesive methodology, despite what can at times appear to be a literal-minded didacticism.

Rather, the behaviour of the fish within the texts and on the pages of the manuscript provokes the kind of understanding of seeming misalignment that Christopher Cannon has spotted in another collection of exemplary texts, Robert Mannyng's *Handlyng Synne* (from which Rate, indirectly or otherwise, retrieved *The Knight who Forgave his Father's Slayer* for this manuscript). Cannon observes that *Handlyng Synne* 'possesses the kind of form that resists analysis because its shape seems so simple and obvious': its careful division into sections on different topics (Ten Commandments, Seven Deadly Sins, and so on) gives the impression that it progresses methodically by rotating among exemplary narratives, moral and spiritual instruction, and introductions of pertinent topics.[1] Cannon observes that many of the narratives in fact connect only indirectly to the *sentence* with which they are presented; he concludes that, rather than being an error or failed afterthought, this mismatch is precisely what encourages audiences' learning through reflection. In fact, Cannon says, 'the bold and extraordinary achievement of these narratives is to unfold doctrine in ways ... requiring such efforts on the reader's part – that their very apprehension makes them a part of lived experience'.[2]

The abundant fish in Ashmole 61, cohabiting in both consistent and idiosyncratic ways with the texts with which they share the page and the book, encourage reflection on this very inconsistency, too. That reflection may, as Cannon suggests, cause the textual river in which the fish swim to become, through the puzzle they present to the reader, an active part of extra-textual experience. Elizabeth

Allen notes that 'even as they detach or disorient readers ... ruptures also encourage symbolic or associative connection'.³ What ruptures and disconnections do not do, *pace* Allen or Cannon, is point towards a single true textual meaning. Similarly, the section of exemplary texts in which *Lybeaus Desconus* appears in Ashmole 61 may gesture through its human–non-human mercy assemblages towards a reliably moral foundation, yet the inconsistencies within and among texts even in the seemingly constrained and univocal interpretive environment of didactic literature point towards acts of learning and discernment rather than a fixed moral answer. Reading the community of texts in Ashmole 61, and doing so through its varied mediations – fifteenth-century manuscript, twenty-first-century print edition, or online version thereof – makes clear the differing agencies that each environment affords individual members, human and otherwise, of the full household book.

Notes

1 Cannon, 'Form', p. 185.
2 Cannon, 'Form', p. 187. I present a similar argument regarding *The Wounds and the Sins* in Chapter 3.
3 Allen, 'Episodes', p. 192.

Appendix

Contents of Oxford, Bodleian Library MS Ashmole 61

Quire Status	Watermark	Foliation	Item	Title	MS
Q.1. ff. 1-8	none	1r-5r	1	[Life of] *Seynt Ewstas* (title in MS)	2
		5v-6r	2	Lydgate's *Ram's Horn*	11
		6r-6v	3	*How the Wise Man Taught his Son*	2
		7r-8v	4	*Good Wife Taught her Daughter*	V
Q.2. ff. 9-18	none	9r-16v	5	[Sir] *Ysombras* (title in MS)	10
		16v-17r	6	*Ten Commandments*	V
		17v-19v	7	Lydgate's *Stans Puer Ad Mensam* (long version)	V
Q.3. ff. 19-30	A	20r-21v	8	*Dame Curtasy*	V
		21v	9	Latin epigram	V
		21v	10	12 rules for purchase of land	15
		21v	11a	Latin epigram	U
		21v	11b	Latin epigram	V
Q.4. ff. 30-45	A	22r	12	Evening prayer	3
		22r-22v	13	Morning prayer	2
		22v	14	*Ten Commandments*	-
		22v-23r	15	Prayer to Mary	51
Q.5. ff. 46-57	A	23r-26r	16	*Debate of the Carpenter's Tools*	U
		26r-26v	17	Prayer at the Levation	7
		26v-27v	18	*The Knight who Forgave His Father's Slayer*	U
Q.6. ff. 58-65	B	27v-38v	19	*Erle of Tolous*	4
		38v-59v	20	*Lybaeus Desconus*	6
Q.7. ff. 66-77	B	59v-62r	21	*Sir Corneus*	U
		62r-65v	22	*The Jealous Wife*	U
		66r-67v	23	*The Incestuous Daughter*	2
		67v-73r	24	*Sir Cleges*	2
Q.8. ff. 78-91	B	73r-78v	25	*The Feasts of All Saints and All Souls* (Latin title in MS)	V
		78v-83r	26	*The King and His Four Daughters*	V
		83r-87v	27	*Ypotis*	14
Q.9. ff. 92-104	none	87v-105v	28	*Northern Passion* (Latin title in MS)	13
		106r	29	*Short Charter of Christ*	21
		106r	30	*The Lament of Mary*	2
Q.10. ff. 105-120	C	107r-108r	31	Lydgate's *Dietary* ("The governans of man" in the MS)	56
		108r-119v	32	Maidstone's *Seven Penitential Psalms* (Latin title in MS)	14
		120r-128r	33	*Prick of Conscience Minor*	7
Q.11. ff. 121-136	C	128r-136r	34	*The Stasyons of Jerusalem* (title in MS)	2
		136r-136v	35a	*The Sinner's Lament*	6
		136v-138v	35b	*The Adulterous Falmouth Squire*	7
Q.12. ff. 137-150	C	138v-144v	36	*Legend of the Resurrection*	V
		145r-150v	37	[*Life of St.*] *Margaret* (title in MS)	2
		150v-151r	38	*The Wounds and the Sins*	9
Q.13. ff. 151-162	C	151r-156r	39	*Kyng Orfew* (title in MS)	3
		156v-157r	40	*Vanyte* (title in MS)	U
		157r-161v	41	*King Edward and the Hermit*	U

Notes

Watermark information and collation are based on the MS Ashmole 61 Collation Chart (REFS LXXIV.27) produced by B. C. Barker-Benfield of Duke Humfrey's Library (Bodleian Library, Oxford) in 1986. The watermarks were identified by A. J. Bliss (*Sir Orfeo*, pp. xi–xiii). My thanks to Dr Barker-Benfield for his generous assistance with these materials. Only a third of the works in Ashmole 61 are given titles in the manuscript (items 1, 5, 20, 25, 28, 30, 31, 32, 34, 37, 39, and 40). Titles used here are generally those used in Shuffelton's edition, themselves adapted from Blanchfield ('The romances in MS Ashmole 61', p. 87) and Guddat-Figge (*Catalogue of Manuscripts Containing Middle English Romances*, pp. 249–51).

Under 'MS status', U means that the Ashmole text is a unique copy of the item; V means that the Ashmole text is considered a unique version of the item (listed as such in the *Digital Index of Middle English Verse*); a number indicates that the Ashmole text is not a unique copy and is not considered a unique version but instead is one among that number of extant copies. This information was informed by Blanchfield, 'The romances in MS Ashmole 61', p. 87, and the *DIMEV*.

When this book was first published, MS Ashmole 61 could be consulted only in person in the Bodleian Library. The included images are copies of photos provided at that time by Bodleian Imaging Services. Now, a complete digitized copy of the manuscript can be accessed online for free through the Digital Bodleian website: https://digital.bodleian.ox.ac.uk/objects/69462c25-b481-4643-9942-34f7243ea921/

Bibliography

Adams, Gillian. 'Medieval children's literature: its possibility and actuality'. *Children's Literature* 26 (1998): 1–24.
Adams, Tracy. 'Introduction: devotions and emotions in the Middle Ages'. *Digital Philology* 1.2 (2012): 173–83.
Ahmed, Sara. 'Affective economies'. *Social Text* 22.2 (2004): 117–39.
Ahmed, Sara. *The Cultural Politics of Emotion*. Abingdon: Routledge, 2004.
Ahmed, Sara. 'Happy objects'. In Melissa Gregg and Gregory J. Seigworth, eds, *The Affect Theory Reader*. Durham, NC: Duke University Press, 2010, pp. 31–51.
Alaimo, Stacy. *Bodily Natures: Science, Environment, and the Material Self*. Bloomington, IN: Indiana University Press, 2010.
Alaimo, Stacy, and Susan Hekman. *Material Feminisms*. Bloomington, IN: Indiana University Press, 2008.
Allen, Elizabeth. 'Death and romance in *Sir Orfeo*'. In Daniel K. Jernigan, Walter Wadiak, and Michelle Wang, eds, *Narrating Death: The Limit of Literature*. Abingdon: Routledge, 2019, pp. 126–46.
Allen, Elizabeth. 'Episodes'. In Paul Strohm, ed., *Middle English*. Oxford Twenty-First Century Approaches to Literature. Oxford: Oxford University Press, 2007, pp. 191–206.
Allen, Elizabeth. *False Fables and Exemplary Truth: Poetics and Reception of Medieval Mode*. Basingstoke: Palgrave Macmillan, 2005.
Allen, Valerie. 'Mineral virtue'. In Jeffrey Jerome Cohen, ed., *Animal, Vegetable, Mineral: Ethics and Objects*. Washington, DC: Oliphant Books, 2012, pp. 123–52.
Amos, Mark Addison. '"For manners make man": Bourdieu, de Certeau, and the common appropriation of noble manners in the *Book of Courtesy*'. In Kathleen Ashley and Robert L. A. Clark, eds, *Medieval Conduct*. Medieval Cultures, 29. Minneapolis, MN: University of Minnesota Press, 2001, pp. 23–48.
Amsler, Mark. 'Affective literacy: gestures of reading in the later Middle Ages'. *Essays in Medieval Studies* 18 (2001): 83–110.
Ankersmit, F. R. *Sublime Historical Experience*. Stanford, CA: Stanford University Press, 2005.

Archibald, Elizabeth. *Incest and the Medieval Imagination*. Oxford: Oxford University Press, 2001.
Aristotle. *History of Animals*. In *Complete Works*, vol. 1. Ed. Jonathan Barnes. Princeton, NJ: Princeton University Press, 1984, pp. 921–3 [8.1].
Ashe, Laura. 'The "Short Charter of Christ": an unpublished longer version, from Cambridge University Library, MS Add. 6686'. *Medium Aevum* 72 (2003): 32–48.
Ashley, Kathleen. '*The Miroir des Bonnes Femmes*: not for women only?' In Kathleen Ashley and Robert L. A. Clark, eds, *Medieval Conduct*. Medieval Cultures, 29. Minneapolis, MN: University of Minnesota Press, 2001, pp. 86–105.
Ashley, Kathleen, and Robert L. A. Clark. 'Introduction. Medieval conduct: texts, theories, practices'. In Kathleen Ashley and Robert L. A. Clark, eds, *Medieval Conduct*. Medieval Cultures, 29. Minneapolis: University of Minnesota Press, 2001, pp. ix–xx.
Bahr, Arthur. *Fragments and Assemblages: Forming Compilations of Medieval London*. Chicago: University of Chicago Press, 2013.
Bahr, Arthur. 'Miscellaneity and variance in the medieval book'. In Michael Johnston and Michael Van Dussen, eds, *The Medieval Manuscript Book: Cultural Approaches*. Cambridge: Cambridge University Press, 2015, pp. 181–98.
Bahr, Arthur, and Alexandra Gillespie. 'Medieval English manuscripts: form, aesthetics, and the literary text'. *Chaucer Review* 47.4 (2013): 346–60, introduction to special issue: *Medieval English Manuscripts: Form, Aesthetics, and the Literary Text*.
Bakhtin, Mikhail. *Rabelais and his World*. Trans. Hélène Iswolsky. Bloomington, IN: Indiana University Press, 1984.
Barad, Karen. *Meeting the Universe Halfway: Quantum Physics and the Entanglement of Matter and Meaning*. Durham, NC: Duke University Press, 2007.
Barad, Karen. 'Posthumanist performativity: toward an understanding of how matter comes to matter'. In Stacy Alaimo and Susan Hekman, eds, *Material Feminisms*. Bloomington, IN: Indiana University Press, 2008, pp. 120–54.
Barker-Benfield, Bruce C. 'MS Ashmole 61 collation chart,' REFS LXXIV.27. Duke Humfrey's Library, Bodleian Library, Oxford, 1986.
Behar, Katherine. 'An introduction to OOF'. In Katherine Behar, ed., *Object-Oriented Feminism*. Minneapolis, MN: University of Minnesota Press, 2016, pp. 1–36.
Benjamin, Walter. 'The work of art in the age of mechanical reproduction'. In *Illuminations*. Trans. Harry Zohn. Ed. Hannah Arendt. New York: Schocken Books, 1969, pp. 217–52.
Bennett, Jane. 'Systems and things: a response to Graham Harman and Timothy Morton'. *New Literary History* 43.2 (2012): 225–33.
Bennett, Jane. *Vibrant Matter: A Political Ecology of Things*. Durham, NC: Duke University Press, 2010.

Blanchfield, Lynne S. '"An idiosyncratic scribe": a study of the practice and purpose of Rate, the scribe of Bodleian Library MS Ashmole 61'. DPhil dissertation, University of Wales, Aberystwyth, 1991.

Blanchfield, Lynne S. 'Rate revisited: the compilation of narrative works in MS Ashmole 61'. In J. Fellows et al., eds, *Romance Reading on the Book*. Cardiff: University of Wales Press, 1995, pp. 208–20.

Blanchfield, Lynne S. 'The romances in MS Ashmole 61: an idiosyncratic scribe'. In Maldwyn Milles, Jennifer Fellows, and Carol Meale, eds, *Romance in Medieval England*. Cambridge: D. S. Brewer, 1991, pp. 65–87.

Bliss, J. A., ed. *Sir Orfeo*. Oxford: Clarendon Press, 1966.

Boffey, Julia. 'Bodleian Library, MS Arch. Selden. B.24 and definitions of the "Household Book"'. In A. S. G. Edwards, Vincent Gillespie, and Ralph Hanna, eds, *The English Medieval Book: Studies in Memory of Jeremy Griffiths*. London: British Library, 2000, pp. 125–34.

Boffey, Julia, and A. S. G. Edwards. 'Bodleian MS Arch.Selden B.24: the genesis and evolution of a Scottish poetical anthology'. *Poetica* 60 (2003): 31–46.

Boffey, Julia, and A. S. G. Edwards. 'Towards a taxonomy of manuscript assemblages'. In Margaret Connolly and Raluca Radulescu, eds, *Insular Books: Vernacular Manuscript Miscellanies in Late Medieval Britain*. Proceedings of the British Academy, 201. Oxford: Oxford University Press for the British Academy, 2015, pp. 263–79.

Boffey, Julia, and John T. Thompson, 'Anthologies and miscellanies: production and choice of texts'. In Jeremy Griffiths and Derek Pearsall, eds, *Book Publishing in Britain 1375–1475*. Cambridge: Cambridge University Press, 1989, pp. 279–315.

Bogost, Ian. *Alien Phenomenology, or What It's Like to Be a Thing*. Minneapolis, MN: University of Minnesota Press, 2012.

Bolter, Jay David, and Richard Grusin. *Remediation: Understanding New Media*. Cambridge, MA: MIT Press, 1999.

Bourdieu, Pierre. *The Logic of Practice*. Trans. Richard Nice. Stanford, CA: Stanford University Press, 1990 [1980].

Brantley, Jessica. 'The pre-history of the book'. *PMLA* 124.2 (2009): 1–15.

Brantley, Jessica. 'Reading the forms of *Sir Thopas*'. *Chaucer Review* 47.4 (2013): 416–38.

Braswell, Laurel. '*Sir Isumbras* and the legend of St Eustace'. *MS* 27 (1965): 128–51.

Brockman, Bennett. 'Children and literature in late medieval England'. *Children's Literature* 4 (1973): 58–63.

Broomhall, Susan. 'Emotions in the household'. In Susan Broomhall, ed., *Emotions in the Household, 1200–1900*. Basingstoke: Palgrave, 2008, pp. 1–37.

Brown, Carleton, ed. *Religious Lyrics of the XVth Century*. Oxford: Clarendon Press, 1957 [1924].

Bryan, Jennifer. *Looking Inward: Devotional Reading and the Private Self in Late Medieval England*. Philadelphia: Penn State University Press, 2008.

Bryant, Levi. *The Democracy of Objects*. Ann Arbor, MI: Open Humanities Press, 2011.
Bynum, Caroline Walker. *Christian Materiality: An Essay on Religion in Late Medieval Europe*. New York: Zone, 2011.
Cadwallader, Robyn. *The Anchoress*. New York: Sarah Crichton Books of Farrar, Straus, and Giroux, 2015.
Caldwell, Ellen M. 'The heroism of Heurodis: self-mutilation and restoration in *Sir Orfeo*'. *Papers in Language and Literature* 43.3 (2007): 291–310.
Calvino, Italo. *The Nonexistent Knight*. Trans. Archibal Colquhoun. Boston: Houghton Mifflin Harcourt, 1962.
Camille, Michael. 'Before the gaze: the internal senses and late medieval practices of seeing'. In Robert S. Nelson, ed., *Visibility Before and Beyond the Renaissance: Seeing as Others Saw*. Cambridge: Cambridge University Press, 2000, pp. 197–223.
Cannon, Christopher. 'Form'. In Paul Strohm, ed., *Middle English*. Oxford Twenty-First Century Approaches to Literature. Oxford: Oxford University Press, 2007, pp. 177–90.
Carruthers, Mary. *The Book of Memory: A Study of Memory in Medieval Culture*. 2nd edn. Cambridge: Cambridge University Press, 2008 [1990].
Carruthers, Mary. 'The concept of ductus, or journeying through a work of art'. In Mary Carruthers, ed., *Rhetoric Beyond Words: Delight and Persuasion in the Arts of the Middle Ages*. Cambridge: Cambridge University Press, 2010, pp. 190–213.
Cartlidge, Neil. 'Sir Orfeo in the Otherworld: courting chaos?' *Studies in the Age of Chaucer* 26 (2004): 195–226.
Caxton, William, trans. *The Book of the Knight of the Tower*. Ed. M. Y. Offord. EETS s.s. 2. London: Oxford University Press, 1971.
Cervone, Cristina Maria. *Poetics of the Incarnation: Middle English Writing and the Leap of Love*. Philadelphia: University of Pennsylvania Press, 2013.
Chickering, Howell. 'Rhetorical stimulus in *The Prick of Conscience*'. In Stephanie Hayes-Healy, ed., *Medieval Paradigms: Essays in Honor of Jeremy DuQuesnay Adams*. New York: Palgrave, 2005, pp. 191–230
Coffield, Kris. 'Interview: Levi Bryant'. *Fractured Politics*, 29 June 2011. www.scribd.com/document/96872695/Interview (accessed 25 August 2020).
Cohen, Jeffrey Jerome. 'An abecedarium for the elements'. *postmedieval* 2 (2011): 291–303.
Cohen, Jeffrey Jerome. *Medieval Identity Machines*. Minneapolis, MN: University of Minnesota Press, 2003.
Cohen, Jeffrey Jerome. *Stone: An Ecology of the Inhuman*. Minneapolis, MN: University of Minnesota Press, 2015.
Coleman, Joyce. *Public Reading and the Reading Public in Late Medieval England and France*. Cambridge: Cambridge University Press, 1996.
Connolly, Margaret. 'The whole book: editions and facsimiles'. In Margaret Connolly and Raluca Radulescu, eds, *Insular Books: Vernacular*

Manuscript Miscellanies in Late Medieval Britain. Proceedings of the British Academy, 201. Oxford: Oxford University Press for the British Academy, 2015, pp. 281–99.

Connolly, Margaret, and Raluca Radulescu. 'Introduction'. In Margaret Connolly and Raluca Radulescu, eds, *Insular Books: Vernacular Manuscript Miscellanies in Late Medieval Britain.* Proceedings of the British Academy, 201. Oxford: Oxford University Press for the British Academy, 2015, pp. 1–29.

Coole, Diana, and Samantha Frost. 'Introducing the New Materialisms'. In Diana Coole and Samantha Frost, eds, *New Materialisms: Ontology, Agency, and Politics.* Durham, NC: Duke University Press, 2010, pp. 1–39.

Cooper, Lisa H. *Artisans and Narrative Craft in Late Medieval England.* Cambridge: Cambridge University Press, 2011.

Copeland, Rita. *Rhetoric, Hermeneutics, and Translation in the Middle Ages: Academic Traditions and Vernacular Texts.* Cambridge: Cambridge University Press, 1995.

Crenshaw, Kimberlé. 'Demarginalizing the intersection of race and sex: a black feminist critique of antidiscrimination doctrine, feminist theory and antiracist politics'. *University of Chicago Legal Forum* 1, article 8 (1989): 139–67.

Critten, Rory G. 'Bourgeois ethics again: the conduct texts and the romances in Oxford Bodleian, Library MS Ashmole 61'. *Chaucer Review* 50.1–2 (2015): 108–33.

Crocker, Holly A. *The Matter of Virtue: Women's Ethical Action from Chaucer to Shakespeare.* Philadelphia: University of Pennsylvania Press, 2019.

Dagenais, John. 'Decolonizing the medieval page'. In Peter Stoicheff and Andrew Taylor, eds, *The Future of the Page.* Toronto: University of Toronto Press, 2004, pp. 37–70.

Dagenais, John. *The Ethics of Reading in Manuscript Culture: Glossing the Libro de buen amor.* Princeton, NJ: Princeton University Press, 1994.

Da Rold, Orietta. 'Materials'. In Alexandra Gillespie and Daniel Wakelin, eds, *The Production of Books in England, 1350–1500.* Cambridge: Cambridge University Press, 2011, pp. 12–33.

Da Rold, Orietta. *Paper in Medieval England: From Pulp to Fictions.* Cambridge: Cambridge University Press, 2020.

'The Debate of the Carpenter's Tools revisited'. *Tools and Trades History Society*, Newsletter 118, winter 2012. http://taths.org.uk/tools-trades/articles/337-the-debate-of-the-carpenter-s-tools-revisited (accessed 25 August 2020).

Deleuze, Gilles, and Félix Guattari. *A Thousand Plateaus.* Trans. Brian Massumi. Minneapolis, MN: University of Minnesota Press, 1988 [1980].

Digital Index of Middle English Verse. Ed. Linne R. Mooney, Daniel W. Mosser, and Elizabeth Solopova. www.dimev.net/ (accessed 25 August 2020).

Dinshaw, Carolyn. *How Soon is Now? Medieval Texts, Amateur Readers, and the Queerness of Time*. Durham, NC: Duke University Press, 2012.
Downes, Stephanie, and Rebecca McNamara. 'The history of emotions and Middle English literature'. *Literature Compass* 13.6 (2016): 1–13.
Dronzek, Anna. 'Gendered theories of education'. In Kathleen Ashley and Robert L. A. Clark, eds, *Medieval Conduct*. Medieval Cultures, 29. Minneapolis, MN: University of Minnesota Press, 2001, pp. 135–59.
Edden, Valerie, ed. *Richard Maidstone's Penitential Psalms*. Heidelberg: Carl Winter, 1990.
Evans, Murray J. *Rereading Middle English Romance: Manuscript Layout, Decoration, and the Rhetoric of Composite Structure*. Montreal: McGill-Queens University Press, 1995.
Falk, Oren. 'The son of Orfeo: kingship and compromise in a Middle English romance'. *Journal of Medieval and Early Modern Studies* 30 (2000): 247–74.
Farina, Lara. 'Get a grip? The tactile object of *Handlyng Synne*'. In Stephanie Downes, Sally Holloway, and Sarah Randles, eds, *Feeling Things: Objects and Emotions Through History*. Oxford: Oxford University Press, 2018, pp. 97–113.
Fein, Susanna. *Moral Love Songs and Laments*. Kalamazoo, MI: Medieval Institute Publications. 1998.
Fein, Susanna, and David Raybin. 'About this issue'. *Chaucer Review* 47.4 (2013): 343–5, introduction to guest-edited special issue: *Medieval English Manuscripts: Form, Aesthetics, and the Literary Text*.
Feros Ruys, Juanita. 'Introduction'. In Juanita Feros Ruys, ed., *What Nature Does Not Teach: Didactic Literature in the Medieval and Early-Modern Periods*. Turnhout: Brepols, 2008, pp. 1–40.
Fitzgibbons, Moira. 'Enabled and disabled "myndes" in *The Prick of Conscience*'. In Seeta Chaganti ed., *Medieval Poetics and Social Practice: Responding to the Work of Penn R. Szittya*. New York: Fordham University Press, 2012, pp. 72–94.
Flannery, Mary C. 'The concept of shame in late-medieval English literature'. *Literature Compass* 9.2 (2012): 166–82.
Flannery, Mary C. 'Personification and embodied emotional practice in Middle English literature'. *Literature Compass* 13.6 (2016): 351–61.
Fletcher, Alan J. '*Sir Orfeo* and the flight from the enchanters'. *Studies in the Age of Chaucer* 22 (2000): 141–77.
Fowler, Elizabeth. 'The romance hypothetical: lordship and the Saracens in *Sir Isumbras*'. In Ad Putter and Jane Gilbert, eds, *The Spirit of Medieval English Popular Romance*. London: Longman, 2000, pp. 97–121.
Furrow, Melissa F. 'Kings and Commoners: introduction'. In *Ten Bourdes*. Ed. Melissa F. Furrow. TEAMS Middle English Texts Series. Kalamazoo, MI: Medieval Institute Publications, 2013. https://d.lib.rochester.edu/teams/text/furrow-ten-bourdes-kings-and-commoners-introduction (accessed 25 August 2020).

Furrow, Melissa F., ed. *King Edward and the Shepherd*. In *Ten Bourdes*. Ed. Melissa F. Furrow. TEAMS Middle English Texts Series. Kalamazoo, MI: Medieval Institute Publications, 2013. https://d.lib.rochester.edu/teams/publication/furrow-ten-bourdes (accessed 25 August 2020).

Furrow, Melissa F., ed. *Ten Bourdes*. TEAMS Middle English Texts Series. Kalamazoo, MI: Medieval Institute Publications, 2013. https://d.lib.rochester.edu/teams/publication/furrow-ten-bourdes (accessed 25 August 2020).

Furrow, Melissa F., ed. *Ten Fifteenth-Century Comic Poems*. New York: Garland, 1985.

Gayk, Shannon, and Robyn Malo, eds. *Journal of Medieval and Early Modern Studies* 44.3 (2014), special issue: *The Sacred Object*.

Gillespie, Alexandra. 'Manuscripts'. In Marion Turner, ed., *Critical Theory Handbooks: Handbook of Middle English Studies*. Oxford: Wiley-Blackwell, 2013, pp. 171–85.

Ginn, R. K. G., ed. *Sir Cleges*. Master's thesis, Queen's University Belfast, 1967.

Gitelman, Lisa. *Always Already New: Media, History, and the Data of Culture*. Boston: MIT Press, 2006.

Goldberg, P. J. P. 'The fashioning of bourgeois domesticity in later medieval England'. In Maryanne Kowaleski and P. J. P. Goldberg, eds, *Medieval Domesticity: Home, Housing and Household in Medieval England*. Cambridge: Cambridge University Press, 2008, pp. 124–44.

Goldberg, P. J. P., and Maryanne Kowaleski. 'Introduction: medieval domesticity: home, housing and household'. In Maryanne Kowaleski and P. J. P. Goldberg, eds, *Medieval Domesticity: Home, Housing and Household in Medieval England*. Cambridge: Cambridge University Press, 2008, pp. 1–13.

Griggs, Eleanor. 'The orchard and the "ympe tre": gardening, mastery, and ecology in *Sir Orfeo*'. *Comitatus* 50 (2019): 97–118.

Guddat-Figge, Gisele. *Catalogue of Manuscripts Containing Middle English Romances*. Texte und Unterzuchungen zur Englischen Philologie, 4. Munich: Münchener Universitäts Schriften, 1976.

Hanawalt, Barbara A. '"The Childe of Bristowe" and the making of middle-class adolescence'. In Barbara A. Hanawalt and David Wallace, eds, *Bodies and Disciplines: Intersections of Literature and History in Fifteenth-Century England*. Medieval Cultures, 9. Minneapolis, MN: University of Minnesota Press, 1996, pp. 155–78.

Hanawalt, Barbara. *Growing Up in Medieval London*. Oxford: Oxford University Press, 1993.

Hanna, Ralph. *London Literature, 1300–1380*. Cambridge Studies in Medieval Literature. Cambridge: Cambridge University Press, 2009.

Haraway, Donna. *When Species Meet*. Minneapolis, MN: University of Minnesota Press, 2008.

Hardman, Philippa. 'Compiling the nation: fifteenth-century miscellany manuscripts'. In Helen Cooney, ed., *Nation, Court and Culture: New*

Essays on Fifteenth-century English Poetry. Dublin: Four Courts Press, 2001, pp. 50–69.
Hardman, Philippa. 'A mediaeval "library *in parvo*"'. *Medium Aevum* 47 (1978): 262–73.
Hargreaves, Henry. 'Lydgate's "A Ram's Horn"'. *Chaucer Review* 10.3 (1976): 255–9.
Harman, Graham. *Object Oriented Ontology: A New Theory of Everything*. New York: Penguin, 2018.
Harman, Graham. 'The well-wrought broken hammer: object-oriented literary criticism'. *New Literary History* 43.2 (2012): 183–203.
Harris, Carissa. *Obscene Pedagogies: Transgressive Talk and Sexual Education in Late Medieval Britain*. Ithaca, NY: Cornell University Press, 2019.
Heidegger, Martin. *Being and Time*. Trans. J. Stambaugh. Albany, NY: SUNY Press, 1996.
Holsinger, Bruce. 'Of pigs and parchment: medieval studies and the coming of the animal'. *PMLA* 124.2 (2009): 616–23.
Holsinger, Bruce. 'Parchment ethics: a statement of more than modest concern'. *New Medieval Literatures* 12 (2010): 131–6.
Hopkins, Andrea. *The Sinful Knights: A Study of Middle English Penitential Romance*. Oxford: Clarendon Press, 1990.
Jirsa, Curtis R. H. 'In the shadow of the ympe-tre: arboreal folklore in *Sir Orfeo*'. *English Studies* 89.2 (2008): 141–51.
Johnston, Michael. *Romance and the Gentry in Late Medieval England*. Oxford: Oxford University Press, 2014.
Johnston, Michael. 'Romance, distraint, and the gentry'. *Journal of English and Germanic Philology* 112.4 (2013): 433–60.
Johnston, Michael. 'Two Leicestershire romance codices: Cambridge, University Library MS Ff.2.38 and Oxford, Bodleian Library MS Ashmole 61'. *Journal of the Early Book Society* 15 (2012): 85–100.
Johnston, Michael, and Michael Van Dussen. 'Introduction: manuscripts and cultural history'. In Michael Johnston and Michael Van Dussen, eds, *The Medieval Manuscript Book: Cultural Approaches*. Cambridge: Cambridge University Press, 2015, pp. 1–16.
Kay, Sarah. *Animal Skins and the Reading Self in Medieval Latin and French Bestiaries*. Chicago: University of Chicago Press, 2017.
Kay, Sarah. 'Legible skins: animals and the ethics of medieval reading'. *postmedieval* 2.1 (2011): 13–32.
Keen, Jill Averil. *The Charters of Christ and Piers Plowman: Documenting Salvation*. New York: Peter Lang, 2002.
Kelly, Meaghan. 'Affective reading in "The Sinner's Lament" and "The Adulterous Falmouth Squire"'. *Chrestomathy: Annual Review of Undergraduate Research, School of Humanities and Social Sciences, School of Languages, Cultures, and World Affairs, College of Charleston* 10 (2011): 220–31.
Kendall, Elliot. 'Family, *Familia*, and the uncanny in *Sir Orfeo*'. *Studies in the Age of Chaucer* 35 (2013): 289–327.

Killian, Ann E. 'Menacing books: *The Prick of Conscience* and the rhetoric of reproof'. *The Yearbook of Langland Studies* 31 (2017): 1–37.
King, Peter. 'Emotions in medieval thought'. In Peter Goldie, ed., *Oxford Handbook of Philosophy of Emotion*. Oxford: Oxford University Press, 2009, n.p.
Kline, Daniel T. 'Introduction: medieval children's literature: problems, possibilities, parameters'. In Daniel T. Kline, ed., *Medieval Literature for Children*. Abingdon: Routledge, 2003, pp. 1–11.
Kuczynski, Michael P. *Prophetic Song: The Psalms in Moral Discourse in Late Medieval England*. Philadelphia: University of Pennsylvania Press, 1995.
Kwakkel, Erik. *Books Before Print*. Medieval Media Cultures. Croydon: ARC Humanities Press, 2018.
Larson, Wendy R. 'The cults of St Margaret and St Marina'. In Samantha J. E. Riches and Sarah Salih, eds, *Gender and Holiness: Men, Women, and Saints in Late Medieval Europe*. Abingdon: Routledge, 2002, pp. 23–35.
Larson, Wendy R. 'Who is the master of this narrative? Maternal patronage of the cult of St Margaret'. In Mary C. Erler and Maryanne Kowaleski, eds, *Gendering the Master Narrative: Women and Power in the Middle Ages*. Ithaca, NY: Cornell University Press, 2003, pp. 94–104.
Laskaya, Anne, and Eve Salisbury, eds. *Erle of Tolous*. In *The Middle English Breton Lays*. TEAMS Middle English Texts Series. Kalamazoo, MI: Medieval Institute Publications, 1995. https://d.lib.rochester.edu/teams/publication/laskaya-and-salisbury-middle-english-breton-lays (accessed 25 August 2020).
Laskaya, Anne, and Eve Salisbury, eds. *Sir Orfeo*. In *The Middle English Breton Lays*. TEAMS Middle English Texts Series. Kalamazoo, MI: Medieval Institute Publications, 1995. https://d.lib.rochester.edu/teams/publication/laskaya-and-salisbury-middle-english-breton-lays (accessed 25 August 2020).
Latour, Bruno. *Reassembling the Social: An Introduction to Actor-Network Theory*. Oxford: Oxford University Press, 2005.
Lemay, Helen Rodnite. *Women's Secrets: A Translation of Pseudo-Albertus Magnus' De Secretis Mulierum with Commentaries*. Albany, NY: SUNY Press, 1992.
Lerer, Seth. 'Artifice and artistry in *Sir Orfeo*'. *Speculum* 60.1 (1985): 92–109.
Lerer, Seth. 'Medieval English literature and the idea of the anthology'. *PMLA* 118 (2003): 1251–67.
Lewis, Katherine J. '"Lete me suffre": reading the torture of St Margaret of Antioch in late medieval England'. In Jocelyn Wogan-Browne, Rosalynn Voaden, Arlyn Diamond, Ann Hutchison, Carol Meale, and Lesley Johnson, eds, *Medieval Women: Texts and Contexts in Late Medieval Britain: Essays for Felicity Riddy*. Turnhout: Brepols, 2000, pp. 69–82.
Lewis, Katherine J. 'The *Life of St Margaret of Antioch* in late medieval England: a gendered reading'. *Studies in Church History* 34 (1998): 129–42.

Libby, Christine. 'The object of his heart: subjectivity and affect in mystic texts'. *Literature Compass* 13.6 (2016): 362–71.
Matlock, Wendy. 'Reading family in the Rate manuscript's *Saint Eustace* and *Sir Isumbras*'. *Chaucer Review* 53.3 (2018): 350–73.
Matlock, Wendy. 'Reworking the household in *The Debate of the Carpenter's Tools*'. *English Studies* 95.2 (2014): 109–30.
McDermott, Ryan. 2016. *Tropologies: Ethics and Invention in England, c. 1350–1600*. South Bend, IN: University of Notre Dame Press.
McDonald, Nicola. 'A polemical introduction'. In Nicola McDonald, ed., *Pulp Fictions of Medieval England: Essays in Popular Romance*. Manchester: Manchester University Press, 2004, pp. 1–21.
McGann, Jerome. 'From text to work: digital tools and the emergence of the social text'. *Text* 16 (2006): 49–62.
McNamer, Sarah. *Affective Meditation and the Invention of Medieval Compassion*. Philadelphia: University of Pennsylvania Press, 2010.
McNamer, Sarah. 'Feeling'. In Paul Strohm, ed., *Middle English*. Oxford Twenty-First Century Approaches to Literature. Oxford: Oxford University Press, 2007, pp. 241–57.
Mehl, Dieter. *The Middle English Romances of the Thirteenth and Fourteenth Centuries*. London: Routledge and Kegan Paul, 1968.
Middle English Dictionary. Ed. Robert E. Lewis, et al. Ann Arbor, MI: University of Michigan Press, 1952–2001. Online edition in *Middle English Compendium*. Ed. Frances McSparran, et al. Ann Arbor, MI: University of Michigan Library, 2000–2018. http://quod.lib.umich.edu/m/middle-english-dictionary/ (accessed 25 August 2020).
Mills, Maldwyn, ed. *Lybeaus Desconus*. EETS OS 261. London: Oxford University Press, 1969.
Minnis, Alastair. '*The Prick of Conscience* and the imagination of paradise'. In Simon Horobin and Aditi Nafde, eds, *Pursuing Middle English Manuscripts and Their Texts: Essays in Honor of Ralph Hanna*. Turnhout: Brepols, 2017, pp. 157–75.
Mitchell, J. Allan. *Becoming Human: The Matter of the Medieval Child*. Minneapolis, MN: University of Minnesota Press, 2014.
Mitchell, J. Allan. 'Dining tables, conduct texts, and human ecology'. In Holly Crocker and D. Vance Smith, eds, *Middle English Literature: Criticism and Debate*. Abingdon: Routledge, 2014, pp. 339–48.
Mitchell, J. Allan. *Ethics and Exemplary Narrative in Chaucer and Gower*. Woodbridge: Boydell and Brewer, 2004.
Mitchell, W. J. T. 'There are no visual media'. *Journal of Visual Culture* 4 (2005): 257–66.
Morse, Mary. 'Alongside St Margaret: the childbirth cult of Saints Quiricus and Julitta in late medieval English manuscripts'. In Emma Cayley and Susan Powell, eds, *Manuscripts and Printed Books in Europe 1350–1550: Packaging and Consumption*. Exeter Studies in Medieval Europe. Liverpool: Liverpool University Press, 2013, pp. 187–206.

Morse, Mary. '"Thys moche more ys oure lady mary longe": Takamiya MS 56 and the English birth girdle tradition'. In Simon Horobin and Linne R. Mooney, eds, *Middle English Texts in Transition: A Festschrift Dedicated to Toshiyuki Takamiya on his 70th Birthday*. York: Boydell and Brewer, 2014, pp. 199–219.

Morton, Timothy. 'Here comes everything: the promise of Object-Oriented Ontology'. *Qui Parle* 19.2 (2011): 163–90.

Morton, Timothy. 'An object-oriented defense of poetry'. *New Literary History* 43 (2012): 205–24.

Nagy, Piroska. 'Historians and emotions: new theories, new questions'. *Cultural History of Emotions in Premodernity*, 24 October 2008. http://emma.hypotheses.org/147 (accessed 25 August 2020).

Nelson, Ingrid. *Lyric Tactics: Poetry, Genre, and Practice in Later Medieval England*. Philadelphia: University of Pennsylvania Press, 2017.

Nichols, Steven G. 'What is a manuscript culture?' In Michael Johnston and Michael Van Dussen, eds, *The Medieval Manuscript Book: Cultural Approaches*. Cambridge: Cambridge University Press, 2015, pp. 35–49.

Nolan, Maura. 'Medieval habit, modern sensation: reading manuscripts in the digital age'. *Chaucer Review* 47.4 (2013): 465–76.

Norako, Leila K. '*Sir Isumbras* and the fantasy of crusade'. *Chaucer Review* 48.2 (2013): 166–89.

Nordal, Guðrún. 'Manuscripts in Iceland in the age of Chaucer: production, texts and literary culture'. Plenary address, New Chaucer Society, Reykjavik, Iceland, 16 July 2014.

Oresme, Nicole. *Nicole Oresme and the Marvels of Nature*. Ed. Bert Hansen. Turnhout: Brepols, 1985.

Orlemanski, Julie. *Symptomatic Subjects: Bodies, Medicine, and Causation in the Literature of Late Medieval England*. Philadelphia: University of Pennsylvania Press, 2019.

Orme, Nicholas. *Medieval Children*. New Haven, CT: Yale University Press, 2001.

Oxford, Bodleian Library MS Ashmole 61. https://digital.bodleian.ox.ac.uk/objects/69462c25-b481-4643-9942-34f7243ea921/

Paxson, James J. 'Personification's gender'. *Rhetorica: A Journal of the History of Rhetoric* 16.2 (1998): 49–179.

Pearsall, Derek. 'The value/s of manuscript study: a personal retrospect'. *Journal of the Early Book Society* 3 (2000): 167–81.

Pearsall, Derek. 'The whole book: late medieval English manuscript miscellanies and their modern interpreters'. In Stephen Kelly and John J. Thompson, eds, *Imagining the Book*. Turnhout: Brepols, 2005, pp. 17–29.

Price, Leah. 'From the history of a book to a "history of the book"'. *Representations* 108 (2009): 120–38.

Purdie, Rhiannon. *Anglicizing Romance: Tail-Rhyme and Genre in Medieval English Literature*. Cambridge: D. S. Brewer, 2008.

Radulescu, Raluca. 'Pious Middle English romances turned political: reading *Sir Isumbras, Sir Gowther*, and *Robert of Sicily* in fifteenth-century England'. *Viator* 41.2 (2010): 333–60.

Radulescu, Raluca. 'Vying for attention: the contents of Dublin, Trinity College, MS 432'. In Margaret Connolly and Raluca Radulescu, eds, *Insular Books: Vernacular Manuscript Miscellanies in Late Medieval Britain*. Proceedings of the British Academy, 201. Oxford: Oxford University Press for the British Academy, 2015, pp. 121–42.

Reames, Sherry L. *The Legenda Aurea: A Reexamination of its Paradoxical History*. Madison, WI: University of Wisconsin Press, 1985.

Reames, Sherry L., ed. *Middle English Legends of Women Saints*. TEAMS Middle English Texts Series. Kalamazoo, MI: Medieval Institute Publications, 2003. https://d.lib.rochester.edu/teams/publication/reames-middle-english-legends-of-women-saints (accessed 25 August 2020).

Rentz, Ellen K. *Imagining the Parish in Late Medieval England*. Columbus, OH: Ohio State University Press, 2015.

Rhetorica ad Herennium. Trans. Harry Caplan. Cambridge, MA: Harvard University Press, 1999.

Rice, Nicole. *Lay Piety and Religious Discipline in Middle English Literature*. Cambridge: Cambridge University Press, 2008.

Robertson, Elizabeth. 'The corporeality of female sanctity in *The Life of St Margaret*'. In Renate Blumenfeld-Kosinksi and Timea Szell, eds, *Images of Sainthood in Medieval Europe*. Ithaca, NY: Cornell University Press, 1991, pp. 268–87.

Robertson, Kellie. 'Exemplary rocks'. In Jeffrey Jerome Cohen, ed., *Animal, Vegetable, Mineral: Ethics and Objects*. Washington, DC: Oliphant Books, 2012, pp. 91–121.

Robertson, Kellie. 'Scaling nature: microcosm and macrocosm in later medieval thought'. *Journal of Medieval and Early Modern Studies* 49.3 (2019): 609–31.

Robinson, Emily. 'Touching the void: affective history and the impossible'. *Rethinking History* 14.4 (2010): 503–20.

Rosenwein, Barbara H. *Emotional Communities in the Early Middle Ages*. Ithaca, NY: Cornell University Press, 2006.

Rosenwein, Barbara H. 'Worrying about emotions in history'. *The American Historical Review* 107.3 (2002): 821–45.

Rudd, Gillian. *Greenery: Ecocritical Readings of Late Medieval English Literature*. Manchester: Manchester University Press, 2007.

Salisbury, Eve. *Chaucer and the Child*. Basingstoke: Palgrave, 2016.

Salisbury, Eve, and James Weldon, eds. *Lybeaus Desconus*. TEAMS Middle English Texts Series. Kalamazoo, MI: Medieval Institute Publications, 2014. https://d.lib.rochester.edu/teams/publication/salisbury-and-weldon-lybeaus-desconus (accessed 25 August 2020).

Sanok, Catherine. *Her Life Historical: Exemplarity and Female Saints' Lives in Late Medieval England*. Philadelphia: University of Pennsylvania Press, 2007.

Saunders, William. 'The symbolism of the pelican'. *Arlington Catholic Herald*. 2003. www.catholiceducation.org/en/culture/catholic-contributions/the-symbolism-of-the-pelican.html (accessed 25 August 2020).

Scheer, Monique. 'Are emotions a kind of practice (and is that what makes them have a history)? A Bourdieuian approach to understanding emotion'. *History and Theory* 51 (May 2012): 193–220.

Seaman, Myra. 'Disconsolate art'. In Eileen A. Joy, Myra Seaman, and Nicola Masciandaro, eds, *Dark Chaucer: An Assortment*. New York: Punctum Books, 2013, pp. 139–49.

Seaman, Myra. 'Late medieval conduct literature'. In Liz McAvoy and Diane Watt, eds, *The History of British Women's Writing, to 1500*, vol. 1. Basingstoke: Palgrave, 2011, pp. 121–30.

Seaman, Myra. 'Renovating the household through affective invention in Manuscripts Ashmole 61 and Advocates 19.3.1'. In Glenn D. Burger and Rory G. Critten, eds, *Household Knowledges in Late Medieval England and France*. Manchester: Manchester University Press, 2019, pp. 74–99.

Seaman, Myra. 'Thomas Chestre's *Sir Launfal* and the Englishing of medieval romance'. *Medieval Perspectives* 15 (2000): 105–19.

Seaman, Myra. 'Tugging at the roots: the errant textography of Middle English romance'. *Journal of Medieval and Early Modern Studies* 39 (2009): 283–303.

Sheldon, Rebekah. 'Form/matter/chora: Object-Oriented Ontology and Feminist New Materialism'. In Richard Grusin, ed., *The Nonhuman Turn*. Minneapolis, MN: University of Minnesota Press, 2015, pp. 193–222.

Shuffelton, George, ed. *Codex Ashmole 61: A Compilation of Popular Middle English Verse*. TEAMS Middle English Texts Series. Kalamazoo, MI: Medieval Institute Publications, 2008. https://d.lib.rochester.edu/teams/publication/shuffelton-codex-ashmole-61 (accessed 25 August 2020).

Shuffelton, George. 'Is there a minstrel in the house? Domestic entertainment in late medieval England'. *Philological Quarterly* 87.2 (2008): 51–76.

Singman, Jeffrey L. *Robin Hood: The Shaping of the Legend*. Westport, CT: Greenwood Press, 1998.

Smith, Vance. *Arts of Possession: The Middle English Household Imaginary*. Minneapolis, MN: University of Minnesota Press, 2003.

Spalding, Mary Caroline. *The Middle English Charters of Christ*. Bryn Mawr, PA: Bryn Mawr College, 1914.

Spearing, A. C. *Textual Subjectivity: The Encoding of Subjectivity in Medieval Narratives and Lyrics*. Oxford: Oxford University Press, 2012.

Sponsler, Claire. 'Eating lessons: Lydgate's "Dietary" and consumer conduct'. In Kathleen Ashley and Robert L. A. Clark, eds, *Medieval Conduct*. Medieval Cultures, 29. Minneapolis, MN: University of Minnesota Press, 2001, pp. 1–22.

Sponsler, Claire. 'Medieval ethnography: fieldwork in the medieval past'. *Assays* 7 (1992): 1–30.

Sponsler, Claire, 'Narrating the social order: medieval clothing laws'. *Clio* 21 (1992): 265–83.
Staley, Lynn. 'Maidstone's *Psalms* and the king's speech'. In Tamara Atkin and Francis Leneghan, eds, *The Psalms and Medieval English Literature: From the Conversion to the Reformation*. Cambridge: D. S. Brewer, 2017, pp. 255–70.
Staley, Lynn. 'The *Penitential Psalms*: conversion and the limits of lordship'. *Journal of Medieval and Early Modern Studies* 37.2 (2007): 221–69.
Stanzaic Life of Margaret [Cambridge University Library MS Addit. 4122, 15th c.]. In *Middle English Legends of Women Saints*. Ed. Sherry L. Reames. Kalamazoo, MI: Medieval Institute Publications, 2003.
Steel, Karl. *How to Make a Human: Animals and Violence in the Middle Ages*. Columbus, OH: Ohio State University Press, 2011.
Steel, Karl. *How Not to Make a Human: Pets, Feral Children, Worms, Sky Burial, Oysters*. Minneapolis, MN: University of Minnesota Press, 2019.
Steiner, Emily. *Documentary Culture and the Making of Medieval English Literature*. Cambridge: Cambridge University Press, 2003.
Stewart, Kathleen. *Ordinary Affects*. Durham, NC: Duke University Press, 2007.
Symes, Carol. 'Manuscript matrix, modern canon'. In Paul Strohm, ed., *Middle English*. Oxford Twenty-First Century Approaches to Literature. Oxford: Oxford University Press, 2007, pp. 7–22.
Talbot, Jen. 'Flat ontologies and everyday feminisms: toward a rhetoric of the body'. In Amanda K. Booher and Julie Jung, eds, *Feminist Rhetorical Science Studies: Human Bodies, Posthumanist Worlds*. Carbondale, IL: Southern Illinois University Press, 2018, pp. 84–113.
Thompson, Anne B. 'Jaussian expectation and the production of medieval narrative: the case of "Saint Eustace" and *Sir Isumbras*'. *Exemplaria* 5.2 (1993): 387–407.
Travis, Peter W. 'Aesop's symposium of animal tongues'. *postmedieval* 2.1 (2011): 33–49.
Trigg, Stephanie. 'Emotional histories: beyond the personalization of the past and the abstraction of affect theory'. *Exemplaria* 26.1 (2014): 3–15.
Truesdale, Mark. *The King and Commoner Tradition: Carnivalesque Politics in Medieval and Early Modern Literature*. Abingdon: Routledge, 2018.
Truesdale, Mark. 'Robin Hood and the King and Commoner tradition: "The best archer of ilkon / I durst mete hym with a stone"'. In Lesley Coote and Alexander L. Kaufman, eds, *Robin Hood and the Outlaw/ed Literary Canon*. Abingdon: Routledge, 2018, pp. 69–88.
Tyler, Tom. *Ciferae: A Bestiary in Five Fingers*. Posthumanities Series. Minneapolis, MN: University of Minnesota Press, 2012.
Van Dyke, Carolynn. 'Touched by an owl? An essay in vernacular ethology'. *postmedieval* 7 (2016): 304–27.
von Contzen, Eva. 'Why medieval literature does not need the concept

of social minds: exemplarity and collective experience'. *Narrative* 23.2 (2015): 140–53.
Wade, James. 'Ungallant knights'. In Neil Cartlidge, ed., *Heroes and Anti-Heroes in Medieval Romance*. Cambridge: D. S. Brewer, 2012, pp. 201–18.
Warren, Michelle. 'Post-philology'. In Patricia Ingham and Michelle Warren, eds, *Postcolonial Moves: Medieval Through Modern*. Basingstoke: Palgrave, 2003, pp. 19–45.
Watson, Nicholas. 'Censorship and cultural change in late-medieval England'. *Speculum* 70 (1995): 822–64.
Watson, Nicholas. 'The politics of Middle English writing'. In Jocelyn Wogan-Browne, Nicholas Watson, Andrew Taylor, and Ruth Evans, eds, *The Idea of the Vernacular: An Anthology of Middle English Literary Theory, 1280–1520*. University Park, PA: Pennsylvania State University Press, 1999, pp. 331–52.
Weiskott, Eric. 'A new text of the Middle English *Short Charter of Christ*'. *Notes & Queries* 65 (2018): 478–80.
Williams, Raymond. *Keywords: A Vocabulary of Culture and Society*. Oxford: Oxford University Press, 1985.
Williams, Tara. 'Fairy magic, wonder, and morality in *Sir Orfeo*'. *Philological Quarterly* 91.4 (2012): 537–68.
Williams, Tara. *Middle English Marvels: Magic, Spectacle, and Morality in the Fourteenth Century*. State College, PA: Penn State University Press, 2018.
Wingfield, Emily. 'The literary miscellany in Scotland'. In Margaret Connolly and Raluca Radulescu, eds, *Insular Books: Vernacular Manuscript Miscellanies in Late Medieval Britain*. Proceedings of the British Academy, 201. Oxford: Oxford University Press for the British Academy, 2015, pp. 209–30.
Winstead, Karen A. *Virgin Martyrs: Legends of Sainthood in Late Medieval England*. Ithaca, NY: Cornell University Press, 1997.
Wooden, Cindy. 'Pope urges revival of traditional devotion to Five Wounds of Christ'. *Catholic Herald*, 22 March 2018. https://catholicherald.co.uk/pope-urges-revival-of-traditional-devotion-to-five-holy-wounds-of-christ/ (accessed 25 August 2020).
Woolf, Rosemary. *The English Religious Lyric in the Middle Ages*. Oxford: Clarendon Press, 1968.
Wyckoff, Dorothy. *Albertus Magnus: Book of Minerals*. Oxford: Clarendon Press, 1967.

Index

actant 26–8, 36–7, 46, 56, 78, 80, 141, 172, 235
actor-network 2, 18, 19, 46, 56, 77, 92, 152
Adams, Gillian 62, 86
Adams, Tracy 31, 51–2
Adulterous Falmouth Squire, The 169, 171, 194–9, 202, 212, 224
Advocates 19.3.1 *see* Edinburgh, National Library of Scotland, MS Advocates 19.3.1
affect 1, 19, 24, 28, 32, 33, 47, 51, 60, 137, 142, 147, 200–1
  affective 1–3, 5, 20, 29–32, 51, 60, 64, 65, 68–70, 73–7, 81, 83, 84, 92, 94, 97, 99, 102, 103, 108–10, 122, 136, 137, 141–4, 147, 148, 158, 161, 165, 171–2, 174, 177, 178, 186, 187, 194, 195, 198, 201
agency 2, 16, 18–21, 23–8 *passim*, 32, 35, 42, 46, 48, 50, 51, 55–7, 59–60, 63, 67, 71, 73, 92, 96, 101–2, 110, 112, 114, 120, 123–4, 128, 135, 136, 141–3, 147, 161, 174, 185, 195, 211, 213–14, 218–19, 236, 241, 245, 255

agent 2, 16–18, 21, 26, 28, 31, 37, 46, 48, 56, 67, 68, 73, 75, 83–4, 91, 102, 110–11, 121–3, 126, 136–7, 163, 169, 172–4, 179, 185, 187–8, 201, 223, 235, 246
agential realism 23–4
Ahmed, Sara 29–32, 51–2, 91, 201, 205
Alaimo, Stacy 24, 49
Albertus Magnus 19, 20, 47
alcohol 16, 81, 206, 246
allegory 20, 62, 64, 80, 87, 136, 153, 155, 160–4, 179
Allen, Elizabeth 91, 94–7, 130, 131, 232, 234, 236, 249, 251–2, 259
Allen, Valerie 19, 20, 47, 97
alms 72, 106, 108, 218
Amos, Mark Addison 63–4, 77, 87, 90
Amsler, Mark 171, 201
angel 67, 69, 71–5 *passim*, 77, 123, 158–61, 196–7, 206, 212–13, 217, 255
animal 1, 17, 19, 26, 29, 34, 47, 65, 67–70, 74–5, 77, 81, 84, 88–9, 112, 114–17, 133, 135, 141, 185, 204, 206, 231–2, 251
  see also beast; bird; crow; dog; falcon; horse; hound; pelican; stag; worm

Index

anthology 40, 45, 255
Archibald, Elizabeth 133
armour 67, 71–3, 109, 112–13
arrows 31, 179, 240, 241, 243–4
Ashe, Laura 153, 168–9
Ashley, Kathleen 77, 87, 90
assemblage 16, 19, 26–7, 29, 32, 37–8, 46, 49–50, 54–60 *passim*, 66, 72, 74, 81, 85, 102, 120, 124, 126, 133, 136, 141, 155, 158, 161, 172, 174, 178, 193, 197, 200, 208, 210, 214, 218, 226, 250, 259
Auchinleck Manuscript *see* Edinburgh, National Library of Scotland MS Advocates 19.2.1
audience 6, 7, 11, 40, 45, 59–61, 64–5, 67, 68, 70–2, 74, 77–9, 81, 98, 102, 107, 108, 121, 126–7, 130, 140, 154–6, 166, 173–4, 190, 213, 220, 228–30, 235, 237, 241–4, 248, 253

Bahr, Arthur 24, 27–8, 43, 49–51, 53, 85
Bakhtin, Mikhail 244, 254
banquet 166, 237–8, 245, 253
baptism 75, 90, 117, 217, 220
Barad, Karen 23–4, 49
Barker-Benfield, Bruce 43, 252, 261
beast 16, 67, 79, 185, 196, 210, 215, 229–33, 239–40, 246, 248, 250
Behar, Katherine 24, 49
Benjamin, Walter 35
Bennett, Jane 1, 18, 21, 23, 46–8, 144, 167, 172, 201
bird 16, 66–7, 69, 73–5, 84, 88, 114, 137, 165, 181, 190, 197, 200, 204, 226, 229, 232–3
Blanchfield, Lynne S. 10, 43–5, 61, 85–7, 89, 130, 261

Bliss, J. A. 224, 261
Boffey, Julia 6, 7, 12, 39, 40, 43, 45, 54
Bogost, Ian 46, 48
Bolter, Jay David 37, 53
book history 26–7, 42
book object 1–2, 28, 33, 38, 55, 56
Brantley, Jessica 42, 87
Braswell, Laurel 87
Brockman, Bennett 62, 86
Broomhall, Susan 51, 52
Bryan, Jennifer 63, 87
Bryant, Levi 46–8
Bynum, Caroline Walker 17, 22, 31, 46, 48, 52, 101–2, 131

Cadwallader, Robyn 247
Caldwell, Ellen 225, 250
Camille, Michael 202
Cannon, Christopher 258, 259
Carruthers, Mary 59, 85, 94, 130
Cartlidge, Neil 223–4, 235, 249–52
Cervone, Cristina Maria 153, 168–9
charter 151–3, 168–9
   see also Short Charter of Christ, The
cherries 21, 32, 136, 148–51, 164, 200, 251
Chickering, Howell 190, 204–5
child 61–2, 79, 86, 113, 154–6, 158, 170
childbirth 191, 208, 210, 218–20, 247–8, 251
children 40, 45, 57, 61–2, 68–9, 75, 82, 84, 86, 90, 107, 120, 122–4, 128–9, 134, 147, 153, 199, 215–16
Children's Corner 9, 12, 43, 61, 86, 90
children's literature 60–5
Christ 22, 25, 48, 72, 75, 86, 92, 99–102, 105–6, 110, 120, 122, 136, 151–5, 158, 162–5, 168–70, 172–85,

187, 189–90, 192–3, 197, 203, 207–8, 211–15, 217, 221, 225, 227, 248–9, 256
Cohen, Jeffrey Jerome 20, 47, 132, 225, 250–2
Coleman, Joyce 44, 202
conduct text 2, 6, 8, 9, 22, 56–7, 61–4, 66, 77–81, 85, 86, 90–3, 107, 144–6, 148, 156, 166, 201, 215, 255
Connolly, Margaret 27, 41, 50
Coole, Diana 46
Cooper, Lisa 51
Copeland, Rita 94, 130
Crenshaw, Kimberlé 23, 48
Critten, Rory G. 44
Crocker, Holly A. 20, 47, 90
crow 181
crucifix 16, 75, 100–2, 119
crucifixion 165, 174, 176, 179, 212
cuckold 141–4, 164, 167, 238

Dagenais, John 42, 94, 130
Dame Curtasy 9, 56–8, 78–9, 81–2, 144
Da Rold, Orietta 50
Debate of the Carpenter's Tools, The 21, 29, 51, 129–30, 136–40, 143–4, 164–6
demon 16, 207–9, 212, 216, 219, 247
devil 120–2, 212, 219, 248, 256
didacticism 2, 57, 59, 61–4, 77, 79, 84–7, 94–7, 169, 201, 258–9
Dietary, The 136, 144–8
  see also Lydgate, John
Digby 86 see Oxford, Bodleian Library MS Digby 86
Dinshaw, Carolyn 41
dog 16, 81, 91, 115, 232
  see also hound
Downes, Stephanie 51
dragon 16, 206–10, 213–19, 225, 246–7, 248, 250
  see also dragon-lady

dragon-lady 110, 118, 119, 130
Dronzek, Anna 80, 90

Earl of Tolous, The see *Erle of Tolous, The*
Edden, Valerie 203
Edinburgh, National Library of Scotland MS Advocates 19.2.1 (Auchinleck Manuscript) 12, 43, 87, 209, 224, 226, 250
Edinburgh, National Library of Scotland MS Advocates 19.3.1 (Heege Manuscript) 6, 39, 41, 44, 53, 61, 71, 88
education 4, 45, 75, 96, 156, 171, 193, 197–8, 215–16, 227
Edwards, A. S. G. 6, 7, 40, 43
Erle of Tolous, The 45, 93, 102–10, 112, 119, 128–30, 132, 256–7
exemplarity see didacticism
exemplum see didacticism
Evans, Murray 44, 77, 85–6, 90
Evening Prayer, An 86, 129

fairy 16, 111, 206, 223–5, 231, 233, 235, 251
  see also Fairy King
Fairy King 221, 223, 225, 228–9, 231, 233–4, 246, 250
  see also fairy
falcon 114–15, 232, 235
Falk, Oren 223, 234, 249, 251
family 4–7, 15–16, 29, 39–41, 43–5, 58, 61, 63, 66–71, 73–7, 88–90, 93, 112, 122–4, 126–9, 139, 145–8, 150, 155, 163, 198, 199, 202, 204, 229, 234, 238
Farina, Lara 53, 60, 85–6
Feasts of All Saints and All Souls, The 136, 155, 158–9, 161, 170, 198

feeling 2–3, 29, 30, 52, 114, 189–90, 195
feelings 29, 31, 32, 59, 64, 114, 148, 186–7, 230
Fein, Susanna 37, 53, 195, 205
female 47, 110, 120, 126, 133, 144, 163, 199, 208–9, 215, 219–21, 246–8
see also woman
feminism 23, 24
Feros Ruys, Juanita 63, 87
fiend 16, 75, 97, 117, 121–8, 133, 134, 170, 197, 212, 214, 217, 242
fier baiser 110–11
fish 11–13, 15, 24–6, 33, 45, 49, 50, 54, 65, 152, 168, 248, 255–8
Fitzgibbons, Moira 194, 205
Flannery, Mary C. 141, 165, 166
Fletcher, Alan J. 223–4, 235, 249–52
flower 11–13, 15, 25, 33, 45, 48–9, 65, 70, 75, 83, 115, 152, 168, 197, 226, 229, 255–7
forest 67–8, 70, 115, 130, 150, 192, 229–30, 232, 237–40, 242–4, 250–4 *passim*
Fowler, Elizabeth 88
Furrow, Melissa 25, 49, 252–4

Gayk, Shannon 131
genre 8, 9, 22, 36, 61–2, 65, 80, 87, 95, 128, 134, 140, 210, 221, 224–6, 234, 238–40, 245–6, 253, 255
giant 16, 97, 111, 116–18
Gillespie, Alexandra 24, 49, 53, 255
Gitelman, Lisa 53
Goldberg, P. J. P. 4, 5, 38, 139, 166
Griggs, Eleanor 233–4, 250–1
Guddat-Figge, Gisela 261

Hanawalt, Barbara 62, 86
Hanna, Ralph 43
Haraway, Donna 91
Hardman, Philippa 39, 61–3, 86
Hargreaves, Henry 80, 90
Harley 237 *see* London, British Library MS Harley 237
Harley 3744 *see* London, British Library MS Harley 3744
Harley 3810 *see* London, British Library MS Harley 3810
Harman, Graham 46, 48, 49
harp 206, 227–8, 230–1, 233–4, 246, 250–1
Harris, Carissa 133
Heege Manuscript *see* Edinburgh, National Library of Scotland MS Advocates 19.3.1 (Heege Manuscript)
Hekman, Susan 49
Heurodis 221, 223–4, 234, 249–51
see also Meurodys
history of emotion 30–2, 51–2
Holsinger, Bruce 26, 50
holster book 9–11, 43, 256
Hopkins, Andrea 88, 128
horn 75, 80, 90, 115, 136, 140–3, 166, 238
horse 67, 73, 75, 100, 132, 185–6, 204, 239–40
hound 67, 115, 212, 216, 231, 239
see also dog
household 1–8, 11, 15–16, 18, 24–9 *passim*, 32, 38, 40, 42, 44, 49, 52, 55–8, 64, 67–9, 71–2, 74, 77–85, 92, 120, 128, 135–40, 143–8, 164–5, 171, 183, 189, 198–9, 201, 206, 231, 255–6, 259
household book 5–12, 26–8, 39, 40, 42, 44, 61, 64, 84, 89, 92–3, 128, 224, 255–6, 259

household manuscript 10, 42, 92, 255
How the Good Wife Taught Her Daughter 9, 56, 58, 78–9, 82–4, 86
How the Wise Man Taught His Son 9, 56, 78–9, 83–4

Incestuous Daughter, The 93, 119, 123–7, 134, 202
Isumbras see Sir Isumbras

Jake Fletcher 242–5
Jealous Wife, The 93, 119–24, 127–9, 134, 202
Jirsa, Curtis 251
Johnston, Michael 7, 11, 27, 39, 41–5, 49, 50
justice 32, 68, 78, 82, 98, 105, 107, 126, 136, 150–1, 161–4, 241, 244

Kay, Sarah 26, 50
Keen, Jill Averil 168
Kelly, Meaghan 205
Kendall, Elliot 223, 234, 249, 251
Killian, Ann E. 205
King and His Four Daughters, The 136, 155, 160–4, 168
King and the Hermit, The see King Edward and the Hermit
King Arthur 94, 111–12, 114–15, 117, 141–4, 166–7, 238
King Edward and the Hermit 200, 206, 221, 236–45, 252–4
King, Peter 52
King Uther 148–51, 168, 251
kiss 21, 97, 100–2, 105, 106, 108–10, 112, 119, 130, 133, 148, 163–4
Kline, Daniel 64, 86–7
knight 39, 43, 47–8, 56, 66, 68, 70, 72–3, 88, 93–4, 97–116, 118–19, 128, 130, 132–3, 139, 143, 144, 160, 168, 229, 232, 236, 238, 244
Knight Who Forgave His Father's Slayer, The 21, 93, 97–106, 109, 110, 112, 116, 119, 120, 124, 230, 257, 258
Kowaleski, Maryanne 5, 38
Kuczynski, Michael P. 270
Kwakkel, Erik 10, 43

Lady of Synadoune 110–12, 115–18, 130, 256
Lament of Mary, The 136, 153, 155, 158, 164, 169, 178, 270
Larson, Wendy R. 208, 246–7
Laskaya, Anne 224, 249
Latour, Bruno 18, 46, 48
laugh 84, 118, 141, 150, 232, 242
laughter 118, 232, 242–3
Legend of the Resurrection, The 201
Legenda Aurea 158, 209, 247
Lemay, Helen Rodnite 46
Lerer, Seth 50, 223, 235, 249, 250, 252
Lewis, Katherine J. 208, 212, 218–20, 246–9
Libby, Christine 60, 85, 86
Libeaus Desconus see Lybeaus Desonus
Life of St Eustace, The see St Eustace
Life of St Margaret, The 201, 206–21, 225, 228, 234–6, 246, 247, 250, 270–2
Lincoln, Cathedral Library MS 91 41, 43, 71
London, British Library MS Harley 237 152, 168
London, British Library MS Harley 3744 26, 50
London, British Library MS Harley 3810 226

Lybeaus Desconus 21, 93, 110–20, 128–30, 132–3, 256–59
Lydgate, John 9, 56, 79, 88, 136, 144, 198, 209, 218–19, 247
see also *Dietary, The*; *Right as a Ram's Horn*

McDermott, Ryan 130, 131
McDonald, Nicola 41
McGann, Jerome 26, 36, 53
McNamara, Rebecca 51
McNamer, Sarah 28, 31, 51, 52
McSparran, Frances 61, 63
magic 116–18, 223, 228–9, 238
Magus 116–17, 133
Maidstone's *Seven Penitential Psalms* 171, 177–81, 183–6, 188–90, 194, 199, 202–4
Malo, Robyn 131
manuscript studies 26–8, 33–8, 43, 53
Matlock, Wendy 51, 88, 90
Mehl, Dieter 87
Meroudys 222, 224–5, 228, 229, 232–6 *passim*, 246, 249
see also Heurodis
Mills, Maldwyn 130
Minnis, Alastair 205
minstrel 9–11, 43, 44, 66, 83, 88, 118, 142, 146–7, 167, 250–1
miscellany 27–8, 40–2, 50, 88
Mitchell, J. Allan 17, 19, 46–7, 49, 53, 57, 81, 85, 91, 94–5, 130–1, 136, 143, 165–7
Mitchell, W. J. T. 36
Morning Prayer, A 86, 129
Morse, Mary 247–8
Morton, Timothy 21, 41, 46–8
MS Advocates 19.3.1 see Edinburgh, National Library of Scotland MS Advocates 19.3.1
MS Digby 86 see Oxford, Bodleian Library MS Digby 86

MS Harley 237 see London, British Library MS Harley 237
MS Harley 3744 see London, British Library MS Harley 3744
MS Harley 3810 see London, British Library MS Harley 3810

Nagy, Piroska 52
Nelson, Ingrid 95, 130, 131
new materialism 2, 17–26 *passim*, 28, 32, 47, 171
Nichols, Stephen G. 50
Nolan, Maura 34–7, 53
Norako, Leila K. 87–9
Nordal, Guðrún 53
Northern Passion 165

object-oriented feminism 24
object-oriented ontology (OOO) 18, 23, 26, 46, 49
Orfeo see *Sir Orfeo*
Orlemanski, Julie 95, 131
Orme, Nicholas 86
Oxford, Bodleian Library MS Digby 86 87–9

paper 6, 8, 10, 24, 26, 37–9, 43–4, 50, 170
Paxson, James 170
Pearsall, Derek 28, 34, 50–1, 53
pelican 180–1, 197
penance 32, 67, 68, 72–4, 77, 89, 124, 127, 134, 142–3, 172, 178, 187, 190, 196, 201, 206, 221, 224, 229–30, 245
Prayer at the Levation, A 48, 129
Prayer to Mary, A 86, 129
Price, Leah 26, 42, 50
Prick of Conscience Minor, The 171, 187–90, 192–6, 198–9, 224

Index

pride 66, 83, 98, 100–1, 119, 173–5, 188, 199, 200, 205, 227
Purdie, Rhiannon 87–8
purgatory 158–60, 187, 191, 193, 198, 224

Radulescu, Raluca 27, 41, 50, 52, 89
Rate 9, 11, 12, 15, 24–6, 33, 43–5, 49, 53–4, 56, 57, 71, 78–80, 82–3, 86–7, 89, 90, 132–3, 152–3, 165, 169–70, 177, 179, 183–6, 195, 200, 203, 205, 209–10, 223, 252, 256–8
Raybin, David 37, 53
Reames, Sherry L. 218, 246–8
Remein, Dan 49
Rentz, Ellen K. 190, 205, 220, 249
Rice, Nicole 205
Right as a Ram's Horn 9, 56, 78–80, 83, 90, 198, 200
   see also Lydgate, John
Robertson, Elizabeth 247–8
Robertson, Kellie 19–20, 22, 47
Robinson, Emily 52
romance 2, 6, 8–10, 12, 22, 38, 39, 41, 43, 45, 50, 59, 61, 64–6, 70, 72, 75, 76, 78, 86–9, 93–4, 102–3, 106, 110–12, 116–17, 128, 130, 132–3, 167, 201, 206, 221, 224–7, 234, 236, 238–40, 243, 253, 255, 261
Rosenwein, Barbara 29–31, 51–2
Rudd, Gillian 231, 250

Salisbury, Eve 86, 112, 114, 132–3, 224, 249
Sanok, Catherine 94, 130
Saunders, Corinne 203
Scheer, Monique 31, 52
scribe 6, 8, 9, 11–12, 15–16, 25–7, 38–9, 41–5 *passim*, 50, 56, 57, 87, 92, 183,
 186, 194, 209, 223, 235, 256
Seaman, Myra 87, 89, 130, 249
Sheldon, Rebekah 23, 48
Short Charter of Christ, The 136, 151–5, 158, 168–70, 178
   see also charter
Shuffelton, George 8, 10, 38–9, 42, 44–5, 49, 85, 88–90, 131, 133, 134, 151–3, 156, 161, 166–70, 172, 175–6, 179, 188–90, 194, 201–5, 207, 210, 216, 226–7, 246–50, 252–4, 256, 261
Singman, Jeffrey L. 254
Sinner's Lament, The 169, 171, 195, 196, 224
Sir Cleges 21, 45, 136, 145–51, 167–8, 251
Sir Corneus 49, 129–30, 136, 140, 142–5, 165, 167, 238
Sir Isumbras 9, 13, 56–8, 61, 65–77, 79, 84, 87–90, 132, 167, 205, 229, 230, 240, 248–50, 254
Sir Orfeo 88, 201, 206, 221–36, 238, 239, 249–52, 254, 261
Smith, D. Vance 5, 38, 39
sorrow 2, 69, 71, 89, 122, 126, 147–8, 155, 174, 187, 190, 192, 195–6, 204–5, 229–30, 233
Spalding, Mary Caroline 168
Spearing, A. C. 59, 85
Sponsler, Claire 63, 85, 87, 144, 167
St Eustace 9, 21, 56–8, 65, 75–7, 79, 80, 87–90, 200, 209, 230, 239, 253
St Margaret *see Life of St Margaret, The*
stag 16, 32, 75, 239
Staley, Lynn 177–8, 186, 187, 202–4
Stans Puer ad Mensam 9, 21, 56, 57, 78–9, 82, 83, 129, 167
Stations of Jerusalem, The 201

Steel, Karl 16, 40, 46, 47
Steiner, Emily 168
Stewart, Kathleen 32, 52, 161, 170
Stimulus Consciencie Minor see Prick of Conscience Minor, The
stone 19, 20, 75, 78–80, 83–4, 118, 152, 156–7, 233, 250
Symes, Carol 41

table 16, 21, 81, 91, 116, 135, 141–4, 146, 166–7, 237, 253
Talbot, Jen 23–4, 48–9
tears 10, 16, 97, 126, 185, 187, 190, 197
Ten Commandments 9, 13–14, 56, 58, 78–80, 83–4, 89, 92, 258
Thompson, Anne B. 87
Thompson, John J. 12, 45, 54
Thornton, Robert 41, 43, 50, 165
Travis, Peter 91
Trigg, Stephanie 28, 31, 51–2
Truesdale, Mark 237, 238, 244–5, 252–4
Tubac, Frederic 95
Tyler, Tom 91

Underhill, Roy 166
Uther *see* King Uther

Van Dussen, Michael 27, 50
Van Dyke, Carolynn 91

Vanity 171, 198–200, 205, 221, 227
von Contzen, Eva 59, 85

Wade, James 130, 132–3
Warren, Michelle 42
water 4, 32, 69, 72, 150, 156–7, 160, 174, 186–7, 191, 210, 217
Watson, Nicholas 205
Weiskott, Eric 168
Weldon, James 112, 114, 132, 133
Williams, Raymond 36, 53
Williams, Tara 202, 223–4, 234, 249–51
Wingfield, Emily 86
Winstead, Karen 219, 247–9
woman 43, 47, 70, 83–4, 93, 107, 114, 117–26, 130, 133, 139, 142, 143, 164, 167, 202, 208, 210, 216, 218–20, 222, 223, 236, 247, 251
Wooden, Cindy 202
Woolf, Rosemary 176, 202
worm 118–19, 185–6, 188
Wounds and the Sins, The 45, 171–6, 178–80, 188, 199, 202, 205, 221–2, 227, 259
wrath 98–9, 103, 105, 109–10, 117, 120–2, 163, 175, 179
Wyckoff, Dorothy 47

Ypotis 133, 155, 156, 158, 161, 170

EU authorised representative for GPSR:
Easy Access System Europe, Mustamäe tee 50,
10621 Tallinn, Estonia
gpsr.requests@easproject.com